TEXTBOOK ON
SUCCESSION

TEXTBOOK ON

SUCCESSION

Andrew Borkowski LLB

BLACKSTONE
PRESS LIMITED

First published in Great Britain 1997 by Blackstone Press Limited,
9–15 Aldine Street, London W12 8AW. Telephone 0181-740 2277

ISBN: 1 85431 627 3

British Library Cataloguing in Publication Data
A CIP catalogue record for this book is available from the British Library.

Typeset by Montage Studios Ltd, Tonbridge, Kent
Printed by Livesey Ltd, Shrewsbury, Shropshire

Contents

Preface

I believe that Succession is one of the most interesting and important of all legal subjects. Everyone is affected by the law of Succession. Whereas we might happily pass through life untouched by several of the major areas of English law, we will inevitably be affected by the distribution of the estates of our loved ones and friends when they die. And how we choose to distribute our property, if any, on death may have a substantial effect on others when we ourselves die. Few other areas of law have such 'human interest' as Succession. The case law is full of strange testators who behave eccentrically or who make wills in bizarre circumstances.

This book is written primarily for use in undergraduate courses in Succession. It deals with the basic principles of the subject, the relevant statutory material and the leading cases. Since most readers of this book will be preparing for examinations, I have attempted to write a text which will be convenient to use, and the contents of which will be readily understood and assimilated. To this end I have sometimes included a coulourful fact or two in the descriptions of cases, so that the latter might be more easily remembered. In similar vein I have emphasised cases where famous personalities have been involved. Mention will be found in the following pages of cases concerning Napoleon Bonaparte, Sullivan, Turner, George Orwell and many others of the Great and the Good. But the personality who features most in this book will be, as yet, unknown to the reader. His name is 'Arthur'. Who is Arthur? He is someone who frequently does not understand the law and does rather bizarre things. He makes invalid wills, or incomprehensible ones, or revokes wills incorrectly: everything he touches seems to go wrong. Frankly, he would have benefited from reading this book. His function is to act as an illustrator of the application of the law and its intricacies. If he helps in doing that, and his antics provoke the occasional chuckle in the reader, he will be content.

I would like to thank the staff at Blackstone Press for their help in preparing this book, and several of my colleagues at the Department of Law, University of Bristol, for their invaluable assistance: Patricia Hammond processed the text with her usual high degree of competence, Roger Kerridge helped me with the section on tax in Chapter 10, and David Clarke clarified my thinking on several issues. Corinne Chamberlain, an enthusiastic student of the subject, helped to check the text.

The law is stated as at 1 March 1997 according to the sources available to me.

Andrew Borkowski
Senior Lecturer in Law
University of Bristol
St David's Day 1997

Table of Cases

Table of Statutes

ONE
Intestacy

1.1 INTRODUCTION

Succession is concerned with the transfer of property on death, particularly through disposition by will and succession on intestacy. Although accounts of the law traditionally deal with wills before intestacy there is much to be said for reversing the order. The law on intestacy is relatively compact and far less extensive than the law relating to wills. It embraces certain fundamental issues — such as the purpose of succession laws — which need to be addressed at the outset of a study of the whole subject. Moreover, a knowledge of the law of intestacy is helpful in understanding cases on the law of wills more clearly. Many of these cases are contests between those entitled under a will and those entitled under intestacy. The law of intestacy thus serves as a very useful introduction to the rest of the subject; and it is highly important in practice, given that most adults die intestate. For those reasons intestacy is considered first.

The material is divided into three main sections. The first consists of an introduction to intestacy, dealing with the basic terms and rules, the incidence of intestacy, and the evolution and theoretical basis of the law. The second section gives a more detailed account of the current law. The third is concerned with issues of reform.

1.1.1 The basic terms and rules

1.1.1.1 Basic terms
What is 'intestacy'? Intestacy can be total or partial. A *total intestacy* occurs when a person dies without leaving a valid will effectively disposing of his property. This situation can occur for several reasons:

    (a)   the deceased never made a will;

    (b)   the deceased made a will but it is invalid owing to lack of capacity or defective execution;

(c)   the deceased made a will but it was revoked;

(d)   the deceased made a will which attempted but wholly failed to dispose of his property — for example, where the sole beneficiary predeceased the testator;

(e)   the deceased made a will which contained no disposition of his property. In *Re Skeats* [1936] Ch 683, the testator appointed his wife as executrix, revoked all previous wills and directed the payment of his debts, funeral and testamentary expenses. There was no disposition of property in the will to any person. It was held that the deceased's property should be distributed under the rules of intestacy.

A *partial intestacy* occurs where a testator makes a will but fails effectively to dispose of *some* of his property. This may be the result of a deliberate omission on his part, but is more likely to have been caused by forgetfulness as to the composition or extent of his property, or by the failure of a particular gift.

The word 'intestate' is used to describe the *person* on whose death a total or partial intestacy occurs. The word is also used to describe the *state* in which such a person died or the state in which he left his property, e.g., 'Arthur died intestate' or 'Arthur's intestate estate was valued at . . .'.

1.1.1.2   The basic rules

The modern law of intestacy is founded on the scheme of distribution enacted by the Administration of Estates Act 1925. On a total intestacy the intestate's property is held on trust by his personal representatives, who will pay off the debts of the estate and then distribute the remainder of the property ('the residuary estate') according to the order of entitlement under s. 46 of the Act. Under that scheme the surviving spouse has the primary right of succession. Indeed, in most cases where the intestate is survived by a spouse, the latter is likely to take the entire residuary estate, as was intended by the 1925 legislation. Where the intestate is survived by a spouse and issue (i.e. children or remoter issue) the spouse is entitled to a fixed sum of £125,000, all the personal chattels of the intestate and a life interest in half of the balance of the residuary estate. The issue are entitled to the other half of the balance and the remainder following the life interest. If the intestate is survived by the spouse but not by issue or a specified relative (see 1.2.2.3), the spouse takes the whole of the residuary estate. If the intestate is survived by a specified relative but not by issue, the spouse takes a fixed net sum of £200,000, the personal chattels of the intestate, and one half of the balance absolutely; the specified relative takes the other half. If the intestate is survived by issue but not by a spouse, the issue take the whole residuary estate. If the intestate leaves no surviving spouse or children, the residuary estate passes to the specified relatives, in the prescribed order (see 1.2.4). If there are no such relatives, the Crown takes the estate as *bona vacantia* ('vacant property', i.e. ownerless property).

As regards partial intestacy, the rules are the same as for total intestacy, but they apply only to the undisposed-of part of the estate.

1.1.2 The incidence of intestacy

The Law Commission's Report, *Distribution on Intestacy* (Law Com. No. 187, 1989) contained the results of a commissioned survey of public opinion concerning the law of intestacy. It found that two in three adults had not made a will. Of those, 60 per cent said that they intended to make a will sometime in the future. The main reason given by those who did not intend to make a will was that they had nothing to leave. Other reasons included the belief that will-making was irrelevant (because of the age of the respondent) and that the surviving spouse would take the whole estate automatically:

Main reasons for not making a will
Nothing to leave/no property/no money	35%
Never thought about it	17%
Youthful/too young to need to	15%
Spouse will get what is left automatically	12%

(Appendix C, para. 1.4)

The survey found that 60 per cent among those aged 60 or over had made a will but only 8 per cent of those in the age group 18–30. There was also a correlation — though less pronounced — between will-making and social class: the proportion of those in classes AB was more than twice that among DEs:

Proportion of each group who had made a will

By age		By class	
18–30	8%	AB	53%
31–44	16%	C1	38%
44–59	41%	C2	26%
60 or more	60%	DE	24%

(Appendix C, para. 1.1)

Moreover, a correlation was found between the incidence of will-making and the marital status of those surveyed: 33 per cent of married persons had made a will, but only 19 per cent of cohabitants and 11 per cent of single persons. Overall, the survey suggests that wills are made typically by middle-aged, middle-class, married (or formerly married) property owners. The typical intestate is more likely to be single, to have less property to leave and to belong to a less privileged socio-economic class. The fact that those dying intestate are more likely to leave a modest estate may be thought relevant in framing a satisfactory law of intestacy.

An earlier survey into the incidence of will-making and intestacy had been carried out for the Law Commission by J.E. Todd and L.M. Jones: *Matrimonial Property* (1972). The survey found that among married couples only 24 per cent of husbands and 10 per cent of wives had made a will. However, more than 80 per cent of those who had not made wills felt that it was important for people to make them, and over 70 per cent thought that they would do so in the future. The two surveys tell a broadly similar story, and suggest that the incidence of will-making has increased in recent decades. However, this is questioned by Finch, J., Mason, J., Masson, J., Wallis, L., and Hayes, L., *Wills, Inheritance, and Families* (1996) a study of 800 wills of testators dying between 1959 and 1989. They conclude that the incidence of adults who die leaving a will which is admitted to probate has remained 'remarkably constant' (p. 50) between those years, and put the figure at 30 per cent. Their work suggests that men and women are equally likely to make a will, but that women are less likely than men to be married at the time of making their last will (often made following the husband's death). The median age for will-making was found to be 69 years for men, 73 years for women. The evidence did not suggest that will-making was confined to the wealthy, although testators were *likely* to be drawn from the higher socio-economic groups.

1.1.3 The evolution of the law

Before the 1925 property legislation there were two separate schemes of intestate succession — one for realty, one for personalty.

1.1.3.1 Realty before 1926

Intestate succession to realty before 1926 was governed by the rules of inheritance — a mixture of common law and custom — which became established in the early medieval period and survived largely unchanged until 1925 (they were given statutory force by the Inheritance Act 1833). The rules were of immense importance, especially for most of the medieval period, when it was not possible to make a will of land. Thus the rules determined the devolution of land on death in the formative period of Anglo-Norman society and the common law.

Realty passed to the heir, who was ascertained by the application of a fixed order of entitlement centred around the concept of male primogeniture — the eldest son was the sole heir. If there were no surviving sons (or their issue), realty was inherited by the daughters of the intestate as coparceners, i.e. in equal shares. Next entitled were the collaterals (primarily brothers and sisters) of the intestate. Ancestors could not inherit realty until the Inheritance Act 1833 when they were given priority over collaterals. If there was no heir under the rules, realty escheated — it passed to the deceased's lord or to the Crown.

What of the intestate's widow? Under the rules of inheritance the widow strictly had no rights of succession. However, it became customary for a husband to make his wife a gift of part of his property — known as dower — usually on marriage. It seems that in the thirteenth century the nature of dower changed from that of a customary gift to an automatic right, the widow becoming entitled to a life interest in one third of her husband's freeholds on his death. But dower gradually waned in importance, mainly because it could be easily defeated. The widower had a corresponding right — known as curtesy — which gave him a life interest in the *whole* of his wife's realty on her death. Curtesy too eventually faded, especially after the Married Women's Property Act 1882, which enabled the wife to defeat it by disposing of her property.

1.1.3.2 Personalty before 1926
The Anglo-Saxon codes commonly contained provisions concerning the distribution of the goods on death, typically giving succession rights to the widow, the children and the kinsmen of the deceased. This basic scheme remained largely unchanged throughout the medieval period, but was subject to considerable local variation in the customary law. There was too a protracted battle between the common law courts and the ecclesiastical courts as to jurisdiction over the administration of estates.

Rules of entitlement to personalty on intestacy — mostly the existing rules — were enacted by the Statutes of Distribution 1670–1685. The scheme of distribution under the Acts remained the basis of the law of intestate succession to personalty until 1925. Indeed, parts of the present law bear close resemblance to the seventeenth-century provisions. Under the statutory rules a widow took one third of the personalty if there were surviving issue, a half if there were none; a widower was entitled to all of his wife's personalty. Issue took the whole of the personalty if the intestate was not survived by a spouse; they took two thirds if the intestate's wife survived him. Other next-of-kin were entitled to half of the personalty if the intestate was survived by a wife but not by issue. Otherwise the next-of-kin took only if there were no issue and no surviving spouse. The Crown was entitled to all the personalty if there were no ascertainable next-of-kin within the prescribed order. The 1670 Act also provided that personalty passed *initially* to the intestate's personal representatives (and not directly to the next-of-kin) to distribute according to the statutory provisions.

The Statutes of Distribution applied only to total intestacy. The position on partial intestacy was that the executor took the undisposed-of personalty beneficially, although in equity he would normally be regarded as holding on trust for the persons entitled under a total intestacy.

1.1.3.3 The 1925 legislation and thereafter
The Administration of Estates Act 1925 enacted a unified scheme of intestate succession applicable to all of the property of the intestate. The previous distinction between realty and personalty was abolished as far as devolution of property was concerned. The Statutes of Distribution were repealed and the rules of inheritance (including dower and curtesy) were largely abolished. However, the pre-1926 rules are not entirely museum pieces. For example, the rules of inheritance still apply to the devolution of entailed interests and — in a modified form — to the succession to the Crown and hereditary titles (in December 1996, a Bill was introduced in the House of Lords proposing to end male primogeniture as regards the succession to the Crown).

The scheme under the 1925 Act gave primacy to the rights of the surviving spouse and equalised the position between widows and widowers. The surviving spouse was given a statutory legacy of £1,000, the personal chattels of the intestate and a life interest in one half of the residue if there were issue (or a life interest in the whole residue if there were specified relatives but no issue). This entitlement sufficed to give the spouse the whole estate in the vast majority of intestacies (as was intended). Thus the 1925 Act marked an important shift in entitlement from issue to spouses, the change being particularly evident in the relative positions of widows and eldest sons before and after the 1925 Act. The considerable improvement in the surviving spouse's position reflected the practice of testators. The 1925 scheme was informed by the results of a survey which had demonstrated that the surviving spouse was given the primary share of the testator's estate in the vast majority of wills.

The policy of improving the surviving spouse's position was again evident in the next major reform of the law of intestacy — the Intestates' Estates Act 1952. The statutory legacy was increased to £5,000 if there were issue (the increase was well in excess of the inflation rate during the intervening period). If there were no issue but there were specified relatives, the legacy was £20,000. Moreover, the spouse was given the right to appropriate the matrimonial home in satisfaction of the statutory legacy. But perhaps the most significant change in the 1952 Act was the extension of the Inheritance (Family Provision) Act 1938 to intestacy. The 1938 Act entitled certain dependants of a deceased testator to apply for reasonable financial provision out of his estate by way of maintenance. The court was given a discretionary power to make provision for such applicants, and thus in effect to alter the effect of the deceased's will. The application of this power to cases of intestacy by the 1952 Act introduced a measure of much-needed flexibility into the operation of the intestacy rules.

The Administration of Estates Act 1925, as amended by the Intestates' Estates Act 1952, remains the foundation of the current law of intestacy. However, important changes were made after 1952 by a series of Acts and Statutory Instruments. The main effects of these changes have been to increase the statutory legacy of the surviving spouse and to improve the position of the illegitimate child. More recently, the Law Reform (Succession) Act 1995 prevents the surviving spouse taking unless he or she survives the intestate by 28 days. Moreover, the Act abolishes the controversial hotchpot provisions of the Administration of Estates Act 1925 under which certain beneficiaries on intestacy (whether total or partial) had to account for other benefits received from the deceased (see 1.2.3.3). These changes were recommended by the Law Commission's Report (No. 187, 1989). However, the Commission's major recommendation — that the surviving spouse should take the whole estate — was rejected by the Government.

1.1.4 The theoretical basis of the law

The intestacy rules inevitably cannot provide for every situation. They can only hope to provide a solution which is fair and reasonable in the general run of cases. (Law Com. No. 187, 1989, para. 6)

The solution embraced currently in English law has been described as a 'safety-net' for those who die intestate. The solution which this safety-net provides is based primarily on the presumed intention of the intestate. But other factors underpin the law, which as a result appears at times to be pulling in different directions.

1.1.4.1 Presumed intention

The scheme enacted by the Administration of Estates Act 1925 was intended to reflect the wishes of the average testator. For that purpose a survey of wills was conducted in order to ascertain the type of provisions that testators commonly made in wills (a similar survey was carried out before the passing of the 1952 Act). The rules of intestacy can thus be regarded as a form of will made for the intestate by Parliament. But is it justifiable to base the law of intestacy on surveys of how *testators* behave? Why equate the intestate with the testate?

That the presumed intention of the intestate is the foundation of the law has been consistently emphasised. For example, the Law Commission stated (Law Com. No. 187, 1989, para. 24):

> There are a number of principles upon which the rules of intestacy might be based and in our working paper [No. 108] we canvassed the respective merits of the presumed wishes of the deceased, the needs or deserts of the survivors, and the status of the surviving spouse. The present law is based upon a combination of these, although the underlying object has been to do what the deceased himself, or herself, might have wished.

It is clear from even a cursory examination of the current law of intestacy that it is largely based on the presumed intentions of the deceased. This can be seen particularly in the primacy of the surviving spouse's position and in the priority given to children over other next-of-kin in the prescribed order of succession. And the entitlement of the spouse to the personal chattels of the intestate and to the appropriation of the matrimonial home no doubt accords with the wishes of most intestates. Moreover, on a partial intestacy the application of the intestacy rules to the undisposed-of property is made specifically subject to 'the provisions contained in the will': Administration of Estates Act 1925, s. 33(7).

1.1.4.2 Other factors

There are, however, aspects of the current law of intestacy which live uneasily with, or do not conform to, the presumed wishes of the deceased. For example, it can safely be said that very few intestates would wish their property to pass to the Crown, and yet that is a possibility under the present law. In this respect the law appears to reflect the ancient custom whereby the Crown (or the lord) took property that had escheated. Neither would the average intestate intend the application of some of the rules relating to the spouse's rights to a life interest, or the rights of issue under the statutory trusts. Many would be surprised to learn, for example, that their property might pass wholly to their last spouse, with no benefit going to the intestate's children by a former marriage; and that it might pass equally to a grandchild as well as to a child, as is possible because of the *per stirpes* rule (see 1.2.3.2). And it can be presumed that most intestates who had cohabited with a partner prior to death would be distressed to learn that their property might pass to a remote relation (or even the Crown) and not to the partner. If the intestacy rules are meant to be a safety-net based on presumed intention, it is a net full of gaping holes.

Nor do the intestacy rules provide the fixed and certain scheme of entitlement envisaged in 1925. As has been seen already, the Inheritance (Family Provision) Act 1938 was extended to intestacy by the Intestates' Estates Act 1952. The discretionary powers thereby given to the court to alter the operation of the intestacy rules have since been considerably widened. The current legislation, the Inheritance (Provision for Family and Dependants) Act 1975, enables certain categories of applicant (including cohabitants) to claim a redistribution of the intestate estate for their maintenance. And a surviving spouse, if dissatisfied with the distribution on intestacy, may claim for 'such financial provision as it would be reasonable in all the circumstances of the case for a husband or wife to receive': s. 1(2)(a). The existence of these discretionary powers helps to smooth, where appropriate, the rigidity of the basic intestacy rules. Some will view this as an uneasy mix between certainty and flexibility, but it is hoped that it will lead to a fairer system overall, and one which caters for *needs* to some extent.

Even if there had been no family provision legislation, the statutory rules on intestacy could not be regarded as mandatory and immutable for they are subject, as are testamentary provisions, to the rule in *Saunders* v *Vautier* (1841) Cr & Ph 240; 41 ER 482. This important rule provides that if all the beneficiaries entitled on intestacy are of full age and are *sui iuris* (of full capacity), they can agree to distribute the estate as they wish — they are not bound by the statutory order. Suppose, for example, that the intestate is survived by three children, one of whom has cared for him in an exemplary way, perhaps in very difficult circumstances. The three will be equally entitled under the statutory rules but they can agree, if they wish, that the property should be divided unequally in recognition of the special care provided by one of them. Another common reason for agreeing to a distribution inconsistent with the statutory rules is to minimise tax liability.

1.2 TOTAL INTESTACY

The law of intestate succession is contained mostly in the provisions of the Administration of Estates Act 1925, as amended. References in the remainder of this chapter to 'the Act' or to 'the 1925 Act' are to be taken as indicating the Administration of Estates Act 1925 unless the contrary is indicated.

1.2.1 Trust with power to sell

Under s. 9 of the Act (as amended), the intestate's estate vests temporarily in the Public Trustee until the grant of administration to personal representatives to administer the estate. On their appointment the personal representatives hold the estate under s. 33(1) of the Act as amended by the Trusts of Land and Appointment of Trustees Act 1996, sch. 2, para. 5(2): 'On the death of a person intestate as to any real or personal estate, that estate shall be held in trust by his personal representatives with the power to sell it.'

Under the previous law the personal representatives held property on trust for sale, but with a general power to postpone sale and a duty not to sell personal chattels and reversionary interests in certain circumstances. The amended s. 33(1) — which applies whether the intestate died before or after the commencement of the 1996 Act (1 January 1997) — affords the personal representatives a greater measure of flexibility in effecting the trust. Where the intestate's estate comprises an interest in a dwelling-house in which a surviving spouse was resident when the intestate died, the personal representatives must not sell or otherwise dispose of the interest, during the year following the first taking out of representation, without the written consent of the surviving spouse 'except in the course of administration owing to want of other assets': Intestates' Estates Act 1952, Second Schedule, para. 4(1). The purpose of this provision is to give the surviving spouse time to decide whether to exercise the power to appropriate the house (normally the matrimonial home). A reasonable period is desirable given that the spouse will often not be able to focus clearly on the future for some time after the intestate's death.

Out of the ready money of the deceased and any net money arising from disposing of any other part of the estate (after payment of costs) the personal representatives must first pay all the funeral, testamentary and administration expenses, debts and other liabilities of the intestate: s. 33(2) of the Administration of Estates Act 1925, as amended. The residue of the money is referred to by the Act as 'the residuary estate of the intestate'. During the minority of any beneficiary or the subsistence of any life interest, the personal representatives have the power to invest the residuary estate (or part of it) in authorised investments prior to its distribution to the beneficiaries: s. 33(3). As regards trusts of land — any trust of property which consists of or *includes* land — personal representatives now appear to have 'all the powers of an absolute owner': s. 6(1) of the Trusts of Land and Appointment of Trustees Act 1996. This includes, for example, delegating their functions to beneficiaries of full age: s. 9(1) of the 1996 Act.

The residuary estate is distributable under the provisions of s. 46 of the Administration of Estates Act 1925. The operation of s. 46 can best be explained by considering the following situations: where the intestate is survived by a spouse; where there is issue but no surviving spouse; where there is neither spouse nor issue; where there are no surviving relatives.

1.2.2 Where there is a surviving spouse

1.2.2.1 Who is the spouse?
Section 46 confers succession rights on 'a husband or wife' but does not define the status, which must thus be determined according to general principles. The spouse is the person who is lawfully married to the intestate when the latter dies. It is irrelevant for this purpose that the parties were in the process of divorcing when the intestate died. In *Re Seaford* [1968] P 53, CA, the wife of the intestate, having obtained a decree nisi of divorce, applied for it to be made absolute. However, the intestate died (as the result of an overdose of sleeping tablets) a few hours before the notice of application for the decree absolute was filed at the District Registry. It was held that the marriage still subsisted when the intestate died. Thus the wife was entitled to seek appointment as the

intestate's personal representative (and presumably was entitled to the spouse's usual succession rights on intestacy). Consider, however, *Re Collins* [1990] 2 All ER 47, where a wife obtained a decree nisi of divorce against her violent husband but died soon afterwards before the decree absolute could be pronounced (there was no proof that her death was the result of a crime). The husband inherited the whole of her estate (valued at about £35,000). Later her children applied under the Inheritance (Provision for Family and Dependants) Act 1975 for reasonable financial provision out of her estate, and one of them was granted a lump sum of £5,000. The case illustrates how a successful application under the 1975 Act may reduce the spouse's entitlement on intestacy.

A party to a voidable marriage is the lawful spouse of the other party. This is because a voidable marriage is regarded as a valid marriage and subsists until a decree absolute of nullity is pronounced. Marriages are voidable on the grounds set out in s. 12 of the Matrimonial Causes Act 1973 — for example, lack of consent, or non-consummation owing to incapacity or wilful refusal. In *Re Roberts* [1978] 3 All ER 225, CA, it was alleged that the intestate lacked capacity to marry on account of mental illness. Nevertheless, the intestate's widow was held to be his spouse for all purposes, including entitlement to rights on his intestacy. As regards void marriages, the position is quite different. A void marriage is a complete nullity, hence the parties never acquire the status of husband and wife. Marriages are void on the grounds enacted by s. 11 of the Matrimonial Causes Act 1973 — for example, marriages that are bigamous or in breach of certain formalities. However, in some circumstances a party to a void marriage may apply for financial provision out of the intestate's estate under the Inheritance (Provision for Family and Dependants) Act 1975 (see 8.2.1.1).

What if the marriage is polygamous? At one time there was considerable doubt whether polygamous marriages could be recognised as having legal effects in English law. But since the Second World War the trend has been towards recognition of polygamous marriages and their consequences. Although there appears to be no reported case which directly holds that a party to a polygamous marriage is entitled to succeed on intestacy, the point can hardly be doubted. In *Re Sehota* [1978] 3 All ER 385, a testator left all his property to his second wife (he had married two wives in India). His first wife applied for financial provision out of his estate under the Inheritance (Provision for Family and Dependants) Act 1975. It was held that a party to a polygamous marriage had *locus standi* to apply under the Act as a spouse. By analogy it seems clear that such a spouse would be regarded as 'a husband or wife' under s. 46 of the Administration of Estates Act 1925.

What if the parties are separated? A marriage is not terminated by separation. Thus a separated spouse has full succession rights under s. 46. However, an exception is provided where the intestate died while a decree of judicial separation was in force and the separation was actually continuing at that time. In that case the surviving spouse is regarded as having predeceased the intestate and thus cannot take any interest on intestacy: Matrimonial Causes Act 1973, s. 18(2). It seems that this exception is confined to judicial separation decrees and does not apply in the case of separation or similar orders made by the magistrates' courts.

It should be noted that cohabitants do not have any rights of intestate succession under s. 46 of the 1925 Act. However, cohabitants can now apply for financial provision out of the intestate's estate under the Inheritance (Provision for Family and Dependants) Act 1975 provided that the intestate died on or after 1 January 1996. This was recommended by the Law Commission in Law Com. No. 187, 1989 and enacted by s. 2 of the Law Reform (Succession) Act 1995 (see 8.2.1.6).

1.2.2.2 Survivorship

The surviving spouse has the primary rights of succession on an intestacy. However, in order to take, whether on total or partial intestacy, the spouse must survive the intestate by 28 days: s. 46(2A) of the Administration of Estates Act 1925. This subsection was inserted into the 1925 Act by s. 1(1) of the Law Reform (Succession) Act 1995. It applies if the intestate dies on or after 1 January 1996, but not if death occurred before that date. The purpose of this reform was explained by the Law Commission (Law Com. No. 187, 1989, para. 57):

> It was also noted that it is the current practice to incorporate a survivorship clause into wills. The object of such clauses is to stop the assets of both spouses going to the parents or relatives of the second to die in cases of not quite simultaneous death, usually in accidents. We consider that this is a practice which it would be useful for the intestacy rules to adopt.

The Law Commission recommended that the survivorship period should be 14 days, fearing that any longer might lead to unacceptable delays in the administration of estates. But an amendment extending the period to 28 days was carried in Parliament. This reform, irrespective of the period chosen, is probably consistent with the presumed intention of most people dying intestate in such circumstances.

1.2.2.3 Basic entitlement

To what is the surviving spouse entitled? The position depends on who else survived the intestate. If the intestate is survived by issue, the spouse takes a fixed net sum — usually referred to as the statutory legacy — of £125,000 (with interest), the intestate's personal chattels absolutely and a *life interest* in half of the residue. The other half of the residue is held on statutory trusts for the issue (see 1.2.3.2). No other relatives of the intestate can take where the intestate is survived by the spouse and issue. If the intestate leaves no issue but is survived by a parent, or brother or sister of the whole blood (or their issue), the surviving spouse takes a statutory legacy of £200,000 (with interest), the personal chattels absolutely and half of the residue *absolutely*. The other half passes to the parents, but if no parents survive, then to brothers and sisters of the whole blood (or their issue). If the intestate leaves no issue, no parent, and no brother or sister of the whole blood (or their issue), the surviving spouse takes the whole of the residuary estate absolutely.

Apart from having rights in the residuary estate, a relative of the intestate will have the right to take property which he had owned jointly with the intestate. This right arises through survivorship and is inherent in the nature of a joint tenancy. The typical scenario is where husband and wife own the matrimonial home under a joint tenancy. If one of them dies intestate, the survivor takes the home *in addition to* all the rights of succession conferred by the 1925 Act. If the home was held by tenancy in common, the intestate's severable share constitutes part of his estate and is distributed under s. 46 in the usual manner.

Summary of rights of surviving spouse

		Spouse takes
(a)	Where issue survives the intestate	1. £125,000 (with interest)
		2. Personal chattels
		3. Life interest in half of the residue
(b)	No issue, but parent, or brother or sister of the whole blood (or their issue)	1. £200,000 (with interest)
		2. Personal chattels
		3. Half of the residue absolutely
(c)	No issue, parent, or brother or sister of the whole blood (or their issue)	The whole residuary estate absolutely

1.2.2.4 The statutory legacy

A statutory legacy was first given by the Intestates' Estates Act 1890 (£500 for widows only). The Administration of Estates Act 1925 raised the legacy to £1,000 and applied it to widows and widowers alike. The legacy was raised to £5,000 by the Intestates' Estates Act 1952 where the intestate left issue, and to £20,000 where there were no issue but there were surviving specified relatives. The amounts were raised to £8,750 and £30,000 respectively by the Family Provision Act 1966, and the Lord Chancellor was given the power by that Act to raise the sum (and has done so several times).

The current amounts — £125,000 and £200,000 respectively — were provided by the Family Provision (Intestate Succession) Order 1993 and apply to deaths on or after 1 December 1993. It appears that the amounts of the legacies have been raised particularly with the rising cost of house purchase in mind. Interest on the legacy is payable from the date of the intestate's death until the legacy is paid or appropriated. The Lord Chancellor has the power to specify the rate by order. The current rate of 6 per cent per annum dates from 1 October 1983.

1.2.2.5 Personal chattels

Under s. 46 of the 1925 Act the surviving spouse is entitled to the intestate's personal chattels absolutely. Why? Presumably the entitlement is justified on the ground that the spouse is the person most closely connected with such chattels — indeed, many of them may have some special significance or sentimental value for the spouse. The entitlement to personal chattels is potentially a most valuable one. There may be cases where such chattels — valuable jewellery or works of art, for example — may constitute the greater part of the estate's value.

Personal chattels are defined by s. 55(1)(x) of the 1925 Act:

> 'Personal chattels' mean carriages, horses, stable furniture and effects (not used for business purposes), motor cars and accessories (not used for business purposes), garden effects, domestic animals, plate, plated articles, linen, china, glass, books, pictures, prints, furniture, jewellery, articles of household or personal use or ornament, musical and scientific instruments and apparatus, wines, liquors and consumable stores, but do not include any chattels used at the death of the intestate for business purposes nor money or securities for money.

This definition has been regularly criticised by the judges. For example, in *Re Chaplin* [1950] Ch 507, at 509, Vaisey J commented that the 'enumeration of specific articles in the definition is neither happy nor clear' and he described the definition as 'an *omnium gatherum*' (a witty Anglo-Latin phrase concocted to emphasise the rag-bag nature of the elements of the definition). *Re Chaplin* was actually not a case of intestacy at all but an example of the occasional use made by testators (presumably on the advice of their solicitors) of the s. 55(1)(x) definition — the testator had left all the residue of 'my personal chattels as defined by the Administration of Estates Act 1925 to my wife absolutely'. The definition certainly shows its age, particularly in the early items listed, which conjure up an image of a bygone era.

The definition specifies certain items as personal chattels but excludes others. The words listing certain items as personal chattels are to be interpreted in their ordinary sense. For example, in *Re Whitby* [1944] Ch 210, CA, the court held that cut but unmounted diamonds were 'jewellery'. Property which does not come within the description of jewellery may nevertheless constitute personal chattels if it qualifies as 'articles of personal ornament' within s. 55(1)(x). In *Re Hutchinson* [1955] Ch 255, 'horses' were interpreted as including racehorses as well as horses used for domestic purposes. Danckwerts J held that the conjunction of 'horses' with 'carriages' and 'stable furniture' in the definition did not restrict the meaning to horses used for domestic purposes. In *Re Reynold's WT* [1965] 3 All ER 686, stamp albums were not regarded as 'books', but were held to be 'articles of personal use' and thus personal chattels. 'Furniture' was held to include a collection of clocks in *Re Crispin's WT* [1974] 3 All ER 772, CA, a generous decision but one in line with the generally wide interpretation given to the definition in s. 55(1)(x). In similar vein one might suppose that 'pictures' include paintings and that 'musical and scientific instruments and apparatus' include the technological paraphernalia now common to many households, such as televisions, videos and personal computers.

A key phrase in s. 55(1)(x) is 'articles of household or personal use or ornament'. Unlike the items specifically included, this phrase is general in its ambit and thus has a potentially wide application. The emphasis is very much on the *use* to which the article is put: it must be 'household or personal use or ornament'. For example, in *Re Chaplin* (above) the court held that a motor-yacht used solely for private pleasure cruises was an article of personal use, and rejected the plausible argument that 'article' was inapt to describe a 60-foot yacht with a paid crew. In *Re Crispin's WT* (above) the testator bequeathed 'all my personal chattels as defined in the Administration of Estates Act 1925'. A few years before his death he inherited a valuable collection of clocks and watches which he preserved (he had to buy a bigger home to house the collection). The collection was valued at £50,000 out of a total estate of £80,000. The clocks were normally kept locked up in rooms. The watches were kept in a special chest which the testator occasionally opened in order to display them. He maintained the watches and was in the habit of wearing them. It was held that the use to which the clocks were put was irrelevant since they fell within the ordinary meaning of 'furniture'. But the watches were articles of personal use, as Russell LJ explained (p. 775):

> A watch is in its nature an article of personal use, and in the present case we regard the cherishing by eye and hand of the collection as well as the wearing of selected items from time to time as bringing them within the definition of articles of personal use.

Whether a collection is an article of personal use depends on the nature of the collection and how it is used. Suppose, for example, that Arthur inherits a valuable collection of pre-First World War teddy bears, which he never displays but keeps locked in a room or deposited in a bank. Such use could hardly be said to be 'personal'. If the only or chief reason for maintaining a collection is for investment purposes — as is sometimes the case with stamp and coin collections — it is less likely to be an article of personal use. In *Re Reynold's WT* (above) the issue was whether a valuable stamp collection was an article of personal use under a bequest of personal chattels as defined by s. 55(1)(x). The collection consisted of several albums together with a number of boxes containing loose stamps. The deceased had built up the collection since childhood (it had been his main hobby). The case was decided by a judge who might have been thought especially qualified for the task — Stamp J. The judge stated (p. 688):

> If the testator had gone into the shop of a stamp dealer and bought a collection of stamps and installed it in his flat it could hardly be said that the collection so bought was an article of personal use. I have, however, to put myself into the testator's armchair and to look at the stamp collection in relation to the way in which he collected it and the way in which he used it.

On this basis it was held that the collection was an article of personal use. Similarly in *Re Collins's Settlement Trusts* [1971] 1 All ER 283, a valuable stamp collection was held to come within a gift of 'personal effects' since the deceased had built up the collection over many years — it was his main hobby and he was recognised in philatelic circles as an experienced collector. The phrase 'personal effects' was treated as analogous with 'personal chattels'.

Section 55(1)(x) specifically excludes money, securities for money and 'any chattels used at the death of the intestate for business purposes'. The exclusion of chattels used for business purposes is understandable but is not expressed with sufficient clarity. If the chattel — a motor car, for example — was used both for business and domestic purposes at the intestate's death, is it excluded? It would have been preferable if the *extent* of business use had been indicated by some such phrase as 'for entirely or mainly business purposes'. Not only is the drafting of the definition unhelpful, but there is also a lack of reported authority on the interpretation of 'business purposes'. It would be plausible to interpret the phrase as excluding any chattels used for business purposes at the intestate's death, however limited the use. But the court is perhaps more likely to follow the Canadian decision, *Re MacCulloch's Estate* (1981) 44 NSR (2d) 666, where it was held that the test was whether the *dominant* use of the chattel was for business purposes. The testator had bought a yacht, allegedly for the personal use of himself and his wife, Patricia Bredin, the actress. He bequeathed to his wife all his 'articles of personal, domestic or household use or ornament'. It was held that she was not entitled to the yacht since the dominant use of the yacht was commercial (hire for pleasure cruises).

1.2.2.6 Interest in balance of the residue

In addition to the statutory legacy (with interest) and the personal chattels, the surviving spouse takes a life interest in half of the residue if there are surviving issue. If there are no issue but the intestate is survived by a parent, or brother or sister of the whole blood (or their issue), the spouse takes half of the residue absolutely.

Where a life interest arises the administration of the estate may be complicated by the need for continuing trusts; and the entitlement to income rather than to capital may prove disadvantageous to the spouse in some circumstances. Thus it will normally be far preferable for the spouse to take the life interest in capitalised form. The easiest way to achieve this is for the spouse and the issue simply to agree how much the spouse should take by way of a capital sum in place of the life interest. This can be done under the rule in *Saunders* v *Vautier* (see 1.1.4.2). Alternatively, resort may be had to the right to capitalise the life interest under s. 47A(1) of the 1925 Act:

Where a surviving husband or wife is entitled to a life interest in part of the residuary estate, and so elects, the personal representative shall purchase or redeem the life interest by paying the capital value thereof to the tenant for life, or the persons deriving title under the tenant for life, and the costs of the transaction; and thereupon the residuary estate of the intestate may be dealt with and distributed free from the life interest.

The value of the sum to which the spouse is entitled on redemption of the life interest is calculated by taking into account the spouse's life expectancy and the average yield on certain Government stocks at the date when the election was made. Tables for this purpose are contained in the schedule of the Intestate Succession (Interest and Capitalisation) Order 1977. The election has to be made by the spouse within 12 months of the date when representation to the estate was first taken out, but the period may be extended if it would otherwise operate unfairly: s. 47A(5). Election is made by the spouse giving written notice to the personal representatives: s. 47A(6). If the spouse is the sole representative, written notice must be given to the Senior Registrar of the Family Division of the High Court: s. 47A(7).

1.2.2.7 The matrimonial home
The destination of the matrimonial home will be of overriding importance in the distribution of the residuary estate. As has been emphasised already, if the home was owned jointly it does not form part of the residuary estate since the surviving spouse is entitled to it by *ius accrescendi* (survivorship). If the home was not owned by joint tenancy, the intestate's interest in it at his death will form part of the residuary estate. The Administration of Estates Act 1925 did not give any specific entitlement in the home to the surviving spouse, although personal representatives have the general power to appropriate any asset in or towards satisfaction of any interest in the estate to which the surviving spouse was entitled: s. 41. Moreover, the Intestates' Estates Act 1952 gave the spouse the right to *require* the personal representatives to appropriate the matrimonial home for that spouse. The Second Schedule, para. 1(1) provides:

> ... where the residuary estate of the intestate comprises an interest in a dwelling-house in which the surviving husband or wife was resident at the time of the intestate's death, the surviving husband or wife may require the personal representative, in exercise of the power conferred by section 41 of the principal Act (and with due regard to the requirements of that section as to valuation), to appropriate the said interest in the dwelling-house in or towards satisfaction of any absolute interest of the surviving husband or wife in the real and personal estate of the intestate.

Several points arise in the operation of this provision. First, the residuary estate must comprise 'an interest' in a dwelling-house. Both freeholds and leaseholds are comprised in the term 'interest', but the Schedule does not apply to leases with less than two years to run from the date of death or those that are determinable within the two years on the landlord giving notice following the intestate's death: Second Schedule, para. 1(2). However, an interest in such a lease may be appropriated if the surviving spouse is entitled to acquire the freehold or an extended lease under s. 7(8) of the Leasehold Reform Act 1967.

Secondly, the interest must be in 'a dwelling-house'. This is a curious phrase to use given that s. 5 of the Intestates' Estates Act 1952 states that the effect of the Second Schedule is to enable the surviving spouse 'to acquire the matrimonial home'. Is 'a dwelling-house' synonymous with 'the matrimonial home'? Most probably not — the Schedule appears to apply to a house that was not necessarily the matrimonial home. This conclusion is strengthened by the fact that under para. 1(1) of the Schedule it is irrelevant whether the intestate was resident or not at the dwelling-house (only the surviving spouse's residence is relevant). Moreover, it is more consistent with the overall thrust of the 1952 Act — the improvement of the surviving spouse's position — that the right should extend to a dwelling-house, because in some cases there may no longer be a matrimonial home owing to marital breakdown.

Thirdly, the surviving spouse must have been 'resident at the time of the intestate's death' in the dwelling-house being appropriated. Since a person may simultaneously be resident in more than one home, it may be that the right to appropriate is not necessarily confined to one dwelling-house, especially as para. 1(1) refers to 'an interest in a dwelling-house' and not to *the* dwelling-house. But this is hardly conclusive since in later paragraphs of the Schedule the references are predominantly to 'the' dwelling-house. Sherrin and Bonehill, *The Law and Practice of Intestate Succession*, 2nd edn., 1994, consider that only one house may be appropriated (p. 245).

Fourthly, what is meant by 'in or towards satisfaction of any absolute interest' of the surviving spouse in the intestate's estate? A plausible interpretation of this phrase would be that appropriation is possible only if the house does not exceed the value of the spouse's absolute interests under the intestacy. However, it is clear that such a restriction was not intended by the legislature since para. 5(2) of the Second Schedule states that appropriation can be made 'partly in satisfaction of an interest' of the surviving spouse, 'and partly in return for a payment of money' by the spouse to the intestate's personal representative. In *Re Phelps* [1980] Ch 275, the Court of Appeal applied this provision and held that a widow could appropriate a house, which exceeded the value of her absolute interests on intestacy, by making an equalisation payment.

Fifthly, what is meant by 'any absolute interest' in the intestate estate? The phrase comprises the statutory legacy (with interest), the personal chattels and the capital value of the life interest (where it arises) which the spouse has elected to redeem. But it does not include a life interest which has not been capitalised.

Where the right to appropriate is exercised, the interest in the dwelling-house will have to be valued (unless the value is agreed by all those entitled on the intestate's death). Before deciding whether to appropriate such an interest, the surviving spouse can require (and usually will) the personal representatives to have the interest valued: Second Schedule, para. 3(2). The relevant value of the interest is the market value at the time of appropriation, not the value when the intestate died. It follows that it is in the spouse's interest to exercise the right to appropriate as quickly as possible during a period of rapid house-price inflation. In *Robinson v Collins* [1975] 1 All ER 321, the intestate's home was valued at £4,200 when he died. A summons was brought to determine the value at which the widow was entitled to have the property appropriated. By the time the issue was determined the value of the house had nearly doubled (and the widow had not yet chosen to appropriate). It was held that the relevant value was that at the time of appropriation.

The right to appropriate an interest in a dwelling-house must be exercised by giving written notice to the personal representatives within 12 months of the first taking out of representation with respect to the intestate's estate: Second Schedule, para. 3(1)(a). But the period may be extended if otherwise it would operate unfairly: para. 3(3). If the spouse is one of the personal representatives, notice must be given to the others: para. 3(1)(c). If the spouse is the sole personal representative, the position appears unclear (the safest course is to have an additional personal representative appointed). During the 12-month period in which the right to appropriate can be exercised, the personal representatives must not dispose of the interest in the dwelling-house without the written consent of the surviving spouse (see 1.2.1).

In certain circumstances the right to appropriate is not exercisable unless the court is satisfied that the exercise of the right 'is not likely to diminish the value of assets in the residuary estate (other than the said interest in the dwelling-house) or make them more difficult to dispose of': para. 2. The circumstances specified in para. 2 are where:

(a)   the dwelling-house forms part of a building and an interest in the whole of the building is comprised in the residuary estate; or

(b)   the dwelling-house is held with agricultural land and an interest in that land is comprised in the residuary estate; or

(c)   the whole or part of the dwelling-house was used as a hotel or lodging house at the time of the intestate's death; or

(d)   a part of the dwelling-house was at that time used for purposes other than domestic purposes.

1.2.2.8   Double entitlement?

It may be possible for a surviving spouse to take on intestacy in two different capacities — as spouse and as next-of-kin of the intestate. An adopted child is regarded in law as the legitimate child of the adoptive parent or parents. The child becomes a brother or sister of the whole blood of the existing children of the adoptive parents (if they were a married couple). Curiously there is no ban in current English law on the marriage of collaterals if their relationship has arisen through adoption. Suppose then that a married couple have a daughter, Sally, and a son, Tim. Later they adopt a boy, Arthur, who thus becomes the brother of Sally and Tim. Later Arthur and Sally marry (as they legally can) and eventually Arthur dies intestate without issue, survived by Sally and Tim. Sally is entitled on his intestacy as his widow; thus she takes the statutory legacy, the personal chattels and half the balance of the residue absolutely. The remaining half passes in this scenario to the intestate's brothers and sisters of the whole blood, that is, Sally and Tim. It would thus seem possible for Sally to take both as the spouse and sister of Arthur.

1.2.2.9   The entitlement of the issue

If the intestate is survived by a spouse and issue, the balance of the residuary estate (after the satisfaction of the spouse's entitlement) passes to the issue on statutory trusts (see 1.2.3.2). The balance comprises two elements:

(a)   the half of the residue not taken by the spouse;

(b)   the remainder in the spouse's life interest. If the spouse capitalises the life interest, the sum freed thereby passes to the issue.

1.2.3   Issue but no surviving spouse

Section 46(1)(ii) of the Administration of Estates Act 1925 provides:

> If the intestate leaves issue but no husband or wife the residuary estate of the intestate shall be held on the statutory trusts for the issue of the intestate.

1.2.3.1   Who are the issue?

The word 'issue' comprises the lineal descendants of the intestate, that is, the children, grandchildren and remoter descendants who are living at the intestate's death, including issue who are *en ventre sa mère* at that time.

(a)   *Illegitimate children.* Before the Family Law Reform Act 1969, the general position was that illegitimate children could not succeed on the intestacy of their parent, or vice versa. Section 14 of that Act provided that an illegitimate child was entitled to succeed on the intestacy of a parent, and vice versa. This reform equated the position of illegitimate with legitimate children as regards the parent-child relationship; but it did not enable illegitimate children to take on the intestacy of grandparents, brothers or sisters, uncles or aunts, or vice versa. The Law Commission recommended further reforms in its report on illegitimacy (Law Com. No. 118, 1982), which were enacted in the Family Law Reform Act 1987 (applicable to persons dying intestate on or after 4 April 1988). Under s. 1 of this Act, references to 'any relationship between two persons shall, unless the contrary intention appears, be construed without regard to whether or not the father and mother of either of them, or the father and mother of any person through whom the relationship is deduced, have or had been married to each other at any time'. Section 18(1) applies the general principle in s. 1 to entitlement on intestacy under the Administration of Estates Act 1925. Consequently, illegitimate children can now take not only on the intestacy of their parents but also of their brothers and sisters, grandparents, and uncles and aunts, and vice versa. Section 18(2) retains the presumption (originally enacted in the Family Law Reform Act 1969) that an illegitimate child shall be presumed not to have been survived by the father unless the contrary is shown. This presumption does not prevent the father from taking but places on him the onus of claiming entitlement.

(b)   *Legitimated children.* Section 5(3) of the Legitimacy Act 1976 provides that a legitimated person, and any other person, shall be entitled to take any interest as if the legitimated person had been born legitimate. Legitimation occurs on the marriage of the parents of an illegitimate child. The effect of legitimation under the 1976 Act is to place the legitimated child in the same position as the legitimate child as regards succession on intestacy. The position of legitimate, legitimated and illegitimate children has thus now been equated.

(c) *Adopted children.* Under s. 39(1) of the Adoption Act 1976, an adopted child is treated as the legitimate child of his adoptive parent or parents. Moreover, the child is treated as if he were not the child of any person other than the adopters: s. 39(2). Thus the child will have succession rights on his adoptive parents' intestacy, but not as regards his previous parents. Because an adopted child is treated as the child of the adoptive parents, its position as regards succession on intestacy is the same as that of a child born of those parents. That basic principle applies to all the new relationships created by the adoption. For example, the adopted child will be able to succeed on the intestacy of his adoptive brothers and sisters, or grandparents or uncles and aunts, and vice versa.

(d) *Stepchildren.* Under the present law a stepchild has no right to take on the intestacy of the step-parent or vice versa. Given the contemporary frequency of such relationships (because of the increase in the incidence of divorce and subsequent remarriage) it may be seen as unfortunate that stepchildren and step-parents have no mutual rights of intestate succession. However, a stepchild may be able to apply for financial provision from an intestate estate as 'a child of the family' under the Inheritance (Provision for Family and Dependants) Act 1975 (see 8.2.1.4).

(e) *Human fertilisation.* Under s. 27 of the Human Fertilization and Embryology Act 1990, only the woman who is carrying or has carried a child as the result of the placing in her of an embryo or of sperm and eggs is to be treated as the mother of the child (whether or not the child is genetically related to her). If the woman was married when the embryo or the sperm and eggs were placed in her, her husband will be treated as the child's father unless it is shown that he did not consent to the placing: s. 28.

1.2.3.2 The statutory trusts

Whenever issue take on intestacy they take their entitlement on 'statutory trusts': s. 46(1) of the Administration of Estates Act 1925. Statutory trusts are defined by s. 47(1)(i), under which the residuary estate is to be held for the issue as follows:

> In trust, in equal shares if more than one, for all or any of the children or child of the intestate, living at the death of the intestate, who attain the age of 18 years or marry under that age, and for all or any of the issue living at the death of the intestate who attain the age of 18 years or marry under that age of any child of the intestate who predeceases the intestate, such issue to take through all degrees, according to their stocks, in equal shares if more than one, the share which their parent would have taken if living at the death of the intestate, and so that no issue shall take whose parent is living at the death of the intestate and so capable of taking.

This definition certainly reads awkwardly, but in defence of the draftsman it must be said that it attempts to describe a rather complicated scenario. The salient elements of this definition are as follows:

(a) *Vested interest*. Children and remoter issue must attain 18 years or marry under that age in order to take a vested interest in the intestate estate. The minimum age of marriage is 16 years, but parental consent is normally required if a party to the marriage is under 18. If issue are under 18, their contingent interests will be held for them on trust. What if issue fail to attain a vested interest? Any contingent share accrues to the shares held by other issue. If all the contingent shares fail — that is, no one attains a vested interest — the residuary estate will be distributed as if the intestate had not been survived by any issue: s. 47(2)(a).

(b) *Entitlement per stirpes*. The statutory trusts operate on the principle of distribution of the estate among the issue *per stirpes* ('through the stems'). Under this principle the estate is distributed through the stems or branches of the family, each of which is entitled to an equal share. The number of branches is determined by the number of children that survived the intestate or who predeceased the intestate but left issue surviving him. For example, if the intestate is survived by two sons, A and B, and by no other next-of-kin, there are two branches of the intestate's family; thus the estate is shared equally by A and B. If only A had survived (and no other next-of-kin), A would take the whole estate, there being only one branch. But suppose that A has survived while B has predeceased the intestate but has left a daughter, C, who has survived the intestate. Then there are two branches of the family surviving the intestate — A and C, the latter representing B. The grandchild, C, takes the share that would have gone to her parent, B, had the latter survived the intestate. Thus A and C share the estate equally. If in this last scenario B had two children, C and D, who survived the intestate, the estate would be split — half to A, one quarter each to C and D (since they take equally the share that would have passed to their parent, B).

(c) *Priority to the nearest*. Where there are different generations of issue within *the same branch* of the intestate's family, the nearest generation excludes the remoter. Thus, if an intestate is survived by a daughter, A, who has a son, B, A takes the whole estate since A is the nearer issue. If the intestate had another child, C, who had predeceased the intestate but had left a child D, who survived the intestate, A and D would take the estate equally. In this case A (a child) does not exclude D (a grandchild) because they constitute different branches of the intestate's family.

Example
The following example illustrates a number of the points discussed above in the operation of statutory trusts. Suppose that Arthur dies intestate leaving a residuary estate of £180,000. He is survived by a son, Alan; a daughter, Beryl, who has a son, Chris; and by David and Erica, the two children of Arthur's deceased son, Frank. David is aged 15; Erica is aged 17 and is married. Arthur had another son, Michael, who predeceased him without issue. The estate will be distributed as follows. There are three branches of issue surviving Arthur — Alan, Beryl, and the children of Frank. The three branches take equally. Thus Alan and Beryl take £60,000 each. Beryl's son, Chris, takes nothing since he is excluded by his mother (she is nearer issue to the intestate within the same

branch). David and Erica, the children of Frank, take his share by representation *per stirpes* (£30,000 each). David's interest is contingent on his attaining 18 years of age. Erica, however, takes an immediate vested interest since she is married. If David dies before attaining 18, his share is taken by Erica.

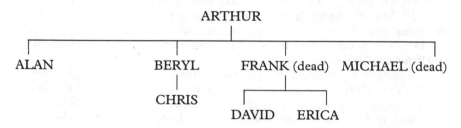

1.2.3.3 Hotchpot

Hotchpot comprises the notion that certain benefits conferred *inter vivos* on a child by his intestate parent have to be brought into account on the distribution of the residuary estate. The concept is analogous to the *collatio bonorum* in Roman law whereby a child entitled on intestacy had to account for benefits acquired as the result of his emancipation by his father. The idea is to achieve equality between children as to the totality of the benefits received from an intestate parent, both *inter vivos* and on death. Besides being dubious in principle — equality may not necessarily have been intended by the parent — the application of hotchpot could be problematic in practice. Not surprisingly hotchpot was abolished by s. 1(2) of the Law Reform (Succession) Act 1995 as regards persons dying intestate on or after 1 January 1996. However, since cases may arise for some time to come in which the pre-1996 law will be relevant, the reader cannot escape some discussion of hotchpot.

The hotchpot rules are contained in s. 47(1)(iii) of the 1925 Act, which applies only if the property held on statutory trusts for issue 'is divisible into shares'. Thus hotchpot does not apply where there is only one child — or branch of the intestate's family — entitled to take. It is only benefits conferred on *children* that need to be brought into account, and not benefits conferred on grandchildren or remoter issue. However, where a child of the intestate predeceases him, and that child's share is taken by the intestate's grandchild (or remoter issue) *per stirpes*, the beneficiary must account for benefits conferred on that predeceased child. Suppose, for example, that the intestate dies leaving a residuary estate of £200,000, and is survived by a daughter, A, and a grandson, B, the son of the intestate's predeceased son, C. Suppose further that the intestate had conferred *inter vivos* benefits worth £20,000 on A, and £10,000 on B (the grandson). Only A's benefits have to be brought into hotchpot. Thus the estate will be distributed — £90,000 to A, £110,000 to B. But if the intestate had conferred benefits of £40,000 on C, B would then have to account for the benefits conferred on his parent. It should be noted that where hotchpot applies, the relevant distribution is calculated by first adding the total amount to be accounted for to the residuary estate, then dividing the resulting sum between the branches of issue entitled, and then subtracting from each share any amount that has to be brought into account. For example, in the last-mentioned scenario, the total amount of benefits to be brought into account was £60,000. Thus the sum to be divided between the issue was £260,000 — notionally £130,000 each to A and B. A has to account for £20,000, B for £40,000. Hence A takes £110,000, B takes £90,000.

Which benefits are to be brought into account? Under s. 47(1)(iii) it is 'any money or property which, by way of advancement or on the marriage of a child of the intestate, has been paid to such child by the intestate or settled by the intestate for the benefit of such child (including any life or less interest and including property covenanted to be paid or settled)' which must be brought into account subject to any contrary intention. Several elements of this description require explanation:

(a) *Advancement.* Curiously there is no definition of advancement in the 1925 Act. The classic case law definition is to be found in *Taylor* v *Taylor* (1875) LR 20 Eq 155, at 157–8, where Jessel MR stated:

> ... an advancement by way of portion is something given by the parent to establish the child in life, or to make what is called a provision for him — not a mere casual payment. ... You may make the provision by way of marriage portion on the marriage of the child. You may make it on putting him into a profession or business in a variety of ways: you may pay for a commission, you may buy him the goodwill of a business and give him stock-in-trade; all these things I understand to be portions or provisions.

Later in his judgment Jessel MR remarked that *prima facie* an advancement must be made 'in early life' and that 'any sum given by way of making a permanent provision for the child would come within the term establishing in life' (p. 159). The case was concerned with whether various benefits received by the intestate's two sons amounted to advancements. One son became a clergyman and was regularly given large sums by the intestate to assist him in paying his housekeeping and other expenses — these payments were held not to be advancements. The other son had a somewhat more diverse, if unsuccessful, career. First he studied law at the Middle Temple with a view to being called to the Bar, but abandoned his attempt; then he entered the army; then he and bought some land in Wales with a view to carrying on mining operations (which proved unprofitable). His father supported him liberally during these ventures. The following payments were held to be advancements: payment of the admission fee to the Middle Temple; the price of the commission and outfit for entry to the army; the price of plant and machinery and other payments made in connection with the mining operations. But the following were held not to be advancements: the fee paid to a special pleader at the Middle Temple in whose chambers the son read law; the cost of the passage of the son and his wife on going to India with his regiment; payment of his debts incurred in the army.

It seems clear that provision of maintenance or temporary assistance does not constitute an advancement; nor does provision for education. Moreover, the age of the child and the amount of the provision are relevant factors. In *Re Hayward* [1957] 1 Ch 528, the intestate made *inter vivos* nominations amounting to about £507 in favour of his elder son, who was aged 43 and employed as a clerk in the War Office. It was not clear what the intestate's purpose was in making these nominations. The court held that they were not advancements (thus the son did not have to account for them). Both the age of the son and the size of the nominations were held to be factors fatal to the argument that the intestate had made an advancement: the sum was not sufficiently large to constitute a permanent provision. If such provision is made, it does not matter that the payment was not intended to *establish* the child. In *Hardy* v *Shaw* [1975] 2 All ER 1052, it was held that a substantial gift of shares in a family company to each of two adult children was by way of advancement — since it was a permanent provision — even though they were already established in the business.

(b) *Marriage.* Benefits conferred by an intestate 'on the marriage of a child of the intestate' must also be brought into hotchpot under s. 47(1)(iii). It is clear that such benefits need not have been made by way of advancement. Strictly this would mean that all wedding gifts from the intestate to his child should be accounted for, but it is doubtful whether the courts would go that far (there appears to be no reported case on this point).

(c) *Paid or settled.* Section 47(1)(iii) applies to money or property which was 'paid to' or 'settled' for the benefit of a child. The drafting is hardly elegant — the reference to property being 'paid' is rather awkward — but it is clear that 'paid' is to be construed widely. In *Hardy* v *Shaw* (above) it was accepted without argument that a transfer of shares came within the expression 'money or property paid'.

(d) *Contrary intention.* Section 47(1)(iii) states that the hotchpot rules apply 'subject to any contrary intention expressed or appearing from the circumstances of the case'. In *Hardy* v *Shaw* (above) the intestate was survived by three children — Mary, Vera and Harold — all of whom worked in the family business. One of the daughters, Mary, married a man of whom her father strongly disapproved. After the marriage Mary ceased to work in the business whereupon the father stated that she should have no further shares in it. He left the whole of his estate to his wife, including his shares in the company. Sometime after his death, his widow gave all her shares to Vera and Harold, and eventually died intestate. The residuary estate passed to the three children. Not surprisingly it was argued that Vera and Harold should not have to account for the transfer of the shares since in the circumstances a contrary intention was evident. The court held, however, that no such intention could be established. The test was subjective: 'looking at all the circumstances, do they require an inference that her intention [the intestate's] was that the gift should not be brought into hotchpot?' (*per* Goff J, at p. 1057). The judge thought it crucial whether the facts showed an intention on the intestate's part to prefer Vera and Harold to Mary as regards provision for them on the intestate's death. He concluded that as there was insufficient evidence that the intestate ever directed her mind to what should happen on her death, a contrary intention could not be demonstrated. Thus Vera and Harold had to account as they had failed to discharge the onus of proof of establishing a contrary intention. Clearly the decision in *Hardy* v *Shaw* resulted in the greater likelihood of the application of hotchpot because it severely restricted the operation of the 'contrary intention' exception.

At what valuation are benefits to be brought into hotchpot? Section 47(1)(iii) provides that the value is to be reckoned 'as at the death of the intestate'. In *Re Reeve* [1935] Ch 110, it was held that a life interest which the intestate had surrendered to his son could be of no value since the interest had to be valued as at the date of the intestate's death.

It needs to be emphasised again that the hotchpot provisions now apply only in the case of intestates dying before 1996. Few will mourn the abolition of hotchpot. The application of the rules demanded some fine (and hardly justifiable) distinctions to be drawn between different types of gift, often based on an assumed intention that the intestate might not have possessed.

1.2.4   No surviving spouse or issue

Where there is no surviving spouse and surviving issue who attain a vested interest, the residuary estate is distributed under s. 46(1) of the 1925 Act in the following order: parents; brothers and sisters of the whole blood (or their issue); brothers and sisters of the half-blood (or their issue); grandparents; uncles and aunts of the whole blood (or their issue); uncles and aunts of the half-blood (or their issue).

1.2.4.1   Parents
Parents take on the intestacy of their children in equal shares absolutely: s. 46(1)(iii). A sole surviving parent takes the whole residuary estate. However, as noted already, the father of an illegitimate child is presumed not to have survived his child unless the contrary is shown (see 1.2.3.1).

1.2.4.2   Brothers and sisters of the whole blood
Brothers and sisters of the whole blood are persons who have both parents in common with the intestate. Under s. 46(1)(v), brothers and sisters of the whole blood take on 'statutory trusts', which have the same meaning as for issue (apart from hotchpot not applying). Thus persons in this category do not take a vested interest unless they attain 18 years of age or marry under that age. Representation *per stirpes* applies: a child of a predeceasing brother or sister of the intestate takes the share that would otherwise have been taken by that brother or sister. Thus, if the intestate is survived by a sister, A, and by a nephew, B, the child of the intestate's deceased brother, C, the residuary estate will be shared equally by A and B. If the nephew, B, was the sole survivor from this category, he would take the whole residuary estate in preference to other next-of-kin lower in the order (e.g., grandparents).

It should be remembered that parents or brothers and sisters of the whole blood (or their issue) may also take where the intestate is survived by a spouse but no issue (see 1.2.2.3).

1.2.4.3 Brothers and sisters of the half-blood
Brothers and sisters of the half-blood have one parent in common with the intestate. Persons entitled in this category take on the same statutory trusts as brothers and sisters of the whole blood: s. 46(1)(v).

1.2.4.4 Grandparents
Where there is no surviving spouse, issue, parent, or brother or sister of the whole or half-blood (or their issue), the residuary estate passes to the grandparents of the intestate in equal shares: s. 46(1)(v). A sole surviving grandparent takes the whole residuary estate. The entitlement of grandparents is absolute — it is obvious that the statutory trusts are inapplicable in their case.

1.2.4.5 Uncles and aunts of the whole blood
An uncle or aunt of the whole blood is a brother or sister of the whole blood of a parent of the intestate. Persons in this category take on statutory trusts: s. 46(1)(v). Thus entitlement can pass *per stirpes*: the issue of a predeceased uncle or aunt of an intestate take the share that would have passed to the uncle or aunt. To illustrate: suppose that the intestate is survived by Tom, who is the child of Harry, the predeceased uncle of the intestate. Tom, who is of course a cousin of the intestate, will take the residuary estate. It is within this category (and the next) that cousins are given entitlement on intestacy.

1.2.4.6 Uncles and aunts of the half-blood
An uncle or aunt of the half-blood is a brother or sister of the half-blood of a parent of the intestate. Persons in this category take on the same statutory trusts as uncles and aunts of the whole blood: s. 46(1)(v).

1.2.5 No surviving relatives: *bona vacantia*

If the intestate is not survived by a spouse, issue or any of the specified relatives, the residuary estate passes to the Crown as *bona vacantia*. The Crown's rights appear to date from the foundation of the monarchy, although the concept of the automatic entitlement of the State as the heir of last resort can be traced back to Roman law. Under s. 46(1)(vi), the Crown may provide 'in accordance with the existing practice, for dependants, whether kindred or not, of the intestate, and other persons for whom the intestate might reasonably have been expected to make provision'. It is clear that no one has a right to a grant under this provision — the making of grants is discretionary, although it should conform to 'the existing practice' (the jurisdiction is exercised by the Treasury Solicitor). The 'grounds' on which grants are more likely to be made include the following:

(a)   where the applicant was a beneficiary under a document intended by the intestate to be his will, but which failed to take effect;

(b)   where there existed between the applicant and the intestate a long and close relationship, e.g., cohabitation as man and wife;

(c)where the intestate made his home with the applicant and came to be regarded as a member of the applicant's family;

(d)   where the applicant performed such essential services or substantial acts of kindness (without payment) that the intestate might reasonably have been expected to benefit the applicant by will (see further Ing, *Bona Vacantia*, 1971, chapter 10).

1.3   PARTIAL INTESTACY

1.3.1   The basic position

A partial intestacy occurs when a testator makes a will which disposes of only part of his estate, or which disposes of the whole estate but not all of the beneficial interests in it — for example, where a testator leaves the whole of his estate to his wife for life but fails to dispose of the remainder. There are various reasons why partial intestacies occur: the testator might simply have forgotten or not understood how much property he owned; or he might have failed to include a satisfactory residuary clause; or he might have revoked a gift but failed to provide a substitutionary provision. In such cases the testator's acts have contributed to the partial intestacy, but in other cases it can arise through reasons mostly beyond his control — for example, where a beneficiary unexpectedly disclaims a gift under a will.

1.3.1.1   Section 49(1) of the Administration of Estate Act 1925
On a partial intestacy the rules of total intestacy apply to the undisposed-of property subject to the provisions of the will. The key statutory provision is s. 49(1):

> Where any person dies leaving a will effectively disposing of part of his property, this Part of this Act [i.e. Part IV dealing with distribution of intestate estates] shall have effect as respects the part of his property not so disposed of subject to the provisions contained in the will . . .

The overall effect of s. 49(1) is to make a will for the intestate to the extent that he failed to do so. It is as if there were a statutory provision at the end of each will giving any undisposed-of property to those entitled on intestacy. As Templeman J stated in *Re Buttle's WT* [1976] 3 All ER 289, at 291: 'The 1925 Act merely fills in the gaps which the testator omits or fails to fill in himself.' In practice it will be rare for anyone other than a surviving spouse to take on a partial intestacy — the spouse's entitlement will nearly always swallow up the whole of the undisposed-of property or interest.

1.3.1.2   Where spouse has a life interest under the will
In applying the rules on partial intestacy problems may arise where there is a surviving spouse to whom a life interest was left in the will. Suppose, for example, that the testator was survived by his spouse and issue and that he left his estate to his wife for life but failed to dispose of the remainder. What is the wife's entitlement on intestacy and when can it be claimed? In *Re Bowen-Buscarlet's WT* [1971] 3 All ER 636, a testator gave his wife a life interest in his

estate but failed to dispose of the remainder. He was survived by the wife and by issue. The wife's entitlement in the remainder comprised the statutory legacy (with interest), the personal chattels and a life interest in half of the residue. Clearly, she could not take the life interest in the residue because its operation was necessarily postponed until after her life interest under the will. The question arose, however, whether she was entitled to immediate payment of the statutory legacy, or whether it was payable to her personal representatives on her death as part of her estate. It was held that the widow's interests under the will and under the intestacy rules merged so that she was entitled to immediate payment of the statutory legacy. The court followed *Re Douglas's WT* [1959] 2 All ER 620 — where a similar approach had been adopted — and declined to follow the conflicting decision in *Re McKee* [1931] 2 Ch 145, which had apparently decided (the point was not argued) that payment of the statutory legacy could be made only after the surviving spouse's death. The approach exemplified by *Re Douglas's WT* and *Re Bowen-Buscarlet's WT* is greatly to be preferred since it enables the spouse to benefit while still alive.

1.3.2   The provisions of the will

Under s. 49(1) of the 1925 Act, the intestacy rules apply to the distribution of undisposed-of property in a partial intestacy 'subject to the provisions contained in the will'. It is readily understandable that on a partial intestacy the provisions of the will should be dominant — the statutory rules only fill in the gaps not covered by the testator's provisions. For example, it was seen in *Re Bowen-Buscarlet's WT* (above) that the decision resulted from the combined effect of the testamentary life interest and the widow's rights on intestacy. In other cases, where the testator's provisions clearly conflict with the statutory rules, precedence is given to will. For example, in *Re McKee* (above) the testator left his residuary estate on an express trust for sale for his wife for life, remainder to such of his brothers and sisters as should survive her. But as none survived the widow, there was an intestacy as regards the remainder. One of the issues in the case was whether the trust under s. 33 of the 1925 Act was superseded by the express trust for sale under the will. It was held that it had been (the case is regarded as good law on this point).

However, the provisions of the will do not take precedence if they have become ineffective. In *Re Sullivan* [1930] 1 Ch 84, the testator was a nephew of Sir Arthur Sullivan, the famous composer, who had bequeathed to the nephew his musical copyrights. The testator gave the income of his residuary estate on trust for his wife for life, and thereafter on trust for his children. In clause 4 of the will the testator stated that it was his wish that royalties payable in respect of the musical copyrights should be treated as capital, not income. The testator never had children, so a partial intestacy arose. The royalties would normally have passed to the widow as income, but this would have contravened the express provision in clause 4. The trustees sought direction whether the royalties could be treated as income if the widow disclaimed her life interest under the will. Readers could be forgiven for thinking that the facts of this case would have provided an appropriate plot for a typical Gilbert and

Sullivan opera. The court held that in s. 49(1) the words 'subject to the provisions contained in the will' should be construed as referring to the effective provisions therein contained. If the widow disclaimed her testamentary life interest, the provision in the will as to royalties would become inoperative (since the testator had died childless). The widow could thus take the royalties as income. *Re Sullivan* was approved in *Re Thornber* [1937] Ch 29, CA. The testator bequeathed an annuity to his mother, Lettice, and then directed his trustees to pay an annuity to his wife, Agnes, out of the income of his residuary estate. He further directed that any surplus income should be accumulated during his wife's life for 21 years from his death, after which the residuary trust fund should be held for his children. The testator died without issue, whereupon his widow claimed that the surplus income should be dealt with as on intestacy and should not be accumulated. It was held that the direction to accumulate was inoperative because the testator had died childless. Hence the surplus income passed under intestacy, there being no effective provision governing its destination.

1.3.3   Hotchpot on partial intestacy

If a person died partially intestate before 1 January 1996, hotchpot may apply in the distribution of the undisposed-of property. Unlike the case with total intestacy, hotchpot in a partial intestacy applies to a surviving spouse as well as to issue.

1.3.3.1   Surviving spouse
Section 49(1)(aa) of the 1925 Act provides that if the deceased leaves a spouse who acquires any beneficial interests (other than personal chattels specifically bequeathed) under the deceased's will, those interests have to be brought into account as against the spouse's entitlement to the statutory legacy. If the beneficial interests under the will exceed the statutory legacy, the spouse's other rights on intestacy are not affected: the maximum that the spouse 'loses' is the amount of the statutory legacy. In some circumstances the surviving spouse may benefit from disclaiming a beneficial interest under the will in order to take the statutory legacy. For example, if the spouse is left a substantial life interest in the testator's residuary estate and disclaims it, the spouse will preserve the statutory legacy and thus be entitled to an immediate capital sum rather than to income for life.

1.3.3.2   Surviving issue
Hotchpot applies in two ways to issue who take on a partial intestacy. First, the duty under s. 47(1)(iii) of the 1925 Act to account for *inter vivos* advancements made to *children* applies where issue take on partial intestacy as well as on total intestacy (see 1.2.3.3). Secondly, issue have to account under s. 49(1)(a) for benefits received under the will:

> The requirements of section 47 of this Act as to bringing property into account shall apply to any beneficial interests acquired by any issue of the

deceased under the will of the deceased, but not to beneficial interests so acquired by any other persons.

Rarely has a statutory provision met with as much judicial and academic criticism as s. 49(1)(a). The problem lies mainly in the incorporation of s. 47 by s. 49(1)(a). The former section deals with essentially a different matter, that is, *inter vivos* advancements made to *children*, whereas s. 49(1)(a) is concerned with testamentary gifts to *issue*. In *Re Morton* [1956] Ch 644, at 647 Danckwerts J stated:

> I think that [i.e. s. 49(1)(a)] is as bad a piece of draftsmanship as one could conceive, in many respects. It says 'the requirements'. What requirements? I am told the requirements are to be found in section 47(1)(iii). There one finds certain provisions which are not by themselves particularly apt for application to something else . . .

Section 49(1)(a) *could* be interpreted as requiring any issue to account for all the testamentary benefits acquired by himself and by all the other issue of the deceased. Such an interpretation would be absurd but is made possible by the failure of s. 49(1)(a) to delineate clearly who is to bring benefits into hotchpot, and against which shares. There are two plausible interpretations of s. 49(1)(a), the distributive and the stirpital. The distributive interpretation has the considerable merit of simplicity and fairness: a person taking as issue on partial intestacy must account for any testamentary benefits conferred on him, but not on any other issue. The stirpital interpretation is more complicated, less fair to the person having to account, but leads to greater fairness between different branches of the deceased's family. It was described as follows by Harman J in *Re Young* [1951] Ch 185, at 189:

> Any member of the family belonging to a certain branch must bring in everything that has been taken or acquired under the will by that branch.

It is the stirpital interpretation that has been followed by the courts. In *Re Young* the testator settled a share of his residuary estate on discretionary trusts for the benefit of his son, Charles, and Charles's children. The testator died intestate as regards another part of his estate. Charles was entitled to share in the partial intestacy, but the question arose as to what he had to account for in hotchpot under s. 49(1)(a). His beneficial interest was actually minimal because he died soon after the testator. Nevertheless it was held that he had to account (through his personal representative) not only for the value of his own benefit but also for that of his children. Harman J clearly preferred (p. 190) the stirpital interpretation of s. 49(1)(a):

> . . . it seems to me that what is to be brought into account is the beneficial interest which the issue acquired. Who are the issue in question? The father

and children, the two generations between them, are the issue, and it seems to me, therefore, that anything that the father and children together acquired under the will is a beneficial interest acquired by the issue.

The decision in *Re Young* can perhaps be justified on the merits of the case in that it would have been unfair to the testator's other children if Charles's estate had to account only for the minimal benefit received by him. Two subsequent decisions — *Re Morton* (above) and *Re Grover's WT* [1971] Ch 168 — followed the stirpital interpretation espoused in *Re Young*, but with less enthusiasm. In *Re Morton*, Danckwerts J thought that the beneficial interests brought into hotchpot should be 'at a valuation appropriate to the nature of the interest' (p. 649). This comment appears to be more consistent with the distributive interpretation but can be explained as being concerned with the *valuation* of benefits rather than with the question as to which benefits should be brought into hotchpot against which share. In *Re Grover's WT*, Pennycuick J clearly preferred (p. 174) the distributive interpretation:

A possible construction ... which, I confess, appeals to me, was ... that any descendant of the testator who acquires a beneficial interest under his will brings that interest, and nothing more, into account against his share under the partial intestacy.

Nevertheless, the judge thought that he should apply the stirpital interpretation to the facts before him because of the unanimity of view (as he perceived it) in the two earlier cases. All three cases are thus consistent in applying the stirpital interpretation to s. 49(1)(a). However, there are several other uncertainties in the interpretation of s. 49(1)(a) and its attendant case law. For example, is the stirpital interpretation to be applied where a grandchild takes on partial intestacy and benefits under the will are given to him and his issue? And what is the position where children and their issue take benefits in different parts of the testator's property? All three cases discussed above were concerned with children and their issue taking successive interests in the same part of the testator's estate.

The position regarding the time at which benefits are to be valued on a partial intestacy is the same as in total intestacy — it is 'as at the death of the intestate': s. 47(1)(iii) as incorporated by s. 49(1). As regards contrary intention, there is some difference between total and partial intestacy. Whereas in total intestacy it will be remembered that hotchpot applies 'subject to any contrary intention expressed or appearing from the circumstances of the case' (s. 47(1)(iii)), in partial intestacy hotchpot applies 'subject to the provisions contained in the will' (s. 49(1)).

It must be emphasised again that hotchpot has been abolished in the case of intestacies arising on or after 1 January 1996. Given the problems of interpreting s. 49(1)(a), and the unsatisfactory case law, the abolition of hotchpot on partial intestacy is particularly to be welcomed.

1.4   ISSUES OF REFORM

1.4.1   Law Commission Report No. 187

The Law Commission published a Working Paper in 1988 raising the issue of intestacy reform: *Distribution on Intestacy*, Working Paper No. 108. There followed a survey of public opinion and a full report which contained the results of the survey, a critique of the law, recommendations for change and a draft Bill: *Distribution on Intestacy* (Law Com. No. 187, 1989). The Commission naturally paid heed to social evolution in the last few decades, especially changes in the nature and distribution of property. The great increase in home ownership (in preference to rented accommodation), pensions and life insurance was noted, as was the trend towards joint ownership of homes and other assets.

The Commission stated that it was guided by two principal considerations:

> The first is that the intestacy rules should be certain, clear and simple both to understand and to operate. They do not lay down absolute entitlements, because the deceased is always free to make a will leaving his property as he chooses. They operate as a safety-net for those who, for one reason or another, have not done this. If the rules can conform to what most people think should happen, so much the better. If they are simple and easy to understand, the more likely it is that people who want their property to go elsewhere will make a will. It is also important to enable estates to be administered quickly and cheaply. The rules should be such that an ordinary layman can easily interpret them and consequently administer them. Also the rules should make it unnecessary for an administrator to have to determine complex or debatable questions of fact. (para. 25)

The second principal consideration was 'the need to ensure that the surviving spouse receives adequate provision' (para. 26). This objective required that, wherever possible, the spouse should be entitled to remain in the matrimonial home and to receive a sufficient income. There were three possible ways to ensure that the spouse received adequate provision:

(a)   substantially to increase the statutory legacy;
(b)   to allow the spouse to take the matrimonial home automatically, together with an increased statutory legacy and possibly a share of any residue; and
(c)   to allow the spouse to take the whole estate.

The Commission concluded that 'the solution which will provide the right result in the great majority of cases is for the surviving spouse to receive the whole estate' (para. 28). This conclusion was consistent with the survey conducted for the Commission: 72 per cent thought that if the intestate was survived by a spouse and independent adult children, the spouse should take the whole estate. The Commission was critical of the current system of periodic uprating of the statutory legacy by statutory instrument, and did not consider that index-linking the legacy would be a sufficient improvement. Allowing the surviving spouse to take the whole estate would considerably simplify the law in the Commission's view. It would no longer be necessary to have special provisions about appropriation of the matrimonial home. Life interests would no longer be created. Nor would statutory trusts apply where the intestate was survived by a spouse and issue.

The Law Commission considered some possible objections to its central proposal that the surviving spouse should take the whole of the estate. For example, it was suggested that children who were minors should not be excluded by the surviving spouse's entitlement. The Commission agreed that one of the purposes of the intestacy rules was 'to provide minors with sufficient resources to meet their needs', but considered that 'the interests of minor children are normally best served by their surviving parent being adequately provided for' (para. 37). The Commission was particularly concerned about the question whether spouses of second or subsequent marriages should be treated differently where the intestate leaves issue of a former marriage. The total exclusion of the intestate's children from entitlement in such circumstances would strike many as indefensible, but the Law Commission thought that unless children were excluded the surviving spouse would not receive adequate provision in some cases:

> Children of former marriages are often middle-aged at the death of their parents and unlikely to need financial provision. By contrast, the surviving spouse will, in most cases, need to receive the whole estate in order to ensure that he or she can remain in the matrimonial home. Since one of the principal aims of the intestacy rules is that the surviving spouse should receive adequate provision, any provision for issue of former marriages would detract from the fulfilment of this goal. (para. 42)

Another objection was that the Law Commission's proposal would not promote efficient tax planning. The Commission's response was admirably principled: '. . . we believe that taxation considerations should not be taken into account in formulating the intestacy rules' (para. 38).

The proposal that the surviving spouse should take the whole estate was not supported by the Government and was not enacted by the Law Reform (Succession) Act 1995. But the Commission's other recommendations were enacted, as has already been seen: the need for the surviving spouse to survive the intestate by 28 days; the abolition of hotchpot on total and partial intestacy; and the right of a cohabitant to apply for financial provision out of an intestate estate under the Inheritance (Provision for Family and Dependants) Act 1975. It has to be remembered when assessing the intestacy rules that certain persons (principally spouses, children, cohabitants and dependants) can apply under the 1975 Act for reasonable provision out of an intestate estate on the ground that the intestacy rules do not make reasonable provision for them. A recurring theme in the Report is the Commission's reliance on the 1975 Act as a remedy of last resort when the intestacy rules appear inadequate. For example, the availability of the Act is used as a partial justification for excluding the intestate's stepchildren from taking on intestacy. Although the 1975 Act can (and does) fulfil the role of a back-stop in hard cases, its discretionary basis inevitably leads to some uncertainty as to the likelihood of an application succeeding under the Act. Is it not preferable to ensure that the intestacy law is as fair as possible *in the first instance* than to proceed on the basis that defects can be put right by an application under the 1975 Act? The Commission's reluctance to allow stepchildren or cohabitants direct entitlement on intestacy is a case in point. The great increase in recent decades in their numbers arguably demanded some recognition in the form of direct entitlement under the intestacy rules.

1.4.2 Should the surviving spouse take the whole estate?

The Law Commission's proposal that the surviving spouse should take the whole of the estate on intestacy provoked a generally lukewarm response. Commentators could see merit in the proposal, but at the same time drew attention to its potential unfairness. For example, S.M. Cretney thought that the proposal had 'much to commend it' but that it could lead to injustice in some cases; and, regarding the use of the 1975 Act, there were substantial concerns about relying on 'a discretionary adjustive code as a means of remedying the inability of the law to deal with changing family structures': (1995) 111 LQR 77. R. Kerridge referred to the possibility of 'substantial unfairness' inherent in the Law Commission's proposal where the intestate remarries and is survived by the spouse and the intestate's children by an earlier marriage. He suggests that it would be preferable for the spouse to take a life interest in the whole estate in such a case: (1990) 54 Conv 358. That would certainly be preferable to the Law Commission's proposal, although the creation of a life interest does complicate the administration of an intestate estate.

A number of factors appear relevant in considering whether children should be excluded from entitlement on intestacy when the intestate is survived by a spouse. For example, should it matter whether a child is a minor or an adult, or whether (if an adult) he is dependent on the intestate? Certainly a stronger case can be made out for the entitlement of minor children or dependent adult children. Should the means of the surviving spouse and children be taken into account? If they were, a fairer distribution might result, but there is a deep suspicion in many quarters of the desirability of means testing. Should the length of the surviving spouse's marriage be relevant, or the number of marriages to which the intestate was a party? Suppose, for example, that Arthur makes a will leaving all his property to his wife for her life, remainder to his children. His wife dies after many years of marriage. Arthur marries again and dies a few months later. Since the effect of the remarriage was to revoke the will (see 5.1), Arthur has died intestate. His wife (of a few months) would take the entire estate under the Law Commission's proposal; his children would not be entitled. Should a marriage of a few months' duration result in the total exclusion of the children under the intestacy rules? Surely not. But then should

Arthur not have made a fresh will? Of course he should have ... but he did not, for whatever reason, and it would indeed be presumptuous to conclude that he did not wish his children to benefit.

The fundamental objection to the spouse-takes-all proposal is that it fails to give sufficient weight to the importance of the parent-child bond. Is there a more important bond within the family? Possibly — many would consider the marital bond to be supreme. But even if the primacy of the marital bond is admitted, is it so pronounced that it should exclude the parent-child bond as regards entitlement on intestacy? Hardly, and yet the Law Commission proposes precisely that. It is rightly concerned that the surviving spouse should be adequately provided for, but that concern need not be translated into the blanket exclusion of children. Their interests need to be balanced against those of the surviving spouse. But where there are no children, a strong case can be made for the spouse taking the whole estate.

The ownership of the matrimonial home — often the most valuable family asset — should obviously be a crucial factor in assessing the extent of the surviving spouse's intestacy entitlement. But under the present law this consideration is irrelevant (the right to appropriate the home does not affect the *quantum* of the spouse's entitlement). This can obviously create anomalies, as the Law Commission recognised. For example, the spouse who is a joint tenant of the matrimonial home will take the home by survivorship *and* the full entitlement on intestacy; whereas, if the home is owned solely by the intestate — or if it is held by tenancy in common — the spouse who wishes to retain the home might in effect 'lose' all or part of the intestacy entitlement. It would be much simpler and fairer in this respect if the matrimonial home were regarded as held jointly. A sensible matrimonial property regime is a pre-condition of a satisfactory intestacy law. Failing any substantial reform to the law of matrimonial property, the present anomalies regarding the spouse's intestacy entitlement will continue. A possible improvement would be to increase the spouse's statutory legacy where the spouse does not own the matrimonial home, to reduce the legacy where the spouse takes the home as joint tenant, and to retain the current level of legacy where the spouse holds a share in the home by tenancy in common.

In conclusion it is worth reiterating the Law Commission's observation that the law cannot possibly cater for all possible cases. Anomalies are bound to arise whatever the system devised. The current law, following the reforms enacted by the Law Reform (Succession) Act 1995, achieves a reasonable balance between the intestate's relations. If the anomalies resulting from the law of matrimonial property could be removed or reduced, the current law would have much to commend it.

TWO

Wills: Nature, Characteristics and Contents

2.1 NATURE AND CHARACTERISTICS OF WILLS

2.1.1 Basic notions

'A will is an instrument by which a person makes a disposition of his property to take effect after his decease and which is in its own nature ambulatory and revocable during his life' (*Jarman on Wills*, 8th edn., 1951, vol. 1, p. 26). This definition expresses the salient features of a will. However, a will is not confined to disposing of property. It may, for example, appoint executors or trustees, or a guardian for a child who is a minor; or it may contain directions about the testator's funeral or disposal of his body; or it may revoke a prior will. But it seems that if a will does not dispose of property, it is inadmissible to probate: *Re Berger* [1989] 1 All ER 591. Another well-known definition is that in *Halsbury's Laws of England* (4th edn., 1984, vol. 50, p. 91):

> A will or testament is the declaration in a prescribed manner of the intention of the person making it with regard to matters which he wishes to take effect upon or after his death.

This definition is preferable to the extent that it does not imply that a will's sole function is to dispose of property; nor does it insist on an 'instrument' — its use of 'declaration' encompasses the possibility that a will can be made orally if it is a privileged will (see 9.1.1). On the other hand, the *Halsbury* definition fails to emphasise two highly important features of wills — that they are ambulatory and revocable (below). It is curious that there is no satisfactory statutory definition. However, s. 3 of the Wills Act 1837, although it does not attempt to define a will, nevertheless has important things to say about the legal significance of a will — it provides that 'it shall be lawful for every person to devise, bequeath, or dispose of, by his will executed in manner hereinafter required, all real estate, and all personal estate which he shall be entitled to, either at law or in equity, at the time of his death ...'. It is this section which in theory at least makes testamentary succession possible (even though it was largely declaratory of the previous law). The general effect of a will is that the legal interest in the deceased's estate passes to his personal representatives, while the beneficiaries obtain the equitable interest.

2.1.1.1 Form, intention and capacity

The *Halsbury* definition of a will (above) speaks of the declaration of the testator's intention 'in a prescribed manner'. Unless the declaration is a privileged will, it must conform to the manner prescribed by s. 9 of the Wills Act 1837. This requires, in essence, that the will should be made in writing and signed by the testator in the presence of witnesses (see Chapter 4).

Apart from satisfying the required formalities the testator must *intend* that his expressed wishes should take effect *on his death* — that is, he must have *animus testandi*. Thus it is an essential characteristic of a will that it is intended to operate on death and not before. In *Cock* v *Cooke* (1866) LR 1 P & D 241, the deceased left a duly executed paper stating 'I wish my sister to have my bankbook for her own use'. The court was satisfied that it was intended to take effect after the deceased's death, and not as an *inter vivos* gift. Wilde J stated (at p. 243):

It is undoubted law that whatever may be the form of a duly executed instrument, if the person executing it intends that it shall not take effect until after his death, and it is dependent upon his death for its vigour and effect, it is testamentary.

The requirement that a will must be intended to operate on death distinguishes wills from *inter vivos* dispositions by deed. The latter are usually intended to have immediate effect. Where, however, a disposition by deed is postponed until the death of the donor, the deed takes effect as a will if it satisfies the formal requirements: *In the Goods of Morgan* (1866) 1 P & D 214, where three deeds of gift conveying property on trust for children were held to constitute the donor's will. Each had been executed with the formalities required for making a will, and each contained a clause emphasising that the deed was not to operate until death.

Besides having *animus testandi* a testator must have capacity to make a will. This means, principally, that he must be at least 18 years old and must have 'a sound and disposing mind and memory' — that is, the mental ability to make a will (capacity and *animus testandi* are considered in detail in Chapter 3).

2.1.1.2 Wills are ambulatory

A will can operate only on the testator's death and not before. Thus a will cannot confer any benefits while the testator is alive — the beneficiary simply has a *potential* interest in the estate but receives no actual benefit until the testator dies. And even then the benefit might not materialise if there are insufficient assets to satisfy the testator's gifts. It follows that if the beneficiary predeceases the testator, the gift to him lapses — that is, the beneficiary's estate will not benefit, as a general rule. Moreover, the testator is generally free, despite having made the will, to deal with and dispose of his property as he wishes. Since the will does not take effect until death, it is capable of encompassing property which the testator acquires after making his will. Hence the potential application of the will is of a mobile, shifting character — and that is what is strictly meant by the will being 'ambulatory' (from the Latin *ambulatorius* — mobile, shifting, mutable).

2.1.1.3 Wills are revocable

The general rule is that a will can be revoked prior to the testator's death. Revocation of a will — literally 'a calling back' — results in the will being nullified and made inoperative, either wholly or partially (revocation is considered fully in Chapter 5). That a testator can revoke a will at any time is a natural consequence of his general right to deal with his property as he wishes. But what if he declares in his will that it is irrevocable? Such a declaration is not binding on the testator: *Vynior's Case* (1609) 8 Co Rep 81b; 77 ER 597. Although this case is commonly regarded as establishing the rule, it should be noted that it was actually concerned with the revocation of bonds, not wills. It would seem that the only circumstance in which a will can become irrevocable is if the testator permanently loses the required mental capacity to revoke a will — the *animus revocandi*. However, even then his will could be revoked if the Court of Protection were to make a subsequent will on his behalf under the Mental Health Act 1983 (see 9.1.2).

If a testator contracts to make or not make a will, the principle of the revocability of wills is unaffected to the extent that the testator cannot in theory fetter his right to revoke. But he might well incur *contractual* liability if he revokes a will (wholly or partially) in breach of his contractual obligations. The importance of this topic merits separate consideration (see 2.1.2). Moreover, where two testators have made mutual wills, whereby they agree not to revoke their respective wills, a trust may arise in favour of a beneficiary under such a will if it is subsequently revoked (see 2.1.3).

2.1.1.4 Codicils

A codicil is a testamentary instrument intended as a supplement to a previous will. The making of a codicil presupposes the existence of a prior will and effectuates additions or alterations to the will. The necessity for making a fresh will is thereby avoided, although the codicil must be made in the same manner as prescribed for a will. The codicil, being the subsidiary instrument, will normally be much shorter than the will. On the testator's death any codicils will be construed together with his will (or wills) — in that sense the various instruments constitute his 'will'. In *Lemage* v *Goodban* (1865) LR 1 P & D 57, at p. 62, Wilde J described a will as 'the aggregate of his [the testator's] testamentary intentions' and held that a will could consist of 'several independent papers'. And in *Douglas-Menzies* v *Umphelby* [1908] AC 224, at 233 Lord Robertson stated:

Whether a man leaves one testamentary writing or several ... it is the aggregate or the net result that constitutes his will, or, in other words, the expression of his testamentary wishes. The law, on a man's death, finds out what are the instruments which express his last will. If some extant writing be revoked, or is inconsistent with a later testamentary writing, it is discarded. But all that survive this scrutiny form parts of the ultimate will or effective expression of his wishes about his estate. In this sense it is inaccurate to speak of a man leaving two wills; he does leave, and can leave, but one will.

Although a codicil is subsidiary to the will it has the important effect of bringing the will down to the date of the codicil. This is because a codicil to a will republishes the will — that is, the will is given a fresh starting date: s. 34 of the Wills Act 1837. Overall, it seems that the use of codicils is 'rare': Finch *et al.*, 1996, p. 65 (see 1.1.2).

2.1.1.5 Other dispositions

A person can make a disposition of his property, effective on his death, by methods other than by a will. For example, property can be disposed of by nomination in certain circumstances. A nomination is a direction (normally in writing) that investments held on behalf of the nominator should be paid on his death to the nominated person. Nominations are typically made, for example, of funds held in Trustee Savings Banks, Friendly Societies and pension schemes. Nominations differ from wills chiefly because of their restricted application, their form — they need not be made in the manner prescribed for wills — and the fact that the funds pass directly to the nominee and not to the nominator's estate (see 9.2.1).

Another important form of disposition of property on death is the gift made in contemplation of death (*donatio mortis causa*). This type of gift has characteristics similar to both an *inter vivos* disposition and a will, but strictly is neither. It is a hybrid form of gift whereby the donor parts with dominion (essential control) over the subject-matter of the gift in contemplation of his death (see 9.2.2).

2.1.1.6 A little history

In the Anglo-Saxon period the law of inheritance was largely custom-based and reflected the importance of the family bond. Local customs probably varied enormously but it seems that land was normally divisible in equal shares between members of the family, sons having the primary right. The basic concept was one of *sharing* property rather than it being taken solely by one individual. The inheritance of land could at first not be altered by will, as a general rule. But eventually wills of land became possible, although the consent of the monarch was necessary (thus such wills were exceptional). Anglo-Saxon wills varied considerably in both form and content. However, the expression *cwaeth his cwide* is commonly found — the testator 'has his say'. It seems that 'bequeath' is derived from *cwaeth*. Once made it was considered to be irrevocable and not ambulatory — the converse of the modern will — and thus in some respects similar to a conveyance.

As regards personalty, under the customary rules of inheritance in the Anglo-Saxon period the deceased's goods were normally divided into thirds, the widow taking one third, the children another, while the remaining third — 'the dead's part' — could be bequeathed by the deceased as he wished. Well, almost; for it was frequently the case that the Church would persuade a dying man to leave 'the dead's part' to religious and charitable purposes.

The short-term effects of the Norman Conquest on devolution by will are unclear, but eventually the redistribution of land within a feudal society led to the emergence in the twelfth century of the rules of inheritance based on the concept of male primogeniture (see 1.1.3.1). The application of the rules meant that for most of the medieval period it was generally not possible to make a will of land: the old Anglo-Saxon written wills became redundant. However, the inability to devise land by will proved to be a very major factor in the development of the 'use'. Landowners found a way to separate the legal and beneficial title to their property by transferring the legal title to feoffees (grantees) while retaining the current enjoyment (the 'use') over the land. They would then make wills in which they disposed of *the use*, thus keeping within the prohibition against wills of land. Although the use was not recognised at common law, Chancery was prepared to enforce uses. Indeed, by the beginning of the sixteenth century it has been estimated that the vast majority of land in England was held by use. The popularity of the use seriously threatened the Crown since the feudal dues payable to the monarch could be avoided to a considerable extent by employment of the use. The result was the Statute of Uses 1536, which attempted to eradicate the use. The effect was again to make it impossible to make wills of land. However, the measure proved very unpopular and was followed shortly afterwards by the Statute of Wills 1540, which made it possible to make a will (writing required) of certain types of tenure. The right was later extended over most other forms of tenure, so that after 1660 it could be said that there was a *general* right to devise land by will (at least for men — the right to devise land by will was not given to a married woman until the Married Women's Property Acts of the late-nineteenth century). The Statute of Frauds 1677 laid down stricter formalities for wills of land, requiring the will to be signed by the testator and to be witnessed by three or four credible witnesses. The Wills Act 1837 reduced the minimum number of witnesses to two and ended the differences (in the formal requirements) between wills of realty and personalty.

As regards wills of personalty after the Norman Conquest, the story is one of growing Church influence. The ecclesiastical courts — staffed by civilians trained in Roman and Canon law — eventually came to exercise sole jurisdiction over wills of personalty, which came to be generally regarded as ambulatory and revocable. Moreover, several forms of will emerged. Wills could be nuncupative (oral) as well as written; in the latter case a seal was necessary. And it seems that a notarial form of will was possible (one made before a notary). The Statute of Frauds 1677 left the formal requirements for wills of personalty largely unchanged, but the Wills Act 1837 insisted on the same formalities as for wills of land — writing, signature, minimum of two attesting witnesses. Although amended several times since, the requirements of the 1837 Act remain the basis of the modern will.

There is some uncertainty as to how much freedom the testator of personalty had. The customary tripartite division of Anglo-Saxon times survived in certain areas until the eighteenth century but was never formally recognised by the common law that emerged in the early medieval period. It seems then that the common law allowed unrestricted testation, but in some areas testators would customarily dispose only of 'the dead's part' and then often in favour of religious and charitable objects.

2.1.1.7 Jurisdiction

In the early medieval period the ecclesiastical courts acquired jurisdiction over wills of personalty. Often the will of personalty consisted of the last words of a dying man, witnessed or recorded by a priest. It was thus natural for the Church to be involved in ensuring that the wishes of the deceased were carried out, especially as the Church was potentially an important recipient of his property. However, in the course of time the deficiencies of ecclesiastical jurisdiction — especially the lack of effective remedies — resulted in litigants preferring to enforce their rights in Chancery. Thus the jurisdiction of the ecclesiastical courts gradually diminished. Eventually a secular Court of Probate and a system of probate registries were created in 1857. The Judicature Acts of the 1870s transferred the jurisdiction of the Court of Probate to the Probate, Divorce and Admiralty Division of the High Court. That jurisdiction is now vested primarily in the Family Division of the High Court.

The historical division of jurisdiction is mirrored in the current jurisdictional arrangements. The Family Division has exclusive jurisdiction over non-contentious and common form probate — the great bulk of probate business — under the Supreme Court Act 1981. In practice much of this business is dealt with in district probate registries; some goes to the principal registry of the Family Division; and a small percentage is heard before a judge of the Family Division. Jurisdiction over contentious or solemn form probate is exercised primarily by the Chancery Division, but the county court has jurisdiction if the net estate at the deceased's death was valued below £30,000. The Chancery Division is also the primary forum for matters relating to the construction of wills. However, wills may be construed in the Family Division in order to ascertain which parts of a will should be admitted to probate, or where a small estate would be depleted by referring the matter to the Chancery Division.

2.1.2 Contracts relating to wills

This section is concerned with the legal consequences of contracts to make testamentary gifts and contracts not to revoke such gifts. Of course, whatever a testator contracts to do, he cannot thereby be prevented from making a fresh will or from revoking a will. This is because of the fundamental principle that wills are revocable (above). But breach of such a contract may result in a contractual remedy. For liability to arise, the agreement must satisfy the standard requirements of a contract: there must be offer and acceptance, consideration (or a deed), certainty of terms, and intention to create legal relations. The courts have increasingly tended to regard arrangements between family members as showing the required intent to create legal relations where property arrangements are concerned. For example, in *Parker* v *Clark* [1960] 1 All ER 93, a promise to leave a house to a niece by will if she and her husband gave up their own home and came to live with the promisors was upheld as a valid contract.

It should be noted that a contract relating to land and made after 26 September 1989 is void unless it is in writing: s. 2 of the Law of Property (Miscellaneous Provisions) Act 1989. If the contract was made on or before that date, it is unenforceable unless it is in writing or is evidenced by a signed memorandum within s. 40 of the Law of Property Act 1925, or the doctrine of part performance applies.

2.1.2.1   Contracts to leave a gift

If a contract is made to leave a legacy of fixed amount in a will, the promisee becomes a creditor of the estate. In *Hammersley* v *De Biel* (1845) 12 Cl & Fin 45; 8 ER 1312, a father promised to leave £10,000 by will in favour of his daughter and her children in consideration of her marriage into a titled German family. He did not make the agreed provision in his will. It was held by the House of Lords that his estate was liable to pay the promised sum (with interest). The position is similar where a specific asset has been promised. The promisee is a creditor of the promisor's estate and can sue for damages if the contract is broken. In *Synge* v *Synge* [1894] 1 QB 466, CA, the defendant promised to leave specified realty to the plaintiff for life as an inducement to her to marry him. She agreed to the proposed terms, and the marriage took place. But the husband then conveyed the property to a third person. The court awarded damages to the wife, based on 'the value of the possible life estate which Lady Synge would be entitled to if she survived her husband'. The fact that the husband had disposed of the property in breach of the agreement entitled his wife to sue immediately on the breach. In an appropriate case specific performance is available for the promisee. The court declined to speculate in *Synge* v *Synge* whether the remedy would have been granted had it been sought, but the court stated that it could order any person — other than a purchaser without notice — who held the asset as the testator's successor in title to transfer it to the promisee.

What if the promise is to leave the promisee all the promisor's property, or a specified share or the residue? In such a case the promisee is entitled to enforce the contract but his position is that of a beneficiary of the estate, not a creditor. Thus his rights are postponed to those of any creditors: *Bennett* v *Houldsworth* (1877) 6 Ch D 671.

2.1.2.2   Contracts not to revoke gifts

If a testator contracts not to revoke a will or a gift in a will, but later breaches the contract, the promisee can sue for damages for the lost benefit. But the breach cannot be prevented by injunction because of the general principle that wills are always revocable.

Wills can be revoked in several ways (see Chapter 5). It seems that damages lie only if the testator revokes his will intentionally. However, if the will is revoked by the testator's subsequent marriage, the action does not lie, even if the testator intended thereby to revoke the will. In *Re Marsland* [1939] Ch 820, CA, the testator made a will benefiting his wife and children, and immediately afterwards covenanted in a separation deed not to 'revoke' the will or the gifts to them. His wife died a few years later. Many years after her death the testator remarried, thus revoking his will. It was held that the children had no action under the covenant since on its construction it was confined to revocation by the testator other than by marriage. Even if the contract (or covenant) not to revoke is drafted so widely that it applies to revocation by marriage, it is void for public policy to the extent that it attempts to restrain marriage. In *Robinson* v *Ommanney* (1883) 23 Ch D 285, CA, the testatrix exercised a power of appointment by will and then covenanted not to do 'any act, deed, matter or thing by means whereof the said will so to be made by her should be revoked, annulled, cancelled, or affected in any manner howsoever'. Later she revoked her will and made another appointing in favour of a different beneficiary. It was held that although the covenant was void to the extent that it restrained marriage, it was divisible in its scope and thus was breached by the making of another will revoking the earlier one.

2.1.2.3 Proprietary estoppel

Where one person (A) has acted to his detriment on the faith of a belief, which was known to and encouraged by another person (B), that he either has or is going to be given a right in or over B's property, B cannot insist on his strict legal rights if to do so would be inconsistent with A's belief. The principle is commonly known as proprietary estoppel, and since the effect of it is that B is prevented from asserting his strict legal rights it has something in common with estoppel. But in my judgment, at all events where the belief is that A is going to be given a right in the future, it is properly to be regarded as giving rise to a species of constructive trust, which is the concept employed by a court of equity to prevent a person from relying on his legal rights where it would be unconscionable for him to do so. (*per* Edward Nugee QC, sitting as a Deputy Judge of the High Court, in *Re Basham* [1987] 1 All ER 405, at 410)

Proprietary estoppel applies to promises or arrangements which lack the formality of a contract or covenant. The estoppel creates an equity the effect of which is not entirely clear (owing to inconsistency in the cases). It appears that the court will endeavour to make good — as fairly as possible between the parties — the expectation of the one party that he has or will be given a proprietary interest in the other party's property. In *Re Basham* the plaintiff worked without payment for her stepfather for some 30 years helping him to manage various public houses and a petrol station. She was very close to him and to her mother, and lived nearby with her husband and children (they were dissuaded by the stepfather from moving away). After the death of her mother, the plaintiff and her husband cared for her stepfather when he became ill and spent their own money on repairs and improvements in the cottage where he lived. They were under the firm impression — as were other members of the family — that he intended that his estate should pass to the plaintiff. He had told the plaintiff that he wanted her to have his cottage, and he reiterated that intention shortly before his death — 'Joan you're to have the house'. He died intestate, his estate being valued at £43,000 (of which the cottage was worth £21,000). On intestacy the whole estate would have passed to his two nieces, his closest next-of-kin. It was held that the plaintiff was entitled to the whole estate by virtue of proprietary estoppel. The four requirements for the operation of the estoppel had been satisfied: the plaintiff had a belief at all material times that she would inherit the whole estate; this belief was encouraged by the deceased; the plaintiff acted to her detriment; and she acted as a result of her belief that she would inherit the whole estate. It was argued for the defendants that the plaintiff's behaviour could be attributed to her natural love and affection for her stepfather, but the court held that her acts went well beyond what could be expected given that there was no blood tie between them. The court also rejected the arguments that proprietary estoppel could apply only if the plaintiff's belief related to an existing right and to an identifiable particular asset. However, in *Layton v Martin* [1986] 2 FLR 227 — which was not cited in *Re Basham* — it was held that a proprietary estoppel must relate to a specific asset. A married man promised 'financial security after my death' to the plaintiff if she agreed to live with him (his wife was in poor health and receiving medical treatment abroad). The court held that the promise was insufficient for a proprietary estoppel.

2.1.2.4 *Quantum meruit*
If the promisee has rendered services for the promisor he may have a claim against the latter's estate — even though there is no enforceable contract between them — on the basis of a *quantum meruit*, according to Commonwealth authority. In *Deglman v Guaranty Trust Co. of Canada* [1954] 3 DLR 785, an aunt made an oral promise to her nephew that she would leave him one of her houses in Ottawa in her will if he performed such services for her as she might request. The services consisted of doing odd jobs in her houses and taking her on trips to Montreal and elsewhere. The aunt died without leaving a house to the nephew in her will. It was held that he could recover for the services performed since they were not given gratuitously but on the footing of a contract (even though unenforceable). Rand J stated (at p. 788) that the nephew was 'entitled to recover for his services and outlays what the deceased would have had to pay for them on a purely business basis to any other person in the position of the respondent' (the nephew). It is likely that a claim for the house would now succeed on similar facts on the basis of proprietary estoppel. In *Hink v Lhenen* (1974) 52 DLR (3d) 301, a *quantum meruit* claim was allowed where a daughter was promised that her father would leave her his house if she lived with him and performed services for him.

2.1.3 Mutual wills

2.1.3.1 The basic doctrine

It has long been established that a contract between persons to make corresponding wills gives rise to equitable obligations when one acts on the faith of such an agreement and dies leaving his will unrevoked so that the other takes property under its dispositions. It operates to impose upon the survivor an obligation regarded as specifically enforceable. It is true that he cannot be compelled to make and leave unrevoked a testamentary document and if he dies leaving a last will containing provisions inconsistent with his agreement it is nevertheless valid as a testamentary act. But the doctrines of equity attach the obligation to the property. The effect is, I think, that the survivor becomes a constructive trustee and the terms of the trust are those of the will which he undertook would be his last will) (*per* Dixon J in *Birmingham* v *Renfrew* (1937) 57 CLR 666, at 683).

The facts of this case provide a typical illustration of the operation of the mutual wills doctrine. A married couple made separate wills on the same occasion in similar terms. The wife left the whole of her estate to her husband, with a gift over to certain of her relatives in the event of his predeceasing her. The husband made a will in the same terms, the court finding that these wills had been made pursuant to an agreement between them. On the wife's death the husband inherited her estate under her will but then made a new will in favour of his own relatives, thus revoking his earlier will. It was held that the deceased wife's relatives could enforce a constructive trust in their favour against the husband's estate.

Mutual wills arise when two or more persons agree to make wills in similar terms and that the survivor will be bound to dispose of his estate in a specified manner. The testators can make separate wills to this effect, or their wishes can be effected by a joint will — that is, *one* will executed by them jointly. Frequently spouses benefit each other, either through reciprocal life interests with a remainder over to a third party (usually their issue) or by giving each other absolute gifts with a substitutionary provision in favour of the third party in the event of the other spouse's predecease. However, it is not necessary that the testators should benefit each other. In *Re Dale* [1993] 4 All ER 129, where a married couple made wills in favour of their children, it was held that the mutual wills doctrine could apply even though the surviving testator had not received any benefit under the will of the first testator to die. It can thus be seen that the Law Reform Committee's definition of mutual wills — 'mutual wills are joint wills in which the testators not only confer reciprocal benefits on each other but in which they agree that the survivor shall be bound by the terms of those wills' (*The Making and Revocation of Wills*, LRC Report No. 22, 1980, para. 3.50) — is misleading on two counts: mutual wills need not confer reciprocal benefits, neither do they need to be joint.

The imposition of a constructive trust on the surviving testator cannot prevent him from revoking his will, because of the basic principle that a will cannot be made irrevocable. Nevertheless, if he revokes, his intentions will inevitably be frustrated to some extent by the operation of the trust in favour of the beneficiaries under his previous (mutual) will. The purpose of the doctrine of mutual wills is to provide a remedy against the unconscionable revocation of a will. It is thus a classic example of equity's traditional jurisdiction in matters where breach of faith is involved, as was emphasised by Lord Camden in

Dufour v *Pereira* (1769) Dick 419; 21 ER 332, at 333, the case which is regarded as establishing the doctrine:

> It is a contract between the parties, which cannot be rescinded, but by the consent of both. The first that dies, carries his part of the contract into execution. Will the Court afterwards permit the other to break the contract? Certainly not.

2.1.3.2   The agreement

In order for the equitable doctrine to apply it must first be shown that the wills were made in pursuance of an agreement by the testators as to the disposal of their property, and that they agreed that the survivor was bound by the agreement, that is, that the survivor's will should not be revoked. The agreement must be proved since it is the very foundation of the doctrine. The terms must be clear and unequivocal: *Walpole* v *Orford* (1797) 3 Ves 402; 30 ER 1076. Moreover, there must be an intention that the agreement should be legally binding. The best proof of the necessary agreement will be a clear statement in the wills themselves but other proof, including the making of an oral agreement, may suffice. It is imperative, however, to show that the wills were made in pursuance of an agreement not to revoke them. Evidence that the wills were made in similar terms and on the same occasion is not *in itself* conclusive proof that they were intended as mutual wills. In *Re Oldham* [1925] Ch 75, a married couple made wills in almost identical terms on the same day, each giving property to the other absolutely with the same alternative provisions in case of the predecease of the other. After the husband's death the wife made a fresh will wholly departing from the earlier will. It was held that the mutual wills doctrine did not apply because there was no proof that the wills alleged to be mutual had been made in pursuance of an agreement not to revoke them. Astbury J stated (at p. 88) that 'the fact that the two wills were made in identical terms does not necessarily connote an agreement beyond that of so making them'. A similar approach (but with a different result) was adopted in *Re Cleaver* [1981] 2 All ER 1018, where Nourse J emphasised that the mere simultaneity of wills and the similarity of their terms was not enough by itself to establish the necessary agreement, but that these factors were a relevant circumstance to be taken into account. There had to be clear and satisfactory evidence — on a balance of probabilities — of the necessary agreement. On the facts such proof was forthcoming, including evidence of conversations of the testators with family, friends and neighbours.

Where the evidence of the agreement is primarily extrinsic the court will probably lean — in cases of doubt — against a finding that the necessary agreement existed. This is because the operation of the doctrine of mutual wills can result in practical difficulties (see 2.1.3.7) and because it constitutes a potentially wide-ranging restriction on the freedom of testators to dispose of their property as they wish. It seems that the court is more likely to lean against mutual wills if they purport to give the surviving testator an absolute interest, or where the whole of the property of the parties is subject to the mutual provisions of the wills. Although it is understandable that the agreement not to revoke should be the basis of the mutual wills doctrine, the position regarding the proof of the agreement seems unduly strict. The insistence on clear proof of an actual agreement is somewhat unrealistic in the typical mutual wills scenario — similar wills made by married couples. The rule that mere identity of terms is not conclusive proof of the agreement is particularly questionable. Is it not reasonable to assume in such a case that the parties intended that the wills should not be revoked?

2.1.3.3   When does the trust arise?

The constructive trust arises when the first of the mutual testators dies without having revoked his will. Death in those circumstances is the determining event because it shows that the deceased carried his part of the agreement into execution, and thus it would be a fraud on the part of the survivor to depart from the agreement. Since the trust arises on the death of the first testator it follows that a gift to a beneficiary who survives that testator but predeceases the surviving testator does not lapse. In *Re Hagger* [1930] 2 Ch 190 a married couple executed a joint mutual will in which they left property to each other for life, remainder to named beneficiaries. One of the beneficiaries, Eleanor, survived the wife (the first to die) but predeceased the husband. The issue was whether Eleanor took a vested interest in the remainder when the wife died. It was held that the trust arose at the wife's death and that consequently the interests passed to Eleanor's estate. Clauson J stated (at p. 195):

> To my mind *Dufour* v *Pereira* decides that where there is a joint will such as this, *on the death of the first testator* the position as regards that part of the property which belongs to the survivor is that the survivor will be treated in this Court as holding the property on trust to apply it so as to carry out the effect of the joint will. As I read Lord Camden's judgment in *Dufour* v *Pereira* that would be so, even though the survivor did not signify his election to give effect to the will by taking benefits under it. (emphasis added)

The last sentence from the above extract raises the issue of the interpretation of Lord Camden's judgment in *Dufour* v *Pereira*. Certain remarks of his leave it unclear whether the coming into operation of the trust depends on acceptance of the benefits under the deceased's will by the surviving testator. Clearly Clauson J thought — rightly it is submitted — that the acceptance or otherwise of benefits was irrelevant. Nevertheless, there have been some doubts (at least in academic quarters) as to when the trust arises under the mutual wills doctrine. Arguments could be suggested for the view that the relevant time is when benefits are accepted by the surviving testator, or when the agreement is initially made or when the surviving testator dies. But it is now beyond dispute that the death of the first testator to die (with his will unrevoked) is *the* determining event that creates the trust. In *Re Dale* (above) the testators did not give each other any benefits under their respective wills, and yet the trust was held to arise (on the assumption that the wills were mutual) on the death of the first testator to die. Morritt J reviewed the cases where there had been a benefit conferred on the surviving testator and concluded that none of them insisted that acceptance of benefit was a *condition* for the imposition of the trust.

2.1.3.4 Position of the survivor

As emphasised already, the mutual wills doctrine cannot prevent the survivor from revoking his will. If the survivor makes a new will, it will be given full effect, subject to the imposition of the constructive trust. Thus the new will is entitled to probate, whereas the previous one is not (assuming it has been totally revoked). But the imposition of the constructive trust will effectively frustrate the survivor's intention to alter his will. It is important to consider the extent to which the trust operates over the survivor's property. The basic rule is that the trust covers all the property of the survivor at his death unless the initial agreement displays a contrary intention. In *Re Green* [1951] Ch 148, a married couple made mutual wills pursuant to an agreement that they would each leave all their property to the other, and that the survivor would leave half of his or her estate to certain named individuals and charities. After the wife's death the husband remarried and made a second will in which he made gifts to different charities and left the residue to his second wife. It was held that the husband's estate was to be distributed according to his second will subject to the constructive trust over half of his estate in favour of the named individuals and charities under his first will.

Moreover, a distinction needs to be drawn between mutual wills which confer a life interest on the survivor and those which leave an absolute interest. In the former case the constructive trust can apply only to the survivor's property and not to the inherited life interest (which must be held by *express* trust). But if the mutual wills confer an absolute interest on the survivor, with a gift to a third party in the case of predecease, then the constructive trust applies *prima facie* to all of the survivor's property, including that inherited from the first testator to die.

What is the precise nature of the obligation imposed by the constructive trust? The survivor must not revoke his mutual will; but that does not prevent him from disposing of his property *inter vivos*. For example, suppose that Arthur and his wife, Edith, make mutual wills leaving their respective estates to one another, with a substitutionary gift to their son, Tom, in the event of the other spouse predeceasing the testator. Edith dies first. Arthur inherits her estate but he dissipates it and his own property through his obsession with gambling. He dies insolvent. Tom will thus take nothing whether or not Arthur had revoked his will. Hence it can be seen that the mutual wills doctrine does not guarantee that the beneficiaries will take anything. The survivor *prima facie* is free to do as he pleases with his property provided that he does not revoke his will. And if he does revoke the will, the trust operates only in respect of his assets, if any, at his death, as explained by Dixon J in *Birmingham* v *Renfrew* (see 2.1.3.1) at p. 689:

> The purpose of an arrangement for corresponding wills must often be, as in this case, to enable the survivor during his life to deal as absolute owner with the property passing under the will of the first party dying. That is to say, the

object of the transaction is to put the survivor in a position to enjoy for his own benefit the full ownership so that, for instance, he may convert it and expend the proceeds if he choose. But if he dies he is to bequeath what is left in the manner agreed upon. It is only by the special doctrines of equity that such a floating obligation, suspended, so to speak, during the lifetime of the survivor, can descend upon the assets at his death and crystallise into a trust. No doubt gifts and settlements, *inter vivos*, if calculated to defeat the intention of the compact, could not be made by the survivor and his right of disposition, *inter vivos*, is, therefore, not unqualified.

It should be noted that the survivor's power of disposition is restricted to the extent that the survivor must avoid transactions 'calculated to defeat the intention of the compact'. In *Re Cleaver* [1981] 2 All ER 1018, Nourse J interpreted these *dicta* as restraining large voluntary dispositions but not 'ordinary gifts of small value' (p. 1024).

What if the survivor marries after the death of the first testator to die? Since marriage revokes a prior will it is arguable that the survivor will thereby have breached his obligation not to revoke his mutual will. However, it will be recalled that in *Re Marsland* (see 2.1.2.2) it was held that a covenant not to revoke a will was not broken by the subsequent remarriage of the covenantor. But if the agreement between the mutual testators was that their wills should not be revoked in any circumstances one would expect a court to hold that subsequent marriage did breach the obligation. In *Re Goodchild* [1996] 1 All ER 670, it was held that the floating trust created by mutual wills was not destroyed by the remarriage of the second testator after the death of the first. The court appeared to lay down a general rule irrespective of the precise nature of the agreement between the testators:

> Whether the mutual wills are simply expressed to be 'irrevocable', or are expressed to be subject to an obligation to give effect to their terms, the intention is presumably the same: that is, that the underlying trust ... is to be respected. In my view, the law will give effect to that intention. (*per* Carnwath J, at p. 677)

Re Marsland was distinguished on the ground that it was not concerned with mutual wills. *Re Goodchild* has brought welcome clarity to this issue but it is dubious in principle. The doctrine of mutual wills is intended to protect beneficiaries against unconscionable conduct on the part of the surviving testator. To describe remarriage as constituting such conduct seems perverse.

2.1.3.5 Revocation during joint lives

What is the position if a mutual will is revoked before the death of the first testator to die? The mutual wills doctrine has no application since the revocation has occurred before the constructive trust arises. In *Stone v Hoskins* [1905] P 194, a married couple made mutual wills, but the wife later made fresh wills without her husband's knowledge. On her death he claimed that the court should pronounce against the fresh wills or, alternatively, that the executors under the later wills should be directed to hold the property of the testatrix in trust for the beneficiaries under the earlier (mutual) will. The husband's claims were rejected by the court.

It seems that the consequences of a revocation during joint lives are at most purely contractual. Clearly mutual wills can be revoked by the joint consent of the testators. In such a case the disappointed beneficiary has no remedy (because of privity of contract). But unilateral revocation will have the effect of releasing the 'innocent' testator from his obligation not to revoke and will give him the right to sue for damages for breach of contract. This right may be of greater theoretical significance than practical value because it could be very difficult to assess damages. How would the plaintiff's loss be calculated, especially if the mutual wills did not confer reciprocal benefits on the testators?

2.1.3.6 Moral obligation?

In *Re Goodchild* (above) the testator and his first wife executed simultaneous wills in identical form in favour of the survivor of them, and then in favour of their adult son. The testator inherited all his wife's estate on her death. He later remarried and then made a new will benefiting his second wife. Although the evidence was insufficient to prove that the original wills had been mutual, the court was satisfied that the first wife had made her will on the understanding that the testator would give effect to what she believed to be their mutual intentions, giving rise to a moral obligation on the part of the testator to benefit the son. This greatly strengthened the son's claim for reasonable provision from the testator's estate under the Inheritance (Provision for Family and Dependants) Act 1975 (see 8.4.2.4).

2.1.3.7 Pitfalls and reform

There are several pitfalls and uncertainties about the operation of the mutual wills doctrine which render it generally inadvisable for testators to make mutual wills. The major problem is that the imposition of the constructive trust may prove a serious restriction on the survivor, who may find that the whole or a substantial part of his property is shackled thereby. This will be particularly inconvenient if the survivor's circumstances have radically changed, as the Law Reform Committee recognised (LRC Report No. 22, 1980, para. 3.52):

> One criticism of mutual wills is that they can create injustice because they are based on the often fallacious assumption that the needs of the beneficiaries will remain constant over a period of time.

Moreover, there may be serious difficulties in some cases in ascertaining which property is subject to the trust unless this is precisely expressed in the original agreement. And there are a number of issues about which the current state of the law is to some extent unclear, especially the ability of the survivor to make *inter vivos* dispositions, the precise nature of his duties (if any) as trustee, and the effect of unilateral revocation during joint lives. However, the Law Reform Committee was not in favour of mutual wills being abolished; and the Committee rejected the proposal that the survivor should be able to amend his will (presumably unrestricted by the constructive trust) to take account of changed family circumstances:

> Whilst we have some sympathy with this proposal, in principle we think it right that people should remain bound by their agreements. That circumstances may change is known to the parties when they make their wills and the fact that it is rarely, if ever, sensible to enter into mutual wills does not of itself justify the creation of the power proposed. (para. 3.52)

2.1.3.8 The constructive trust

The constructive trust that lies at the heart of the mutual wills doctrine may arise in several other situations. The common feature in these cases is that equity is prepared to enforce rights under an agreement which would not normally be enforceable at common law but which nevertheless is essentially contractual. In *Re Cleaver* (above) Nourse J referred to mutual wills as 'only one example of a wider category of cases, for example secret trusts, in which a court of equity will intervene to impose a constructive trust' and continued (at p. 1024):

> The principle of all these cases is that a court of equity will not permit a person to whom property is transferred by way of gift, but on the faith of an agreement or clear understanding that it is to be dealt with in a particular way for the benefit of a third person, to deal with that property inconsistently with that agreement or understanding. If he attempts to do so after having received the benefit of the gift equity will intervene by imposing a constructive trust on the property which is the subject-matter of the agreement or understanding.

The judge's reference to equitable intervention *after* receipt of 'the benefit of the gift' should not be interpreted as stipulating that such intervention is possible *only* after the benefit has been received. As already seen (at 2.1.3.3), the constructive trust in mutual wills arises on the death of the first testator to die, irrespective of the receipt of any benefit by the survivor.

Of the situations in which a constructive trust arises, the one that most approximates to mutual wills is the secret trust. The essence of a secret trust is the agreement by a beneficiary (A) under a will to hold his benefit for another person (B) on the trusts communicated to him by the testator. The trust is 'secret' because it is not openly expressed in the will. Equity enforces the trust in favour of B should A attempt to depart from the agreement. The essential conditions for the creation of this species of constructive trust are that the testator should have the necessary intention, that he should communicate that intention to A, and that A should accept or acquiesce. In *Ottaway* v *Norman* [1972] Ch 698, Harry left his house and contents to Eva, his cohabitant, on the understanding that she would leave the property by will to William, Harry's son. After Harry's death, Eva made a will carrying out his intentions, but some years later she made a new will which disposed of the property in favour of different beneficiaries. It was held that a secret trust had been established in

favour of William in respect of the house and such of the contents as had passed
to Eva under Harry's will.

2.1.3.9 Joint wills
Joint wills must not be confused with mutual wills. A joint will is simply *one* will
executed by two or more testators. It lacks the mutuality of provision based on
an agreement not to revoke that is the essential characteristic of a mutual will.
A joint will operates as the separate will of each testator and may be revoked by
each (to the extent that it applies to him) irrespective of the consent of the
other. Joint wills are uncommon in practice; the most likely reason for making
them is to exercise a joint power of appointment. They are sometimes used to
make mutual wills. In such a case the will is both joint and mutual — that is,
one will executed jointly, containing an agreed disposal of property with an
agreement not to revoke. The fact that a will containing reciprocal provisions is
made jointly may be some evidence of an intention to make mutual wills. Some
Canadian cases show that in such circumstances the court may more readily
infer that wills are mutual, e.g., *Re Gillespie* [1968] 2 OR 369.

2.2 THE CONTENT OF WILLS

Although most wills are primarily concerned with the disposition of the
testator's property, they can perform various other functions. Wills vary
enormously in content, reflecting the multitude of circumstances that affect
individual testators and the will-making process. And they vary greatly in
length — from wills containing many clauses and extending over several pages
to those where testators show remarkable economy of expression, as in *Thorn* v
Dickens [1906] WN 54, where a will consisting of three words — 'All for
mother' — was upheld as valid.

2.2.1 Reasons for making wills

2.2.1.1 Disposing of property
The primary reason for making a will is to effect a disposition of the testator's
property on his death in accordance with the will's provisions. The disposition
of property will consist typically of a series of specific gifts and pecuniary
legacies followed by a gift of the residuary estate. Disposal of property will
always be the primary function of a will, but probably less so than formerly. The
trend is for people to dispose of more of their assets *inter vivos* to pay for their
care in old age.

2.2.1.2 Appointing executors
The appointment of one or more executors is another highly important
function of a will. The executor's main duties are to obtain probate, to ensure
the burial of the deceased, to pay his debts and administer his estate, and to
effect the provisions of the will. Obviously the executor should be someone who

is adult and responsible, in whom the testator can reside his trust with complete confidence. It is strictly not necessary to appoint an executor — the court can appoint one instead — but failure to do so by the testator is definitely not recommended as the estate will be diminished by the costs of applying to the court for an appointment. Banks and solicitors are often chosen as executors or act as advisers to 'lay' executors. Where the will confers benefits other than immediate absolute gifts — for example, where a life interest is created — it is usually advisable for the testator to appoint trustees. It is common to appoint the executors as trustees.

2.2.1.3 Disposing of the testator

As the executors are responsible for burying the testator, the general rule is that they are entitled to the possession of the body until burial. Some testators may wish to include directions about their funeral and the disposal of their body. It seems that such directions are not binding. Consider the remarkable case, *Williams* v *Williams* (1881) 20 Ch D 659: the testator directed in a codicil that after his death his body should be given to his friend Eliza to be dealt with in such manner as he had specified in a private letter to her. He gave her a Wedgwood vase for the purpose — the letter directed that his body should be burned under a pile of wood and the fragments put in the vase (the testator was 'an advocate for cremation'). He further directed that his executors should pay Eliza for her expenses. Following his death the testator was buried by the direction of his widow in Brompton Cemetery with the approval of the executors. But enter Eliza. She obtained the Home Secretary's permission to remove the body and then had it cremated. The ashes were placed in the vase and buried. The court dismissed her action against the executors for expenses, holding that directions by will as to the disposition of the testators' body were unenforceable. The same principle appears to apply in the case of intestacy. In *Saleh* v *Reichert* [1993] 104 DLR (4th) 384, the deceased had expressed the clear view that she wished to be cremated (she abhorred the prospect of burial). Her husband, the administrator of her estate, accordingly sought to have her remains cremated; but her father wished her to be buried in accordance with the tenets of the Muslim faith (she had been brought up as a Muslim). It was held that the wishes of the deceased are not legally binding. Nevertheless, the executor or administrator has the duty to dispose of the deceased's remains 'in a decent and dignified fashion', and, in carrying out that duty, may follow the deceased's wishes. The court dismissed the father's action to prevent cremation.

Although executors are not bound by the testator's directions, they will usually feel at least morally obliged to follow them if they can reasonably do so. If the testator wishes to donate his organs for medical purposes, he is best advised to communicate his views in some form other than a will (a donor card for example).

2.2.1.4 Appointing guardians

Another reason for making a will is to appoint a guardian for a child who is a minor. Under s. 5 of the Children Act 1989, a parent who has parental responsibility for his child may appoint a guardian for the child in the event of the parent's death. Similarly a guardian may appoint another guardian as a substitute in the event of death. As a general rule a guardian's appointment becomes operative only when the child no longer has a parent with parental responsibility over him.

2.2.1.5 Revoking wills
The revocation of prior wills and codicils is one of the most important functions that a will can perform. Indeed, every properly drawn will should contain a revocation clause even if there are no prior testamentary instruments to revoke. The presence of the clause will usually avoid the necessity for searching after the testator's death for prior wills.

2.2.1.6 Expressing a view
The making of a will offers the testator an opportunity to express personal feelings on a wide range of matters, especially the behaviour of family and friends, secure in the knowledge that no cross-examination will follow. For example, testators sometimes describe the reasons why a particular individual has or has not received a benefit in the will. A court must have regard to such reasons — if considered relevant — in an application for reasonable provision from the testator's estate under the Inheritance (Provision for Family and Dependants) Act 1975 (see 8.4.2.7). Moreover, testators will occasionally express a heartfelt exhortation to a relative or friend, such as in *In the Estate of Cook* [1960] 1 All ER 689 — 'Please Leslie be kind to Dot'. Or they will take the opportunity to express their religious or philosophical leanings or their views on the state of the world. Such musings may lack dispositive effect but will nevertheless form part of the will unless omitted from probate (see 10.2.1.4).

2.2.1.7 Estate planning
For those testators who are likely to leave a large estate on death, the making of a will is an opportunity for estate planning, a means whereby tax liability may be minimised. The testator who has a spouse and children will be advised to provide for them in such a way as to take maximum advantage of the exemptions and reliefs offered by the current tax regime. Of course, some testators will have a fixed view as to how they wish their estates to be distributed, so that in such cases the saving of tax will be a minor consideration to them. But it can be safely assumed that many wealthy testators will be interested in making tax-effective wills, and it would be negligent of their legal and financial advisers to fail to inform them of the tax implications of their intended provisions. However, Finch *et al.*, 1996 (see 1.1.2) found that, overall, there was little evidence of tax planning as a major factor in wills. The vast majority of estates were not large enough to be subject to taxation. Most solicitors did not profess expertise in taxation and tended to refer appropriate clients to accountants.

2.2.2   Typical structure of a will

The drafting of wills is an area of expertise which is outside the scope of this book. Nevertheless it is important for the student of Succession to have some appreciation of the structure of a typical will. It may be that the 'typical will' is something of an illusion since home-made wills vary enormously in format and content, whilst even professionally drawn wills show some differences. However, professional wills *generally* exhibit a certain similarity in their content and tend to follow a familiar, if not fixed, structure. Finch *et al.*, 1996, found that the number of professionally drawn wills had increased in recent decades, accounting for nearly 90% of all wills.

2.2.2.1   Commencement

There is no set way of starting a will. In former times, when testators perhaps tended to be more god-fearing than now, it was quite common to start a will with an exclamation of a religious character such as 'In the name of God, Amen'. But these days the commencement is usually more prosaic — 'I Arthur Regis of 15 Camelot Close, Glastonbury, Somerset revoke all testamentary dispositions previously made by me and declare this to be my last will . . .'; or 'This is the last will of me Arthur Regis of . . .'. Often the phrase 'my last will and testament' is used, but 'testament' appears to add nothing of significance and can be readily omitted. The testator should indicate at the outset that he is making a will (or a codicil) by describing the document as such. Sometimes a description of the testator's occupation is inserted in the commencement, e.g., 'stuntman' or 'accountant'. This is unnecessary, although it could sometimes be helpful in indentifying the testator.

2.2.2.2   Preliminaries

The will should contain a revocation clause revoking all previous testamentary dispositions, either in the commencement or immediately after it. The revocation clause is often followed by the appointment of executors and trustees, which should contain their addresses. Unless a bank or a solicitors' firm is appointed, it is good practice to appoint substitutes in case the first choices are unable to act. If the testator'wishes to leave directions about the disposal of his body, these too are frequently contained in a preliminary clause.

2.2.2.3   Gifts

The heart of the will consists of the gifts that the testator makes to beneficiaries. It is usual to begin with specific gifts (gifts of a specified part of the testator's estate) and pecuniary legacies. It is important to make a residuary gift since failure to do so may result in an unwanted intestacy. Often the residuary gift is by far the largest in the will. It is good practice to provide for substitutional gifts where appropriate, especially if no residuary gift is made. A survivorship clause is commonly used in association with a substitutional gift, e.g., 'to Frank if he survives me for the period of two calendar months, otherwise to Tom'. The dispositive clauses should also contain directions about the source from which debts (including tax liability) and gifts are to be satisfied. For example, the testator may wish to provide that a certain gift should be 'free of inheritance tax'. Such directions will normally be followed where possible if the estate is solvent. If the estate is insolvent, the directions are overridden by the statutory order applicable to the payment of debts (see 10.2.3.4).

2.2.2.4 Additional powers

In certain circumstances executors and trustees may have some difficulties in administering an estate if they can rely only on the powers automatically vested in them by reason of their office. A common scenario where such problems might occur is where the will creates trusts for the testator's children under the age of majority. In such cases the professionally drawn will is very likely to contain clauses giving the executors and trustees additional powers as regards matters such as maintenance, making investments, appropriating property, carrying on a business and taking receipts. In the case of a trust of land the need to grant additional powers has been largely obviated by the Trusts of Land and Appointment of Trustees Act 1996, under which personal representatives have 'all the powers of an absolute owner': s. 6(1). If the testator intends that the executors or trustees should be able to charge for their services — for example, where a solicitor acts as executor or trustee — a clause known as a 'charging clause' is necessary because of the general rule that personal representatives and trustees cannot charge for their services.

2.2.2.5 Execution formalities

The will normally ends with a testimonium and an attestation clause. The testimonium recites that the testator signed in order to execute the will and often states the date, e.g., 'IN WITNESS of which I have signed this as my will on the 1st day of April One thousand nine hundred and ninety-six'. However, the date is sometimes inserted in the commencement. Strictly, it is not essential that a will should have a date or that it should contain a testimonium, but it is obviously good practice to have both. The attestation clause recites that the testator signed in the joint presence of the witnesses and that they signed in his presence, e.g., 'signed by the testator in our presence and attested by us in the presence of the testator and of each other'. Again, an attestation clause is not strictly necessary, but is *very* desirable because its presence leads to a presumption of due execution and thus greatly eases the grant of probate. Whereas professionally drawn wills do not always contain a testimonium, they invariably include an attestation clause. It would be negligent of a solicitor to omit an attestation clause when drafting a will. The signatures of the testator and witnesses normally follow the attestation clause, alongside it or under it. The signatures need not be placed at the end of the will but that is the most sensible place for them.

2.2.3 A specimen will and codicil

Let us suppose that our testator, Arthur, has a wife, Mabel, two adult children, Michael and Diana, and a brother, Cyril. Arthur is an enthusiastic member of his local Round Table (a society that raises funds for worthy causes). A simple will — without the creation of any trusts, and not necessarily attempting to minimise tax liability — might take the following form:

This is the LAST WILL of me Arthur Regis of 15 Camelot Close, Glastonbury, Somerset.

1. I revoke all my previous testamentary dispositions.
2. I appoint as my executors my wife Mabel Regis of 15 Camelot Close, Glastonbury, Somerset and my brother Cyril Regis of 6 Lancelot Gardens, Tintagel, Cornwall.
3. I wish to be cremated and for my ashes to be placed in an urn in the family grave at Merlin Park Cemetery, Glastonbury.
4. I give the following specific legacies free of inheritance tax:
    (a) To my brother Cyril my collection of pre-1940 Polish postage stamps
    (b) To my daughter Diana my personal copy of the original edition of Malory's *Morte d'Arthur*
    (c) To my son Michael my silver antique sword known as 'Excalibur'.
5. I give the following pecuniary legacies:
    (a) £1,000 (one thousand pounds) to the Glastonbury Round Table for the general purposes of the society
    (b) £2,000 (two thousand pounds) to my niece Camilla Regis, daughter of my brother Cyril Regis.
6. I give the residue of my estate, out of which shall be paid my debts, funeral and testamentary expenses, to my wife Mabel absolutely provided that she survives me for the period of two calendar months, otherwise to my daughter Diana and my son Michael in equal shares absolutely.

IN WITNESS of which I have signed this as my will on the 1st day of April One thousand nine hundred and ninety-six.

SIGNED by the testator   )
in our presence and attested   )
by us in the presence   )   [Signature of Arthur Regis]
of the testator and   )
of each other   )
            [Signatures, addresses and occupations of witnesses]

Unfortunately, a few months after executing this will, Arthur had a row with Camilla and decided to exclude her from his will. Moreover, he wished to increase the legacy to the Glastonbury Round Table. So he made a codicil in the following terms:

This CODICIL dated the 15th day of October One thousand nine hundred and ninety-six is made by me Arthur Regis of 15 Camelot Close, Glastonbury, Somerset.

1. I revoke the gift of £2,000 to my niece Camilla Regis in clause 5(b) of my will.
2. I give to the Glastonbury Round Table the sum of £3,000 (three thousand pounds) in place of the legacy of £1,000 in clause 5(a) of my will.

3. In all other respects I confirm my will dated the 1st day of April One
    thousand nine hundred and ninety-six.

SIGNED by the testator   )
in our presence and attested   )
by us in the presence   )   [Signature of Arthur Regis]
of the testator and   )
of each other   )
          [Signatures, addresses and occupations of witnesses]

2.3 THE WILL AS A SOCIAL DOCUMENT

A study of a large number of wills of testators dying over a sizeable period, such
as that carried out by Finch *et al.*, 1996, can reveal much about the transfer of
wealth in society. Finch *et al.* describe wills as 'a social and cultural form of
expression' (at p. 177). The authors analyse patterns in will-making and
identify three interlocking factors as forming 'underlying principles of bequeathing': genealogical position, generational position, and whether the
beneficiary occupies the position of 'next-of-kin' (at p. 124). The operation of
these factors helps one to understand the ways in which testators distinguish
between kin when deciding on the appropriate form of gift. Moreover, the
authors claim that such understanding enables one to 'identify with considerable accuracy the type of gift likely to be received by each' (at p. 124).

The authors' study of wills leads them to classify wills as 'total estate' or
'composite' wills. In total estate wills 'no distinction is made between different
types of property; all property is simply added together and then bequeathed'
(at p. 83). A typical total estate will would be where the testator leaves all his
property to his wife. Composite wills, on the other hand, specify 'certain types
of property' to be given to named individuals, before adding the remainder of
the estate together to form the residue. It was found that the proportion of total
estate wills was 52 per cent and that in about half of such wills the surviving
spouse was the sole beneficiary. The number of beneficiaries in total estate wills
averaged 1.5 compared with 5.6 in composite wills (p. 84). In the latter,
beneficiaries tended to be drawn from a wider range of people.

Patterns of substitution were analysed too. Sixty-two per cent of all wills were
found to have at least one substitute beneficiary. The incidence of substitution
was similar in total estate and composite wills, but there was 'a difference in the
comprehensiveness of the coverage' (p. 129): 60 per cent of total estate wills
provided substitutes for all bequests and beneficiaries, whereas in composite
wills only 7 per cent provided substitutes for all bequests, and 13 per cent for
all beneficiaries.

THREE

Making a Will: Capacity and Intention

In order to make a valid will a testator must have the capacity and intention to make a will. Moreover, the required formalities must be satisfied (the subject of the next chapter).

3.1 CAPACITY TO MAKE A WILL

To have capacity means that a person is legally competent to make a will. What makes a person competent to make a will? First, the testator must have attained the required minimum age and, secondly, he must possess the necessary level of mental competence.

3.1.1 Age

Section 7 of the Wills Act 1837 (as amended) provides that 'no will made by any person under the age of 18 years shall be valid' (under the original s. 7 the relevant age was 21). The current minimum of 18 years was introduced by the Family Law Reform Act 1969 and applies to wills made after 1969. A number of common law jurisdictions do allow minors, if married, to make wills, or even if they are contemplating marriage to a particular person.

Should there be a maximum age limit? Given the importance of will-making, the idea of having an upper age limit may have some point. Many aged testators may be somewhat confused in their thinking, even though they satisfy the relatively undemanding test of mental competence necessary to make a valid will (see 3.1.2). Should such testators have an unrestricted right to make a will? It would be difficult to suggest any particular age as a dividing line. Admittedly, statute has done precisely that at the other end of the age-scale, but there is a difference: whereas there is an element of consensus as to when minors reach an age at which they can generally be regarded as sufficiently mature and responsible, no such consensus is likely as to when old age begins to diminish mental faculties. A possible compromise, however, is to require persons of a certain age — say 80 or over — to acquire a doctor's certificate as to their mental competence in order to make a will, something that already happens in practice in many cases (but without the element of compulsion). Thus old age would not be a bar *per se* but would put the onus on aged testators to demonstrate a basic level of mental fitness to make a will. But then exceptions would be necessary to cater for emergency situations and death-bed wills.

There is an important exception to s. 7 of the Wills Act 1837: persons who are in actual military service or who are seamen at sea are entitled to make a will below the age of 18 (see 9.1.1).

3.1.2 Mental competence

3.1.2.1 The *Banks* v *Goodfellow* test
The classic exposition of the degree of mental competence required to make a will in English law is contained in *Banks* v *Goodfellow* (1870) LR 5 QB 549, at 567 *per* Cockburn CJ:

> As to the testator's capacity, he must, in the language of the law, have a sound and disposing mind and memory. In other words, he ought to be capable of making his will with an understanding of the nature of the business in which he is engaged, a recollection of the property he means to dispose of, of the persons who are the objects of his bounty, and the manner in which it is to be distributed between them. It is not necessary that he should view his will with the eye of a lawyer, and comprehend its provisions in their legal form. It is sufficient if he has such a mind and memory as will enable him to understand the elements of which it is composed, and the disposition of his property in its simple forms. In deciding upon the capacity of the testator to make his will, it is the soundness of the mind, and not the particular state of the bodily health, that is to be attended to; the latter may be in a state of extreme imbecility, and yet he may possess sufficient understanding to direct how his property shall be disposed of; his capacity may be perfect to dispose of his property by will, and yet very inadequate to the management of other business, as, for instance, to make contracts for the purchase or sale of property.

The *Banks* v *Goodfellow* test is a working guide: no test could be expected to do more in as complicated an area as that of the functioning of the human mind. It appears that the *Banks*-competent testator must possess a 'sound and disposing mind and memory'. That requires four criteria to be satisfied:

(a) 'nature of the business': the testator must understand 'the nature of the business in which he is engaged'. Thus he must be aware that he is engaged in a testamentary act, i.e. expressing wishes — normally concerning the disposition of property — that will take effect on his death. It is a broad understanding that is required of the testator: he need not view the will 'with the eye of a lawyer'.

(b) 'recollection of the property': the testator must have 'a recollection of the property he means to dispose of'. Again, it is a *general* awareness that is required: the testator need not recollect every item of his property. In *Waters* v *Waters* (1848) 2 De G & Sm 591; 64 ER 263, a case concerning the lengthy will of a wealthy but illiterate testator, Coleridge J stated (at p. 276) that 'a specific and accurate knowledge of every atom of his property' was not required of the testator but that 'he ought to know generally the state of his property and what it consists of'. The required level of recollection will depend on the circumstances: a testator with extensive proprietary assets may be expected to have the awareness appropriate to the amount of property that he owns.

(c) 'the objects of his bounty': the testator must recollect 'the persons who are the objects of his bounty'. Thus the testator must at least be aware of the existence of persons who might be considered to have a moral claim on his estate — whether relatives or friends — even if he chooses not to benefit them. In *Harwood* v *Baker* (1840) 3 Moo PC 282, 13 ER 117, the testator appears to have suffered a stroke after visiting the Bank of England. A few days later he executed a will shortly before he died in which he left all his property to his wife, thus excluding a number of relatives. The will was held to be invalid because the testator, in the opinion of the court, was too ill to give sufficient consideration to the potential claims of his relatives. Erskine J stated (at p. 120) that the question before the court was whether the testator was capable of recollecting who were his relatives, of understanding 'their respective claims upon his regard and bounty, and of deliberately forming an intelligent purpose of excluding them from any share of his property'. The case is not authority, however, for saying that testators must engage in a careful exercise of recollecting all their relatives and friends in order to make a valid will.

(d) 'manner' of distribution: the testator must have a recollection of 'the manner' in which the property is to be distributed between 'the objects of his bounty'. It is not altogether clear what 'manner' comprises, but most probably it refers to the division of the testator's estate: he must be broadly aware of how he has shared out his estate. That may require an understanding of the closeness of his ties with potential beneficiaries and the nature of their claims: *Boughton* v *Knight* (1873) LR P & D 64. In that case Hannen J stated (at pp. 65–6) that apart from the need to recall 'fitting objects of the testator's bounty' a testator had to have 'an understanding to comprehend their relationship to himself and their claim upon him'.

Medical science has advanced considerably since the time when *Banks* v *Goodfellow* was decided, especially in the field of mental health. Although it is questionable to what extent the test put forward in the case is medically sound, the courts continue to regard the test as *the* indicator of the level of mental competence required. In *Wood* v *Smith* [1992] 3 All ER 556, CA, the testator made a will two days before he died. He was aged 82 and had been transferred to hospital following a serious accident in his home. There was compelling evidence — especially from a solicitor who had visited the testator shortly before the latter died — that the testator was confused and incoherent. The court held that the onus of establishing testamentary capacity had not been

Making a Will: Capacity and Intention

discharged: there was insufficient evidence that the testator was able to comprehend the extent of his property or the nature of the claims of those he was excluding. On the other hand, not every form of mental illness will be fatal to testamentary capacity, as *Banks* v *Goodfellow* made clear. For example, in *Brown* v *Pourau* [1995] 1 NZLR 352, the testatrix's will was upheld even though she was occasionally subject to trances in which, believing that a Maori curse had been placed on her, she talked to 'the spirits' and 'the fairies'.

Whether a testator is *Banks*-competent may depend on the level of complexity of a will. Consider *In the Estate of Park* [1953] 2 All ER 1411, CA, where the testator was aged 78 and in very poor health. He had been seriously affected by two strokes so that he was unable to look after his financial affairs — he had previously been a successful businessman — and became forgetful and occasionally confused. Eventually he decided that he wanted to marry the cashier at his club, whom he scarcely knew. When he informed his chauffeur of his intentions the latter responded: 'Well, I don't think you even know the lady yet, sir.' But the testator was not to be discouraged and three weeks later the couple married at Kensington register office. The testator executed a new will at the reception following the wedding — an unusual form of diversion at such gatherings. He died some days later. The will, a complicated one, was held to be invalid on the grounds of lack of mental competence (although the marriage was upheld). The Court of Appeal drew a distinction between simple and complicated wills, implying that the mental competence required would differ accordingly.

3.1.2.2 A testator can be capricious

It is not a rule of English law that a testator must make a sensible will. As long as the *Banks* v *Goodfellow* test is satisfied a testator can make a will that is eccentric, or lacking in judgment. As Hannen J said in *Boughton* v *Knight* (above) 'the law does not say that a man is incapacitated from making a will if he proposes to make a disposition of his property moved by capricious, frivolous, mean, or even bad motives' (at p. 66). Similarly, in *Bird* v *Luckie* (1850) 8 Hare 301; 68 ER 375, Knight Bruce VC described the position thus (at p. 378):

> ... no man is bound to make a will in such a manner as to deserve approbation from the prudent, the wise, or the good. A testator is permitted to be capricious and improvident, and is, moreover, at liberty to conceal the circumstances and the motives by which he had been actuated in his dispositions. Many a testamentary provision may seem to the world arbitrary, capricious and eccentric, for which the testator, if he could be heard, might be able to answer most satisfactorily.

There are numerous examples of capricious and eccentric testators in English law. Some regard a will as an opportunity to express strong feelings. For example, the will of Henry, Earl of Stafford — who accompanied James II into exile — described his wife as 'the worst of women' and guilty of 'all crimes'. He left her 'five and forty brass halfpence, which will buy a pullet for her supper'.

One will provided 'To my son William one shilling and I hope he burns his fingers with it' (for these and other examples see Turing, J. (1982) 79 LSG 1361). Although eccentricity, caprice or foolishness are not in themselves fatal to a will, they are nevertheless best avoided. Apart from the considerable anxiety that such wills may cause to family and friends, their validity will be more difficult to establish because the propounders may have the onus of establishing the mental competence of the testator: it is less likely that they will be able to rely on the presumption — applicable to rational wills — that the testator was mentally competent (see 3.1.2.5). Furthermore, even if formally valid, the capricious will may be more easily challenged under the Inheritance (Provision for Family and Dependants) Act 1975 on the grounds that it does not make reasonable provision for the applicant.

3.1.2.3 Delusions
A will may be invalid if it was made while the testator was suffering from a delusion. What is a delusion? It is an irrational belief which cannot be eradicated by rational argument. In *Dew* v *Clark* (1826) 3 Add 79; 162 ER 410, Nicholl J described a delusion as follows (at p. 414):

Wherever the patient once conceives something extravagant to exist, which has still no existence whatever but in his own heated imagination; and wherever, at the same time, having once so conceived, he is incapable of being, or at least of being permanently, reasoned out of that conception; such a patient is said to be under a delusion ...

It is not every delusion that will negate testamentary capacity, only those that influence a testator in making the provisions of his will and prevent him from being *Banks*-competent. In *Dew* v *Clark* the testator gave his daughter, his only child, a small gift out of his large estate (derived mostly from his lucrative practice as 'medical electrician' to the rich and famous). He treated her with great cruelty in her youth and appears to have formed an irrational aversion to her, describing her *inter alia* as 'a fiend, a monster, Satan's special property' and 'a very devil'. The evidence suggested, however, that the daughter was of exemplary character. It was held that the will was invalid since the meagre provision for the daughter was clearly influenced by the testator's delusion. Similarly, in *Boughton* v *Knight* (above) a will which left the bulk of the estate to virtual strangers was held invalid because of the testator's insane dislike of his sons. These cases do not decide that a testator cannot disinherit his children. He can do so — he can even be capricious — provided that he is not acting under a delusion. Thus, if the daughter in *Dew* v *Clark* really had been as the testator imagined her to be, the will would have been valid.

A variety of interesting delusions can be found in the reports. In *Smee* v *Smee* (1879) 5 P & D 84, a testator believed that he was the son of George IV, that his father had defrauded him by preventing him from benefiting from a trust fund, and that this fund had been diverted in favour of his brothers. In his wills the testator excluded his brothers from any benefit. In directing the jury, Hannen P stated (at p. 92) that the verdict should be against the will 'unless your minds are satisfied that there is no reasonable connection between the delusion and the bequests in the wills'. The jury found against the will. In *Battan Singh* v *Amirchand* [1948] 1 All ER 152, PC, the testator made a will in which he declared that he had no relatives; he left his property to two friends. He was in the last stages of tuberculosis and died the following day. His statement was incorrect: he had four nephews to whom he had left his property in a will made only five weeks earlier. The Privy Council found against the last will since it was 'the product of a man so enfeebled by disease as to be without sound mind or memory at the time of execution and that the disposition of his property under it was the outcome of the delusion touching his nephews' existence' (pp. 156–7). In *Re Nightingale* (1974) 119 SJ 189, a testator who was dying from cancer cut out his adopted son — the principal beneficiary under his previous will — from his second will. There was evidence that during the six weeks between the execution of the two wills there were two occasions on which the testator tried to sit up in bed while struggling for breath. On each occasion the son had pushed him gently back onto his pillows. The court pronounced against the later will on the ground that most probably the father made it while under the delusion that the son was trying to murder him (there was a paucity of evidence as to what the testator really thought).

Perhaps the most remarkable case of all is *Smith* v *Tebbitt* (1867) 1 P & D 398. The testatrix left the bulk of her huge estate to a Dr Smith, her doctor, and comparatively little to her sister, her only next-of-kin. The testatrix suffered from monomania. She believed *inter alia* that she was part of the Holy Trinity — she was the Holy Ghost and Dr Smith was the Father; that she would give birth to the Saviour, for which event she provided baby-linen; that she was the Bride of Christ and the Virgin Mary; that she would one day possess Buckingham Palace and Windsor Castle; that the final judgment would take place in her own drawing-room, with her sitting in judgment on her fellow creatures; that Dr Smith had at one time resurrected her, giving her a new body; and that her sister was 'a child of the devil' who would have 'the hottest place in hell' and whom the Father (i.e. Dr Smith) had told her to 'cut off'. Not surprisingly the court held that the will was invalid as it had clearly been influenced by the delusions concerning Dr Smith and the testatrix's sister.

However deluded a testator may be, his will is valid provided that the delusion did not affect the making of the will. In *Banks* v *Goodfellow* the testator left most of his estate to his niece who had lived with and cared for him. The testator had at one time been confined in a lunatic asylum and continued thereafter to be afflicted by two particular delusions: first, that he was being pursued by devils or evil spirits, and, secondly, that a man long dead 'still pursued and molested him'. However, the testator was capable of managing his affairs — especially the leasing of his property in the Lake District — and had given sensible instructions about the drafting of his will. The court upheld the will, Cockburn CJ stating (at p. 566):

> . . . a degree or form of unsoundness which neither disturbs the exercise of the faculties necessary for such an act, nor is capable of influencing the result, ought not to take away the power of making a will . . .

The distinctions between caprice and delusion, or between delusions that affect testamentary capacity and those that do not, can in theory be easily drawn. In practice, however, the dividing line may be much more difficult to draw. As Fust J said in *Mudway v Croft* (1843) 3 Curt 671; 163 ER 863, at 866, 'the same acts which would constitute insanity in one eccentric individual might not do so in another'. Both the capricious and the deluded testator act in the same way: they make eccentric provisions. But the deluded testator does so because he is driven by an irrational belief — one that no rational person would hold. But then what is meant by a 'rational person', and what are the limits of a rational person's thinking? Another complicating factor is that rationality is tested by how the outside world — more specifically, the judge — views the testator's beliefs and actions. Obviously the judgment can be made only on the evidence before the court. And yet there may have been some explanation — which has not come to light — which would make the testator's provisions seem rational. Suppose that Arthur excludes his wife from benefiting under his will because he believes that she is 'in league with the devil'. Assuming there is no evidence for his belief, the will is unlikely to survive: Arthur's delusion affected his provisions. But what if Arthur knew that his wife had been an active member of a secret Satanic cult, and he had kept the information to himself? Can it still be said that his will is 'irrational'?

3.1.2.4 When must the testator have capacity?

The basic rule is that the testator must be mentally competent when the will is executed. If competence at the relevant time is established, the fact that the testator lacked such competence before or after the execution will not invalidate a will. Hence a will made in a lucid interval is valid. In *In the Estate of Walker* (1912) 28 TLR 466, the testatrix had been declared a lunatic and was kept under supervision. She suffered from delusions by virtue of which she was potentially violent and dangerous. However, she took an intelligent interest in general topics, kept corresponding with relatives and friends, and in other respects was 'a shrewd, clever woman' with an excellent memory. She made a will attested by three doctors who were prepared to certify that she was mentally competent to make a will at the time of the execution. The will was upheld. *Chambers and Yatman v Queen's Proctor* (1840) 2 Curt 415; 163 ER 457, concerned a barrister of the Inner Temple, alleged to be of 'strange and eccentric habits' (i.e. the barrister, not the Inner Temple). He suffered from various delusions, principally that he was an object of 'scorn and contempt' to his friends and the whole world — not an uncommon delusion — and that he would be disbarred because he had concealed the fact that his father was 'only a chemist'. He made a perfectly sensible will, his conduct when executing the will being described by the witnesses as 'cool, collected and rational'. The following day he executed himself: he committed suicide. The court upheld the will as it was satisfied that it had been made in a lucid interval.

There is an important exception to the rule that the testator must be mentally competent when the will is executed. Where a competent testator gives instructions as to the making of his will but then loses mental competence before the will is executed, the will is nevertheless valid if the instructions were given to a solicitor, the will was prepared in accordance with those instructions, and the testator executed the will while understanding that he was executing a will for which he had given instructions. The rule was enunciated in *Parker* v *Felgate* (1883) 8 PD 171 by Hannen P (at p. 173):

> If a person has given instructions to a solicitor to make a will, and the solicitor prepares it in accordance with those instructions, all that is necessary to make it a good will, if executed by the testator, is that he should be able to think thus far, 'I gave my solicitor instructions to prepare a will making a certain disposition of my property. I have no doubt that he has given effect to my intention, and I accept the document which is put before me as carrying it out'.

In that case the testatrix, a young woman in her late twenties, contracted Bright's disease. She consulted her solicitor and gave him instructions to draft a will in which she gave the bulk of her estate to a children's hospital in preference to relatives. Before the will could be executed the testatrix lapsed into a partial coma from which she was occasionally roused. On one such occasion her doctor rustled the will in front of her face and said, 'This is your will'. It was then signed on her behalf with her consent. The court found that the testatrix did not 'remember and understand' the instructions given to the solicitor and that she could not have understood the clauses in the will. Nevertheless the will was upheld since she understood that 'she was engaged in executing the will for which she had given instructions'. The rule in *Parker* v *Felgate* was applied by the Privy Council in *Perera* v *Perera* [1901] AC 354, where the instructions were given to a licensed notary (an official with jurisdiction over the authentication of documents such as wills). In *Battan Singh* v *Amirchand* (see 3.1.2.3) the instructions were given to a lay intermediary to pass to the solicitor. On the facts the Privy Council refused to apply the rule in *Parker* v *Felgate*. Lord Normand stated (at p. 155):

> ... the principle enunciated in *Parker* v *Felgate* should be applied with the greatest caution and reserve when the testator does not himself give instructions to the solicitor who draws the will, but to a lay intermediary who repeats them to the solicitor. The opportunities for error in transmission and of misunderstanding and of deception in such a situation are obvious, and the court ought to be strictly satisfied that there is no ground for suspicion, and that the instructions given to the intermediary were unambiguous and clearly understood, faithfully reported by him and rightly apprehended by the solicitor, before making any presumption in favour of validity.

The rule in *Parker* v *Felgate* appears to be confined to where instructions are given to a solicitor (or notary) or to an intermediary to give to a solicitor. Given that the rule constitutes a major exception to the fundamental principle that the testator should have capacity when the will is executed, it would be inadvisable to extend it further. However, in the Irish case, *Re Glynn* [1990] 2 IR 326, the rule was applied where the testator instructed two friends — neither of whom was legally qualified — to draw up his will (they were not intermediaries).

3.1.2.5   The burden of proof

... the *onus probandi* lies in every case upon the party propounding a Will; and he must satisfy the conscience of the Court that the instrument so propounded is the last Will of a free and capable Testator.

This basic principle was stated by Parke B in *Barry* v *Butlin* (1838) 2 Moo PC 480; 12 ER 1089, at 1090. The burden of proof must be satisfied on a balance of probabilities. However, if the will is rational on its face, there is a presumption that the testator was mentally competent to make the will. The evidential burden of proof then shifts to the party opposing the will to rebut the presumption by evidence to the contrary. If such evidence is forthcoming, the burden of proof shifts back to the propounder. This form of legal ping-pong was fully explained in *Waring* v *Waring* (1848) 6 Moo PC 341; 13 ER 715, a case concerning a testatrix with a multitude of delusions, one of which was that Lord Melbourne (the Prime Minister of the time) used to visit her house, disguised as a fish-pedlar, in order to have 'an improper connection' with her. The position can be illustrated by *Symes* v *Green* (1859) 1 Sw & Tr 401; 164 ER 785. The testator made a will which was challenged by his nephew, his only relative, who had been excluded. As the will was rational and correctly executed, it was presumed to have been made by a mentally competent testator. However, evidence was produced that when he made the will the testator was suffering from insanity, induced partly by his belief that he was destined for 'eternal perdition' as he had partaken in a church sacrament while 'unworthy'. The evidence rebutted the presumption of mental competence. Thus the burden of proof shifted to the propounder, who was unable to satisfy the court of the testator's mental competence.

What if the will is irrational on its face? It seems that the testator will be presumed to have lacked mental competence, but this presumption is probably weaker than the presumption of capacity which arises from a rational will. As usual, appropriate evidence can rebut the presumption. In *Austen* v *Graham* (1854) 8 Moo PC 493; 14 ER 188, the testator left only a small gift to his brother, his only relative, and the residue of his estate to the Turkish Ambassador to be applied for the benefit of the poor in Constantinople and for the erection of a cenotaph in the city 'with a light burning, and a description of the Testator engraved thereon'. The Privy Council thought that these provisions might be considered 'absurd and irrational in a native of England and a Christian according to English habits', but they were explained by the fact that the testator had in early life adopted 'the manners and mode of living of a Mohamedan'.

The evidential burden of proof may also be affected by the presumption of the continuance of a mental state. If the testator is shown to have been mentally competent prior to the making of a will, it is presumed that he continued to be competent at the time of execution. If, on the other hand, the testator is known to have suffered from serious mental illness before the will was executed, the presumption arises that the illness continued so that the testator lacked capacity at the time of the execution. The presumption may be rebutted by evidence showing that the testator had recovered his mental competence before executing the will, or that the execution occurred during a lucid interval. In *Cartwright* v *Cartwright* (1793) 1 Phill 90; 161 ER 923, the will of the testatrix was rational on its face: hence the presumption arose that she was mentally competent to make it. However, proof that she had been declared insane six months prior to its execution led instead to the presumption that her mental state continued at the time of execution — a reversal of presumptions. Nevertheless the will was upheld because of evidence that the testatrix had 'full and complete capacity to understand what was the state of her affairs and her relations, and to give what was proper in the way she has done' (at p. 933).

3.1.2.6 Effect of mental incompetence

If a testator lacked the mental competence to make a will, the effect is that the whole will fails. But if it is shown that the incapacity affected only part of the will, then exceptionally the rest of the will may be upheld, as occurred in *Re Bohrmann* [1938] 1 All ER 271. The testator, diagnosed as a paranoid psychopath, was a man of 'exceptional acumen in managing his private affairs'. He left substantial gifts to charity in his will and subsequent codicils. In the last codicil he inserted a clause revoking gifts to English charities and substituted American charities. At the time he was suffering from a delusion that he was being persecuted by the London County Council, his local authority, and that he might be dispossessed of his home because of a grudge held against him by one of the authority's valuers. Langton J upheld the codicil with the omission of the offending clause. This decision broke new ground: a testamentary instrument apparently had never been divided before in similar circumstances. The judge justified his approach thus:

> It has been the practice in this court for many years to delete from instruments of testamentary disposition anything which the court is satisfied is not brought to the knowledge and approval of the testator. I conceive that I am doing no more now in declaring for this codicil without clause 2 than I should be doing in deleting from the codicil something which I believe was never brought to his knowledge and approval as a sane, balanced man. (p. 282)

This decision reflects the traditional preference of English judges for upholding wills or codicils wherever possible. And it adds a measure of flexibility to the options available to a judge — for that reason it is to be welcomed. However, it is questionable how confident a judge can be in deciding that a testator is simultaneously mentally competent as to one part of the will but not another.

It is obviously good practice in cases where there is any doubt as to a testator's mental capacity to arrange for the testator to be examined by an experienced medical practitioner. In *Kenward* v *Adams* (1975) *The Times*, 28 November, Templeman J suggested a 'golden if tactless rule' in cases where the testator was old and infirm (applicable equally where there is doubt as to his mental state): the making of his will should be witnessed and approved by a medical practitioner, who should satisfy himself as to the capacity of the testator and make a record of his findings. The advice was repeated in *Re Simpson* (1977) 121 SJ 224, where a testator, suffering from Parkinson's disease and close to death, made a will which was held to be invalid for want of knowledge and approval. The Law Reform Committee's Report, *The Making and Revocation of Wills* (LRC Report No. 22, 1980) expressed the hope that the 'golden if tactless rule' would continue to be followed but did not recommend that the rule should be enacted. The Committee feared that complications could arise regarding the confidential relationship between solicitor and testator, and added:

> Further, because a complicated will dealing with large amounts of property requires a greater degree of mental alertness than a simple will dealing with a small estate, the doctor might well have to be told of the terms of the will and possibly also of the testator's family situation which may be relevant, in order to assess whether or not the testator had sufficient capacity to make the kind of will he in fact made. In our view many testators might well take exception to revealing the contents of their wills or their family circumstances to unknown medical practitioners. (para. 2.19)

If a person is mentally incapable of making a valid will, a 'statutory' will may be made on their behalf by the Court of Protection under the Mental Health Act 1983 (see 9.1.2).

3.1.2.7 Miscellaneous factors

A testator who is blind or illiterate is able to make a valid will: his condition does not in itself deprive him of testamentary capacity. However, the propounders of the will must show that the testator knew and approved of the contents of the will (Non-Contentious Probate Rules (NCPR) 1987, r. 13). Reading the will to the testator provides strong evidence of knowledge and approval (though not conclusive) and should be recited in the attestation clause since a presumption will thereby arise that the testator knew and approved of the contents. But other proof may suffice. Consider *In the Goods of Geale* (1864) 3 Sw & Tr 431; 164 ER 1342, where the testator was deaf, dumb and could neither read nor write. He conversed with his family and friends by signs which were well understood by all of them. He was considered to be 'shrewd and intelligent, and possessed of considerable mechanical skill and ingenuity'. A will was drafted for him at his request and properly executed, the testator and witnesses communicating by signs at the appropriate time. The will was upheld on proof of the signs used. For example, to indicate money the testator touched his pockets; to indicate all his property or all things, he looked around while raising his arms with 'a sweeping motion all round'; to indicate his wife he pointed to the ring-finger of his left hand and crossed his arms — females were indicated by crossing arms, males by crossing wrists. In *Fincham* v *Edwards* (1842) 3 Curt 63; 163 ER 656, the will of a virtually blind testatrix (her hand had to be guided to the point where she was supposed to sign) was upheld even though it had not been read over to her when she executed it. The court was satisfied that she had sufficient knowledge of the contents.

What if the testator made the will while under the influence of drink or drugs? There is no presumption that a person addicted to drink lacks testamentary capacity: *Ayrey* v *Hill* (1824) 2 Add 206; 162 ER 269. But if evidence is forthcoming that the will was executed while the testator was under the influence of drink, the propounders must prove that the testator had the necessary mental competence. In *In the Estate of Heinke* [1959] CLY 3449, the testator made a codicil in a public house during a bout of heavy drinking. He revoked a substantial gift to a woman who had been 'his housekeeper and mistress' for the last 16 years of his life. Sachs J held that the codicil was void on the ground that the deceased had not been of sound mind, memory and understanding when he executed it and did not know and approve the contents. The same principle will apply where the testator makes a will when under the influence of drugs.

3.2 INTENTION TO MAKE A WILL: *ANIMUS TESTANDI*

3.2.1 Introduction

It is a fundamental principle that a will is invalid unless the testator had the intention to make it — he must have the *animus testandi*. More specifically, the requirement is that the testator must have intended that his wishes — as expressed in the appropriate form — should take effect on his death. It follows that these wishes must be entirely the result of his volition: the testator must know and approve of the contents of his will. Hence *animus testandi* can be vitiated by factors such as mistake or undue influence.

If a testator uses the services of a solicitor to make a will, it is very likely that the *animus testandi* is present. The intention is perhaps less obvious in the case of a home-made will, but even then one can assume that people are unlikely to go through the rigmarole of executing a will unless they intended to make one. Therefore a presumption arises that a document which appears on its face to be a will — executed in accordance with the required formalities — was made with *animus testandi*. The presumption is rebuttable. In *Lister* v *Smith* (1868) 3 Sw & Tr 282; 164 ER 1282, at 1285, Wilde J stated:

> . . . if the fact is plainly and conclusively made out, that the paper which appears to be the record of a testamentary act, was in reality the offspring of a jest, or the result of a contrivance to effect some collateral object, and never seriously intended as a disposition of property, it is not reasonable that the Court should turn it into an effective instrument.

Suppose that Arthur, a law lecturer, wanting to demonstrate to his students how to make a will, executes one in class. It leaves all his property to the students in the class. Can they propound the will on his death? Only if he executed the will with *animus testandi*, which on the facts was very unlikely. In *Nichols* v *Nichols* (1814) 2 Phill 180; 161 ER 1113, the children of the deceased propounded the following document as the last will of the deceased: 'I leave my property between my children; I hope they will be virtuous and independent; that they will worship God, and not black coats.' The mention of 'black coats' was a reference to lawyers: the deceased, a solicitor himself, was in the habit of ridiculing the way that lawyers 'employed a vast number of unnecessary words'. The document was executed after a convivial dinner when the deceased wanted to illustrate how short a will could be. Evidence showed that the deceased never again alluded to the document (which was kept by a witness) and that he subsequently regarded himself as not having made a will. Not surprisingly the court pronounced for an intestacy.

3.2.2 Wishes intended to take effect on death

The testator must make an expression of wishes — normally disposing of his property — to be carried out on his death. Thus, if he executes a document and there is no evidence that it is intended to take effect on death, the document lacks testamentary character and thus cannot constitute a will. In *Hodson* v *Barnes* (1926) 43 TLR 71, the testator wrote '17 — 1925. Mag. Everything i possess. — J.B.' It was held that these words were insufficient to show *animus testandi* as they could not be said to dispose of property on his death. In *In the Estate of Knibbs* [1962] 2 All ER 829, the testator, a barman on a liner, was chatting about his sister Iris with the head barman. The testator stated that she had always been good to him and that 'If anything ever happens to me, Iris will get anything I have got'. In deciding that the words were 'the mere exchange of gossip' spoken without *animus testandi*, Wrangham J stated (at p. 832):

> ... in order to be a testamentary act there must be a statement of the deceased's wishes for the disposition of his property which is not merely imparted to his audience as a matter of information or interest, but is intended by him to convey to that audience a request explicit or implicit to see that his wishes are acted on.

Cases such as *Hodson* v *Barnes* and *In the Estate of Knibbs* vividly illustrate the necessity for there to be testamentary intention, but they seem distinctly ungenerous. Had the testator in *Hodson* v *Barnes* written the word 'to' before 'Mag.' that may have sufficed; similarly, if the barman in *Knibbs* had expressed a request, e.g., 'I want Iris to get everything'. In *Re Jones* [1981] 1 All ER 1, the words uttered by a mortally wounded soldier — 'If I don't make it, make sure Anne gets all my stuff' — were held sufficient. That the validity of a will should turn on such fine distinctions is questionable and is bound to lead to hard cases such as *Re Knibbs*. A more readily justifiable decision is *In the Estate of Beech* [1923] P 46, CA. The testator wrote two letters — while on active service in France in the First World War — in which he incorrectly summarised the provisions of an earlier will. The issue arose whether the letters could have testamentary effect. The Court of Appeal held that the letters lacked *animus testandi* as they were simply an expression of what the testator thought that he had done. Similarly in *Re Donner's Estate* (1917) 34 TLR 138, the deceased spoke to a fellow officer about making a will shortly before participating in offensive action on the Somme in 1916. The deceased was informed (incorrectly) that if he died intestate his mother would inherit all his property. He responded, 'That is just what I want. I want my mother to have everything'. It was held that his statement did not show *animus testandi* since the deceased was simply confirming what he understood to be the legal position.

Although a testator must express a wish intended to take effect on death, it is not necessary that he should have intended to make a will admissible to probate under English law. In *Re Berger* [1989] 1 All ER 591, the Court of Appeal granted probate to documents written by the deceased in Hebrew and known as *zavah*. They contained religious exhortations to his family and dispositions of property. They were intended by the deceased to be enforceable in the Jewish rabbinical court, but there was no indication whether he intended them to be enforceable in the English courts. Nevertheless the *zavah's* execution conformed with the formalities required under the Wills Act 1837; and it did contain directions as to the disposal of the deceased's property on his death, thus showing *animus testandi*.

Moreover, a testator can have *animus testandi* even though he is not aware that he is making a will: *Milnes* v *Foden* (1890) 15 PD 105, at 107, where Hannen P stated that it was not necessary 'that the testator should intend to perform or be aware that he has performed a testamentary act'. In *Re Stable* [1919] P 7, the deceased, a young soldier who was engaged to be married, consulted his family solicitor about making a will shortly before going to the front in France. The solicitor's grasp of the law was somewhat inadequate since the deceased was informed that as he was a minor he could not make a will (but see 9.1.1.6). Soon afterwards, while visiting an acquaintance, he said to his fiancée, 'If anything happens to me, and I stop a bullet, everything of mine will be yours'. Clearly the deceased did not think that he was making a will as he had been told that he was too young to do so. Nevertheless it was held that his statement was made with *animus testandi* since he expressed his wishes as to what should be done with his property in the event of his death. However, was *Re Stable* correctly decided on the facts? It is arguable that the deceased's words did not demonstrate *animus testandi* since they can be interpreted as simply conveying information rather than expressing a request to be effected on death. Wherein lies the difference between 'Iris will get anything I have got' (*Re Knibbs*, will invalid) and 'everything of mine will be yours' (*Re Stable*, will valid)? Perhaps it lies in the fact that in *Re Stable* the words were actually spoken to the beneficiary rather than *about* the beneficiary, and thus can more easily be interpreted as having a dispositive effect than those in *Re Knibbs*.

3.2.3   Conditional wills

3.2.3.1   Will inoperative unless condition satisfied
Testators sometimes make wills conditional on the occurrence of some specified event. The basic rule is that such wills take effect only if the condition

is fulfilled. For example, in *In the Goods of Hugo* (1877) 2 PD 73, a married couple executed a joint will 'in case we should be called out of this world at one and the same time and by one and the same accident'. It appears that they were nervous about undertaking a lengthy railway journey, there having been a number of serious railway accidents beforehand. They survived the journey. On the husband's death over two years later the issue was raised whether the joint will had revoked an earlier will of his. It was held that the joint will was inoperative as it was conditional upon a contingency that never occurred. A similar decision was reached in *Re Govier* [1950] P 237. A married couple made a joint will at a time (May 1941) when the county of Devon — where the parties were living — was subject to severe bombing raids. They were conscious of the risk of being killed together by the same bomb. The will stated, 'In the event of our two deaths . . .' and then appointed an executor and made a number of bequests. The will did not refer to the possibility of one spouse surviving the other. It was held that the will was conditional on their dying together; hence it had no effect (the husband survived the wife). The judge concluded that the words 'in the event of our two deaths' referred to the couple dying together and were not simply expressing a general contemplation of death sometime in the future. In *In the Goods of Robinson* (1870) LR 2 P & D 171, a seaman on a return voyage from London to Sicily made a will in a French port 'in case anything should happen to me during the remainder of the voyage from hence to Sicily and back to London'. He survived the journey and died two years later. The will was held to be inoperative: it had been made dependent on an event that had not occurred (the court sensibly refusing to interpret the phrase 'in case anything should happen to me' literally).

3.2.3.2 Motive or condition?

Where a testator expresses a motive or reason for making a will rather than a condition, the position is different: the will is regarded as unconditional. But the distinction between motive and condition may not always be obvious. Consider *In the Goods of Spratt* [1897] P 28: the testator, a British soldier serving in New Zealand in 1864 during the Maori War, wrote a letter to his sister stating that if the war continued 'the chances are in favour of more of us being killed, and as I may not have another opportunity of saying what I wish to be done with any little money I may possess in the case of an accident, I wish to make everything I possess over to you . . . Keep this until I ask you for it'. The testator died many years later, long after the conclusion of the Maori War. The court held that as the testator's intention to make a will was not conditional the will was operative. Jeune P explained (at p. 30) that a will is conditional if it is 'clearly expressed to take effect only on the happening, or not happening, of any event'; it is unconditional if the testator says that he is led to make his will by reason of the uncertainty of life in general, or for some special reason. The judge then addressed the position where the distinction was not clear:

> But if it be not clear whether the words used import a reason for making a will or impress a conditional character on it, the whole language of the document, and also the surrounding circumstances, must be considered. In

such cases there are two criteria which are especially useful for determining the problem: first, whether the nature of disposition made appears to have relation to the time or circumstances of the contingency; and, secondly, where the contingency is connected with a period of danger to the testator, whether it is coincident with that period, because, if it is, there is ground to suppose that the danger was regarded by the testator only as a reason for making a will, but, if it is not, it is difficult to see the object of referring to a particular period unless it be to limit the operation of the will.

Applying these tests, the phrase 'in case of an accident' was held to point only to the reason for making the will. The fact that the testator asked his sister to keep the will until he asked for it was regarded as significant: it showed that he did not have in mind any particular time when the will was to cease to be operative. This decision was followed in *Re Panapa* [1993] 1 NZLR 694, where the testatrix made a will 'in anticipation of my marriage' to her intended husband. She died the following day (the day prior to the intended wedding). It was held that the will had not been made conditional on the marriage. The phrase 'in anticipation of' expressed a reason for making the will, not a condition (the testatrix did not want the will to be revoked by the marriage).

3.2.3.3   Proof of the condition

Proof that the testator intended a conditional will must appear on the face of the will, although extrinsic evidence is admissible to resolve any ambiguity in the expression of the condition in the will: *Re Govier* (above). But extrinsic evidence is not admissible to prove that a will appearing on its face to be unconditional is in fact conditional. In *Corbett v Newey* [1996] 2 All ER 914, CA, the testatrix made it clear to her solicitor that she wanted to make *inter vivos* gifts of her farms in Cornwall and instructed him to prepare a new will excluding any reference to the farms. Moreover, she emphasised that she regarded the transactions as interrelated and that she did not intend to sign the new will until the *inter vivos* gifts were in place. She eventually executed the new will but, because of a misunderstanding over the relevance of dating a will, the execution occurred before the *inter vivos* gifts had been made. The issue arose whether the new will was a conditional will operative only on completion of the *inter vivos* gifts. It was held that the testatrix had failed to make an effective new will. She could not by words or conduct outside the terms of the will impose a condition postponing the will's operation. A conditional will was possible only if the condition appeared on the face of the will. Moreover, the testatrix lacked the *animus testandi* to make an unconditional will since when she signed it she did not intend to create a document which would operate unconditionally, as explained by Waite LJ (at p. 921):

Since a will operates from the moment of execution, it necessarily follows that to possess the necessary *animus testandi* the testator must intend that this dispositive (although revocable and ambulatory) regime will be called into play immediately — and not postponed to, or made dependent upon, some future event or condition. That is why — surprising though the distinction may be at first sight to a layman — it is possible to have a will which is on its face conditional, and yet impossible to have a will which though unconditional on its face purports, through some direction imposed externally by the testator at the time of its execution, to be made conditional in its operation.

3.2.4 Knowledge and approval

Since a testator must have *animus testandi* in order to make a will, it follows that he must know and approve of the contents of his will. This is a fundamental requirement of every will, as was made suitably clear by Lord Penzance in *Cleare* v *Cleare* (1869) 1 P & D 655, at 657:

> That he knew and approved of the contents is a proposition implied in the assertion that a will was made by him. For if a man were to sign a paper of the contents of which he knew nothing, it would be no will. ... That the testator did know and approve of the contents of the alleged will is therefore part of the burthen of proof assumed by every one who propounds it as a will.

Although knowledge and approval is a general requirement, it is of particular relevance where doubt exists whether the document propounded as the deceased's will was the product of his volition, e.g., where there are 'suspicious circumstances' (see 3.2.5). Failure to prove knowledge and approval will result in the failure of the whole or part of the will.

3.2.4.1 The presumption
The burden of proof is on the propounder of the will; but if the will is shown to have been duly executed and made by a testator of the necessary mental capacity, a presumption arises that the testator knew and approved of the contents: *Barry* v *Butlin* (1838) 2 Moo PC 480; 12 ER 1089. The effect of the presumption will be to shift the evidential burden to the person challenging the will, who must then produce evidence to rebut the presumption. If such evidence is forthcoming the burden of proving knowledge and approval reverts to the propounder: *Cleare* v *Cleare* (above). In practice, knowledge and approval will be presumed in the vast majority of wills admitted to probate. The presumption probably does not arise when the circumstances are suspicious or abnormal, e.g., if a person who prepares a will takes a benefit under it. Neither does the presumption arise in the case of a will made by a blind or illiterate testator, or a will signed by another person on behalf of the testator; but it will be different if an attestation clause recites that the testator had knowledge and approval.

3.2.4.2 The time factor
When must the testator know and approve of the contents of the will? It must be at the time when the will was executed: *Hastilow* v *Stobie* (1865) 1 P & D 64. However, where the testator did not have knowledge and approval at the time of execution but did so when instructing his solicitor to prepare a will, the rule in *Parker* v *Felgate* (see 3.1.2.4) is applicable. For example, in *In the Estate of*

Wallace [1952] 2 TLR 925, the testator wrote out a document, headed 'Last wish', which provided that the beneficiaries were 'to have all I am possed [*sic*] of'. In accordance with his instructions a will was drafted embodying the terms of the 'Last wish'. It was executed the day before the testator's death, when his condition had deteriorated. The evidence established that he knew and approved of the contents of the 'Last wish', and that when he executed the will he understood what he was doing and accepted the will as a document that carried out his wishes. The will was upheld.

3.2.4.3 Type of proof
Where proof of knowledge and approval is required, i.e. when the presumption has been rebutted or does not arise, the court must be satisfied by proof that the will was made by a free and capable testator. The most common form of proof is evidence showing that the testator read over the will when executing it, or that it was read **over** to him. At one time evidence of reading over the will was regarded as conclusive proof of knowledge and approval: *Guardhouse* v *Blackburn* (1866) 1 P & D 109. That such a rule should have become established is surprising, given the potential for abuse and the uncertainty as to what 'reading over' might entail. The rule began to lose its force when in *Fulton* v *Andrew* (1875) LR 7 HL 448 the House of Lords held that there was no 'unyielding' rule of law that 'all further enquiry is shut out' on proof of reading over. More recently Latey J held in *Re Morris* [1970] 1 All ER 1057 that reading over is still regarded as weighty evidence, but not conclusive.

3.2.5 Suspicious circumstances

Affirmative proof of knowledge and approval is necessary whenever circumstances exist which 'excite the suspicion of the court', as Lindley LJ stated in *Tyrrell* v *Painton* [1894] P 151, CA. He continued (at p. 157):

> ... wherever such circumstances exist, and whatever their nature may be, it is for those who propound the will to remove such suspicion, and to prove affirmatively that the testator knew and approved of the contents of the document, and it is only where this is done that the onus is thrown on those who oppose the will to prove fraud or undue influence, or whatever else they rely on to displace the case made for proving the will.

This rule, sometimes described as 'the suspicious circumstances doctrine', requires the propounder of the will to prove knowledge and approval at the outset of the case: the normal presumption of knowledge and approval is not operative. The case law shows that the rule is concerned with the circumstances surrounding the execution of a will.

3.2.5.1 Will prepared by beneficiary
In *Barry* v *Butlin* (see 3.2.4.1) Parke B stated (at p. 1090):

> If a party writes or prepares a Will, under which he takes a benefit, that is a circumstance that ought generally to excite the suspicion of the Court, and calls upon it to be vigilant and jealous in examining the evidence in support of the instrument, in favour of which it ought not to pronounce unless the suspicion is removed, and it is judicially satisfied that the paper propounded does express the true Will of the deceased.

In this case the testator executed a will prepared for him by his attorney under which the latter took a substantial legacy. Nothing was given in the will to the testator's son, his only next-of-kin. On the facts the court's suspicions were removed by evidence that *inter alia* the testator had been very friendly with the attorney for some time, that the will was executed 'fairly and openly' in the presence of 'respectable witnesses' (including a doctor), that comparison with an earlier draft showed that the testator's mind 'was employed on the subject' and 'cognizable' of the contents, and that he had long broken off relations with his violent son.

The leading case on suspicious circumstances is *Wintle* v *Nye* [1959] 1 All ER 552, HL. It is as famous a case as any in Succession, having featured in newspaper headlines and been the subject of television programmes. The case concerned a solicitor, Nye, who prepared a will and a codicil for an elderly testatrix under which Nye in effect took the bulk of her large estate as residuary beneficiary. She was 'unversed in business' and totally reliant for advice on Nye who had acted as the family solicitor and had known her for many years. The will was complicated and rather beyond the understanding of the testatrix (who was described as of limited intelligence). No independent advice was received by the testatrix, and Nye did little or nothing to persuade her to seek it. He retained the will and did not give her a copy. The subsequent codicil revoked charitable legacies thus increasing the size of Nye's residuary benefit. Although the will and codicil were upheld at first instance and by the Court of Appeal, the House of Lords held that the codicil and the gifts in the will to Nye were invalid (but the rest of the will took effect). There was a heavy burden on him in these circumstances to prove that the testatrix knew and approved of the contents of the will and the codicil, a burden which on the facts he failed to discharge. Viscount Simonds stated (at p. 557):

> It is not the law that in no circumstances can a solicitor or other person who has prepared a will for a testator take a benefit under it. But that fact creates a suspicion that must be removed by the person propounding the will. In all cases the court must be vigilant and jealous. The degree of suspicion will vary with the circumstances of the case. It may be slight and easily dispelled. It may, on the other hand, be so grave that it can hardly be removed. In the present case, the circumstances were such as to impose on the respondent as heavy a burden as can well be imagined.

This case turned on the issue whether the testatrix knew and approved of the contents of the will and codicil. It was *not* about undue influence or fraud (see 3.2.7), neither of which was alleged. Nye was opposed by Colonel Wintle who claimed to be interested in the event of the testatrix's intestacy. The challenge took an unusual form: Wintle, an eccentric with a colourful past, physically assaulted Nye outside the Law Courts. Moreover, he personally prepared the legal challenge to the will and codicil and conducted the case in court himself, losing in the High Court and Court of Appeal, but succeeding in the House of Lords.

The smaller the benefit to the preparer of the will, the lesser will be the degree of suspicion. For example, Parke B gave the opinion in *Barry* v *Butlin* (above) that if a man 'of acknowledged competence and habits of business' left a legacy of £50 to his attorney out of an estate of £100,000, this would be a suspicious circumstance 'of no weight at all' (p. 1091). However, standards of professional conduct have become more exacting since *Barry* v *Butlin* was decided. According to the Law Society's *Guide to the Professional Conduct of Solicitors 1993* (p. 325):

> Where a client intends to make a gift *inter vivos* or by will to his or her solicitor, or to the solicitor's partner, or a member of staff or to the families of any of them and the gift is of a significant amount, either in itself or having regard to the size of the client's estate and the reasonable expectations of prospective beneficiaries, the solicitor must advise the client to be independently advised as to that gift and if the client declines, must refuse to act.

These guidelines reflect the decision in *Re A Solicitor* [1974] 3 All ER 853, where a solicitor was struck off the Roll of Solicitors for failing to advise two sisters-in-law to seek independent advice when they sought to make wills partially in his and his family's favour.

3.2.5.2 Other suspicious circumstances

Affirmative proof of knowledge and approval will be required in situations analogous to those where a will is prepared by a beneficiary, e.g., where it is prepared by a close relative of a beneficiary. In *Tyrrell* v *Painton* (above) the testatrix made wills in favour of the defendant, a trustee of her marriage settlement, with whom she was on friendly terms. She later became dissatisfied with him and made another will, mainly benefiting her cousin. Two days later, her health deteriorating, she was visited by the defendant's son and his friend, 'a strange young man'. She executed a will — while she was exhausted and drowsy — in favour of the defendant. It was written in the son's handwriting and was witnessed by the son and his friend. The Court of Appeal held that the rule which threw upon the propounder of a will (prepared by a beneficiary) the burden of showing that it was the true will of the deceased was not confined to cases where the will was prepared by a beneficiary. It extended to any 'well-grounded suspicion' (*per* Davey LJ, at p. 159). Moreover, on the facts the evidence of the attesting witnesses was insufficient to remove the suspicion: thus the will failed. In *Thomas* v *Jones* [1928] P 162, the testator's solicitor prepared a will which included a residuary clause substantially benefiting the solicitor's daughter. The will was prepared after lengthy interviews with a testator whose mental capacity was failing; no attempt was made to obtain independent medical advice as to the testator's competence. The residuary clause was excluded from probate.

In *Re Ticehurst* (1973) *The Times*, 5 March, an elderly testatrix made a new will leaving her three houses to relatives (rather than to her tenants as under the previous will). The new will was prepared by a solicitor after correspondence between him and the testatrix. However, as her eyesight was poor, she used the wife of a nephew as an amanuensis to conduct the correspondence. The nephew was one of the recipients of a house under the new will. There was evidence that a draft of the new will was read over to the testatrix prior to execution, but this was held insufficient to override the court's suspicions: the whole will failed.

3.2.6 Mistake

A testator may lack knowledge and approval of the whole or part of his will because of a mistake on his part. However, it is not every mistake which will affect knowledge and approval. It is thus important to differentiate between the types of mistake that occur.

3.2.6.1 Mistake as to whole will

This occurs where the testator executes a will by mistake. Such cases are rare, but when they occur the will clearly fails as the testator lacked knowledge and approval of the will that was executed. For example, suppose that Arthur drafts a will leaving all his property to his brother Harold, who drafts one in similar terms in favour of Arthur, but they execute the other's will by mistake. It seems that neither will can be upheld as neither was executed with the necessary knowledge and approval: there was no *animus testandi*. Similar facts occurred in *Re Meyer* [1908] P 353, where each of two sisters attempted to make a codicil in favour of the other but mistakenly executed the other's codicil. When the first of them died it was held that the codicil she executed could not be admitted to probate as she had not intended to sign it. However, a different result was reached in *Guardian, Trust, and Executors Company of New Zealand* v *Inwood* [1946] NZ LR 614, on virtually identical facts. Two sisters made wills in which they left each other life interests in their respective residuary estates, but each executed the other's will by mistake. When the first (Jane Remington) died the issue arose whether the will that she had signed — but which was that of her sister, Maude Lucy — could be admitted to probate. The will left a life interest to 'my sister Jane Remington'. The New Zealand Court of Appeal upheld the will omitting the word 'Jane'.

3.2.6.2 Mistake as to legal effect

It is the contents of a will that the testator must know and approve, not the consequences. Hence a mistake as to the legal effect of the testator's provisions does not affect the validity of the will (or part of it). The justification for this rule may be that it prevents litigation arising about what exactly the testator was aiming to achieve, a question which would be difficult to answer in the regrettable absence of the chief witness. Nevertheless the rule inevitably results in hard decisions. Consider *Collins* v *Elstone* [1893] P 1: the testatrix left two wills and a codicil to the first will. The second will disposed of only a small policy of life insurance, but did contain a clause revoking all previous testamentary dispositions. The testatrix did not wish to revoke any earlier dispositions but was assured by an executor (who had prepared the second will) that the second will had no application to earlier dispositions. The advice was honestly given but erroneous and disastrous in its consequences. It was held (with regret) that since the testatrix knew and approved of the inclusion of the revocation clause — even though she did not understand its effect — the clause was part of the will and thus revoked the earlier will.

3.2.6.3 Mistake as to contents
If any part of a will has been included by mistake without the testator's knowledge and approval, it can be omitted from probate provided the sense of the rest of the will is not thereby altered. In *Re Phelan* [1971] 3 WLR 888, the testator was the perfect lodger — he made a will leaving all his property to his landlady and her husband. A few weeks later he made three more wills (executed on the same day) each disposing of a block of shares in the couple's favour. He had mistakenly become convinced that it was necessary to dispose of each block of shares by separate wills. The three wills were made on will forms, each of which contained a revocation clause which the testator failed to delete. The court held, somewhat generously, that the revocation clauses could be omitted since the testator had no knowledge and approval of them — he was in effect mistaken as to the contents of his will. A similar decision was reached in *In the Goods of Oswald* (1874) 3 P & D 162, where a testatrix executed a later will not realising that it contained a revocation clause — she did not read the will over, neither was it read to her. The court held that the revocation clause in the later will could be excluded from probate since its presence was unknown to the testatrix. The distinction between the above cases and *Collins* v *Elstone* (above) is that in the latter case the testatrix was aware of the presence of the revocation clause. But should cases turn on this distinction? Would it not be preferable if the test was whether there was a true intention on the facts to revoke prior dispositions?

A mistake as to the contents of a will may arise through a clerical error (e.g., wordprocessing) made either by the testator or by another person such as a professional adviser. Consider *In the Goods of Boehm* [1891] P 247, where a testator instructed that a bequest should be given to each of his unmarried daughters 'Georgiana' and 'Florence'. The conveyancing counsel who drafted the will made the unfortunate mistake of inserting the name 'Georgiana' in both the bequests. The court held that the name Georgiana could be omitted from the bequest intended for Florence since the error was never brought to the testator's notice. That bequest would then contain blanks (instead of 'Georgiana') which the court of construction would have in its power to construe as intended to benefit Florence. The court of probate lacked at that time the power to insert words. Now, however, words may be added by rectification in some circumstances (see 3.2.6.5).

What if the clerical error results in the *omission* of a part of the will? In *Re Morris* [1970] 1 All ER 1057, clause 7 of the testatrix's will contained 20 pecuniary legacies, numbered from 7(i) to 7(xx). Later she instructed her solicitor to draft a codicil revoking clauses 3 and 7(iv), but a clerical error resulted in the omission of '(iv)': thus the codicil appeared to revoke the whole of clause 7. When the testatrix was executing the codicil she cast her eyes over it but did not notice the omission. The court held that since the testatrix had not intended to revoke the whole of clause 7 — the glancing over the will being insufficient to show knowledge and approval — the reference to '7' would be omitted. Nor was she bound by the mistake of the draftsman as it had been made without his knowledge and approval. Clause 7 was thus preserved in its entirety — not quite what the testatrix intended but closer to her intentions than revoking the whole clause. The court of probate could not add '(iv)' since it then lacked the power to insert words.

3.2.6.4 Remedies: omission

Where a testator lacks knowledge and approval because of a mistake as to the contents of the will, there are two possible remedies — omission and rectification. As we seen already, the court can omit words from probate if they were not intended by the testator to be part of the will. But the sense of the remainder of the will must not be altered as a result (the omitted words will be regarded as blank spaces). Thus omission is more likely in the case of independent, severable parts of the will such as revocation clauses, as in *Re Phelan* (above). In *Morrell* v *Morrell* (1882) PD 68, the testator instructed that all his 400 shares in his family company should pass to his nephews. Conveyancing counsel misunderstood the instructions and drafted the gift as comprising 'forty' shares. There was no evidence that the testator had read the will before executing it. It was held that since the testator had not approved the inclusion of 'forty', the word could be omitted from probate with the result that all the shares in the company passed to the nephews. Compare, however, *Re Horrocks* [1939] 1 All ER 579: the testatrix left the residue of her estate in trust for such 'charitable or benevolent' objects in Preston as her trustees should select. The word 'and' should have been used instead of 'or': as it stood the gift would fail for uncertainty. Had the solicitor drafted the will mistakenly, not realising the effect of the word 'or', the mistake would have been as to legal consequences, and thus not remediable. Not surprisingly it was claimed that the mistake was a clerical error in typing the will, and probate was sought with the omission of 'or'. The court refused, holding that the phrase 'charitable benevolent' would have a cumulative meaning — the omission would thus alter the sense of the remainder of the will.

At the time *Re Horrocks* was decided the court lacked the power to rectify the will by replacing 'or' with 'and'. Words could only be omitted, not replaced, since to allow otherwise would be to give the court the power to make wills, something not intended by the Wills Act 1837. The inability to add words was again illustrated by *Re Reynette-James* [1975] 3 All ER 1037, where a typing error by a solicitors' firm resulted in gifts being bequeathed to the wrong beneficiary. The gifts were omitted from probate. A partial intestacy thus arose under which the intended beneficiary (the testatrix's son) benefited, thus being partly compensated for the loss of the gifts. Templeman J regretted the absence of the power to rectify wills.

3.2.6.5 Remedies: rectification

Decisions such as *Re Horrocks*, *Re Morris* and *Re Reynette-James* (above) invited
consideration of the introduction in *probate* cases of a power to rectify wills, that
is, to amend them by substituting or adding words. The concept was not
entirely new since the court of *construction* has long been able to construe wills as
though they contained words not actually written in them (see 6.2.1.2). The
introduction of a power of rectification was considered by the Law Reform
Committee (*Interpretation of Wills*, LRC Report No. 19, 1973). The Committee
recommended that rectification should be possible in two instances — clerical
error and failure to understand the testator's instructions. These recommendations were enacted by s. 20 of the Administration of Justice Act 1982, applicable
to testators dying after 31 December 31 1982. Section 20(1) provides:

> If a court is satisfied that a will is so expressed that it fails to carry out the
> testator's intentions, in consequence —
>   (a) of a clerical error; or
>   (b) of a failure to understand his instructions,
> it may order that the will shall be rectified so as to carry out his intentions.

Under s. 20(2), an application for rectification shall not be made 'after the end
of the period of six months from the date on which representation with respect
to the estate of the deceased is first taken out'. The phrase 'is first taken out' has
been construed as meaning 'is first *effectively* taken out' in an identical provision
in the Inheritance (Provision for Family and Dependants) Act 1975 (see 8.2.3).
The period of six months is intended to achieve a reasonable balance between
the interests of those who wish to have the will rectified and those content to
take under the unrectified will. The court has a discretion to allow applications
outside the normal period.

What is a 'clerical error'? The statute does not provide a definition, but
clarification is to be found in the case law. In *Wordingham* v *Royal Exchange
Trust* [1992] 3 All ER 204, 'clerical error' was construed as an error made in the
process of recording 'the intended words of the testatrix' in the drafting or
transcription of her will. In that case the testatrix instructed her solicitor to alter
an existing will. He prepared a new will in which he inadvertently omitted a
clause while transcribing the provisions of the previous will. It was held that his
action amounted to a 'clerical error' and that the court could rectify the new
will by including the omitted clause. In *Re Segelman* [1995] 3 All ER 676, it was
held that s. 20(1)(a) was not limited to cases in which 'the intended words'
could be identified with precision. Chadwick J decided that the jurisdiction to
rectify under para. (a) extended to cases where the relevant provision in the will
has been introduced — or has not been deleted — 'in circumstances in which
the draftsman has not applied his mind to its significance or effect', i.e. has
acted *per incuriam* (p. 686). The court rectified a will by deleting a proviso
which would have restricted the class of beneficiaries contrary to the testator's
wishes. The testator's solicitor had inserted the proviso on his own initiative in
the draft will and had failed to delete it despite receiving a schedule of named
beneficiaries which rendered the proviso inappropriate.

What if the clerical error was made by the testator rather than by his draftsman, as, for example, where the testator fails to transcribe provisions correctly from an earlier will when making a fresh one? It is very probable that an error by the testator is covered by s. 20(1)(a). That was certainly the intention of the LRC Report No. 19 and finds support in the cases — see *Wordingham* v *Royal Exchange* and *Re Williams* [1985] 1 All ER 964, where Nicholls J stated (at p. 969):

> It was suggested in the course of argument that s. 20 could not apply to a home-made will such as the one before me, because 'clerical error' in s. 20(1)(a) suggests a clerk. I do not accept this. A testator writing out or typing his own will can make a clerical error just as much as someone else writing out or typing a will for him.

As regards s. 20(1)(b) — failure to understand the testator's instructions — the Law Reform Committee explained:

> In our view, where it can be established, first, that the will fails to embody the testator's instructions, and secondly what those instructions were, it ought to be open to the court to rectify the will so as to make it embody them. Those instructions, if faithfully carried out, may not achieve what the testator really wanted. That is another question. But if the testator said to his solicitor: 'I want my wife to have my house for her life and then it is to go to my son John', and if the solicitor draws a will which, on its literal construction, leaves the house to the wife absolutely, then we see no reason why the court should not be able to rectify the will. (para. 21)

How would cases decided before the enactment of s. 20 be decided now? *Re Morris* would clearly be a strong candidate for rectification under s. 20(1)(a): the court could add '(iv)' after '7' in the provision concerning clause 7, thus achieving exactly what the testatrix intended. In *Re Horrocks* rectification would depend on the nature of the mistake made. If it was a clerical error then clearly the court could substitute 'and' for 'or' under s. 20(1)(a); but rectification would probably not be possible if the original inclusion of 'or' rather than 'and' was because of the solicitor's failure to appreciate the legal effect of using one word rather than the other (assuming he had applied his mind to the effect of the provision). Rectification would clearly be available in *Re Reynette-James* to correct the clerical error whereby gifts were given to the wrong beneficiary (similarly *In the Goods of Boehm*).

Section 20 is a modest provision allowing rectification in two particular cases only. It is a matter of regret that the Law Reform Committee did not recommend a wider scope for rectification. For example, s. 20 does not appear to apply where there is uncertainty as to the meaning intended by the testator, or where he misunderstood the legal effects of the words used. In these cases the only available remedy — and a very limited one — is omission of words from probate. Misunderstanding the effect of the words used is perhaps the most likely reason why rectification might be needed, so it is all the more surprising that it was omitted from s. 20. Cases such as *Collins v Elstone* (see 3.2.6.2) would probably be unaffected by s. 20 and thus decided the same way.

3.2.7 Fraud and undue influence

A testator lacks *animus testandi* if he makes his will as the result of the fraud or undue influence of another person. Fraud and undue influence may be conveniently considered together as there are important similarities between them. For example, the consequence of proving that a will (or part of it) was made either through fraud or under undue influence is that the will fails either wholly or partially. Moreover, persons alleging fraud or undue influence must have clear proof otherwise they may be heavily penalised in costs. The basic difference is that fraud misleads the testator whereas undue influence coerces him.

3.2.7.1 Fraud

Fraud consists of intentionally misleading the testator, thereby affecting the making of his will or its provisions. The testator must have been deceived: a failed attempt to deceive him is irrelevant. The case law on fraud is somewhat thin, indicative of the rarity of this means of challenging a will due to the gravity of the allegation and the availability of easier and less gladiatorial alternatives — alleging lack of knowledge and approval on the grounds of mistake, mental competence or even suspicious circumstances.

In *Allen v M'Pherson* (1847) 1 HLC 191; 9 ER 727, the testator, having made large bequests to the appellant in his will, executed a final codicil containing a much smaller gift. It was alleged that this was the result of false representations being made about the appellant's character to a testator 'feeble in mind and in body from age, and his previous habits of drinking wine and spirits'. It was held that this was a clear case of fraud. Lord Lyndhurst stated (at p. 735):

> There cannot be a stronger instance of fraud than a false representation respecting the character of an individual to a weak old man, for the purpose of inducing him to revoke a bequest made in favour of the person so calumniated.

In *Wilkinson v Joughin* (1866) LR 2 Eq 319, the testator married a woman who was already married. She deliberately concealed the fact from him, the court refusing to believe her claim that she thought that her previous husband had died. In his will the testator described her as his 'wife'. It was held that the gift to the woman was void because of her fraud. However, a gift to her daughter — described by the testator as his 'stepdaughter' — was upheld since she was an innocent legatee. Compare *Re Posner* [1953] 1 All ER 1123, where the facts were similar apart from the crucial difference that the testator was not deliberately misled since neither party knew at the time of their marriage that the wife was still a married woman. The gift to the 'wife' was upheld since there had not been any *fraudulent* assumption by her of the character of wife.

It is clear from the cases on fraud that there must be a deliberate misleading of the testator. Should it matter whether he was *deliberately* deceived or not? Arguably it should not. The important question should be whether the testator's will represents his true intentions: was he misled or not in making his provisions? Once it is established that he was misled, and that the deception influenced his provisions, why should it matter how the deception arose? However, clearly it would be inappropriate to describe innocent deception as 'fraud'; it could be regarded perhaps as a case of mistake as to contents caused by error of fact (see 3.2.6.3).

Need it be the testator who is misled? Presumably not: misleading the testator's solicitor, for example, might suffice. And attempting to deceive even after the testator's death can clearly amount to fraud — for example, where a person alters the will or forges one: see *Re Raphael* [1973] 3 All ER 19.

3.2.7.2 Undue influence

In the law of succession 'undue influence' has a different meaning than the one it bears in some other areas of the law: it means coercion, duress. *Animus testandi* is obviously lacking where a will (or part of it) is made by a testator who is coerced. Persuasion, however, is legitimate; and in practice the problem is in determining whether the influence exerted on the testator amounted to persuasion or coercion. Suppose, for example, that Arthur is contemplating making a will in favour of his local zoo. His wife, Mabel — very much the dominant partner — is furious when she discovers his intentions. She tells him to make the will in her favour 'or else'. Arthur complies. Has he been persuaded or coerced? It is not unnatural for spouses to press their claims, especially when in competition with a zoo. On the other hand, if the evidence points to Arthur being totally dominated by his wife and very concerned about the consequences posed by the threat of 'or else', the facts may point to coercion. The test is whether the testator was led or driven, as explained by Wilde J in *Hall* v *Hall* (1868) 1 P & D 481, at 482:

... pressure of whatever character, whether acting on the fears or the hopes, if so exerted as to overpower the volition without convincing the judgment, is a species of restraint under which no valid will can be made. Importunity or threats, such as the testator has not the courage to resist, moral command asserted and yielded for the sake of peace and quiet, or of escaping from distress of mind or social discomfort, these, if carried to a degree in which the free play of the testator's judgment, discretion or wishes, is overborne, will constitute undue influence, though no force is either used or threatened. In a word, a testator may be led but not driven; and his will must be the offspring of his own volition, and not the record of someone else's.

In that case the will of a prosperous farmer and land valuer failed because it was proved that it had been made for the sake of peace in consequence of the violence and threats from the sole beneficiary, his wife.

The leading case on undue influence is *Parfitt* v *Lawless* (1872) 2 P & D 462, where the relevant principles were fully considered. The testatrix made a will under which the chief beneficiary to her large estate was a Roman Catholic priest. It is possible that the testatrix intended that the property should be used for saying masses or other religious purposes. The priest had resided for many years with the testatrix and her husband as domestic chaplain, and for most of the time acted as her confessor. There was no evidence, however, that the priest had influenced the testatrix in the making of the will, or that he had exercised any role in her business affairs. The court held that as there was no evidence of undue influence the will was valid. It was argued against the will that the relationship between the testatrix and the priest raised a presumption of undue influence, an analogy being drawn with the equitable rules applicable to *inter vivos* gifts. However, the court distinguished wills from *inter vivos* gifts, first, because in the case of the latter there is 'a transaction in which the person benefited at least takes part' whereas in the case of a legacy the beneficiary often has 'no part in or even knowledge of the act'. Lord Penzance continued (at pp. 469–70):

A more material distinction is this: the influence which is undue in the cases of gifts *inter vivos* is very different from that which is required to set aside a will. In the case of gifts or other transactions *inter vivos* it is considered by the Courts of equity that the natural influence which such relations as those in question involve, exerted by those who possess it to obtain a benefit for themselves, is an undue influence.... The law regarding wills is very different from this. The natural influence of the parent or guardian over the child, or the husband over the wife, or the attorney over the client, may lawfully be exerted to obtain a will or legacy, so long as the testator thoroughly understands what he is doing, and is a free agent. There is nothing illegal in the parent or husband pressing his claims on a child or wife, and obtaining a recognition of those claims in a legacy, provided that the persuasion stops short of coercion, and that the volition of the testator, though biased and impressed by the relation in which he stands to the legatee, is not overborne and subjected to the domination of another.

The importance of *Parfitt* v *Lawless* is that:

(a)   it establishes that no presumption of undue influence arises from proof of a relationship — however close — between the testator and the other party; and
(b)   it emphasises that to prove undue influence it is necessary to prove coercion, i.e. that the testator was not a free agent — that his volition was overborne.

(a)   No presumption   Undue influence cannot be presumed from the relationship between the parties. In *Craig* v *Lamoureux* [1920] AC 349, PC, a husband was instrumental in having a will prepared for, and executed by, his very ill wife under which he was the sole beneficiary. She died two days later. Undue influence was alleged against the husband but it was not proved since there was

no evidence of coercion. However, a presumption of undue influence can arise from the *circumstances* surrounding the will's execution. For example, in *Mynn v Robinson* (1828) 2 Hagg Ecc 169; 162 ER 823, the presumption arose — and was not rebutted — from proof that the will of a married woman was procured by the 'active agency' of her husband nine days before her death while she was in an extremely weak state. The husband had a record of deceptive behaviour, and the will wholly departed from a previous will made only a few months earlier. The presumption arose not from the relationship between husband and wife but because of the circumstances of the will's execution.

Concern has been expressed about anecdotal evidence of undue influence being brought to bear on elderly testators by some proprietors of residential and nursing homes. The Justice Committee recommended in *Report on Home Made Wills* (1971) that a presumption of undue influence should arise where testators aged 60 or over left property — other than small gifts — to persons who were providing them with residential care under a contract. This recommendation has not been enacted, not surprisingly. It is offensive to those who provide residential care, and patronising to middle-aged testators.

(b)   Coercion   In *Wingrove* v *Wingrove* (1886) 11 PD 81, Hannen P stressed that it was insufficient to prove that a person has the power to coerce the testator — it had to be shown that the power was exercised. Coercion could take various forms:

> The coercion may of course be of different kinds, it may be in the grossest form, such as actual confinement or violence, or a person in the last days or hours of life may have become so weak and feeble, that a very little pressure will be sufficient to bring about the desired result, and it may even be, that the mere talking to him at that stage of illness and pressing something upon him may so fatigue the brain, that the sick person may be induced, for quietness' sake, to do anything. This would equally be coercion, though not actual violence. (pp. 82–3)

Coercion, then, may take various forms ranging from direct physical threats to a more subtle domination over the testator's mind. But the test is always — was the testator's volition overborne? In *Betts* v *Doughty* (1879) 5 PD 26, the testatrix, aged 80, attempted to alter her will so as to exclude the plaintiffs. She approved a draft of a new will but was told by the plaintiffs that if she executed the will, she could no longer reside in their house. A solicitor's clerk brought the will for her to execute it but was not allowed to see her. This was an unusual case: coercion was exercised not to force but to prevent the making of a will. The court found a bold and sensible solution, upholding the earlier will but imposing a trust on the plaintiffs to hold their shares as trustees for the beneficiaries under the intended will. In *Re Harden* [1959] CLYB 3448, the undue influence consisted of the domination of the testatrix by a man who purported to have occult powers as a medium: he passed messages from 'the other side' as to how the testatrix should dispose of her estate in two wills made by her. The court pronounced against them.

The weaker the testator — whether physically, mentally or both — the easier it will be to prove undue influence. In *Hampson* v *Guy* (1891) 64 LT 778, CA, the testamentary dispositions of an elderly testatrix of feeble mental capacity were held invalid on the grounds of undue influence exercised by the nuns of a convent at which she resided. Kay LJ stated (at p. 780):

> ... the amount of influence which would induce a person of strong mind and in good health to make a will according to the wishes of the persons who were attempting to induce such a testator must be very much greater than the amount of inducement which would improperly influence the mind of a person who was weak partly from mental infirmity and partly from ill-health ...

3.2.7.3   Burden of proof

Anyone who challenges a will on the grounds of fraud or undue influence must prove the allegation — the onus is not on the propounder to disprove such allegations: *Boyse* v *Rossborough* (1857) 6 HLC 2. Although the usual civil standard of proof applies — the balance of probabilities — strong evidence of fraud or undue influence must be adduced since the allegation imparts an element of moral condemnation. Consequently, if allegations are made on insufficient evidence, the party making them (or possibly his legal adviser) runs the risk of being penalised in costs. In *Re Cutcliffe's Estate* [1959] P 6, CA, an old and very ill testator executed a will in favour of his stepdaughter (with whom he had previously quarrelled) and two female companions when she brought a prepared will for him to sign. Undue influence was alleged against the stepdaughter, the evidence suggesting that the testator was frightened of her and that a crescendo of words 'sign, sign, sign' was apparently heard while the testator was executing the will. The court disbelieved the evidence and Hodson LJ stated (at p. 21):

> ... where pleas of undue influence and pleas of fraud are made, the probability, at any rate, if they are unsuccessfully made, is that the people who make such charges and fail will be condemned in the costs not only of that charge but of the whole action.

In practice it is preferable for the challenger of a will to allege suspicious circumstances, whenever possible, rather than fraud or undue influence. If there is evidence of suspicious circumstances the onus shifts to the propounder to show knowledge and approval on the part of the testator; hence the challenger is not saddled with the difficulty of proving fraud or undue influence with the attendant risks. *Wintle* v *Nye* is a case in point (see 3.2.5.1). If in that case the will had been challenged on the grounds of fraud or undue influence, the challenge would almost certainly have failed. But because the allegation was that the will was made in suspicious circumstances (of which there was evidence) the onus fell on the propounder to remove the suspicion by proving knowledge and approval by the testatrix, a task which the propounder was unable to do. In *In the Estate of Fuld (No. 3)* [1968] P 675, Scarman, J stated (at p. 722):

It may well be that positive charges of fraud and undue influence will not feature as largely in the pleadings of probate cases, now that *Wintle* v *Nye* has been decided, as they have done in the past; clearly it would be preferable if they did not . . .

3.2.7.4   Overlap with suspicious circumstances?

Should fraud and undue influence be treated separately (as here) or should they be regarded as aspects of the rule concerning suspicious circumstances (see 3.2.5)? Clearly, a layman would describe fraud and undue influence as examples of suspicious circumstances. Moreover, in *Vout* v *Hay* [1995] 125 DLR (4th) 431, the Supreme Court of Canada took a very wide view of the suspicious circumstance doctrine:

> The suspicious circumstances may be raised by (1) circumstances surrounding the preparation of the will; (2) circumstances tending to call into question the capacity of the testator; or (3) circumstances tending to show that the free will of the testator was overborne by acts of coercion or fraud. (*per* Sopinka J, at p. 439)

However, the English courts have tended to confine suspicious circumstances to cases where the beneficiary has been involved — directly or indirectly — in the preparation of the will, yet no fraud or undue influence was proved. Moreover, the differing rules on the burden of proof (above) indicate that fraud and undue influence are not synonymous with suspicious circumstances.

FOUR

Making a Will: Formalities

4.1 INTRODUCTION

We think it of great importance that, as a general rule, Wills of every description should be required to be executed according to one simple form which may be easily and generally understood. (Real Property Commissioners: Fourth Report, 1833, p. 12)

The commissioners should be congratulated for this admirable, principled statement. Of course the legal requirements for making a will should be simple and easily understood, and to a large extent this aim has been achieved in English law. The fact that numerous 'do-it-yourself' guides to will-making are readily available does indicate that this area of the law is considered not to be unduly difficult for the layman to understand. Indeed, executing a will is considerably simpler than buying or selling a house (even a car in some respects).

The 1833 Report was written at a time when English law was undergoing considerable change. The so-called 'Age of Reform' led to a general demystification of the law, evident chiefly in the jettisoning of arcane forms and procedures. The formalities for making a will were a case in point. The law at the time of the 1833 Report was unnecessarily complicated and unwieldy, the formalities differed according to which type of property was being disposed of: some wills required three or four witnesses, some only two, others none at all. The 1833 Report stimulated reform, leading to the enactment of the Wills Act 1837, which greatly simplified the requirements for executing a will. It is still s. 9 of the Wills Act 1837 (as amended) that continues to govern the execution of wills in English law. There can be few instances, if any, of a statute older than the Wills Act 1837 having such important practical application in today's world.

The execution requirements under s. 9 were considered by the Law Reform Committee's Report, *The Making and Revocation of Wills* (LRC Report No. 22,

1980). Although some changes were recommended — later enacted in the Administration of Justice Act 1982 — the Committee thought that the law concerning the making of wills was generally satisfactory and that little change was necessary. A survey (carried out for the Committee) of wills submitted to probate during a three-month period in 1978 showed that only 93 out of 40,664 were rejected because of invalid execution under s. 9 (see LRC Report No. 22, Annex 2). It thus appears that the requirements of s. 9 do not result in a substantial failure-rate of wills. Of course, the figures reveal only the number of rejected wills. It has been surmised — with some anecdotal evidence in support — that s. 9 is probably breached in many more cases than the above figures suggest but that the breaches do not necessarily come to light.

The case law on s. 9 is rich and diverse: we will meet a number of very eccentric testators, and cases that are among the most unusual and interesting in English property law.

4.2 SECTION 9 OF THE WILLS ACT 1837

Section 9 (as amended) provides:

No will shall be valid unless —
    (a)   it is in writing, and signed by the testator, or by some other person in his presence and by his direction; and
    (b)   it appears that the testator intended by his signature to give effect to the will; and
    (c)   the signature is made or acknowledged by the testator in the presence of two or more witnesses present at the same time; and
    (d)   each witness either —
        (i)   attests and signs the will; or
        (ii)   acknowledges his signature,
in the presence of the testator (but not necessarily in the presence of any other witnesses),
but no form of attestation shall be necessary.

This provision applies where the testator dies after 31 December 1982. The position concerning testators who died before 1983 will be considered later (see 4.2.9). The constituent elements of s. 9 will now be considered in turn.

4.2.1 A will must be 'in writing'

A will is invalid unless it is in writing. However, there is an important exception: an oral will can be made by a privileged testator (see Chapter 9). The LRC Report No. 22 rejected the idea of allowing non-privileged testators to make oral wills as this might 'create uncertainty and give rise to litigation because of the difficulties of proving and interpreting oral statements' (para. 2.20).

What is meant by the requirement that a will must be 'in writing'? Curiously s. 9(a) offers no explanation even though there are obvious uncertainties in interpreting the phrase. However, according to the Interpretation Act 1978 'writing' includes 'typing, printing, lithography, photography and other modes of representing or reproducing words in a visible form' (sch. 1). Thus there appear to be no particular restrictions on the agent used for the writing. A will written in pencil — no doubt something of a rarity — is valid. But if a will is written partly in pencil, partly in ink, it will be presumed that the pencil part was intended only as a draft. In that case the words written in pencil will be excluded from the will unless there is evidence that they were clearly intended by the testator to be part of it: *In the Goods of Adams* (1872) LR 2 P & D 367.

Which language should be used? A will can be written in any language provided that there is reliable evidence as to what the language means. In *Whiting v Turner* (1903) 89 LT 71, a French testatrix made a will in France headed 'Mon Testament' and written in French. The will was correctly executed according to English law and thus was held to be admissible to probate. In *Re Berger* (see 3.2.2), documents written in Hebrew were held to constitute a will. The test is whether the writing is decipherable: if it is then s. 9 is satisfied even if the writing does not constitute a 'language'. Consider *Kell v Charmer* (1856) 23 Beav 195; 53 ER 76: the testator left to one son 'the sum of i.x.x.' and to another 'the sum of o.x.x.'. These were private symbols used by the testator in his jewellery business to denote prices or sums of money. Extrinsic evidence was admissible to show that the symbols represented £100 and £200 respectively, and the will was upheld. The report of this well-known case will be greatly appreciated by the tired law student — it is remarkable for its extreme brevity. Resort to extrinsic evidence may not be necessary, however, if there is evidence in the will as to the meaning of the testator's writing: for example, where the testator provides his own 'dictionary' in the will.

On what materials must the writing appear? Again s. 9(a) offers no guidance on this issue, but cases and the practice of probate registries suggest that any materials suffice provided that a permanent form of visual representation results. Valid wills have been made, for example, on telegrams, calendars, the backs of cheques, and even on a nurse's petticoat! In *In the Estate of Murray* [1963] CLY 3621, a will made on a small piece of cardboard during a snooker game was upheld. The vast majority of wills are written on paper, but some testators display a preference for the abnormal. Consider *Hodson v Barnes* (1926) 42 TLR 71. The testator worked as a pilot on the Manchester Ship Canal. Because of dietary problems he regularly ate eggs for lunch while at work. After his death the empty shell of a hen's egg was discovered (in his bedroom) on which his alleged will was written in his handwriting (see 3.2.2). This was one of the shortest wills to have been propounded in English law, but then wills written on egg-shells are never likely to tax the reader. The court rejected the will principally because of lack of *animus testandi*, but the use of the egg-shell was not thought to be fatal even though described as 'grotesque'.

There appears to be no theoretical restriction on the *size* of the materials used. Thus a will made, say, on a large plank of wood would be valid. Indeed, in common law jurisdictions probate has apparently been granted to wills made on step-ladders, stable doors and tractors.

4.2.2 'Signed by the testator'

4.2.2.1 The signature

What, in law, is a signature? The case law on the subject shows an admirable degree of flexibility on the part of the judges. Given the important consequences of making wills, it is remarkable what the courts have accepted as a 'signature'. For example, in *In the Estate of Finn* (1935) 52 TLR 153, a smudged, inky thumb-print which produced 'a mere blot' on the will was held sufficient. The testator was illiterate and the judge accepted that the mark was intended by him as his signature. Even if the testator can sign 'normally', but chooses to make a mark instead, s. 9 is satisfied provided the mark was intended to represent the signature: *Baker* v *Dening* (1838) 8 Ad & E 94; 112 ER 771.

The classic explanation of what is a signature was given by Lord Campbell LC in *Hindmarsh* v *Charlton* (1861) 8 HL Cas 160 (at p. 167): '... there must either be the name or some mark which is intended to represent that name.' Thus it would suffice to use a stamped name or a seal intended as a signature. Even the use of an assumed name satisfies the test. For example, in *In the Goods of Redding* (1850) 2 Rob Ecc 339; 163 ER 1338, the testatrix — whose true name was Charlotte Redding — executed a will in the name of 'Charlotte Higgins'. She used that name for several years, probably in order to conceal details about her whereabouts. Later she altered her name in the will to Redding but the alteration was invalidly executed. The court nevertheless upheld the validity of the will as it originally stood since 'Higgins' constituted the mark of the testatrix.

In *In the Estate of Cook* [1960] 1 All ER 689, the testatrix's will ended, 'Please Leslie be kind to Dot. Your loving mother'. Did those words amount to a signature? Collingwood J held that the will had been validly signed as the words 'Your loving mother' were meant to represent the name of the testatrix. The judge purported to be applying the test in *Hindmarsh* v *Charlton*, but it is arguable that the testatrix did not satisfy it. She neither wrote a name nor made a 'mark' (the argument that 'Your loving mother' is a mark is rather strained). Should there not be a distinction between cases where testators cannot write their name because of some temporary or permanent incapacity (as in *In the Estate of Finn*) and those where they can do so but choose not to? On the other hand, would it not have been unduly harsh to have invalidated the will in *In the Estate of Cook*, given that the hand-written words 'Your loving mother' were clearly intended to authenticate the will?

Within this arguably lenient approach to the meaning of 'signed by the testator' there is a counter-balancing rule: the will is not regarded as signed if the testator did not complete what he intended to write. In *Re Colling* [1972] 3 All ER 729, the testator attempted to make a will while in hospital. He started to sign the will in the presence of a patient in the next bed and the ward-sister, but she had to leave to attend to another patient before the testator completed signing. It was held that the will had not been validly signed in the presence of both witnesses since the testator had not completed what he intended to do (i.e. sign the will) at the moment when the ward-sister left. Consider, on the other hand, *Re Chalcraft* [1948] 1 All ER 700. The testatrix was close to death when she was handed a codicil to sign. She had been given a large dose of morphine shortly beforehand. She started to write her name but was unable to complete the signature because of her weak condition. She wrote 'E. Chal' instead of 'E. Chalcraft'. Willmer J held that the codicil was valid:

> ... this lady was in an extremely weak condition and was lying, if not quite on her back, very nearly on her back, in a position in which it must have been very difficult to write at all. I must ask myself the question whether on all the facts I can draw the inference that what she wrote was intended by her to be the best she could do by way of writing her name. (p. 702)

On that basis the judge accepted that 'E. Chal' sufficed as a signature. This was a generous decision, but an understandable one on the facts. However, the test whether the testatrix did 'the best she could do' lacks precision. Is it not arguable that the testator in *Re Colling* did the best he could do up to the moment of the ward-sister's departure?

4.2.2.2   'By the testator'
What is the position where the testator is too weak to sign unaided? This occurred in *Wilson* v *Beddard* (1841) 12 Sim 28; 59 ER 1041, where the testator signed the will with a mark the day before he died. He was so ill that his hand had to be guided. The court generously held this to be a valid signature. It is probable — although not clear from the report — that it was one of the witnesses who guided the testator's hand, but that was not fatal to the will's validity.

4.2.2.3   Attachment
The requirement that the will must be signed can lead to difficulties where the will consists of two or more sheets of paper (or appropriate material). Need the testator sign every sheet? If he does not, then questions may arise whether a particular unsigned sheet is part of the will. The rule in such cases used to be that all the sheets must be attached or connected at the moment of execution. The rule was primarily intended to minimise the possibility of fraud, but could have inconvenient consequences if applied strictly. Not surprisingly the rules have become eroded with the passage of time. First, the notion of attachment has been given a wide interpretation so as to include holding or pressing sheets down when signing. In *Re Little* [1960] 1 All ER 387, the testator's will consisted of five sheets of paper. He signed the fifth sheet, which at the moment of execution was covering the other sheets. It was held that as the five sheets were pressed together when the testator signed there was 'a sufficient nexus' between them to form a single will. Secondly, it has been held that the rule of attachment does not necessarily apply to cases where an envelope forms part of the will, e.g., where the testator signs not the will but the envelope intended to contain it. This occurred in *In the Goods of Mann* [1942] 2 All ER 193, where the testatrix wrote out her will on a piece of paper but did not sign it. She wrote on an envelope, 'The last will and testament of Jane Catherine Mann', and placed the will in the envelope. Langton J held that the envelope was part of the will despite the absence of any form of attachment:

... if an unattached paper is to be admitted at all, there is much to be said in favour of an envelope which may reasonably be held to have a far closer relationship to a document which it encloses than a second and wholly disconnected piece of paper. Envelopes are, by their nature, designed to have what may be described as a dependent and secondary existence rather than an independent and primary life of their own. (p. 195)

Thirdly, there is some authority to suggest that all the parts of a will are admissible to probate if, even though unattached, they were in the same room in which the execution took place: *In the Goods of Tiernan* [1942] IR 572; *Sterling* v *Bruce* [1973] NI 255. If this is a further exception to the attachment rule — the authority is unconvincing — it has little to commend it. Ensuring certainty as to what constitutes a will, and preventing fraud, are hardly facilitated if unsigned sheets are given testamentary effect simply because they were in the same room at the moment of execution.

4.2.3 'Some other person in his presence and by his direction'

Section 9(a) allows 'some other person' to sign the testator's will on his behalf: the testator need not sign personally. Which name should the other person write when signing? Perhaps it is less confusing if the testator's name is written, but it is possible to sign in the signer's name. In *In the Goods of Clark* (1839) 2 Curt 329; 163 ER 428, the testator, being close to death, requested the vicar attending him to write out a will on his behalf and to sign it. The vicar signed his own name thus: 'Signed on behalf of the testator, in his presence, and by his direction, by me, C.F. Furlong, Vicar of Warfield, Berks.' The signature was held to be valid.

4.2.3.1 'Some other person'
It is not clear what is the capacity required of the signer: must he be capable, for example, of appreciating that he is signing a *will*? And is there an age requirement? Since minors cannot make wills (as a general rule) it is arguable that they should not be able to sign wills on behalf of testators. But the analogy is a false one because merely signing a will — as opposed to making one — is a ministerial rather than a creative act. It was held in *Smith* v *Harris* (1845) 1 Rob Ecc; 163 ER 1033, that an attesting witness can sign on behalf of the testator, which supports the view that a minor qualifies as 'some other person' (since minors can act as witnesses).

4.2.3.2 'Presence'
'Presence' most probably has the same meaning as in s. 9(d): the testator must be both mentally and physically present (see 4.2.6.4).

4.2.3.3 'Direction'
There is a shortage of authority on the meaning of 'direction', and yet there are some obvious problems of interpretation. For example, need there be some positive act on the part of the testator? The most likely scenario where someone

signs on behalf of the testator is where the latter is too ill to sign. In such cases it is not obvious what might constitute 'direction'. And when must the 'direction' occur: need it be contemporaneous with the signing? Suppose that Arthur hands his will to a friend and asks him to sign it on his behalf; the friend complies and signs it while Arthur is pouring himself a gin and tonic. Has the will been signed 'by his direction'? It would be harsh to hold that this was not 'direction': surely a request to sign suffices.

The fact that s. 9(a) allows the possibility of 'some other person' signing the testator's will is prime evidence of the relative flexibility of will-making formalities in English law. The provision is obviously useful in cases where testators are too ill to sign; but s. 9(a) does not limit signing by another person to such cases. Presumably it would be valid for a perfectly fit testator to have his will signed by another. While the flexibility of s. 9(a) is welcome there is nevertheless bound to be some suspicion raised by any will which is not signed by the testator, especially if it was signed instead by one of the witnesses. Testators are best advised to sign their will personally whenever possible.

4.2.4   Signature intended 'to give effect to the will'

Section 9(b) requires that the testator must have intended by his signature 'to give effect to the will'. This was one of the amendments made to the original s. 9 of the Wills Act 1837 by the Administration of Justice Act 1982. The previous requirement had been that the will should be signed 'at the foot or end' of the will (see 4.2.9.1). That requirement — and its subsequent attempted clarification by the Wills Act Amendment Act 1852 — had caused considerable problems of interpretation, and the failure of many wills. The LRC Report No. 22 recommended change:

> Whilst we accept that the end of the narrative is the normal place for putting the signature of any document, we see no compelling reason why a will should be invalid where the signature is at the top ... the test should simply be whether the testator intended his signature to give effect to his will, regardless of where that signature was placed. We therefore conclude and recommend that a will should be admitted to probate if it is apparent on the face of the will that the testator intended his signature to validate it. (para. 2.8)

As a result of the amendment introduced by s. 9(b), the testator can in effect sign anywhere provided that he intended thereby to give effect to the will. In *Weatherhill* v *Pearce* [1995] 2 All ER 492, the testatrix wrote out an attestation clause as follows: 'Signed by the said Testator Doris Weatherhill in the presence of us present at the same time who at her request in her presence and in the presence of each other here subscribed our names as witnesses.' One of the issues in the case was whether the name at the beginning of the attestation clause sufficed as a signature to the will. It was held that it did as the testatrix intended to give effect to her will by writing her name there. But in practice testators are advised to sign at the end of the will — the most natural place, as Report No. 22 suggested.

4.2.4.1 'By his signature'

It must be emphasised that it is 'by his signature' that the testator must have intended to give effect to the will. The question is not what the testator intended but what he intended by his signature. In *Re White* [1990] 3 All ER 1, the testator made a will in 1981 which he altered in 1984. However, the alterations were invalidly executed since they were not signed by him. Nevertheless the beneficiaries under the altered will argued that it should be regarded as a newly executed will because the signature of 1981 could be deemed to be a signature to the 1984 'will'. The argument failed since the signature and the later alterations were not one operation: there was no conceivable basis on which, by signing the will in 1981, the testator could have intended to give effect to the altered will of 1984.

4.2.4.2 Signature first?

Where the testator writes out a will and then signs at the top it is clear that under s. 9(b) the will may be valid. But what if the signature is placed first at the top of a sheet of paper and the testator then writes out the will's provisions? This occurred in *Wood* v *Smith* [1992] 3 All ER 556, CA, where the testator wrote out his will in hospital two days before he died. He began with the words 'My will by Percy Winterbone of 150 High Street, Margate', and then wrote out some dispositions but did not sign them when he had finished. When the witnesses pointed out that he had not signed at the end of the will, he replied that he had already done so in the opening sentence. One of the issues in the case was whether the testator had signed the will validly. At first instance it was held that the execution of the will was invalid because when he wrote his name there were no dispositions; hence he could not have intended at that moment 'to give effect to the will' — there was no will. The Court of Appeal, however, held that there was clear evidence — the testator's remarks to the witnesses — that he regarded his name at the top as giving effect to the will, which was signed and written out in one continuous operation. Scott LJ stated (at p. 562):

> ... if the writing of the will and the appending of the signature are all one operation, it does not matter whereabouts on the document or when in the course of writing the signature is appended.

It is not clear from *Re White* and *Wood* v *Smith* what is meant by 'one operation'. Suppose that Arthur writes his name at the top of his intended will and then decides to go for a walk. On returning he writes out the dispositions in his will. Is this 'one operation'? Probably not; but what if he had gone on the walk to think about whom to benefit in the will? And what if, having signed at the top, he is then interrupted by a telephone call, after which he writes out the will? Should a distinction be drawn between voluntary and involuntary interruptions, or between short and long interruptions?

It was held in *Wood* v *Smith* that extrinsic evidence can be used to prove the intention to give effect to the will. Thus 'it appears' in s. 9(b) is not to be construed as 'it appears from the will' despite the recommendation of the LRC Report No. 22, para. 2.8 (above). It should be noted that the will in *Wood* v *Smith* failed for lack of testamentary capacity.

4.2.4.3 The envelope cases

The so-called 'envelope' cases provide instructive scenarios to test the application of s. 9(b). Although they were decided before the enactment of s. 9(b), the statutory provision applicable to them was similar in some respects: under the Wills Act Amendment Act 1852 the test was whether the testator intended to give effect by his signature to the writing signed as his will. It will be recalled that in *In the Goods of Mann* the testatrix wrote her signature on the envelope in which the dispositive part of the will was to be contained (see 4.2.2.3). The words constituting her signature were 'The last will and testament of Jane Catherine Mann'. The court held that she intended her signature on the envelope to be her signature to the will. However, compare *In the Estate of Bean* [1944] 2 All ER 348, where the testator wrote his name, address and the date on the back of a printed will form and on an envelope. He did not sign the will form. Hodson J held that the writing on the envelope did not constitute a signature: the testator's failure to sign the will form was accidental and the words on the envelope were put there for the purpose of identifying the contents of the envelope.

The crucial distinction between the cases concerns the testator's intention: did he intend the words on the envelope to be a signature to the will or simply an identification of the contents? The same approach was adopted in *Re Beadle* [1974] 1 All ER 493. The testatrix made her will in the presence of two friends (a married couple) to whom she referred as 'Charley' and 'Maisy'. The testatrix signed her will; Charley also signed as a witness — but not Maisy. The testatrix then wrote on an envelope 'My last will and testament, E.A. Beadle, to Charley and Maisy' and the will was then sealed in the envelope. Both witnesses signed the back of the envelope. Since the paper in the envelope was not properly attested as only one witness had signed, the propounders of the will needed to show that the testator's writing on the envelope constituted a signature: the witnesses' signatures on the back of the envelope would then arguably satisfy the attestation requirements. The court held that the testatrix could not have intended her name on the envelope to be her signature as she thought that she had already signed the will: her writing on the envelope was simply an identification of the contents. The problem with this line of reasoning is that it assumes that a testator can intend to sign only once: the argument seems to be that if the first writing of the name is intended as a signature then the second cannot be so intended. But is it not plausible that a testator might intend — when writing his name on an envelope — to be both signing it and identifying its contents?

4.2.5 Signature made or acknowledged in presence of witnesses

Section 9(c) states that the signature must be 'made or acknowledged by the testator in the presence of two or more witnesses present at the same time'. At the outset it must be emphasised that the requirement is for two *or more* witnesses to be present. Thus to assert that a will must be witnessed by two witnesses is clearly inaccurate, although a very common error. Even the Law Reform Committee failed to state the law correctly in Report No. 22: 'The present law requires the testator to sign or to acknowledge his signature of his will in the presence of two witnesses' (para. 2.9). The need for at least two witnesses is intended to minimise the possibility of forgery or undue influence. It seems a sensible formality but can cause difficulties in practice. The survey carried out for the Committee showed that failure to have two witnesses was the most common reason for invalid execution, accounting for roughly a third of rejected wills (see LRC Report No. 22, Annex 2).

The thrust of s. 9(c) is that the execution of a will should be a witnessed act. There are four elements to be considered: the capacity to act as witness; the making of the signature in the presence of witnesses; alternatively the acknowledgment of the signature in the presence of witnesses; and the joint presence of the witnesses.

4.2.5.1 Capacity to act as witness

Who can witness a will? Given the importance of witnesses, there is surprisingly little authority on this question. The statute does not define what is meant by a 'witness'. But it does require 'presence' of witnesses, from which it can be implied that a witness must have certain attributes. In *Hudson* v *Parker* (1844) 1 Rob Ecc 14; 163 ER 948, Dr Lushington stated that witnesses 'should see and be conscious of the act done, and be able to prove it by their own evidence' (p. 952). The ability to see was emphasised particularly in *In the Estate of Gibson* [1949] 2 All ER 90, where a codicil was signed in the presence of two witnesses, one of whom was blind. In holding the execution invalid Pearce J stated (at pp. 91–2):

> ... for the purposes of the Act a 'witness' means one who in regard to things audible has the faculty of hearing and, in regard to things visible, has the faculty of seeing. The signing of the will is a visible matter, and, therefore, I think a will is not signed 'in the presence of' a blind person, nor is he a 'witness' for the purposes of the section.

However, it may be possible for a blind person to witness a will signed in braille if the signature was acknowledged by the testator to that witness.

Another necessary attribute of a witness that can be implied from the statue is the ability to sign the will (since it is required by s. 9(d)). Provided that a person has the above attributes it seems that anyone can witness a will. Surprisingly no minimum age limit is laid down by the Act: thus minors can act as witnesses provided that they satisfy the requirements of the Act. In *Wilson* v *Beddard* (see 4.2.2.2), a 14-year-old boy was accepted as a valid witness. It seems absurd for this to be the position in view of the importance of will-making. Of course, in practice the sensible testator will choose a sensible witness. Given that witnesses are sometimes required to give evidence after the testator's death as to the execution of the will, what is the profile of a suitable witness? The paradigm is that the witness should be adult, literate, of fixed address, able to see, conscious of witnessing a testamentary act, capable of giving evidence, have a reliable memory, be in reasonable health and likely to survive the testator (this might seem to rule out most of the human race!)

Although not defining the meaning of a 'witness', the Wills Act 1837 contains several provisions about the suitability of witnesses. Section 14 states:

> If any person who shall attest the execution of a will shall at the time of the execution thereof or at any time afterwards be incompetent to be admitted a witness to prove the execution thereof, such will shall not on that account be invalid.

This is a rather curious provision. As it stands s. 14 appears to lead to a strange result: a will might not be invalid simply because of the incompetence of the witnesses at the time of execution. Such an interpretation would appear to make a nonsense of the vital requirement that a will should be witnessed. The most likely explanation of this provision is that 'incompetent' refers to persons who at the time of the passing of the 1837 Act were regarded as legally incompetent to give evidence to the court, e.g., persons of no religious belief, parties to the action (or their spouses). Thus the section is of little relevance today. Section 15 provides that if a person witnesses a will to whom — or to whose spouse — a gift is made in the will, the gift is 'utterly null and void' but the attestation is valid (see 7.2.2). Section 16 regards a creditor — whose debt is charged on any property by the will — as a valid witness. Under s. 17, an executor of a will can be admitted to prove its execution.

4.2.5.2 Signature made in presence of witnesses

What is meant by 'presence' under s. 9(c) as regards the making of the signature? It is clear that 'presence' means both mental and physical presence.

(a) *Mental presence*: the witness must be conscious of the act done. In *Brown* v *Skirrow* [1902] P 3, Gorell Barnes J stated (at p. 5):

> You cannot be a witness to an act that you are unconscious of; otherwise the thing might be done in a ball-room 100 feet long and with a number of people in the intervening space. In my view, at the end of the transaction, the witness should be able to say with truth, 'I know that this testator or testatrix has signed this document'.

However, it is clear that the witnesses need not know that the testator is signing a will; nor need they know what the testator is writing. What they must be conscious of is an act of writing by the testator. In *Smith* v *Smith* (1866) 1 P & D 143, the witnesses saw the testatrix write something on the will but did not know it was a will; neither did they see *what* she wrote. The will was nevertheless upheld on the ground that the witnesses were aware that the testator was writing *something* (which the judge was satisfied was the signature). In practice the witnesses should be told they are witnessing a will in case they have to give evidence in the future about the will's execution.

(b) *Physical presence*: the test is whether the witnesses *could* have seen the testator signing — in the sense of having an opportunity to see — not whether they actually saw the signing. There must be an unobstructed line of sight between the witnesses and the testator at the moment of the signing of the will. Suppose that Arthur takes his will to his neighbours and asks them to witness him signing it. They agree, but rather reluctantly as they are watching their favourite TV series, 'Registrar', about life in a probate registry. While he signs in one room they continue watching TV in another. The signature has not been made in their presence since they could not have seen Arthur signing at the moment when he signed. But s. 9 would have been satisfied if a glass door had separated the two rooms through which they could have seen him signing: they had the opportunity to do so, even if they chose not to take it.

A classic illustration of the application of the rules on presence — both mental and physical — is *Brown* v *Skirrow* (above). The testatrix took her will to her local grocer's in order to sign it there. She did so observed by a shop assistant. When she signed, the other witness, the manager, was engaged with a commercial traveller who was standing between the manager and the testatrix. At that moment the manager had no idea what the testatrix was doing: it was only a little later that he was asked to sign the will as a witness. Had the witnesses been present when the testatrix signed the will? The court held that the will had been invalidly executed: the manager could not have seen the testatrix signing — his view was obstructed by the commercial traveller — and, in any case, the manager was not mentally present as he was not conscious of what was happening.

The courts seem to have focused exclusively on the 'line of sight' rule as a test of physical presence. But *physical* presence should mean something more than just the opportunity to see the testator signing. Surely it connotes *bodily* presence at the execution of a will. The case law appears to assume this without specifying it. The idea, say, that a testator can be signing his will in a TV studio while the witnesses to the will are attesting by watching him on their TV screens at home is nonsensical and should not be countenanced. To regard such an execution as valid would be to make a mockery of the will-making process; and it would run counter to the spirit of the Wills Act 1837.

4.2.5.3 Acknowledgment in presence of witnesses
If the testator does not sign in the presence of witnesses, he must acknowledge his signature in their presence.

(a) *Acknowledgment* The testator must demonstrate that he accepts the signature as his own. It follows that the signature must be in existence prior to its acknowledgment. The acceptance of the signature may take several forms. The most obvious form of acknowledgment is for the testator to say 'that is my signature', but 'that is my will' also suffices. In *Hudson* v *Parker* (1844) 1 Reb Ecc 14; 163 ER 948, Dr Lushington stated (at pp. 952–3):

> it is quite true that acknowledgment may be expressed in any words which will adequately convey that idea, if the signature be proved to have been then existent; no particular form of expression is required either by the word 'acknowledge', or by the exigency of the act to be done. It would be quite

sufficient to say 'That is my will', the signature being there, and seen at the time.

Even if such phrases are not used, a request by the testator for witnesses to sign his will constitutes an acknowledgment. In *Weatherhill* v *Pearce* (see 4.2.4), the testatrix called at the home of two friends and asked them to sign her will, which ended with an attestation clause containing her signature. The will was held to be validly acknowledged. Kolbert J stated (at p. 498):

It is plain that a signature which has already been written can be acknowledged in many ways and no set form is required. It is sufficient to proffer a document which all concerned know is a will for the witnesses to sign, and no express declaration is necessary.

Both the witnesses in that case knew that they were attesting a will, but it seems that even a request for witnesses to sign the *document before them* suffices. In *Keigwin* v *Keigwin* (1843) 3 Curt 607; 163 ER 841, the witnesses were two carpenters working in the testatrix's home. She came into the room where they were working, placed before them a document (her will, already signed), a pen and an inkstand, and asked them 'to sign this paper', pointing to the place where she wished them to sign. The will was so folded as to conceal the contents, but her signature was plainly visible. This was held to be a valid acknowledgment even though the witnesses were not aware that the paper was a will.

It seems that the testator need not say anything at all. He might indicate in writing what he is doing. Indeed, mere gesture may be sufficient. Thus in *In the Goods of Davies* (1850) 2 Rob Ecc 337; 163 ER 1337, evidence that the testatrix pointed to her will and 'by gestures intimated that she had signed the same' was held to amount to an acknowledgment. However, it may be that mere gesture is insufficient where the will was signed by another person on the testator's behalf. If the testator was acknowledging such a signature it is difficult to see how gestures alone could convey to the witness what was happening with sufficient clarity. It is probable that in such a case some form of express recognition by the testator of the signature is necessary: *In the Goods of Summers* (1850) 2 Rob Ecc 295; 163 ER 1323.

(b) *Presence* The witnesses must be mentally and physically present when the testator acknowledges his signature. Mental presence connotes that the witnesses must be conscious of the act done, i.e. aware of the words or conduct of the testator that constitutes the acknowledgment. But they need not realise that it is a will that is being acknowledged. As regards physical presence, the requirement is that the witnesses should see or have the opportunity of seeing the testator's *signature*. That differs from the position concerning the making of a signature in the presence of witnesses, as Brett LJ explained in *In the Goods of Gunstan* (1882) 7 PD 102, CA, at p. 113:

... it seems obvious that where an acknowledgment has to be relied upon, the witnesses must see or have the opportunity of seeing the signature. When they are required to attest the signature, they must see or have the opportunity of seeing the person signing the document.

It seems that there must be a line of sight between the signature and the witnesses at the moment of acknowledgment. In *Re Groffman* [1969] 2 All ER 108, the testator asked his friends to witness his will, gesturing towards his coat: the will, folded in four, was in an inside pocket of the coat. As the witnesses at that moment did not see the signature, nor had the opportunity to do so, the acknowledgment was held to be invalid. It was argued that opportunity to see means that the witnesses could have seen if they had expressed a desire to do so. The argument was rejected. On the other hand, in *Daintree* v *Butcher* (1888) 13 PD 102, CA, the witnesses did not recollect seeing the testatrix sign but evidence was accepted that her signature had already been made when they were asked to witness the document. They were not told that the document was a codicil but the signature was visible to them. The acknowledgment was valid. Cotton LJ stated (at p. 103):

In my opinion, when the paper bearing the signature of the testatrix was put before two persons who were asked by her or in her presence to sign as witnesses that was an acknowledgment of the signature by her. The signature being so placed that they could see it, whether they actually did see it or not, she was in fact asking them to attest that signature as hers.

4.2.5.4 'Present at the same time'
To satisfy s. 9(c), at least two witnesses must have been present *at the same time* when the testator signed or acknowledged. This requirement was introduced by the Wills Act 1837 in order to minimise the possibility of fraud. Moreover, the need for the simultaneous presence of witnesses furnishes more reliable evidence of the testator's capacity.

The requirement of simultaneous presence may be usefully illustrated by two contrasting cases. In *Weatherhill* v *Pearce* (above) the testatrix acknowledged her will in the home of the two witnesses. The evidence was inconclusive as to whether the witnesses were 'present at the same time'. However, the front door opened directly into a large room which took up virtually the whole of the ground floor, and it was clear that the acknowledgment took place on that floor. The judge thought it highly likely that all three ladies were at some time present together in the large ground-floor room. Moreover, there was no evidence to suggest that the witnesses were not at some stage together with the testatrix to witness the will's execution. The court upheld the will, applying the presumption of due execution (see 4.2.8). In *Re Groffman*, it will be recalled that the testator's gesturing towards his coat was held to be an insufficient acknowledgment (above). As there was not enough space in the lounge for the witnesses to sign the will, one of them took the testator into the adjacent dining room. The latter removed the will from his pocket and the witness signed it, the testator's signature being visible to him. When the first witness returned to the lounge he suggested that the second witness should go to the dining room to sign; the latter did so, in the testator's presence. This was held to be an invalid execution as the will had not been acknowledged in the presence of the two witnesses 'present at the same time'. It was argued (unsuccessfully) that what occurred in the lounge and the dining room was essentially one transaction, the two witnesses signing within 'a matter of seconds' of each other. This decision appears ungenerous although it is justifiable as a technically correct application of s. 9(c) to the facts. When comparing *Re Groffman* with *Weatherhill* v *Pearce*, however, a lot seems to turn on a fine distinction. In the latter case the will was upheld even though there was no conclusive evidence that the witnesses were simultaneously present. In the former, the will failed because there was evidence that simultaneous presence was lacking at the crucial moment, albeit by a matter of seconds.

The LRC Report No. 22 considered the requirement that the witnesses should be 'present at the same time'. The Committee was not persuaded by the argument that the rule was unnecessary and that it should be sufficient if the testator executed the will in the presence of *each* witness, whether they were together or not:

> ... we do not consider that this requirement causes any great injustice and on the whole we think it is right that the three necessary participants in the 'ritual' of execution of a will should be present together during the essential part of it, namely the signature or acknowledgment of this signature by the testator. (para. 2.10)

4.2.6   What must the witness do?

Section 9(d) requires that each witness should either attest and sign the will or acknowledge his signature, either act to be done in the presence of the testator (but not necessarily in the presence of any other witness).

4.2.6.1   The order of execution

When s. 9(d) is read in conjunction with the rest of s. 9 it appears — although this is not expressly stated — that the section as a whole lays down a chronological order of events that must be followed. There are two successive steps:

(a)   the testator must first complete signing or acknowledging his signature in the simultaneous presence of at least two witnesses; and

(b)   the witnesses must then sign or acknowledge their respective signatures.

It follows that if a witness signs the will before the testator has completed the first stage, the execution is invalid. In *Wyatt* v *Berry* [1893] P 5, the two witnesses were father and son, both working at the same workshop, although on different floors. The testator took his will (already signed) to the father and asked him to sign. After the father signed his son was called in to sign, the testator saying 'It is a bit of ordering of my affairs. I have signed it, and your father has signed it'. The son then signed, all three being present. The will was held not to be duly executed since the father had signed before the testator had completed the first stage. Similarly, in *Re Davies* [1951] 1 All ER 920, the testatrix marked her will in the presence of one of the witnesses who was then given the will to sign. While the witness was signing, the second witness entered the room whereupon the testatrix acknowledged her signature and requested him to sign (which he did). The execution was held invalid as the first witness had signed before the testatrix had acknowledged her signature to the second witness.

However, there is an important exception to this rule: under s. 9(d), a witness may acknowledge his signature. The LRC Report No. 22, recommended this possibility after the unsatisfactory decision in *Re Colling* (see 4.2.2.1). It will be recalled that the testator started to sign his will in the presence of another patient and the ward-sister who left to attend to another patient before the signature was completed. The testator completed signing and the other witness then signed. When the ward-sister returned, the testator and the other witness acknowledged their signatures, and the sister then added her signature. Under the law applicable at that time the judge had to find, reluctantly, that the execution was invalid since the testator had not completed his signing or acknowledging before a witness signed — the first stage was unfinished when the second stage was commenced. But following the amendment to s. 9 the execution would be valid on these facts since it seems that the fellow patient acknowledged his signature *after* the testator completed the first stage. Suppose, however, that when the ward-sister returned the patient acknowledged his signature before the testator acknowledged his: would s. 9(d) be satisfied? It seems not as the first stage would not have been completed before the second stage was commenced. The recital of the facts in *Re Colling* does not make it clear whether in fact the testator did acknowledge before the patient did so: the report merely states (at p. 730) that when the ward-sister returned 'the testator and Mr Jackson [the patient] acknowledged their signatures to her'. The order of acknowledgment was irrelevant as the law stood at that time (since a witness could not acknowledge a signature), but *Re Colling* would still be decided the same way now if the evidence was that the testator acknowledged after the witness did so. *Wyatt* v *Berry* and *Re Davies* (above) would also be decided the same way because there was no acknowledgment by the first witness in either case.

4.2.6.2 Attest and sign
Each witness must attest and sign the will or acknowledge his signature. To attest means to witness the signature of the testator (or his acknowledgment). The requirement to attest and sign raises several issues.

(a) *Signature* The rules as to what constitutes the signature of a witness are the same as those for a testator — the witness must make a mark intended to be his signature. Thus the witness does not need to use his name. In *In the*

Goods of Sperling (1863) 3 SW & T 272; 164 ER 1279, the testator signed his will in the presence of his solicitor and a servant. When the solicitor had signed he said to the servant 'Now sign yourself here as servant to Mr Sperling'. The servant simply wrote 'Servant to Mr Sperling'. This was probably not quite what the solicitor had meant but, being in a hurry to leave, he folded up the will without looking at it. Nevertheless the court upheld the will since the servant intended the words he wrote to be his signature.

(b) *Personal act* The witness must sign personally. Thus, unlike the position with testators, another person cannot sign on behalf of the witness: *In the Estate of Bulloch* [1968] NI 96. However, it is possible for the hand of the witness to be guided by another person. In *In the Goods of Lewis* (1861) 31 LJP 153, the names of the witnesses were written by another person — as they were unable to write — with each of the witnesses holding the top of the pen when their respective names were written. The execution was held valid since by holding the pen each witness was 'taking some share in the act of writing his name' (*per* Cresswell J at p. 153). This was a very generous decision and another vivid example of the considerable flexibility that English law allows in the making of wills. *In the Goods of Lewis* also prompts the question whether the validity of a will should turn on the distinction between another person writing the witness's name (invalid) or writing it but with the witness holding the top of the pen (valid).

(c) *Position of signature* Section 9(d) does not specify where the witness should sign. Obviously the most sensible place is close to the testator's signature — alongside or just below — but the signature may be anywhere on the will provided that it was intended to attest the testator's operative signature. What if the signatures of the witnesses are not on the same paper as that on which the will is written? Then the signatures are valid provided that they are on paper physically connected with the will. These rules are illustrated by *In the Goods of Braddock* (1876) 1 PD 433: the testatrix validly executed a will occupying one side of a sheet of paper. Some years later she made a codicil to the earlier will. The witnesses to the codicil saw her sign it whereupon they signed the back of the *will* at her request. While the codicil was being executed it was attached to the will by a pin. Upholding the codicil Hannen P stated (at pp. 434–5):

> The law does not require that the attestation should be in any particular place, provided that the evidence satisfies the Court that the witnesses in writing their names had the intention of attesting. But the attestation, if not on the same sheet of paper as the signature of the testator, must be on a paper physically connected with that sheet.

Consider the fruitless attempt to make a will in *In the Goods of Hatton* (1881) 6 PD 204. The testator called in two neighbours, William and John, to help him make a short and simple will. William wrote out the will as instructed by the testator. But John thought he knew better: thinking that the language of the will might be improved, he wrote out another will with different words, but to the same effect. The testator signed the first paper but William and John signed the other. It was held that neither paper was a validly executed will. The paper that the testator signed was the only possible will but the witnesses' signatures were on a separate, independent document — in effect a duplicate of the will — and that was insufficient.

(d) *Intention to attest* The witnesses must sign as witnesses, i.e. with the intention that their signatures should be an attestation of the will. There is a presumption that a person who signed a will — other than the testator — did so as a witness: *In the Estate of Bravda* [1968] 2 All ER 217, CA. However, the strength of the presumption will vary according to circumstances. For example, the presumption will be less strong if the position of the signature is unusual — different, say, from that of the other witnesses. The presumption is rebuttable by evidence showing that the signer did not sign as a witness. In *In the Goods of Sharman* (1869) 1 P & D 662, the testator made a will a few hours before his death, benefiting his sister Adelaide. The will was signed by two witnesses in the presence of the testator and Adelaide. One of the witnesses then suggested that Adelaide should sign to indicate that she was the intended beneficiary. The testator was rightly sceptical of this advice, but Adelaide signed just below the signatures of the witnesses after a further request from the officious witness. She simply signed her name and did not describe herself as the beneficiary. The court was satisfied that Adelaide did not sign as a witness; her benefit was therefore unaffected by s. 15 of the Wills Act 1837 (see 7.2.2). A similar decision was reached in *Kitcat* v *King* [1930] P 266. The signature of the testatrix was followed by the phrase 'Signed and witnessed in the presence of each other', and below that four persons had signed, two of whom were beneficiaries. The court held that the beneficiaries had not signed as witnesses: there was evidence that they signed 'to make it legal' — with the intention merely of expressing assent to the manner of the testatrix's dispositions.

(e) *The operative signature* The witness must attest the testator's operative signature, i.e. the one purported to execute the will. In *In the Estate of Bercovitz* [1962] 1 All ER 552, the testator signed his will at the top and the bottom. The signature at the top was invalid according to the law applicable at the time, but the witnesses only attested that signature not the valid signature at the bottom. Consequently the execution was invalid. Although the law on position of signature has since changed, this case is still good authority for the proposition that the witnesses must attest the testator's operative signature. It will be recalled that in *Re Beadle* (see 4.2.4.3) the testatrix signed on the front of an envelope — intended to contain her will — and the witness signed on the back. Her signature on the envelope was held to be an identification of the contents rather than an operative signature to execute the will. Hence the attestation of the witnesses was defective. The testatrix had also signed the will itself — her operative signature — but the attestation was again invalid since only one witness had signed the will.

4.2.6.3 Acknowledgment by witness

Section 9(d) provides that a witness may ackowledge his signature. The opportunity for a witness to acknowledge a previously made signature was enacted in order to reverse the effect of *Re Colling* (above). The meaning of 'acknowledgment' in this context is probably the same as in the case of testators under s. 9(c). Thus the witness must demonstrate through words, gesture or conduct that he accepts the signature as his own. In *Couser v Couser* [1996] 3 All ER 256, the testator took his will to be attested and signed by a married couple — a farmer and his wife. The wife signed while her husband was absent feeding animals. When the husband returned she said that she had signed but expressed doubts about the validity of her attestation. The testator produced the will and showed it to the husband with the signatures of the wife and the testator visible. The husband signed the will while the wife was making coffee in the same room some 10 feet away. She continued to protest her doubts about the validity of her signature and urged the testator to go to a bank and have the will executed. It was held that the testator had acknowledged his signature in the presence of two witnesses together, and that the wife's protestations during the transaction as to the validity of her signature constituted an acknowledgment of that signature. The court took the view that the same principles applied to the acknowledgment of a witness's signature as in the case of a testator's signature.

To whom should acknowledgment be made? Presumably it must be to the testator since s. 9(d) requires the presence of the testator but not necessarily of any other witness. That being the case, the provision appears somewhat curious: after the testator's death there may be no one able to verify whether an acknowledgment was made. It would have made better sense if the acknowledgment had to be made to the other witnesses as well.

4.2.6.4 Presence of the testator
Section 9(d) requires a witness to sign or acknowledge his signature 'in the presence of the testator'. The purpose of this requirement appears to be to minimise the possibility of the substitution of a spurious will. 'Presence' has the same meaning as in s. 9(a) and s. 9(c): the testator must be mentally and physically present.

(a)   *Mental presence*: the testator must be conscious of the act done by each witness, i.e. their signing or acknowledging. If, therefore, the testator loses consciousness before the witnesses have completed those acts, the will fails. In *Right v Price* (1779) 1 Doug 241; 99 ER 157, the attestation by the witness was held invalid because it was attempted while the testator was insensible: 'He was a log, and totally absent to all mental purposes' (p. 159) and had been in that condition for the previous two days. Compare, however, *Re Chalcraft* (see 4.2.2.1), where it will be recalled that the testatrix was so weak that she managed to write only half her name on her codicil before slipping into unconsciousness. She had been given a large dose of morphine just beforehand. The witnesses hurriedly picked up the codicil and added their signatures. The court held that the witnesses had signed in her presence because they did so *while* she was becoming unconscious. Referring to the effect of the morphia, Willmer J stated (at p. 704):

The process, though swift, would be a gradual process inducing drowsiness and relief from pain, which would in turn induce sleep on the part of the patient. . . . That operation, or expected operation, of the drug seems to me to be inconsistent with a sudden departure of the mental faculties of the deceased. In my opinion the proper inference to draw is that throughout all these critical moments the deceased was losing her faculties through being overcome by drowsiness, but losing them gradually.

(b) *Physical presence*: the testator must have seen or had the opportunity of seeing the witnesses sign at the moment when they did sign; or, in the case of acknowledgment by a witness, the testator must have seen or had the opportunity of seeing the witnesses's signature when that witness acknowledged it. Again, it is the 'line of sight' rule which provides the basic test of physical presence. In *Shires* v *Glascock* (1688) 2 Salk 688; 91 ER 584, the testator asked the witnesses to go to another room ('seven yards distant') to attest his will. In that room was a broken window through which the testator could see the attestation. The execution was held to be good since the signing was in the view of the testator: 'he might have seen it, and that is enough'.

It seems that the 'opportunity to see' means that the testator must have been able to see, if he had chosen to look, from the actual position that he was in when the attestation occurred. In *Norton* v *Bazett* (1856) Deane 259; 164 ER 569, the testator signed his will in the inner room of his office in the presence of the witnesses, his clerks. Since the table in the room was full of papers the witnesses returned to the outer room (where they worked) and signed the will. Although the door between the rooms was open, the testator could not have seen the witnesses signing from his chair at his desk without moving (the report includes a useful plan of the office). It was held that where the witnesses sign in a different room from that in which the testator is, he must be proved to have been in a position from which he could have seen the attestation. Consequently the will failed.

Tribe v *Tribe* (1849) 1 Rob Ecc 775; 163 ER 1210, helps to clarify the line of sight test. A will was executed a few hours before the testator died. The witnesses signed at the dressing-table in her bedroom. The testatrix lay in bed with her back towards the dressing-table; she was unable to see the attestation and could not turn herself in the right direction. There was a conflict of evidence as to whether heavy bed curtains were drawn around the bed at the relevant moment. Nevertheless, the court held that even if the curtains were not so drawn, the attestation had not occurred in her presence since it was impossible — given her weak state — for her to have turned herself so as to have seen the witnesses sign.

Perhaps the most remarkable illustration of the line of sight test is *Casson* v *Dade* (1781) 1 Bro 99; 28 ER 1010. The testatrix travelled by carriage to her attorney's office in order to execute her will. Since the office was very hot, and she suffered from asthma, she decided to leave the office and signed the will in her carriage in the presence of the witnesses. They, however, returned to the office to complete the execution. It seems that the attestation might have been observed by the testatrix because at the relevant time 'the carriage was accidentally put back to the window of the office, through which, it was sworn by a person in the carriage, the testatrix might see what passed'. It is possible that the carriage moved because the horses backed at the relevant time (although the behaviour of the horses is not clear from the report). Whatever the explanation the court accepted that there was a sufficient line of sight, had the testatrix chosen to look. The Lord Chancellor 'inclined very strongly to think the will well executed'. It may strike the reader that this is not a particularly sensible way for a will to be executed.

What if the testator is blind? Can he be physically present when that concept requires him to be able to see? It would seem that the requirement of presence effectively prevents a blind person from making a will. However, the judges have taken the sensible approach that a blind testator is to be attributed with notional vision. Thus the test is whether the testator, had he possessed sight, could have seen the witnesses signing or acknowledging their signatures. In *In the Goods of Piercy* (1845) 1 Rob Ecc 278; 163 ER 1038, the will of a totally blind testatrix was prepared according to her instructions, read over to her, and then signed by her while lying in bed (one of the witnesses having placed her hand at the relevant part of the will). Since there was no table in the bedroom on which the witnesses could sign, they took the will to an adjoining room and signed there. The room was on the same floor, across a landing or passage, the doors of both rooms being open. Since the attestation by the witnesses was 'within view of the bedroom' the will was upheld.

4.2.6.5 Presence of other witnesses?
Section 9(d) states that witnesses need not 'necessarily' sign or acknowledge in the presence of each other. Therefore, if the testator signs his will in the presence of two witnesses, one of whom then signs the will and departs the scene before the other witness signs, the execution is valid. However, the best course is for the witnesses to sign in their joint presence. The LRC Report No. 22, commented on the practice of signing in joint presence:

> Because it provides a further safeguard against the dangers of duress and undue influence, we think it right that witnesses should sign or acknowledge their signature in each other's presence and that the present practice should be continued and encouraged. However, we have not received any evidence that a change in the law is necessary and consistently with our policy not to recommend change unless we consider that a clear case in its favour is made out, we do not recommend that this practice become an additional statutory requirement. (para. 2.12)

This is not one of the most convincing paragraphs in the Report: how can the Committee 'think it right' that witnesses should sign or acknowledge in each other's presence, but consider that there is an insufficient case for the enactment of such a requirement?

4.2.7   Attestation clause?

Section 9 ends with the words 'but no form of attestation shall be necessary'. Nevertheless, although an attestation clause is not strictly essential, it is highly desirable. The purpose of the clause is to recite that the will was executed in accordance with the required formalities; hence it is normal to end the will with such a clause. There is no one standard form of attestation clause but a typical one might read as follows:

> Signed by the above named testator in our presence and attested by us in his presence and in the presence of each other.

Why is an attestation clause so desirable in practice? Because it saves a lot of trouble: it makes it easier for the propounders of the will to obtain probate. The presence of the clause raises a presumption of due execution, whereas under the Non-Contentious Probate Rules 1987, a registrar must require affidavit evidence of the due execution of the will (before admitting it to probate) if the will lacks an attestation clause, or has a defective one.

4.2.8   Presumption of due execution

The traditional desire of English judges to uphold wills whenever at all possible is further illustrated by the application of the maxim *omnia praesumuntur rite esse acta*: 'all formalities are presumed to have been correctly carried out'. This presumption is very important in practice, saving wills where there is a lack of conclusive evidence that the required formalities were satisfied. The classic explanation of the presumption is to be found in *Harris* v *Knight* (1890) 15 PD 170, CA, in which Lindley LJ stated (at pp. 179–80):

> The maxim, *Omnia praesumuntur rite esse acta* . . . expresses an inference which may reasonably be drawn when an intention to do some formal act is established; when the evidence is consistent with that intention having been carried into effect in a proper way; but when the actual observance of all due formalities can only be inferred as a matter of probability. The maxim is not wanted where such observance is proved, nor has it any place where such observance is disproved. The maxim only comes into operation where there is no proof one way or the other; but where it is more probable that what was intended to be done was done as it ought to have been done to render it valid. . . .

The presumption applies where a document appears to be a will that has been executed in compliance with the statutory requirements. Thus it is not essential for there to be positive evidence of due execution. However, if there is evidence of faulty execution, then the presumption is not applicable. In *In the Estate of Bercovitz*, it will be recalled that the witnesses attested the 'wrong' signature — the one at the top of the will instead of the operative signature at the bottom (see 4.2.6.2). The propounders of the will asked for the presumption to be applied, but this was refused since there was clear evidence of faulty execution.

4.2.8.1 'A matter of probability'

It is when there is an absence of evidence one way or the other that the presumption operates. Thus it is of particular use where the attesting witnesses are dead, or cannot be traced, or have become incapable of testifying or are simply unable to recall the circumstances of the execution. But, as was emphasised in *Harris* v *Knight*, the presumption rests on the notion of probability: the court must be able to infer that it is probable that the due formalities were carried out. In *Weatherhill* v *Pearce*, it will be recalled that there was no clear evidence that the testatrix acknowledged her signature in the simultaneous presence of both witnesses (see 4.2.5.4). But Kolbert J thought it 'highly likely' that all three ladies were at some point present together during the execution of the will. He was prepared to apply the presumption because the will purported to be valid and there was no evidence of invalidity:

> ... the correct approach is for the court to give effect to clear testamentary wishes if it is possible and proper to do so and that as the law leans against intestacy the court should not be astute to undermine a will unless there is clear evidence of non-compliance with the rules to be observed in its making. (p. 498)

A less clear-cut example of the application of the presumption is to be found in *Re Denning* [1958] 2 All ER 1. The testatrix's hand-written will consisted of a small single sheet of writing paper. One side was dated and contained her brief dispositions, followed by her signature. On the other side two names were written upside down in different hands. There was no attestation clause and no evidence as to the identity of the names on the back. Nevertheless, Sachs J applied the presumption of due execution because he thought that there was 'no other practical reason why those names should be on the back of the document unless it was for the purpose of attesting the will' (p. 2). This was a generous decision: Sachs J recognised that he was applying the presumption at its furthest limit.

4.2.8.2 The strength of the presumption

A variety of factors may be relevant as to how obliged the court considers itself to apply the presumption. It will definitely feel more obliged in the case of a will executed on professional advice and containing an attestation clause, than with a home-made will without such a clause. The application of the presumption varies considerably in home-made wills because the circumstances of their making are so diverse. For example, the court is more likely to apply the presumption to a home-made will made on a will-form and containing an attestation clause than to one made on an egg-shell without such a clause.

Important also are the characters of the testator and the witnesses, and their capacity to perform the statutory requirements. The presumption cannot apply unless the testator had *animus testandi*; the clearer that intention appears to have been, the stronger the presumption. And the court will be interested to know how competent the testator and witnesses normally were in managing their affairs, and what was the level of their knowledge about the execution requirements. In *Whiting* v *Turner* (see 4.2.1) the court applied the presumption of due execution to a will (written in France in the French language) despite 'exceedingly hazy' evidence from the witnesses as to what had occurred when the will was executed. Pivotal in the court's decision was its estimation that the testatrix understood well what was necessary to execute a will under English law and that she was a lady who was 'very particular as to the way in which things were done'. In *Weatherhill* v *Pearce* (above) the presumption was strengthened by persuasive evidence of the testatrix's intention to make a will. She had made her intention clear in her diary and in a long letter to her daughter, a copy of which was left with the will. And the application of the presumption was probably helped — although this was not emphasised in the judgment — by the fact that the attesting witnesses were 'conscientious and careful ladies with an eye for detail in the best traditions of the Civil Service' (p. 494).

4.2.9   Testators dying before 1983

The formalities applicable to wills made by testators who died before 1983 were the same as those required by the current law with two exceptions:

(a)   position of testator's signature;
(b)   acknowledgment of a witness's signature.

Since the validity of the wills of testators dying before 1983 is decreasingly likely to be an issue, the previous law will be dealt with briefly.

4.2.9.1   Position of testator's signature
Under the original s. 9 of the Wills Act 1837, the testator's signature had to be 'at the foot or end' of the will. The over-strict interpretation of this phrase necessitated reform. The Wills Act Amendment Act 1852 provided that the testator's signature was valid if it 'shall be so placed at or after, or following, or under, or beside, or opposite to the End of the Will, that it shall be apparent on the Face of the Will that the Testator intended to give Effect by such his Signature to the Writing signed as his Will'. Moreover, the Act provided that any part of a will which was written underneath the signature or written after it (in time) would not have effect. In *Re Stalman* (1931) 145 LT 339, CA, a will was held to be invalid because the signature of the testatrix appeared at the top of the will (there had been no room at the bottom). The position of the signature was clearly contrary to the 1852 Act. The decision would now be different provided that the signature was intended 'to give effect to the will': Wills Act 1837, s. 9(b).

Re Stalman was not typical: the general trend of decisions under the previous law was towards leniency in interpreting the 1852 Act. Some cases went as far as holding that a signature could be regarded as being at the end of the will — even though it was not — if the testator intended it to be at the end. In *In the Goods of Hornby* [1946] P 171, the testator placed his signature in an oblong space drawn on the right-hand side of the sheet on which the will was written out. The signature appeared half-way down the sheet: thus some of the dispositions were beneath it. The word 'signed' appeared above the signature which, together with the signatures of the witnesses, was written in ink different from the rest of the will. The execution was held to be valid since the testator's intention was that his signature should be read as being at the end of the will, and he thereby intended to give effect to the will. Similarly, words which appeared after a signature — but which had been written before the testator signed — could be regarded as part of the will if they had been intended to be read as preceding the signature. The intention could be shown if the testator used an interpolation in the duly executed part of the will such as 'continued on the other side' or 'see over': *Paling* v *Ponting* [1930] P 185. Moreover, in cases where a will consisted of two or more sides of paper, and it was not clear where the will began or ended, the courts tended to regard the will as commencing with the dispositions and ending with the signatures. For example, in *In the Estate of Long* [1936] P 166, a will was written on two sides of paper, one of which contained the heading, attestation clause and signatures of the testatrix and witnesses, while the other contained her dispositions. As the evidence was that the dispositions had been written before execution the court upheld the will.

4.2.9.2   Acknowledgment by a witness

Before 1983 a witness could not acknowledge a signature. Therefore, if a witness signed the will before the testator completed signing or acknowledging his signature, the will was invalid: the witness could not later validly acknowledge his earlier signature. The failure on these grounds of the will in *Re Colling* led the Law Reform Committee to recommend that a witness should be able to acknowledge his signature. Consequently, s. 9 of the Wills Act 1837 was amended to make this possible (see 4.2.6.3).

4.3   THE QUESTION OF REFORM

Although the LRC Report No. 22, recommended little change to s. 9 of the Wills Act 1837, it can be argued that the present state of the law is unsatisfactory. The statutory requirements lack precision in some crucial respects and the case law is replete with arcane distinctions and questionable decisions. Even if the requirements were articulated more precisely, some would argue that they are in any case too lax given the importance of will-making. Others, on the other hand, would argue that the requirements are too strict, and that wills should be upheld if they have *substantially* complied with the necessary formalities. But these issues cannot be properly addressed without first considering the purpose of formalities.

4.3.1   Why formalities?

In his article 'Substantial Compliance with the Wills Act' (1975) 88 *Harvard Law Review*, 489, J.H. Langbein examines the role of formalities in will-making. Formalities are said to have four main functions — evidentiary, channelling, cautionary and protective — their cumulative aim being to ensure that the testator's property will be distributed according to his wishes. The evidentiary function of formalities, probably the most important of all, is to provide the court with 'reliable evidence of testamentary intent and of the terms of the will' (p. 492). The need for writing, testator's signature and attestation by witnesses all serve this purpose. The channelling function of formalities achieves 'considerable uniformity in the organisation, language, and content of most wills' (p. 494). The formalities channel the participants in will-making into standardised forms of behaviour — writing, signing, acknowledging, witnessing. This benefits both the administration of the law — millions of estates are disposed of in a familiar manner — and the testator since he has at hand a convenient mode of effecting his wishes. The cautionary function is to remind the testator of the seriousness of what he is doing: making a will becomes 'a ceremony impressing the participants with its solemnity and legal significance' (p. 495). The necessity for writing, the testator's signature, and attestation by the witnesses fulfil this function. The protective function serves to protect the testator against forgery, fraud and undue influence. For example, the necessity for witnesses to sign in the testator's presence is meant to reduce the possibility of the substitution of a surreptitious will.

The LRC Report No. 22 adopted a similar approach:

> ... we took as our starting point the principle that the purposes of the law are, first, to ensure that documents genuinely representing the testator's intentions should be valid, and secondly, to prevent the admission to probate of wills which, because they are forged or for any other reason do not represent the true wishes of the testator.... The existing requirements impart an element of formality or ceremony into the making of a will which we think is appropriate for so important an act as the disposition of an estate. Moreover the evidence we received supported the view that the present rules provide a safeguard not only against forgery and undue influence, but against hasty or ill-considered dispositions which can lead to family dissension and consequent litigation. (para. 2.2)

In *Wills, Inheritance, and Families* (1996) Finch *et al.* emphasise that a will is both a public and a private document, and that there is a public interest in ensuring that the formalities of will-making are 'tightly regulated to ensure that property is transmitted in a manner which is clear and orderly' (p. 40). The public interest requires that close attention be paid to the circumstances of the making of a will since so much depends on it. The authors regard the provision that a will must be signed in the presence of at least two witnesses, and attested and signed by them, as the 'clearest symbolic expression of the public interest in the process of will-making' (*ibid.*).

4.3.2 The need for reform?

4.3.2.1 Relaxation of formalities
Potentially the most important way of relaxing the formalities is through the substantial compliance doctrine. The idea is to give the courts a dispensing

power whereby a will could be regarded valid despite defective execution if the court is satisfied that the will is genuine. The doctrine is discussed at length by J.H. Langbein in his 1975 article (above). He begins thus: 'The law of wills is notorious for its harsh and relentless formalism' (p. 489). This is a highly questionable statement. Certainly one can find numerous cases where judges reluctantly have had to fail wills (*Re Groffman, Re Colling* for example); but equally one can point to cases which show the judges applying the law in a very flexible, generous manner (*Re Chalcraft, Casson v Dade* and others). The evidence is at best equivocal on this issue. However, one can disagree with Langbein's opening sentence but still accept the thrust of his arguments in favour of the substantial compliance doctrine. He summarises the essence of the doctrine as follows (at p. 489):

> The finding of a formal defect should lead not to automatic invalidity, but to a further inquiry: does the noncomplying document express the deceased's testamentary intent, and does its form sufficiently approximate Wills Act formality to enable the court to conclude that it serves the purposes of the Wills Act?

Langbein argues that introduction of a dispensing power for the courts would minimise the failure of wills on minor formal grounds. Litigation would not necessarily be increased thereby: one type of dispute would be substituted for another. The 'awkward formalistic question' would be replaced with a more manageable question — did the conduct of the participants in making the will 'serve the purpose of the formality' (p. 526)?

The substantial compliance doctrine — or variations of it — operates in a number of jurisdictions. In South Australia, for example, a defectively executed will may receive probate 'if the Supreme Court ... is satisfied that there can be no reasonable doubt that the deceased intended the document to constitute his will': s. 12(2) of the Wills Act 1936. This subsection is frequently used, as is evident from the judgment of White J in *In the Goods of Greenslade* (1988) 48 SASR 414. The opening sentence indicates a certain element of weariness and *déjà vu*: 'This is yet another application under s. 12 of the Wills Act 1936. There have been four in this month's list' (p. 414). The case concerned a testator who altered his will incorrectly: indeed, he failed to comply with any of the required formalities for alterations. Nevertheless the altered will received probate since the court was satisfied that the alterations embodied his intentions. A similar dispensing power has recently been introduced in Hong Kong. In Queensland the dispensing power appears to be exercised more stringently since there must be 'substantial compliance' with the formalities: Queensland Succession Act 1981, s. 9.

Although the substantial compliance doctrine has operated for years in a variety of jurisdictions, the LRC Report No. 22 did not recommend its introduction into English law. The Committee thought that litigation might well be increased because of the inevitable uncertainty that would arise as to whether a formally defective will would nevertheless receive probate:

While the idea of a dispensing power has attractions, most of us were more impressed by the argument against it, namely that by making it less certain whether or not an informally executed will is capable of being admitted to probate, it could lead to litigation, expense and delay, often in cases where it could least be afforded, for it is home-made wills which most often go wrong. (para. 2.5)

Even in the absence of a dispensing power for the courts, a laxer regime could be achieved simply by reducing the amount of form required or by providing more informal alternatives. For example, the US Uniform Probate Code 1969 eschews the need for the witnesses to sign in the testator's presence. Another possibility is to allow civilians to make oral wills. However, such wills may give rise to problems in proving and interpreting oral statements. In those jurisdictions where oral wills are allowed it is normal to fix an upper limit on the amount of property that can be disposed. A third possibility is to allow an informal holograph will — one written entirely or substantially in the testator's handwriting but without some of the usual requirements such as the need for witnesses. Such wills are allowed in many jurisdictions. To some extent they are 'self-proving' since, being written in the testator's hand, they demonstrate strong internal evidence of genuineness. However, a major problem is that they hardly fulfil the cautionary function: a holograph will may take effect even though it was made very casually. A famous illustration of this is the decision of the Supreme Court of Pennsylvania in *Re Kimmel's Estate* (1924) 31 ALR 678. The semi-literate testator wrote a short, casual letter to his sons in which he *inter alia* predicted a cold winter, dispensed advice on how to pickle pork and made some dispositions 'if enny thing hapens'. The letter was admitted to probate as a valid will, the court being satisfied that the letter demonstrated testamentary intent. As the judge remarked, why else would the testator have written (towards the end of the letter) 'Kepp this letter lock it up it may help you out'?

The LRC Report No. 22 did not recommend that informal holograph wills should be valid in English law:

Despite the fact that there is no evidence that holograph wills do not operate successfully elsewhere, the majority of our witnesses thought that they would be likely to be confused with draft wills, would give rise to difficulties of interpretation and would provide no safeguard against forgery, insanity or undue influence. (para. 2.22)

4.3.2.2 Stricter formalities?

The previous account of the requirements under s. 9 revealed some highly questionable, over-generous decisions. Moreover, it was argued that s. 9 is hardly a model of clarity: it is drafted with a surprising lack of precision, thus making it possible that very dubious wills might receive probate. For example, 'writing' is not defined: hence there is the rather silly possibility of wills being written on backs of cheques, egg-shells, or nurses' petticoats. 'Signed' by a testator allows all sorts of strange possibilities, including guiding the testator's hand. 'Direction' needs clearer articulation. So does 'presence' in its various appearances in s. 9: the strained, arcane line of sight test is difficult to defend. There is lack of precision too as to the meaning of 'witness' and what constitutes an acknowledgment. Section 9 can be a trap for the unwary.

However, defenders of the efficacy of s. 9 might argue that there is a limit to the precision that can be expected of a statute, and that it is for the courts to clarify the grey areas and even to supply the missing detail. Such arguments would be more convincing if judges were consistent and predictable in their interpretation of s. 9. It may also be argued that the call for greater precision in the statutory requirements does not necessarily point towards a stricter regime. Perhaps so, but in the case of s. 9 that would be the most probable effect. Should the law countenance wills on egg-shells, testators' hands being guided by others, or wills being witnessed by 10-year-olds? Section 9 does not even require that a will be dated, although it is obviously sensible to do so. In *Corbett* v *Newey* [1996] 2 All ER 914, Waite LJ stated (at p. 920) that 'there is no requirement in law that a will should be dated. Lack of a date or the inclusion of the wrong date cannot invalidate a will'. Given the widespread dating of official communications and documents, the non-requirement of dating a will is surprising. Moreover, where a testator makes two or more wills or codicils, their validity may depend on the sequence in which they were executed: that wills need not be dated seems all the more remarkable. However, dating can bring its own problems. The experience in jurisdictions where wills must be dated suggests that litigation can arise from having to decide what constitutes a date, and what is the effect of an incorrect or wrong date. Moreover, exceptions need to be made to prevent hard cases.

The Justice Committee recommended a stricter regime for will-making in its *Report on Home Made Wills* (1971). It was concerned that the comparative ease with which wills could be made in English law concealed from the ordinary testator 'the difficulties in disposing of his estate' (para. 5). The Committee recommended that as an alternative to wills executed under s. 9, testators should be able to make wills in the presence of a commissioner for oaths or similar officer. The problem of invalid execution would largely disappear in such wills. The concept of executing a will before an official — and thereby furnishing the will with probative force — is well-known in continental systems, e.g., the 'notarial' will in France and Germany. The notary is a public official with jurisdiction over the authentication of legal forms and documents. In the United States the Uniform Probate Code provides for a 'self-proving' will whereby a testamentary document can be acknowledged in the presence of an officer authorised to administer oaths. The utility of notarial wills was doubted by the LRC Report No. 22: they would not be used 'by those testators who prefer to make their wills without assistance' (para. 2.23). But there has been some judicial approval of the idea in the past. For example, in *Brown* v *Skirrow* [1902] P 3, Gorell Barnes J said (at p. 7):

I have long held the view that it would be a good thing if wills were required to be signed in the presence of some public official who should be able to see that they are properly executed.

The Law Reform Committee was also opposed to the idea that recourse to a solicitor should be made compulsory, fearing that 'it would deter some people from making a will at all' (para. 2.23). But consider the potential advantages of such a system. Failure of wills on the ground of defective execution would virtually cease to be a problem; the importance of what the testator was doing — the cautionary function — would be made even more evident to him; and the provisions of his will would have had the benefit of professional advice. There would have to be exceptions for death-bed wills, emergencies, and other circumstances where recourse to a solicitor could not reasonably be expected. Nevertheless, one need not necessarily be a solicitor to appreciate the attractions of the idea.

4.4 INCORPORATION

4.4.1 Introduction

Documents which are not executed in accordance with s. 9 may nevertheless form part of the will if they have been incorporated by the will. The rule applies not only to separate documents, but also to the incorporation of words contained in the *same* document, e.g., a will written on a piece of paper may incorporate other words written on the paper even though they were not executed as part of the will. The effect of incorporation is that the incorporated material becomes part of the will and is thus admissible to probate. It may be wondered why anyone would wish to incorporate documents into their will rather than just include the relevant material in the will in the first place. One reason is to reduce the size of what might otherwise be an over-long will. For example, *In the Goods of Balme* [1897] P 261, the testator made a bequest to Selwyn College, Cambridge of all his books as enumerated in his library catalogue ('a voluminous document'). The catalogue was thus incorporated by the will and was admitted to probate, although in the unusual circumstances the court agreed that the catalogue need not be deposited in the Probate Registry but could be held by the college on behalf of the Registry.

4.4.2 The requirements of incorporation

In order for a document to be incorporated three conditions must be satisfied:

    (a)   the document must be identified in the will;
    (b)   the document must be in existence when the will is made;
    (c)   the document must be referred to in the will as existing when the will is made.

4.4.2.1 Document must be identified

To be incorporated a document must be sufficiently described in the will so as to be identifiable: *Croker* v *Marquis of Hertford* (1844) 4 Moo PC 339; 13 ER 334, where a testator directed his executors to pay any legacies that he might afterwards give by any testamentary writing, witnessed or not. The issue was whether an unattested codicil made many years later was incorporated by the will. It was held that such a general reference was insufficient to identify the codicil, Dr Lushington stating (at p. 344) that 'certainty and identification is the very essence' of incorporation, and that if any doubt existed as to the instrument to be incorporated, the principle of incorporation was inapplicable. However, the need for certainty has not been consistently applied in the cases. Indeed, sometimes it is difficult to discern any appreciable degree of identification. For example, in *In the Estate of Saxton* [1939] 2 All ER 418, the testator made a will leaving his property 'to the following persons', but he omitted to state in the will who the persons were. On his death a number of lists were found (with the will) commencing with the statement 'I wish to leave the following amounts'. It was held (dubiously) that the lists were incorporated since this statement established a cross-reference with the words in the will. *In the Estate of Mardon* [1944] P 109 is a more understandable decision. A codicil instructed solicitors to sell the furniture and belongings of the testatrix 'with the exception of the articles mentioned in the schedule attached hereto'. It was held that this was a sufficient identification to incorporate the schedule attached.

Where the incorporated material is written on the same piece of paper as the will, the identification rule fully applies. Thus the words cannot be incorporated unless they have been sufficiently identified, but it seems that a slight reference may suffice. For example, in *In the Goods of Widdrington* (1866) 35 LJP 66, the testatrix executed a will on the first side of a sheet of paper; on the back was found a codicil which was invalidly executed. Below the codicil there was another codicil (duly executed) which made no reference to the first codicil other than that a legacy given by the first codicil had been revoked. It was held that the reference (even though partly erroneous) was sufficient to incorporate the first codicil.

Even though there is sufficient identification, a document will not be incorporated unless it satisfies the description: *In the Goods of Gill* (1869) 2 P & D 6. In that case the testator made a will and soon afterwards executed a document which he described as directions to his executors. He later made a will revoking all prior testamentary dispositions, and disposing of certain chattels 'according to the written directions left by me and affixed to this my will'. This identification in itself was clearly expressed but no paper was found affixed to the will. However, it was argued that the earlier directions to executors should be incorporated. The court held that this was not possible since those directions were in a document which did not answer to the description in the final will.

4.4.2.2 Document must be in existence

The document must already be in existence at the time of the will's execution. The onus of proof is on the party alleging incorporation. In *Singleton* v *Tomlinson* (1878) 3 App Cas 404, the testator wrote his will on 'three sides of a sheet of paper' (according to the report). He directed his executors to sell certain property that he was possessed of 'as stated in the annexed schedule'. The schedule was written on the fourth side, and bore the same date as the will. However, the witnesses to the will did not see the schedule when they were attesting. The House of Lords held that in the circumstances there was insufficient proof of the existence of the schedule when the will was executed; hence the schedule could not be incorporated.

4.4.2.3 Document must be referred to as existing

The will must refer to the document as already in existence. Thus incorporation does not occur if the reference in the will can be construed as applicable to a document coming into existence after the will's execution. The rationale is that the testator should not be able to reserve for himself the power to alter his will in the future by an unattested document — that would undermine the fundamental requirement that a will must be executed according to s. 9. In *Re Jones* [1942] 1 All ER 642, the testator made a gift by will in favour of Tettenhall College on the terms of a deed of trust 'executed by me bearing even date with this my last will and testament, or any substitution therefor or modification thereof or addition thereto which I may hereafter execute'. Although the deed was executed on the same day as the will, it could not be incorporated since the reference in the will included the possibility of the substitution of a future document. In *University College of North Wales v Taylor* [1908] P 1401, CA, the testator left a legacy by a will executed in June 1905 to be held on such terms 'as are contained and specified in any memorandum amongst my papers written or signed by me relating thereto'. On his death a memorandum (dated March 1905) was found with his papers; it contained the terms of the gift to the college. It was held that the memorandum could not be incorporated since 'the testator in using those words has intended to reserve to himself the right to declare from time to time the rules and regulations and the trusts which he desires to apply to his gift' (*per* Farwell LJ, at p. 147).

4.4.3 The effect of republication

If a will is republished (normally by a subsequent codicil) the will is regarded as having been executed on the date of republication: s. 34 of the Wills Act 1837 (see 5.6). So what is the position if a document did not exist when the will was originally executed but came into existence before the will was republished? Such a document is incorporated when the will is republished provided that the will refers (in its republished form) to the document as already in existence. Consider *In the Goods of Lady Truro* (1866) 1 P & D 201: the testatrix bequeathed 'such articles of silver plate and plated articles as are contained in the inventory signed by me and deposited herewith'. Such an inventory did not exist when the will was made but was drawn up thereafter. Later a codicil was executed which republished the will. It was held that the inventory was incorporated. Compare *In the Goods of Smart* [1902] P 238, where the testatrix directed trustees to give certain articles 'to such of my friends as I may designate in a book or memorandum that will be found with this will'. She drew up a memorandum some years later and executed a codicil thereafter republishing her will. It was held that although the memorandum was in existence when the will was republished, it could not be incorporated since it was referred to as a future document ('I may designate'). Gorell Barnes J stated (at p. 240):

... if a testator, in a testamentary paper duly executed, refers to an existing unattested testamentary paper, the instrument so referred to becomes part of his will; in other words, it is incorporated into it; but it is clear that, in order that the informal document should be incorporated in the validly executed document, the latter must refer to the former as a written instrument then existing — that is, at the time of execution — in such terms that it may be ascertained.

4.4.4   The consequences of incorporation

A document which has been validly incorporated forms part of the will and is admissable to probate. What if the incorporated document itself gives the testator the power to vary the disposition of property in the future, as, for example, where an existing settlement is incorporated? This occurred in *Re Edwards' WT* [1948] 1 All ER 821, CA: the testator left his residuary estate to be held on the trusts of a settlement already in existence when the will was made, and which was clearly identified in the will. The settlement allowed the testator to substitute new trusts by memorandum (which he later did). It was held that the settlement as a whole was properly incorporated but not the power allowing the testator to vary dispositions by future memorandum. The Court of Appeal sensibly rejected the argument that because the settlement contained a power to vary in the future, the whole settlement was incapable of incorporation. The decision incorporated the settlement as it stood when the will was made.

The document that is incorporated may consist of an earlier invalid testamentary disposition. For example, if a testator makes a will which is not property executed, a subsequent codicil may incorporate that will: the invalid will then becomes part of the codicil. This is a potentially important application of incorporation in practice. In *Allen* v *Maddock* (1858) 11 Moo PC 427; 14 ER 757, the testatrix made a will which was invalidly attested. She later executed a codicil which commenced 'This is a Codicil to my last Will and Testament'. It was held that since the requirements of incorporation were satisfied, the codicil incorporated the invalid will. Since no other will was found the invalid will was sufficiently identified by the phrase 'last Will'. The same principle was applied in *In the Goods of Almosnino* (1859) 29 LJP 46: the testatrix made an invalid will which on her death was found placed in a sealed envelope. On the envelope were found the following words, 'I confirm the contents written in the enclosed document'. The statement was signed by the testatrix and duly attested. It was held that the words on the envelope (amounting to a codicil) incorporated the enclosed will.

4.5   THE SOLICITOR'S DUTY OF CARE

4.5.1   Introduction

Testators are strongly advised to seek professional advice in the preparation of a will, both as regards its drafting and its execution. Given the importance of the consequences of making a will, the 'do-it-yourself' testator takes huge risks. Fortunately, such testators appear to be in the minority — the vast majority of wills are made with professional advice. But even then things can go wrong.

When a solicitor prepares a will he owes a duty of care not only to the testator (the client) but also to the intended beneficiaries under the will. The testator will be able to recover for the cost of rectifying the solicitor's mistake, 'though in that case the damages would, I think, be merely for the cost of making a new and valid will, or otherwise putting matters right' (*per* Megarry VC in *Ross* v *Caunters* [1979] 3 All ER 580, at 583). If the mistake is discovered after the testator's death, his estate can recover damages; but since financial loss to the estate will probably not have resulted, the damages are likely to be only nominal.

4.5.2   Position of beneficiaries

As regards the solicitor's duty of care (in the preparation of wills) towards intended beneficiaries, it was once doubted whether such a duty was owed. However, in *Ross* v *Caunters* (above) it was held that a solicitor who was instructed to prepare a will conferring a benefit on an identified beneficiary owed a duty of care to that beneficiary to use proper care in carrying out the instructions. The testator's solicitors sent the will to him for execution but failed to warn him that if a beneficiary's spouse witnessed the will, the gift to the beneficiary would fail. On the return of the will to them, the solicitors failed to notice that it had been witnessed by the spouse of a beneficiary. The solicitors admitted negligence but denied that they owed a duty of care to the disappointed beneficiary. The court held otherwise: liability could be imposed for pure economic loss in this case on ordinary tortious principles. *Ross* v *Caunters* proved to be a seminal decision which gained broad academic and judicial approval, even though its precise scope was not clear. The principle that solicitors (or similar professional advisers) should be liable to beneficiaries is surely right and is broadly consistent with the position in continental and Commonwealth jurisdictions. For example, in *Gartside* v *Sheffield* [1983] NZ LR 37, Richardson J remarked (at p. 51) that 'drafting a will is perhaps the classic instance of the performance of tasks for clients that lawyers know will directly affect third parties'. Cooke J stated (at p. 43):

> To deny an effective remedy in a plain case would seem to imply a refusal to acknowledge the solicitor's professional role in the community. In practice the public relies on solicitors ... to prepare effective wills. It would be a failure of the legal system not to insist on some practical responsibility.

It was held in *Gartside* v *Sheffield* that a solicitor, who had accepted instructions to prepare a will, owed a duty of care to a beneficiary to act with due diligence and present the will for execution by the client within a reasonable time. A similar approach was taken by the House of Lords in *White* v *Jones* [1995] 1 All ER 691. The testator executed a will excluding his two daughters from his estate following a family row. On becoming reconciled with them he sent instructions to his solicitors to prepare a new will containing gifts of £9,000 each in their favour. The instructions were received on 17 July, but nothing was done for a month until the solicitors' managing clerk asked the firm's probate department to draw up a new will. The clerk then went on a fortnight's holiday. On his return he arranged to visit the testator on 17 September. Unfortunately the testator died on 14 September. The plaintiffs (the daughters) brought an action for negligence against the solicitors, but it was dismissed on the ground that no duty of care was owed to the plaintiffs in the circumstances of the case. The Court of Appeal unanimously reversed the decision and awarded £9,000 damages to each plaintiff. The House of Lords affirmed the Court of Appeal's decision by a 3:2 majority. Lord Goff thought that an ordinary action in tortious negligence for pure economic loss was not sustainable and that consequently *Ross* v *Caunters* was a doubtful decision. He justified his decision to find the solicitors liable as follows (at pp. 710–11):

> ... your Lordships' House should in cases such as these extend to the intended beneficiary a remedy under the *Hedley Byrne* principle by holding that the assumption of responsibility by the solicitor towards his client should be held in law to extend to the intended beneficiary who (as the solicitor can reasonably foresee) may, as a result of the solicitor's negligence, be deprived of his intended legacy in circumstances in which neither the testator nor his estate will have a remedy against the solicitor. Such liability will not of course arise in cases in which the defect in the will comes to light before the death of the testator, and the testator either leaves the will as it is or otherwise continues to exclude the previously intended beneficiary from the relevant benefit.... Let me emphasise that I can see no injustice in imposing liability upon a negligent solicitor in a case such as the present where, in the absence of a remedy in this form, neither the testator's estate nor the disappointed beneficiary will have a claim for the loss caused by his negligence.

4.6 DEPOSIT AND REGISTRATION

If a will cannot be found at the testator's death, the potential consequences are serious. It will be presumed to have been revoked. Even if the presumption is rebutted, there may be obvious difficulties in proving the will's contents. A solicitor's firm will no doubt make arrangements to ensure the safety of the wills which they hold on behalf of their clients; but sometimes wills are mislaid or destroyed by accident or some disaster. Testators of home-made wills are advised at least to keep the will in a safe place and to ensure that the whereabouts are known to some responsible persons so as to avoid time-consuming and possibly unsuccessful searching. Apart from such private methods of caring for the safety of wills, an official system of voluntary deposit is available.

4.6.1 Voluntary deposit of wills

Under s. 126 of the Supreme Court Act 1981, 'safe and convenient depositories for the custody of the wills of living persons' must be provided where a person may deposit his will on payment of a nominal fee. The deposit procedure is regulated by the Wills (Deposit for Safe Custody) Regulations 1978. A will may be deposited by the testator (or his authorised agent) at the Principal Registry of the Family Division or any district probate registry or sub-registry. Or a will may be sent for deposit (but only to the Principal Registry). The will must be deposited in a sealed envelope bearing an endorsement which must contain *inter alia* the names and addresses of the appointed executors and a statement by the testator that he has notified the executors of their appointment and of the deposit.

The voluntary deposit scheme has not been heavily used in the past. This is hardly surprising in the case of the testators of home-made wills as most will probably not have heard of the possibility of depositing a will. As regards professionally made wills, Finch *et al.* (1996) confirm that many solicitors' firms tend to store clients' wills on the firm's premises, thus increasing the likelihood of obtaining the resulting probate business in due course. However, it seems that the deposit scheme is becoming more widely used.

4.6.2   Registration of wills

In 1966 the Law Commission suggested a system of compulsory registration of wills (Law Commission PWP No. 4, 1966). The Commission was impressed by the system in force in The Netherlands under which a will is invalid unless deposited with a notary, who has a duty to inform the central registry of wills that a will has been deposited with him. The information is entered in a register open to inspection by interested parties. The Commission's suggestion was not implemented, mainly it seems because of fears that home-made wills might be invalidated. However, a system of registration of wills deposited *voluntarily* was enacted by ss. 23–25 of the Administration of Justice Act 1982. When brought into force (if ever) these provisions will replace the current arrangements under s. 126 of the Supreme Court Act 1981 (above). The new scheme is founded on the Council of Europe Convention on the Establishment of a Scheme of Registration of Wills (1972) and is aimed at facilitating the discovery of the existence of wills after testators' deaths. In outline the scheme provides for the voluntary deposit of wills with the Principal Registry of the Family Division. Once deposited the will must be registered by the Registry. Moreover, wills already deposited under s. 126 and previous statutory arrangements will be automatically registered. A testator will be able to request the Principal Registry to arrange for the registration of his will in other Contracting States.

It may be that the reader's pulse is not perceptibly quickened by encountering the rules on the deposit and registration of wills, but the subject can at least claim arguably the most exciting case name in English civil law, *Re Napoleon Bonaparte* (1853) 2 Rob Ecc 606; 163 ER 1429. Following his death in St Helena in 1821, Napoleon's will and seven codicils were proved and deposited in England in 1824. In 1853, Lord John Russell, then the Foreign Minister, applied to the court for delivery to him of the will and codicils in order to transfer them to the French Government. The request was granted.

FIVE

Revocation

The previous two chapters have considered the legal requirements for *creating* a will. In this chapter we consider the opposite — the requirements for undoing what has been created. Revocation is literally the action of 'calling back', in the sense of rescinding or annulling. It is a fundamental characteristic of wills that they are revocable wholly or partially at any time before a testator's death (see 2.1.1.3). This chapter also considers topics related to revocation: alterations (5.4), revival (5.5), and republication (5.6).

A will may be revoked by four different methods:

    (a)   by marriage;
    (b)   by another will or codicil;
    (c)   by a duly executed writing;
    (d)   by destruction.

Revocation by marriage is governed by s. 18 of the Wills Act 1837, the other methods by s. 20. It should be noted at this stage that a testamentary gift to a spouse will *fail* if the marriage subsequently ends in divorce or nullity, but strictly this is not a method of revocation. It is a form of failure of a gift and will be considered later (see 7.2.4).

5.1   REVOCATION BY MARRIAGE

Section 18(1) provides that subject to certain exceptions 'a will shall be revoked by the testator's marriage'. Revocation by marriage thus occurs automatically, irrespective of the testator's knowledge or wishes. No other change in circumstances — for example, the birth of a child, or the death of a spouse — results in automatic revocation: s. 19.

5.1.1 Justification of the rule

Why should marriage revoke a prior will? The LRC Report No. 22 considered the following reasons as justifying the rule:

(a)   Marriage represents a fundamental change in a person's life and with it he or she acquires new personal and financial responsibilities. It is, therefore, a time for starting with a clean slate.

(b)   A spouse and children should not inadvertently be deprived of the rights which they would have upon the intestacy of the other spouse and parent. In so far as people fail to make fresh wills after marriage, or at least fail to revoke a pre-marriage will, this is normally the result of inadvertence and most persons marrying would wish their spouse and children to benefit from their estate: the deceased's intentions are, therefore, more likely to be achieved by the statutory imposition of an intestacy than by preservation of his earlier will. This may, indeed, prevent hardship to the family.

(c)   The present rule is well known and accords with the intentions and expectations of the great majority of those who marry. (para. 3.2)

On the other hand, revocation disadvantages children of a prior marriage who might otherwise take under the will; and gifts to friends and charities are automatically cancelled. Moreover, it has been argued that the rule is unnecessary since, if the will fails to make reasonable provision for the spouse, an application can be made for provision under the Inheritance (Provision for Family and Dependants) Act 1975. Nevertheless, on balance the Law Reform Committee recommended retention of the rule since it was 'well known to lawyers and laymen, it has operated satisfactorily since 1837 and the social and legislative changes which have taken place since then have not created a need to amend it' (para. 3.7). It may be doubted just how 'well known' this rule is to laymen; it is clearly the duty of a solicitor to advise testators intending to marry of the effect of s. 18. The Committee considered the suggestion that the prior will should be preserved but have superimposed on it a statutory legacy in favour of the testator's spouse and, possibly, children. This idea has its attractions, but the Committee saw no clear advantage in this 'half-way house' (para. 3.4).

5.1.2 Void and voidable marriages

A void marriage does not revoke a prior will since such a marriage is regarded in law as never having subsisted (see 1.2.2.1). In *Mette* v *Mette* (1859) 1 Sw & Tr 416; 164 ER 792, the testator, a naturalised British subject, went through a ceremony of marriage in Germany with his late wife's half-sister (a relationship which was then within the prohibited degrees of marriage in English law). Although the marriage was valid according to German law, it was void in English law (which was held to be applicable on the facts). Thus the marriage did not revoke an earlier will made by the testator.

A voidable marriage, on the other hand, is regarded as a valid marriage. If it is annulled it will be regarded as having existed until the annulment (Matrimonial Causes Act 1973, s. 16). Hence voidable marriages revoke prior wills. In *Re Roberts* [1978] 3 All ER 225 CA, the testator went through a marriage ceremony with the plaintiff while suffering from senile dementia and other mental disorders. Some years earlier he had made a will in favour of the defendant. The testator died 18 months after the marriage (which had not been annulled). It was held that the marriage had revoked the will with the result that the plaintiff took on intestacy.

It may seem surprising that a will should be revoked by a marriage which lacks the true consent of one or both of the parties. This is partly the consequence of a quirk in the law of nullity whereby marriages lacking consent are deemed to be voidable rather than void. A number of proposals for changes were considered by the Law Reform Committee (see LRC Report No. 22, para. 3.23) as a result of the decision in *Re Roberts*. One suggestion was that all voidable marriages should be treated like void ones for the purpose of s. 18 of the 1837 Act, so that no voidable marriage would revoke a will. A less radical suggestion was that marriages voidable for lack of consent should not revoke prior wills. The Committee felt that such changes could create as many problems as they would solve, and preferred the following suggestion (which has not been enacted):

> We are attracted by the proposal that where the deceased had entered into marriage while incapable through mental disorder of managing and administering his property and affairs, the court should have a discretion to make financial provision for any person who can show firstly that he would have benefited under a will which was revoked by such marriage and secondly that he was a person for whom the deceased might have been expected to provide by will if he had not been mentally disordered (para. 3.2.5).

5.1.3   Exceptions

There are two exceptions to the rule that marriage revokes prior wills, the position differing according to whether the will was made after 1982.

5.1.3.1   Expectation of marriage
Section 18(3) of the Wills Act 1837 provides:

> Where it appears from a will that at the time it was made the testator was expecting to be married to a particular person and that he intended that the will should not be revoked by the marriage, the will shall not be revoked by his marriage to that person.

This provision, inserted into the Wills Act by the Administration of Justice Act 1982, applies to all wills made after 1982. As yet there appear to be no reported cases on the interpretation of s. 18(3), but pre-1982 Act cases are relevant as the previous provision (requiring 'contemplation' of marriage) was similar. Section 18(3) has several constituents:

(a)   'Where it appears from a will': s. 18(3) is satisfied only if the testator's expectation of marriage and intention not to revoke appear in the will that he made. Thus his mental reservations on the subject are irrelevant: only the words in the will can demonstrate the expectation and the relevant intention. However, extrinsic evidence will be admissible to explain the testator's intention as expressed in the will, but not to supply an intention not indicated therein.

(b)   'At the time it was made': the testator must have had the relevant expectation and intention at the time when the will was made. 'Made' presumably refers to the moment when the will's execution was completed.

(c)   'Expecting to be married': it is not clear what 'expecting' means. An obvious difficulty is whether the word connotes some element of likelihood or probability. Suppose that Arthur fantasises about Mabel, a woman whom he has met briefly. He makes a will which clearly expresses that he is expecting to marry Mabel. Arthur's expectation may be rather far-fetched; indeed, Mabel may be blissfully unaware of his intentions. Can Arthur really be said to have been 'expecting to be married' to her? Probably — the Act simply requires that it should appear in the will that the testator was expecting to be married. It seems that the expectations or otherwise of the other party are irrelevant.

How can the testator show *in the will* that he was expecting to be married? The safest course is to make an express statement to that effect in the will. But the expectation of marriage may also be implied from the use of such phrases as 'my fiancée' (or 'fiancé') or 'my future wife'. Consider *In the Estate of Langston* [1953] P 100, where the testator left his property to 'my fiancée Maida Edith Beck' in a will made two months before their marriage. The court held that the testator had expressed a contemplation of marriage to that lady. In *Burton* v *McGregor* [1953] NZLR 487, a different decision was reached because the judge regarded the word 'fiancée' as a mere description of an existing state of affairs. However, cases decided since 1953 have tended to follow *Re Langston* — for example, *Re Coleman* [1975] 1 All ER 675, in which Megarry J stated (at p. 680):

> When a man speaks of 'my fiancée' he is speaking of 'the woman to whom I am engaged to be married'. It seems to me that in ordinary parlance a contemplation of marriage is inherent in the very word 'fiancée'. The word 'wife' is a word which denotes an existing state of affairs. . . . I do not think that it could reasonably be said that there inheres in the word 'wife' any contemplation of a change of that state of affairs, whether by death or divorce. 'Fiancée' seems to me to be quite different, in that it not only describes an existing state of affairs but also contemplates a change in that state of affairs.

Although it is clear that describing someone as 'wife' normally denotes an existing state of affairs, there may be unusual circumstances where the word can have a different connotation. In *Pilot* v *Gainfort* [1931] P 103, the testator made a will in which he left all his property to 'Diana Featherstone Pilot my wife'. But Diana was not his wife; he was legally married to another woman, who had left him some six years earlier and whom he had been unable to trace. The testator married Diana 18 months after making the will, relying on the legal presumption of the death of his wife (seven years having elapsed since her disappearance). The court held that the will was not revoked since the incorrect description 'wife' expressed contemplation of the marriage that took place. Compare, however, *Re Gray* (1963) 107 SJ 156: the testator's will left everything to Edith, incorrectly describing her as 'my wife'. In fact the testator had married her bigamously. Years later Edith executed a will benefiting the testator. Later still the testator discovered that his legal wife was still alive, Edith learning of her existence for the first time. The wife died shortly afterwards, whereupon the testator and Edith went through another ceremony of marriage. The issue was whether this ceremony revoked their wills. Simon P held that it did: at the time when the testator made his will it was unlikely that he was intending to go through another ceremony of marriage with Edith; and her will could not possibly have expressed a contemplation of marriage since she assumed that she was already married. The decisions can be reconciled. In *Pilot* v *Gainfort* it seems that when the testator described his cohabitant as 'wife' he was definitely intending to marry her, whereas this was hardly the case in *Re Gray*.

(d) 'To a particular person': the will must show that the testator had a particular person in mind. In *Sallis* v *Jones* [1936] P 43, the testator was in something of a hurry to marry after the death of his first wife in February 1927. He made a will in June of that year, the final sentence of which declared 'that this will is made in contemplation of marriage'. There was evidence that the testator had a lady in mind, although he had not yet proposed to her when he made the will. There was no indication in the will, however, that the testator intended to marry anyone in particular. The marriage took place in November 1927. It was held that the will was revoked since the reference to marriage was expressed too generally. Need the 'particular person' be named? It is obviously desirable to do so, but there can be circumstances where s. 18(3) applies even though the intended spouse is not named, e.g., where there is a sufficiently clear description of the person.

(e)   'Intended that the will should not be revoked by the marriage': it must appear from the will not only that the testator was expecting to marry a particular person, but also that he intended that the marriage should not revoke the will. Again, the simplest and most sensible way of expressing the required intention is to make a clear statement to that effect in the will. Whether the court would be prepared to *imply* the intention is not clear.

(f)   'Will shall not be revoked by his marriage to that person': for the exception to apply the testator must have married the person whom he expected to marry (as shown in the will). Thus, if he marries someone else, the marriage will revoke the will.

Even if s. 18(3) does not apply in a particular case to save a will from revocation, a *disposition* in a will shall take effect despite the testator's subsequent marriage if it appears from the will that 'at the time it was made the testator was expecting to be married to a particular person and that he intended that a disposition in the will should not be revoked by his marriage to that person': s. 18(4). Moreover, 'any other disposition in the will shall take effect also, unless it appears from the will that the testator intended the disposition to be revoked by the marriage': s. 18(4)(b). In effect s. 18(4)(b) raises a presumption that the whole will survives marriage if *any part* of it was intended (as shown in the will) not to be revoked. Section 18(4) applies to wills made after 1982 and was introduced into the Wills Act in order to avoid the consequences of *Re Coleman* (see 5.1.3.3).

5.1.3.2 Exercise of power of appointment
Section 18(2) of the Wills Act 1837 provides:

> A disposition in a will in exercise of a power of appointment shall take effect notwithstanding the testator's subsequent marriage unless the property so appointed would in default of appointment pass to his personal representatives.

This provision applies to wills made after 1982. Its meaning appears to be somewhat obscure: in effect the provision contains an exception within an exception. The purpose of s. 18(2) is to preserve the exercise of powers of appointment in wills that are revoked by subsequent marriage unless the revocation would result in the property passing as if on the deceased's intestacy. If it does so pass, then the deceased's family will benefit; hence there is no point in saving the disposition from being revoked. In *Re Gilligan* [1950] P 32, Pilcher J explained the purpose of this provision (at p. 39):

> I think the intention of the section was that a will exercising a power of appointment should only be wholly revoked by the subsequent marriage of the testator in those cases in which the instrument creating the power provides that in default of appointment the fund shall devolve as on an intestacy....

To illustrate the operation of s. 18(2), suppose that Arthur has been given a power to appoint property by will as he chooses, but that on default of appointment the property is to pass to his future wife, if any. Arthur makes a will in which he appoints in favour of the National Trust and subsequently marries. The effect of s. 18(2) would be that his will would be totally revoked and the appointment would fail since the property *would* pass in default of appointment (caused by the revocation) as if on Arthur's intestacy. But if under the instrument creating the power of appointment the property was to pass on default to Arthur's chess club, any appointment by Arthur would be saved from revocation: there would be no point in revoking since Arthur's family could not benefit thereby.

5.1.3.3 Wills made before 1983
As issues concerning wills made before 1983 will occur with decreasing frequency the position will be dealt with briefly. There are again two exceptions to the rule that marriage revokes prior wills.

(a) *Contemplation of marriage*: under s. 177 of the Law of Property Act 1925, 'a will expressed to be made in contemplation of a marriage . . . shall not be revoked by the solemnization of the marriage contemplated'. The leading decisions on the meaning of 'contemplation of marriage' have already been discussed in relation to s. 18(3) of the Wills Act 1837. The decision in *Re Coleman* (see 5.1.3.1), however, needs further consideration. The testator made a will containing substantial gifts 'unto my fiancée Mrs Muriel Jeffrey' (a widow) and leaving the residue to close relatives. He married Muriel two months later. It was held that the will was revoked since the whole of it had not been expressed to be made in contemplation of marriage. As the residuary gifts were not trivial and did not express the required contemplation, the testator's will did not satisfy s. 177. The construction of s. 177 in *Re Coleman* was widely criticised, resulting in the changes enacted by the Administration of Justice Act 1982 (above).

(b) *Exercise of power of appointment*: the original s. 18 of the Wills Act 1837 provided in effect that appointments by will were not revoked by subsequent marriage if the property subject to the power would not pass on default of appointment to persons entitled under the pre-1926 intestacy rules. The LRC Report No. 22 recommended that the wording of s. 18 should be updated, and this was implemented in s. 18(2) for wills made after 1982 (see above). The purpose and effect of the original s. 18 and the new s. 18(2) are the same in all essentials.

5.2 REVOCATION UNDER SECTION 20 OF THE WILLS ACT 1837

Apart from revocation by marriage, a will or codicil can be revoked only by one of the three methods contained in s. 20 of the Wills Act 1837 which states (emphasis added):

> No will or codicil, or any part thereof, shall be revoked otherwise than as aforesaid, or *by another will or codicil* executed in manner hereinbefore required, or *by some writing* declaring an intention to revoke the same, and executed in the manner in which a will is hereinbefore required to be executed, or *by the burning, tearing, or otherwise destroying* the same by the testator, or by some person in his presence and by his direction, with the intention of revoking the same.

Thus the three methods of revocation under s. 20 are:

(a) revocation by another will or codicil;
(b) revocation by some writing;
(c) revocation by destruction.

Whatever method of revocation is used under s. 20, the testator must have the mental capacity to revoke. What is the degree of mental capacity required? In *Re Sabatini* (1969) 114 SJ 35, a testatrix in her nineties, suffering from mental illness, tore up her will. Baker J concluded that she had acted irrationally, not being possessed of a 'sound disposing mind, memory and understanding'. The judge thought that as a general rule a testator must have the same standard of mind and memory, and the same degree of understanding, when destroying his will as when making it. Hence the revocation was ineffective and probate was granted to a copy of the destroyed will. Although the case was concerned with revocation by destruction, the rule clearly applies to the other methods under s. 20 since they require the creation of a will, codicil or some writing executed like a will. It is perhaps surprising that a testator must have the same capacity when destroying a will as is required under the rule in *Banks* v *Goodfellow* (see 3.1.2.1) to make one. Does not the creative act require greater mental competence than the destructive one? On the other hand, to allow a lower degree of mental competence for destroying a will than for revocation by the other methods under s. 20 could cause confusion as there would then be differing standards of capacity for revoking wills.

5.2.1   Revocation 'by another will or codicil'

5.2.1.1   Express revocation
A testator may revoke a prior will or codicil, either wholly or partially, by express words to that effect in a later will or codicil. A professionally drawn will normally contains an express revocation clause, even if there are no prior wills. Often the revocation clause is placed at the beginning of the will, although it may be placed anywhere as long as it is part of the will. No set form of words is necessary but clauses such as 'I hereby revoke all wills, codicils and testamentary dispositions previously made by me' are common. It is insufficient — for the purposes of *express* revocation — for the testator to state that the will is his 'last' or 'only' will. Thus the commonly used phrase, 'This is my last will and testament', does not have the effect of expressly revoking prior wills: *Cutto* v *Gilbert* (1854) 9 Moo PC 131; 14 ER 247.

The operation and scope of a revocation clause will depend on its construction. An unambiguous general revocation clause will normally revoke all prior testamentary dispositions since the testator will be presumed to have knowledge and approval of the clause. In *Lowthorpe-Lutwidge* v *Lowthorpe-Lutwidge* [1935] P 151, the issue was whether the testator had revoked an earlier exercise of a testamentary power of appointment by a later will containing a revocation clause stating 'I revoke all former wills this being my last will and testament'. The significant words in this clause were the opening ones: had the testator simply stated 'This is my last will and testament' it would have been insufficient for an express revocation. Langton, J held that the earlier dispositions were revoked because the burden of proving that the testator had not intended to revoke them had not been discharged:

> It is a heavy burden upon a plaintiff who comes into this Court to say: 'I agree that the testator was in every way fit to make a will, I agree that the will which he has made is perfectly clear and unambiguous in its terms, I agree that it contains a revocatory clause in simple words: nevertheless I say that he did not really intend to revoke the earlier bequests in earlier wills'. (p. 156)

A similar decision was reached in *Sotheran v Denning* (1882) 20 Ch D 99, CA: the testatrix executed a will exercising a power of appointment over realty. Later she made another will revoking all former wills, and later still a third will bequeathing only her personalty, but again revoking all former wills. She had no realty other than that subject to the power of appointment. It was held that the first will was revoked by the second, and the second by the third. Hence the realty passed as on default of appointment.

Nevertheless, a revocation clause will not be operative if a contrary intention can be established from the will or surrounding circumstances. Consider *In the Estate of Wayland* [1951] 2 All ER 1041, where the issue was whether two wills made in Brussels, and disposing only of the testator's Belgian property, were revoked by a later will made in England which contained a revocation clause. The clause was closely followed by the declaration 'this will is intended to deal only with my estate in England'. The court held that the revocation clause was intended to revoke former wills dealing with English property but not the Belgian wills. In *Gladstone v Tempest* (1840) 2 Curt 650; 163 ER 538, Jenner J stated (at p. 540):

> ... it has been over and over again laid down that probate of a paper may be granted of a date prior to a will with a revocatory clause, provided the Court is satisfied that it was not the deceased's intention to revoke that particular legacy or benefit.

It follows that if a revocation clause was included by mistake, and the testator did not know and approve of it, the clause will be inoperative, as occurred in *Re Phelan* [1971] 3 WLR 888 (see 3.2.6.3). However, where the testator did know and approve of the clause, it is operative even though the testator was mistaken as to its legal effect: *Collins v Elstone* [1893] P 1 (see 3.2.6.2). This case is difficult to justify since the surrounding circumstances indicated that the testatrix did not wish the revocation clause to have the effect that it was held to have. Thus the decision seems inconsistent with the principle that the testator's intention should be conclusive, as expressed in *Gladstone v Tempest* (above) and other cases. Nor will a revocation clause be operative (i) if it was contained in a conditional will that failed to take effect, or (ii) where the doctrine of conditional revocation applies (see 5.3).

5.2.1.2 Implied revocation

Even if a will does not expressly revoke prior dispositions, it will impliedly do so to the extent of any inconsistency: the later in time prevails. Sometimes the whole will may be impliedly revoked by a later one — for example, where they are totally inconsistent, or where the later one covers the same ground or is meant as a substitute for the earlier. The documents will be read together to ascertain which provisions the testator intended to apply on his death. In *Lemage v Goodban* (1865) 1 P & D 57, Wilde J stated (at pp. 62–3):

> The will of a man is the aggregate of his testamentary intentions, so far as they are manifested in writing, duly executed according to the statute....

And so this court has been in the habit of admitting to probate, such, and as many papers (all properly executed), as are necessary to effect the testator's full wishes, and of solving the question of revocation, by considering not what papers have been apparently superseded by the act of executing others, but what dispositions it can be collected from the language of all the papers that the testator designed to revoke or to retain.

Dempsey v *Lawson* (1877) 2 PD 98, illustrates that implied revocation can result in the total failure of an earlier will. The testatrix made a will in 1858 and another one in 1860, each containing *inter alia* a number of bequests to Roman Catholic charities. However, the later will — which did not contain a revocation clause — showed significant differences: a major legatee under the 1858 will was omitted and certain other establishments were given considerably smaller and different types of bequest. It was held that the 1858 will was wholly revoked since the intention of the testatrix, as shown by the whole scheme of the 1860 will, was that the latter should be a substitution for the 1858 will. In *Re Hawksley's Settlement* [1934] Ch 384, the testatrix made a will in 1922 with professional advice, then a home-made will in 1927 which did not contain a revocation clause but which described itself as her 'last will and testament' and referred to the earlier will as the 'cancelled will'. The provisions of the later will were wholly inconsistent with the earlier will. The court held that the phrases 'last will' and 'cancelled will' did not in themselves constitute express revocation, but that the earlier will was nevertheless totally ineffective because it was impliedly revoked by the 1927 will.

A remarkable example of implied revocation occurred in *Thorn* v *Dickens* [1906] WN 54. The testator made a will and a codicil, the substantial effect of which was to leave his widow a life interest, with remainder to his children. Some years later he executed a will of startling brevity, one which those with a short concentration span will appreciate. It consisted of three words, 'All for mother'. Barnes J described the document as 'probably the shortest will ever known' (indeed, it is scarcely possible for a will to be shorter). It was proved that 'mother' meant the widow. It appears from the brief report that the earlier documents were wholly revoked by the later will.

The rule that the later testamentary instrument impliedly revokes the earlier to the extent of any inconsistency applies with less force where a will is followed by a codicil. Since codicils are essentially supplementary wills, their existence dependent on an earlier will, they are construed restrictively so as to interfere with wills as little as possible. In *Doe d Hearle* v *Hicks* (1832) 1 Cl & Fin 20; 6 ER 823, the testator devised his copyhold house to his wife for life, but later made a codicil which appeared to revoke earlier dispositions and devised all his freehold, copyhold and personal estate to his daughter. The court held that the codicil was insufficiently specific to revoke the clear gift of the house to the wife. Tindal LCJ stated (at p. 825):

If such devise in the will is clear, it is incumbent on those who contend it is not to take effect by reason of a revocation in the codicil to show that the intention to revoke is equally clear and free from doubt as the original intention to devise.

The rule in *Hearle* v *Hicks* was applied in *Re Stoodley* [1915] 2 Ch 295: the testator made a will dividing the residue of his estate between the vicar of Illminster (for church extensions) and the Society for Promoting Christian Knowledge. Two years later he made a codicil in which he referred to his will and stated 'The residue of my estate not bequeathed by the above will I give and bequeath to Mabel Abbie Locock'. Mabel claimed that the codicil should be interpreted as wholly revoking the gift of residue in the will, but the court held that what passed under the codicil was such portion (if any) of the residue as might ultimately turn out not to have been effectually disposed of by the will. The reason was that the words of gift in the codicil were not as clear and unambiguous as those in the will.

5.2.1.3   Proof of revocation

Revocation by another will or codicil, whether express or implied, occurs when that will or codicil is executed. Thus there must be proof of the contents of the later instrument — that it expressly or impliedly revoked earlier dispositions — and that it was validly executed. What if the revoking instrument is itself later revoked? That would not affect the position: the original will remains revoked. Consider *In the Goods of Hodgkinson* [1893] P 339, CA: the testator gave all his property to his friend Jane. Later he made another will (which did not contain a revocation clause) devising his realty to his sister Emma, but he subsequently revoked that will. The issue was whether Jane was entitled to the whole of the estate or only to personalty. It was held that the first will was partially revoked by the second — as to the gift of realty — and that the revocation of the second will did not revive the revoked part.

Provided that there is proof of the content and execution of the revoking instrument, the revocation will occur even though the instrument is lost or has been destroyed. In *Wood* v *Wood* (1867) 1 P & D 309, the testator made two wills, but the later one could not be found after his death. The court accepted evidence (from the managing clerk of the deceased's attorney) that the later will had been validly executed and that it contained a revocation clause. An intestacy was pronounced for by the court: the earlier will had been revoked by the missing will which itself was presumed to have been revoked by destruction. In *Re Howard* [1944] P 39, the testator made a will in 1933 leaving his estate to his son. In 1940 he executed two further wills on the same day, but there was no evidence as to the order of execution. One of the wills left his estate to his son, the other will left the estate to the testator's wife. Each will contained a revocation clause. The family was wiped out by enemy action a few months later. One of the issues in the case was whether the 1933 will was revoked by the later wills. The court held that although the later wills were irreconcilable, and therefore not admissible to probate, they were effective to revoke the 1933 will.

5.2.2   Revocation 'by some writing'

Under s. 20 of the Wills Act 1837, a will or codicil can be revoked 'by some writing declaring an intention to revoke the same' and executed in the manner required for a will. This is a useful provision in cases where the testator has not revoked by another will or codicil but has executed a document showing an intention to revoke. A total or partial revocation can be effected in this way. Presumably, implied revocation is not possible under this method since the writing must *declare* an intention to revoke — the words of s. 20 point to express revocation. In the remarkable case of *Ford* v *De Pontes* (1861) 30 Beav 572; 54 ER 1012, 'an attachment' occurred between a young Englishwoman and a Frenchman when she visited France. On returning to England she was forced to break off the attachment and entered an unhappy marriage with a wealthy English landowner. Some 30 years later she resumed her friendship with her old flame (by now a general in the French army). She devised her estate to him charged with the payment of some pecuniary legacies. Later she conveyed the estate to him by deed free of the charges. The issue arose whether the deed revoked the will. It was held that the deed did not have a revocatory effect since it did not declare an intention to revoke the will. The case was complicated by the issue whether the deed was invalid for immoral consideration — the testatrix, while still married, was proposing marriage or cohabitation with the general. Those who like a good yarn with a romantic bent will find this case intriguing.

The most likely form of 'writing' under s. 20 is a letter, as in *In the Goods of Durance* (1872) 2 P & D 406. The testator made a will before emigrating to Canada. Soon after becoming resident in Toronto he sent two letters (both executed like wills) to Joe, his brother, in England. One letter authorised the testator's solicitor to deliver the will to Joe; the other instructed Joe to burn the will 'as soon as you receive it without reading it'. Lord Penzance held that the will was revoked by the letter since it was a duly executed writing declaring an intention to revoke the will. *In Re Spracklan's Estate* [1938] 2 All ER 345, CA, the testatrix dictated a letter (while she was seriously ill) which was then duly executed. It was addressed to her bank manager and requested him to destroy her will which she had deposited at the bank. The court held that the will was revoked by the letter.

At what moment does the letter revoke the will? Suppose that Arthur writes a duly executed letter to his solicitor requesting him to destroy Arthur's will but forgets to post the letter. Or suppose that the letter is posted, but is then lost in the post; or that the solicitor receives it but fails to act on it. In all these scenarios the answer is the same: the will is revoked as soon as 'some writing' that satisfies s. 20 comes into existence, i.e. when the letter is duly executed.

5.2.3 Revocation by destruction

Under s. 20 of the Wills Act 1837, a will or codicil can be revoked 'by the burning, tearing, or otherwise destroying the same by the testator, or by some person in his presence and by his direction, with the intention of revoking the same'. It is clear from s. 20 that there are two essentials in revocation by destruction. There must be (i) an act of destruction and (ii) the intention to revoke, as emphasised by James LJ in *Cheese* v *Lovejoy* (1877) 2 PD 251, CA (at p. 253):

All the destroying in the world without intention will not revoke a will, nor all the intention in the world without destroying; there must be the two.

As regards the act of destruction, there are two issues to be considered: (i) what form of destruction is required; and (ii) by whom must the act be done?

5.2.3.1 Destruction: the act?

There must be an act which amounts to a 'burning, tearing, or otherwise destroying' of the will or codicil. These words point to the need for an actual act of destruction. For example, in *Doe d Reed* v *Harris* (1837) 6 A & E 209; 112 ER 79, the testator threw his will (contained in an envelope) on a fire intending to revoke it. His housekeeper snatched it from the fire. It seems that only a corner of the envelope was burnt, not the will itself. The court held that the will had not been revoked. Nor will a 'symbolic' act such as a cancellation suffice. In *Stephens* v *Taprell* (1840) 2 Curt 458; 163 ER 473, the name of the testator was crossed out and the body of the will, the attestation clause and names of the witnesses were run through with a pen. In holding that the will had not been revoked, Jenner J stated (at p. 476):

> ... it could not have been the intention of the Legislature that the striking the will through with a pen should be a mode of revocation. 'Cancellation' and 'revocation' are different terms, though sometimes confounded, cancellation being an equivocal act ... if they did consider cancellation to be a mode of revocation, they would have taken care to render their mentioning clear.

In *Cheese* v *Lovejoy* (above), a testator drew a pen through various parts of his will — but left the words legible — and wrote 'All these are revoked' on the back. The will was thrown among a heap of papers on the sitting-room floor. A housemaid retrieved the will and put it on the kitchen table. It remained in the kitchen for some years but the testator never asked for it. It was held that the will had not been revoked since the testator's acts had not actually 'injured' the will; they were at most an attempt at a symbolic destruction. Criticisms of the decision were considered by the LRC Report No. 22, but no change was recommended, partly because such cases were thought to be rare.

The requirement of an actual act of destruction does not necessitate that the whole will should be destroyed; it is sufficient if 'the essence of the instrument' is destroyed: *Hobbs* v *Knight* (1838) 1 Curt 768; 163 ER 267, at 270. The signature of the testator or of a witness is certainly an essential part of the will. In *Hobbs* v *Knight* the testator cut off his signature at the end of the will but the rest was left intact. It was held that this amounted to a revocation of the will. In *Re Adams* [1990] 2 All ER 97, the testatrix telephoned her solicitor, requesting him to destroy her will. Wisely he sent the will to her and advised her to destroy it herself (implementing her instructions would not have revoked the will: see 5.2.3.2). The will was found after her death with all the signatures very heavily scored out by a ballpoint pen so that they were not apparent to the eye. This was held to amount to a total revocation of the will, the judge rightly declining to distinguish the case from those where signatures are actually removed, e.g., by being cut off.

But what if the testator destroys the signatures of the witnesses but not his own? *Prima facie* this should make no difference: if either or both of the witnesses' signatures are destroyed, this should suffice to revoke the whole will since an essential part of it will be missing. However, the question arises — why would a testator destroy the signatures of the witnesses but not his own if he wished to revoke his will? Such strange conduct might make the court doubt whether the testator intended to revoke. Consider, for example, *In the Goods of Wheeler* (1879) 49 LJ P 29: the testator's will was found with the portion containing the second witness's signature cut off or torn from the document. The excised part was found in a mutilated but legible condition close to the will in the testator's desk (where he kept important papers). Hannen P held that the will had not been revoked since it was 'difficult to conceive the idea of a testator destroying a will by merely tearing off the name of one of the witnesses' (p. 30). Although the judge thought that tearing off the signature of *both* witnesses would definitely revoke a will, it is arguable that similar doubts arise as to the testator's true intentions if he does not destroy his own signature.

What if the testator fails to complete what he intended to do by way of destruction? In *Doe d Perkes* v *Perkes* (1820) 3 B & A 489; 106 ER 740, the testator began to tear his will 'in a fit of passion' during a quarrel with one of the beneficiaries. A by stander seized his arms and prevented him from further tearing the will, while the beneficiary apologised for having upset the testator. The latter calmed down and folded the will (now in four pieces) saying 'It is a good job it is no worse'. The will was found in four pieces after the testator's death. It was held that the will had not been revoked as the testator had not completed the intended act of destruction. Best J stated (at p. 742):

> The real question in these cases is, whether the act be complete. If the testator here, after tearing it twice through, had thrown the fragments on the ground, it might have been properly considered, that he intended to go no further, and that the cancellation was complete; but here there is evidence that he intended to go further, and that he was only stopped from proceeding by an appeal made to his compassion by the person who was one of the objects of his bounty.

In *Elms* v *Elms* (1858) 1 Sw & Tr 155; 164 ER 672, the testator intended to make a new will exclusively benefiting the principal beneficiary under his existing will. After drinking 'almost a pint of brandy' he started to tear the existing will, but was stopped by a friend from tearing it in two. He never made another will, and after his death the partly torn will was found among his papers. The court accepted that he had intended to revoke the will but that he had failed to do so because he had not completed the intended act of destruction. The issue was also raised whether a will had to be torn into at least two pieces to satisfy s. 20. It was held that it was not necessary to tear the will into more pieces than it originally consisted of as long as the testator completed what he intended to do. *Dicta* in the case imply that if the testator intended to make only a small tear, and succeeded in doing so, that would be sufficient to revoke. But that appears to ignore that there must be an actual tearing of sufficient degree to satisfy s. 20.

The rule that there is insufficient destruction unless the testator completed what he intended to do is clearly problematic. For example, how is the intention of the testator in this respect to be ascertained? Should it not matter whether the testator's failure to complete the act of destruction was voluntary or involuntary? And suppose that Arthur, intending to revoke his will by burning it to ashes, sets light to the will but in the process sets light to himself and dies. His will survives half-burnt. Is a court really going to uphold the will on the ground that the testator did not complete what he intended?

A will need not be totally revoked by destruction: partial revocation can occur when a non-essential part of the will has been destroyed. For example, in *In the Estate of Nunn* [1936] 1 All ER 555, the testatrix, an 'expert needlewoman', appears to have cut out a section from the middle of her will and then stitched the two halves together. The court held that only the excised part had been revoked. *In the Goods of Woodward* (1871) 2 P & D 206 was similar: the testator's will consisted of seven sheets of paper, but the first seven or eight lines had been partly cut and torn off. It was held that the mere mutilation of the opening lines did not lead to an inference of intent to revoke the whole will. Thus probate was granted without the mutilated section. But partial revocation can occur only if the will is intelligible and can operate without the destroyed part. In *Leonard* v *Leonard* [1902] P 243, the testator amended his will on a number of occasions. It consisted of five sheets, but on his death it was found that two of the original sheets had been destroyed and replaced by two other sheets (which lacked testamentary effect). The remaining three sheets were unintelligible and unworkable without the destroyed sheets. It was held that the whole will failed. In *Re Everest* [1975] 1 All ER 672, the testator's will contained a gift of personalty to his widow and directed that all his realty and the residue of his personalty should be held by his bank on certain trusts. It was not possible to ascertain the objects of these trusts since part of the will had been cut off. The court granted probate to the will as it stood since there was sufficient remaining of the will to show that the testator intended that what remained should be effective.

It should be noted that the act of destruction need not be witnessed. Destruction is the only method of revocation which can be effected without a witness. It may be queried whether the revocation of a will — with such potentially important consequences — should be allowed by an unwitnessed act. However, the LRC Report No. 22 found little support for the idea of requiring the act of destruction to be witnessed:

> ... it would frequently frustrate the testator's intentions and would create complications in practice. For example, it would be necessary to record the witnessed destruction of the will and to prove the contents of a will which has been destroyed without witnesses would often be difficult, if not impossible. (para. 3.43)

5.2.3.2 Destruction: by whom?
Section 20 requires the destruction to have been effected by the testator or 'some person in his presence and by his direction'. Clearly, then, if Arthur

directs his dog to chew up his will, s. 20 is not satisfied; but what if he directs his five-year-old child to destroy the will? The statute does not define what is meant by 'some person', but presumably the person must be at least sufficiently mentally competent to be capable of being *directed*. Moreover, since a 'person' is required to effect the act of destruction it follows that s. 20 is not satisfied where a will is destroyed by an accidental fire: *Re Booth* [1926] P 118.

It would seem that 'presence' and 'direction' have the same meaning as in the formalities for making a will under s. 9 of the Wills Act 1837 (see 4.2.3). Thus 'presence' requires the testator to be mentally and physically present when the destruction occurs. Physical presence necessitates that there be a line of sight between the testator and the act of destruction. Consider *In the Goods of Dadds* (1857) Deane 290; 164 ER 579: the testatrix asked for a codicil to her will to be burnt and destroyed. She directed that it should be taken to a room (on the floor below the bedroom occupied by her) where there was a fire. Her wishes were followed and the codicil was wholly destroyed. It was held that the codicil had not been revoked since it had not been destroyed in her presence. Similarly, in *In the Estate of Kremer* (1965) 110 SJ 18, a will was held not to be revoked when it was burned by a solicitor in his office after the testatrix had telephoned him with a request to destroy it. The solicitor was adjudged to have made 'a considerable professional error'.

Not only must the will be destroyed by some person in the testator's presence, but also 'by his direction'. The need for 'direction' clearly suggests some positive act on the part of the testator. Thus if Arthur stands passively by watching someone destroying his will without his authorisation, this cannot be 'direction'. And it makes no difference if Arthur subsequently ratifies or acquiesces in the act. In *Gill* v *Gill* [1909] P 157, the testator's wife tore up his will in a fit of temper after he had irritated her while he was drunk. As Bargrave Deane J put it — in one of the more colourful judicial comments to be found in the reports — 'It was about as silly a thing to do as could possibly be imagined; but she was at the time beside herself with anger, just as he was beside himself with drink' (p. 161). It was held that the will had not been revoked since the tearing of the will had not been authorised (it was doubtful, in any case, whether the testator was capable of authorising anything, given his state). The judge stated that no amount of authority afterwards could ratify an act done without authority at the time, but this was strictly *obiter* since there was no evidence of subsequent ratification. On the contrary, the testator treated the tearing up of the will as a joke and as of no effect in law.

5.2.3.3 Intention to revoke (*animus revocandi*)

The testator must have the intention to revoke the will. The necessary degree of mental capacity is the same as is required to make a will: *Re Sabatini* (see 5.2). Thus in *Brunt* v *Brunt* (1873) 3 P & D 37, a will was held not to be revoked where it was torn to pieces by a testator who was 'very drunk' and suffering from an attack of *delirium tremens*. An important distinction must be drawn between the intention to revoke and the intention to destroy. It does not follow that merely because the testator intended to destroy his will he therefore intended to revoke it. Suppose that Arthur intentionally destroys his will believing that the will is invalid — has he destroyed it with the intention of revoking it? Hardly. In *Giles* v *Warren* (1872) 2 P & D 401, the testator formed the mistaken impression that his will was invalid during a conversation with an acquaintance. Consequently he tore the will to pieces. It was held that the will was not thereby revoked, Lord Penzance stating (at pp. 402–3):

> There can be no intention to revoke a will, if a person destroys the paper under the idea, whether right or wrong, that it is not a valid will. Revocation is a term applicable to the case of a person cancelling or destroying a document which he had before legally made. He does not revoke it if he does not treat it as being valid at the time when he sets about to destroy it.

Similarly, *animus revocandi* is absent where a testator destroys the will thinking that it has already been revoked. In *Scott* v *Scott* (1859) 1 Sw & Tr 258; 164 ER 719, the testator, having executed a new will, burnt his previous will and codicil thinking that they had been revoked by the new will. However, it transpired that the new will was not duly executed. Probate was granted to a copy of the original will as the testator had lacked the intention to revoke. The testator must have the intention to revoke *when* the will is destroyed: s. 20 makes it clear that the concurrence of act and intention is necessary. In *Gill* v *Gill* (above) there was clearly no such concurrence: the husband lacked the necessary intent when the wife tore up the will. It follows that if the testator forms the necessary intention after the destruction, the will is not revoked; similarly where he forms the intention before the destruction but the intention ceases by the time the act is done.

If a testator revokes a will, does he thereby revoke a codicil to that will? Since a codicil is a supplementary will it could be argued that the destruction of the 'parent' will shows an intention to revoke the codicil, and that it would be thereby revoked automatically. But that would be to ignore the statute, as was emphasised in *In the Goods of Savage* (1870) 2 P & D 78 by Lord Penzance, who stated that a codicil could not be revoked simply by the destruction of the will because that is not a form of revocation recognised by s. 20:

> ... when a testator has once executed a testamentary paper, that paper will remain in force unless revoked in the particular manner named in the statute. (p. 80)

5.2.3.4 Presumptions

There are two important presumptions concerning revocation by destruction:

(a) *Mutilated will*: if a will or codicil is found on the testator's death in a mutilated condition, and was known to have been in his possession prior to his death, the presumption arises that the testator mutilated it with the intention of wholly or partially revoking it: *In the Goods of Lewis* (1858) 1 Sw & Tr 31; 164 ER 615. In that case the testator executed a will shortly before his death. When his body was being laid out following his death the will was discovered under the bed on which he was lying. His signature and those of the attesting witnesses were torn off and could not be found. An intestacy was declared since the will was presumed to have been revoked.

The presumption may be rebutted by appropriate evidence — for example, where it can be shown that the will was mutilated by someone acting without the testator's authority. Consider, however, *Bell* v *Fothergill* (1870) 2 P D 148, where a will was found after the testator's death in his drawer where he had kept important papers. The testator's signature had been cut out with scissors, but was then restored with gum in its original position. It was held that the fact of the gumming — even assuming that it had been done by the testator — was insufficient to rebut the presumption of revocation. All that it showed was that the testator had probably changed his mind and wanted to revive the will (having revoked it). Moreover, alleged declarations by the testator after the date of the will of an intention to benefit his wife were insufficient to rebut the presumption since they were 'general' and did not refer to the will as in existence.

(b)   *Lost will*: if a will or codicil cannot be found on the testator's death, but was last known to have been in his possession, it will be presumed to have been destroyed by the testator with *animus revocandi*: *Sugden* v *Lord St Leonards* (1876) 1 PD 154, CA. The presumption may be rebutted by evidence to the contrary. In *Re Webb* [1964] 2 All ER 91, there was evidence that the will had been destroyed in an air-raid which had severely damaged the solicitor's office where it was kept. Moreover, references by the testatrix to a draft of the will as 'her will' shortly before her death helped to rebut the presumption. If a will is missing at the testator's death, and it is shown that he became insane after executing it (and remained so until his death), the presumption will not apply. Thus the burden will be on the party alleging revocation to show that the will was destroyed whilst the testator was of sound mind: *Sprigge* v *Sprigge* (1868) 1 P & D 608.

If the will is missing but the presumption of revocation is rebutted, how are the contents to be proved? The best form of proof will be a draft or copy of the will, as in *Re Webb* (above) where one of the witnesses remembered signing the completed draft in the presence of 'a little man in a Homburg hat' (taken to refer to the testator's solicitor). However, the court may accept oral evidence of the contents, even from alleged beneficiaries. This may seem highly dubious but can be justified as a last resort to save a will. In *Sugden* v *Lord St Leonards* (above), the testator, a former Lord Chancellor, made a complex will and eight codicils in the last few years of his life. The will could not be found on his death but was proved largely on the oral testimony of his daughter who had acted as his amanuensis, had read the will several times and had often been instructed by her father in the niceties of the law. Although she was a principal beneficiary under the will (or so she testified), the court accepted her evidence as she was an exceptionally competent and unimpeachable witness.

5.3   CONDITIONAL REVOCATION

Usually the intention of the testator to revoke his will is absolute, in which case
revocation takes effect immediately. But if the intention is conditional,
revocation does not occur until the condition is satisfied. This simple rule once
had a cumbersome and confusing name — 'the doctrine of dependent relative
revocation'. The LRC Report No. 22 recommended that the name 'conditional revocation' should be used.

5.3.1   Evolution of the rule

The rule appears to have first been formulated in the late seventeenth century
as a means of preventing intestacy. As a result of the Statute of Frauds 1677
prescribing strict formalities for the making of wills, there was a danger that
where a testator revoked a will in order to make another, the subsequent will
might fail for invalid execution, an intestacy thus resulting. To save the earlier
will — which often contained provisions similar to the later one — the courts
began to rule that the revocation had been conditional on the efficacy of the
later. The most important of the early cases was *Onions* v *Tyrer* (1716) 1 P Wms
343; 24 ER 418, where a testator made a will devising land on certain trusts.
He later executed a fresh will containing the same provisions (apart from
altering the trustees) and destroyed the earlier will. As the later will was
invalidly executed the court held that the first will had only been revoked by
'accident' and thus was still operative. The rule came to be formulated in
subsequent cases as turning on whether there was a conditional intent to
revoke.

The adoption of this approach by the courts was quite understandable in the
circumstances then prevailing. But the rule was based on something of a fiction
because it deemed the testator to have had an intention to revoke conditionally
when, in reality, he had meant to revoke absolutely. The indiscriminate
application of the rule could lead to abuse in that a result could easily be
achieved which ran counter to the testator's intentions. A classic example of
this was *In the Goods of Middleton* (1864) 3 Sw & Tr 583; 164 ER 1402, where
a testatrix made a will leaving some personalty to her niece and various
bequests to other beneficiaries. Later she executed a similar will but excluded
the niece from benefiting; and later still she cut out the names of the attesting
witnesses from the earlier will. However, the later will had been invalidly
executed. The court pronounced for the earlier will since the testatrix had 'only
intended to revoke it on the assumption that the later will had been duly
executed'. The niece thus benefited even though clearly not intended to do so
by the testatrix. It seems perverse that in a case turning on the alleged intentions
of the testatrix, the decision in fact thwarted those intentions in a material
respect. The undesirability of the approach exemplified by *In the Goods of
Middleton* has since been recognised. The LRC Report No. 22 stated:

> The chief criticism of the rule is that the preservation of a prior will may be
> directly contrary to the testator's wishes. The testator might have intended

the revocation of his earlier will to survive in any event and preferred his property to pass as on an intestacy on failure of the later will. It was suggested that the rule should be abolished in favour of a discretion enabling the Court to validate a later will in such a case. However, most witnesses [i.e. those giving evidence to the Committee] welcomed the approach in *Re Jones* [1976] Ch 200, which makes it clear that a revocation will not be held to be conditional unless there is evidence that such was the testator's intention. We think that the rule, which is a flexible and useful compromise between a complete discretionary power and rigid rules, should be retained. In our view, *Re Jones* not only limits its scope but also provides clear guidance as to its application. (para. 3.47)

Re Jones concerned a testatrix who had 11 nephews and nieces. She made a will by which she left her smallholding to two of her nieces. Shortly before her death a few years later, she informed her bank manager that she had decided to leave the smallholding to other beneficiaries. The testatrix went to her solicitor's office intending to make a will, but her solicitor was unable to take her instructions on that day. She died a few days later not having made a new will. Her original will was found in a mutilated condition, all the relevant signatures having been cut out. At first instance it was held that the will had not been revoked since the revocation had been conditional on the making of a new will. However, the Court of Appeal reversed the decision on the ground that the correct inference from the facts was that the testatrix had intended to revoke her will absolutely.

There may be circumstances where the testator had both a conditional *and* an absolute intention to revoke. Consider *Re Finnemore* [1992] 1 All ER 800: the testator made a will leaving his house, contents thereof and three quarters of the residue to the first defendant, the remaining quarter being left to the second defendant. Two years later the testator made a second will in similar terms, except that the gift of the quarter of the residue was made to two charities, the second defendant receiving only a gift of £500. Three weeks later the testator made a third will, identical with the second apart from increasing the number of charities to three. The second and third wills contained a revocation clause revoking all prior wills. The gift to the first defendant in the second and third wills was void under s. 15 of the Wills Act 1837 since they had been witnessed by her husband (see 7.2.2). It was argued on her behalf that the testator had intended to revoke the first will only on condition that the gift to the first defendant took effect: there was a clear and consistent intention throughout the wills to benefit her. The problem for the court was that if the first will was held not to have been revoked, the second defendant would take a quarter of the residue — a result clearly contrary to the testator's wishes. The court took the imaginative step of construing the revocation clause in the last will as intending an absolute revocation as far as the second defendant was concerned, but a conditional revocation as regards the gifts to the first defendant. Hence the gift in the original will to the first defendant took effect, but the gift to the second defendant was revoked.

The operation of the conditional revocation rule is in theory potentially wide-ranging. The rule will be applied whenever the testator's intention to revoke can be said to have been truly conditional, provided the condition was not satisfied. In practice the cases have tended to fall into two main groups — the 'fresh will' cases, and those where the testator acted under a mistaken belief unrelated to making a fresh will.

5.3.2   Fresh will cases

The origins of the rule on conditional revocation are to be found in cases where the testator revoked a prior will intending to replace it with another will, such as *Onions* v *Tyrer* (above). And it is predominantly in this type of case that the conditional revocation rule has been applied. 'Fresh will' cases may themselves be grouped (for the purposes of exposition) according to the reason why the intended will failed to be operative.

5.3.2.1   Failure to create another will
This may occur, for example, where the testator dies before the fresh will is executed, as occurred in *Re Jones* (above). In *Dixon* v *Treasury Solicitor* [1905] P 42, the testator cut out his signature from his will thinking that this was necessary in order to make another will. This act earned a somewhat harsh comment from Gorell Barnes J: 'It was just one of those stupid acts without which this Court might almost cease to exist' (p. 45). The testator then gave instructions to his solicitor to draft a new will, but died without executing it. The revoked will was admitted to probate since the jury found that the will had been destroyed on condition that a new one was executed.

A similar result occurs where the testator's attempt to make a fresh will results in a document which is not a will. In *Dancer* v *Crabb* (1873) 3 P & D 98, the testatrix decided to exclude a beneficiary from her will 'as she wished to get rid of him'. She dictated alterations to a friend who wrote them down in a memorandum. The testatrix then tore off and burnt the altered part of the will. The memorandum was locked away with the rest of the will, the testatrix mistakenly believing that these papers constituted a new will. It was held that the revocation was dependent on the papers amounting to a new will. As they did not, probate was granted of the original will.

5.3.2.2   Invalid execution
Where the testator revokes a will conditionally on making another, and the new will is invalidly executed, the revocation will be of no effect. Most of the early cases were examples of this scenario. Moreover, where the presumption of the destruction of a will *animo revocandi* arises, it may be rebutted by showing that the destruction was conditional on the making of a validly executed will. For example, in *In the Estate of Botting* [1951] 2 All ER 997, the testator's first will was presumed to have been destroyed as it was missing at his death. However, the court was satisfied that the presumed destruction was conditional on another will being made. As the second will was invalidly executed, the first will (draft copy) was admitted to probate.

5.3.2.3 Ineffective will or disposition

In this scenario the testator makes a valid fresh will but it (or part of it) lacks effect. If the testator had revoked the earlier will conditionally on the later will being effective (or dispositions in it) then the earlier one is not revoked if the condition is not satisfied, as occurred in *Re Finnemore* (above). Another illustration is *In the Goods of Hope Brown* [1942] P 136. A testator executed a holograph will expressly revoking an earlier will that had been professionally drafted. The later will was incomplete. It directed that pecuniary legacies should be paid free of estate duty, but the will did not provide any such legacies. And it divided the proceeds of the future sale of realty among 'the after-mentioned beneficiaries ... in following proportions', but there was no mention of the names of the beneficiaries or their interests in the blank spaces that the testator had left. It was as if the testator was trying to demonstrate how not to draft a will. The court held that the first will was not revoked.

5.3.2.4 Failure to revive a will

A will which has been revoked by a subsequent will cannot be revived by the revocation of the subsequent will. Thus, if a testator revokes a will with the intention of thereby reviving an earlier one, the revocation will be ineffective on the ground that it was conditional. In *Powell v Powell* (1866) 1 P & D 209, the testator made a will leaving all his property to his grandson. Later he made a second will leaving all his property to his nephew. But he became uneasy about the second will and eventually destroyed it whilst holding the first will under his arm and declaring it to be the will that he wished to stand. It was held that the second will had not been revoked since the revocation had been conditional on the revival of the first will. A similar decision was reached in *Re Bridgewater* [1965] 1 All ER 717.

5.3.3 Mistaken belief cases

The conditional revocation rule has also been applied in cases where the testator did not attempt to execute or revive another will but revoked his existing will as the result of a belief which transpires to have been mistaken. In *Campbell v French* (1797) 2 Ves 321; 30 ER 1033, the testator made a will containing legacies to the grandchildren of his sister. Later he executed a codicil revoking the gifts to the grandchildren (who lived in America) 'they all being dead'. But they were alive. It was held that the revocation failed as it had been conditional on the beneficiaries being dead. It is questionable whether this really was a conditional revocation: was not the testator expressing a reason for the revocation rather than a condition? In effect he was saying 'I am revoking *because* they are dead' rather than 'if they are dead' — he acted under a mistake of fact. This would suggest that cases based on a mistaken belief are not true examples of conditional revocation. That they are so regarded is due largely to the confusion between conditional revocation and mistaken revocation evident from the early cases such as *Onions v Tyrer*. Similar comments apply to *Re Carey* (1977) 121 SJ 173, where a testator destroyed his will because he considered that he had nothing to leave. His assessment may have been correct at the time of the revocation, but he later inherited under his sister's intestacy. It was held that the revocation had been conditional on the testator having nothing to leave *at his death* (since a will is ambulatory). Hence the will was admitted to probate. But again, was not the testator's belief the reason rather than the condition for revoking? Was not his thought process, 'I am destroying this will *because* I have no property to leave'?

The classic mistaken belief case is *In the Estate of Southerden* [1925] P 177, CA, where the testator burnt his will under the mistaken impression that the whole of his estate would pass to his widow if he died intestate. The will was held not to have been validly revoked, Atkin LJ stating (at pp. 185–6):

> Cases of dependent relative revocation are mostly cases where the testator has supposed that if he destroyed his will his property would pass under some other document. But the condition is not necessarily limited to the existence of some other document. The revocation may be conditional on the existence or future existence of some fact . . . when the testator destroyed his will in the presence of his wife he did it on condition that she would take the whole of the property. The condition was not fulfilled, and therefore the revocation was not operative.

On the other hand, in *Re Feis* [1964] Ch 106, the court refused to apply the conditional revocation rule. The testatrix made a will dealing with property in England and Germany. Later she made a codicil revoking the provisions applicable to her German estate since she thought (mistakenly) that she had effectively disposed of it by a power of attorney executed after the original will. The court held that she had intended an absolute and not a conditional revocation because the inference from the facts was that she wanted to exclude the legatees under the will in any case and make some totally different provision. In *Re Churchill* [1917] 1 Ch 206, the testator made a will bequeathing his valuable coin collection to Manchester University. Later he purported to make an *inter vivos* gift of the collection to the University, but the gift was imperfect as there was no delivery of the coins at that time. Soon afterwards he executed a codicil revoking the legacy and declaring that he had transferred to the University all the coins which he intended to leave. A few months later he transferred the bulk of the collection to the University, but part of it remained in his possession. On his death the University claimed the remainder of the collection on the ground that the revocation by codicil, being based on a mistaken belief of fact, was conditional and therefore inoperative. The judge held that the revocation was not conditional because the testator had thought that he had done all that was necessary to transfer the coin collection by *inter vivos* gift.

Why a mistaken belief of fact is sometimes held to result in absolute revocation but conditional at other times is not altogether clear. The difficulty of reconciling these decisions stems from the nature of the 'mistaken belief' cases — they are arguably not cases of conditional revocation at all, although treated as such by the courts. And some of the 'fresh will' cases fall into the same category. From a historical perspective it does indeed seem that the conditional revocation rule has frequently been applied in dubious circumstances, when the testator's true intentions have been far from evident. Hence the decision in *Re Jones* (above), limiting the operation of the rule to cases where there is clear evidence of the intention to revoke conditionally, is to be greatly welcomed.

5.4 ALTERATIONS

Alteration is not strictly the same as revocation. To 'alter' means to change, whereas to 'revoke' means to annul. This distinction is emphasised by the Wills Act 1837 which does not include alteration as one of the methods of revocation under ss. 18 and 20. Nevertheless, the consequences of an alteration will often be the same as that of revocation — in each case the affected part of the will (whether altered or revoked) may fail to take effect. And in some cases an alteration may amount to revocation through destruction within s. 20, as occurred in *Re Adams* (heavy scoring out of signatures with ballpoint pen: see 5.2.3.1).

5.4.1 Alterations after execution of will

Section 21 of the Wills Act 1837 provides:

> No obliteration, interlineation, or other alteration made in any will after the execution thereof shall be valid or have any effect, except so far as the words or effect of the will before such alteration shall not be apparent, unless such alteration shall be executed in like manner as hereinbefore is required for the execution of the will....

5.4.1.1 Formal requirements
The effect of s. 21 is that alterations made after the execution of a will are invalid unless executed like a will. Thus the alteration must be signed and attested in the manner required by s. 9, except that s. 21 specifically directs that the signature of the testator and the witnesses must be made 'in the margin or on some other part of the will opposite or near to such alteration, or at the foot or end of or opposite to a memorandum referring to such alteration, and written at the end or some other part of the will'. It follows that an alteration must be signed by the testator or by someone in his presence and under his direction. In *Re White* [1990] 3 All ER 1, the testator dictated certain alterations which were copied onto his will. The testator checked the alterations and wrote in a blank space at the end of the will 'Alterations to Will dated 14.12.84' and asked two witnesses to sign just below. They did so but the testator did not sign. It was held that the alterations had not been duly executed.

If the testator signs the alteration without witnesses, s. 21 is satisfied if he later acknowledges the signature to the witnesses who then attest that signature. But it seems it is insufficient for the testator to acknowledge his signature *to the will*: there must be a fresh signature and attestation in respect of the alterations (unless the testator re-executes the whole will). A duly executed memorandum that refers to the alteration will suffice, as s. 21 indicates. For example, in *In the Goods of Treeby* (1875) 3 P & D 242, the testator made a will disposing of 19 leasehold houses in favour of his children. Later he struck through the description of one of the houses, the obliteration being signed by him but not by any witnesses. Near the end of the will an interlineation appeared by which he left the house to his wife. At the end of the will, following the signatures of the testator and the witnesses, there was a memorandum stating that 'No.1, Westbourne Terrace is struck out for the benefit of my dear wife'. Since the memorandum was signed by the testator and attested by two witnesses, and referred to both alterations (the obliteration and the interlineation), the will was admitted to probate in its altered state. Section 21 does not specify the means whereby the alteration is to be made, but there is a presumption that if a will is written in pencil and ink, the pencilled parts are deliberative only. Hence pencilled alterations to a will written in ink will be presumed to have no effect even though validly executed: *Hawkes* v *Hawkes* (1828) 1 Hagg Ecc 321; 162 ER 599.

5.4.1.2 Exception: words not apparent
An invalidly executed obliteration will have the effect of revoking the obliterated words to the extent that they (or the effect of the will prior to alteration) are 'not apparent': s. 21. What is the meaning of 'apparent'? The case law establishes that whether words are 'apparent' turns on whether they are optically apparent: they must be apparent on the face of the will to the eye. Thus the words are 'not apparent' if they can be discovered only by means of an infra-red photograph, as occurred in *Re Itter* [1950] P 130, where Ormerod J stated (at p. 132):

> If the words of the document can be read by looking at the document itself, then I think that they are apparent within the meaning of the section, however elaborate may be the devices used to assist the eye and however skilled the eye which is being used; but if they can only be read by creating a new document, as in this case by producing a photograph of the original writing on the codicil, then I cannot find that the words are apparent.

The court in *In the Goods of Brasier* [1899] P 36 accepted the evidence of a handwriting expert who used a powerful magnifying glass to decipher a series of gifts to beneficiaries whose names had been erased. In *Ffinch* v *Combe* [1894] P 191, the testator had pasted four strips of paper over certain words in different parts of the will. It was held that the pasted strips could not be removed as that would amount to a physical interference with the will; but nevertheless the words were apparent because they could be read by placing a piece of brown paper around the relevant passages and holding the document against a window pane. Hence the words were admitted to probate as part of the will. What if the words are 'not apparent'? The will is then admitted to probate as if the affected words were blanks: *In the Goods of Ibbetson* (1839) 2 Curt 337; 163 ER 431.

It must be remembered that for alterations to have a revocatory effect the testator must have had an intention to revoke. Thus an accidental obliteration would not suffice to revoke. Moreover, if the testator's intention to revoke was conditional, and the condition is not satisfied, the conditional revocation rule applies. In that case any means of proof — including the use of scientific techniques — is permitted in order to discover the original words in the will; the question is no longer whether the words are 'apparent' but whether they can be deciphered by any means. In *Re Itter* (above) the testatrix had pasted strips of paper over the amounts of legacies bequeathed by her will. On top of these strips she wrote different amounts, but failed to execute these alterations correctly. Ormerod J inferred that her intention had been to revoke the pasted-over legacies only if new legacies were effectively substituted. Hence the strips could be removed or 'any other means' used (including infra-red photography) to ascertain the original amounts. The LRC Report No. 22 commented that as a result of the decision in *Re Itter* 'any difficulty caused by a narrow construction of the word "apparent" will usually be avoided' (para. 3.44). A similar decision had been reached in *In the Goods of Horsford* (1874) 3 P & D 211, where it was held that strips of paper pasted over amounts of legacies could be removed where the conditional revocation rule applied.

5.4.2 Alterations before execution of will

An alteration made before the will is executed is valid provided that it was intended by the testator to form part of his will. The subsequent execution of the will amounts to an execution of the alteration: no additional execution is strictly necessary. In practice, however, it is very advisable for the alteration to be signed and attested because there is a presumption that an unattested alteration was made *after* the execution of the will: *Cooper v Bockett* (1846) 4 Moo PC 419: 13 ER 365. The presumption is rebuttable: in *Greville v Tylee* (1851) 7 Moo PC 320; 13 ER 904, it was held that the *onus probandi* lies upon the party who propounds the alteration as part of the will to prove that it was made before the will's execution with the sanction of the testator. On the facts the presumption was not rebutted; hence an unattested alteration — which would have resulted in the bulk of the testator's estate passing to his doctor rather than to the testator's wife — was not admitted to probate.

The presumption may be rebutted by internal or extrinsic evidence (or a combination of the two). In *Birch v Birch* (1848) 1 Rob Ecc 675; 163 ER 1175, the testator's will was found to contain blanks left for legacies. The body of the will had been written in black ink, and that was the medium used to fill in some of the blanks, but others were filled in with red ink. The writing in the blanks was unattested and there was no clear evidence as to when the blanks had been filled in. The legacies in red ink were not admitted to probate as they were presumed to have been inserted after the execution of the will. But the legacies in black ink were admissible since otherwise it would be difficult to explain why anyone would wish to execute a will containing blanks. While lacking the passion of Stendahl's novel *Le Rouge et le Noir*, *Birch v Birch* is a vivid illustration of the application of the presumption and its rebuttal by internal evidence. Extrinsic evidence may consist, for example, of declarations made by the testator, or the evidence of witnesses and those involved in the will's preparation. In *Keigwin* v *Keigwin* (see 4.2.5.3), the testatrix's will was found to have an unattested alteration. The court accepted evidence from the draftsman of the will (a friend whom the testatrix frequently consulted regarding her affairs) that the alterations had been made prior to the will's execution.

5.5 REVIVAL OF WILLS

Revival is the process by which a revoked will is resurrected and thereby becomes operative.

5.5.1 Methods of revival

Section 22 of the Wills Act 1837 provides:

> No will or codicil, or any part thereof, which shall be in any manner revoked, shall be revived otherwise than by the re-execution thereof, or by a codicil executed in manner hereinbefore required and showing an intention to revive the same ...

Thus there are two methods of reviving a revoked will: either by re-execution of the will, or by a subsequent codicil showing an intention to revive.

5.5.1.1 Re-execution of the will
A re-execution of the will requires that the formalities of s. 9 of the Wills Act 1837 be satisfied again. Thus the will must be duly signed by the testator (or by some person in his presence and by his direction) and must be attested and signed by the witnesses.

5.5.1.2 Codicil showing an intention to revive
Since revival is a drastic act — the resurrection of a 'dead' will — the court must be satisfied that there was a clear intention to revive the will. Before 1837 it was enough for a codicil simply to refer to a previously revoked will, but s. 22 emphasised the need for the testator's intention to revive to be clearly demonstrated, as appears from the important judgment of Wilde J in *In the Goods of Steele* (1868) 1 P & D 575, at 578:

> ... the legislature meant that the intention of which it speaks should appear on the face of the codicil, either by express words referring to a will as revoked and importing an intention to revive the same, or by a disposition of the testator's property inconsistent with any other intention, or by some other expressions conveying to the mind of the Court, with reasonable certainty, the existence of the intention in question. In other words, I conceive that it was designed by the statute to do away with the revival of wills by mere implication.

It is clear from this judgment that the intention need not be stated expressly. Consider *In the Goods of Davis* [1952] P 279, where the testator made a will leaving his estate to Ethel Phoebe Horsley. They married a year later, but the testator was unaware of the effect of the marriage on his will until some years afterwards when it was pointed out to him that his will had been revoked. On being told that he could revive the will by making a codicil, he produced the envelope containing the will and wrote on it 'The herein name Ethel Pheboe [*sic*] Horsley is now my lawful wedded wife'. This statement was duly signed and attested. It was held that the words on the envelope constituted a codicil and that they fell within the third of the situations expounded in *In the Goods of Steele* (above), namely 'some other expressions' conveying the existence of the intention to revive. Willmer J inferred the intention from the testator's words on the envelope because 'what other intention can possibly be imputed to him?'. Accordingly, the testator's will was held to be revived.

It is clear from *In the Goods of Davis* that a writing may qualify as a codicil under s. 22 even though it does not describe itself as such. Another example is *In the Goods of Terrible* (1858) 1 Sw & Tr 140; 164 ER 665, where the testator made a will leaving residuary property to his wife. Following her death he married his second wife (the marriage thereby revoking the will). On the day preceding his death he told his nurse that he wished his first wife's name to be erased from the will, and the name of his second wife to be substituted for it; and he requested that a memorandum be added to the will to effect his wishes. Accordingly, the nurse wrote the following words on the will under the signatures of the attesting witnesses: 'I give and bequeath to my wife Martha Terrible, my wife Sarah Terrible being void by death.' The memorandum was signed by the testator and duly attested. Although the memorandum did not describe itself as a codicil and did not directly refer to the will, it was held to be a codicil reviving the will within s. 22.

On the other hand, it is insufficient for the testator simply to attach a codicil to a revoked will. In *Marsh v Marsh* (1860) 1 Sw & Tr 528; 164 ER 845, the testator — clearly obsessed with making testamentary dispositions — left 27 executed wills and codicils and a large number of incomplete testamentary papers. On his death a codicil was found attached by tape to an earlier revoked will. It was held that the attachment was insufficient to show an intention to revive the will since such an intention must appear in the contents of the codicil. Moreover, it is insufficient for the codicil merely to refer to the revoked will by date, e.g., by a statement such as 'This is a codicil to my will of . . .'. In *Goldie v Adam* [1938] P 85, the testator made a will dated 9 June 1929 and three subsequent codicils. He made another will in 1932 revoking the earlier will and codicils. A year later he executed a codicil expressed to be the fourth codicil to his 'last will' dated 9 June 1929 and ending with the words 'In all other respects I confirm my said will'. The evidence suggested that the testator (through his draftsman) had mistakenly referred to the wrong will. It was held that the mere reference to the 1929 will was insufficient to revive it. But if the codicil not only refers to the revoked will by date but also to its provisions, s. 22 is likely to be satisfied, as in *In the Goods of Stedham* (1881) 6 PD 205. The testator made wills in 1877 and 1878, and a codicil in 1880 which mistakenly described itself as a codicil to the will of 1877. However, although the reference to the 1877 will was mistaken, the draftsman had applied his mind to the 1877 provisions and had employed the language of that will so as to express the testator's wishes at the time of the execution of the codicil. In those circumstances the codicil was held to revive the 1877 will so that all three documents were admitted to probate. *Goldie* v *Adam* (above) was different because there the draftsman had not applied his mind to the provisions of the earlier will.

5.5.1.3   Existence of revoked will?

In order to revive a will under s. 22, it appears that the will must be in existence; a destroyed will cannot be revived. In *Rogers* v *Goodenough* (1862) 2 Sw & Tr 342; 164 ER 1028, the testator had his first will burnt after making another which contained a revocation clause. Later he made a codicil purporting to revive the first will. It was held that the purported revival was ineffectual since the will could only be revived in its original condition. The case did not decide that a destroyed will could never be revived whatever the circumstances. The judge emphasised that his judgment was limited to the facts before him — an intentional destruction of the will — and he declined to state what the position would have been if the destruction had occurred without the testator's knowledge. It might seem harsh to disallow the revival of a will in such circumstances if a copy of it exists. On the other hand, is it too much to expect of a testator in such a case simply to execute a fresh will?

The two methods of revival contained in s. 22 are exhaustive: there is no other method of reviving a will. Thus, if a will has been revoked by a subsequent will, the revocation of the later will does not in itself revive the earlier one: *In the Goods of Hodgkinson* (see 5.2.1.3).

5.5.2   The effect of revival

Revival has the effect of resurrecting a revoked will. According to s. 34 of the Wills Act 1837, the will shall be deemed to have been made at the time when it was revived. Thus a document which was not in existence when the original will was made but came into existence thereafter, prior to the revival, may be incorporated into the revived will (for incorporation see 4.4). Similarly, invalid alterations made after the will's execution may be validated by the revival of the will: *Neate* v *Pickard* (1843) 2 N of C 406.

What is the effect of the revival of a will on an intervening will? Suppose that Arthur makes a will, then another revoking the first, and then a codicil reviving the first will. Which documents are admissible to probate? Clearly the first will and the codicil are operative, but is the second will? Since the first will is deemed by s. 34 to have been made after the second will, it follows that the latter is totally revoked if the first will (or the codicil) contains a revocation clause; otherwise the second will is partially revoked to the extent of any inconsistency with the first will and the codicil. For example, in *Re Pearson* [1963] 3 All ER 763, the testator's second will revoked his first will. He then made a codicil which revived the first will. Since the first will contained a revocation clause, the second will was held to be revoked. The facts in *In the Goods of Dyke* (1881) 6 PD 205 were similar apart from the fact that the first will did not contain a revocation clause. Both wills and the codicil were admitted to probate since the second will was only partially revoked (to the extent of any inconsistency with the first will and the codicil).

It was suggested to the Law Reform Committee that the law would be simplified if the possibility of reviving wills was abolished: it was as easy to make a new will as to revive an old one. The LRC Report No. 22, whilst stating that 'the ways in which a revoked will may be revived ought to be narrowly circumscribed' (para. 3.49), did not recommend the abolition of revival. And rightly so, for whatever the difficulties that may occasionally arise in practice, the non-availability of revival would remove a valuable option for testators. There may be circumstances — emergencies, for example — where reviving a will by re-executing it is more convenient than making a fresh will.

5.6   REPUBLICATION OF WILLS

Republication is the confirmation of a valid existing will, giving it a new starting date. The concept was particularly important prior to the Wills Act 1837 since testamentary gifts of realty applied only to the real estate that the testator had when he made the will: after-acquired realty did not pass. Hence a testator would have to republish his will (or make a new one) in order for it to extend to the newly-acquired realty. But once s. 24 of the Wills Act 1837 enacted that a will extended to all the property which the testator had at death (see 6.3.3.1), a major function of republication was removed. Nevertheless, republication remains a useful option for testators, although one that must be carefully exercised since it may have unexpected consequences.

5.6.1   Methods of republication

Unlike revival, the methods of republication are grounded in case law, not statute. There are two methods: either the will must be duly re-executed, or it must be referred to in a subsequent codicil.

5.6.1.1   Re-execution of will
The re-execution of the will must conform to the requirements of s. 9 of the Wills Act 1837 and must have been intended to be a re-execution. In *Dunn* v *Dunn* (1866) 1 P & D 277, the testatrix wanted to transfer possession of her will to the chief beneficiary. She insisted on making a ceremony of the transfer, signing the will again and requesting it to be signed by witnesses. It was held that the will had not been re-executed since the purpose of the ceremony had been merely to effect a transfer of the will.

5.6.1.2   Subsequent codicil
A duly executed codicil which refers to an earlier will republishes that will provided that the testator intended to republish: the court will infer the required intention much more readily than in the case of revival (where a clear

intention to revive is necessary). This is hardly surprising given that republication is a far less drastic act than revival — confirmation of a will rather than resurrection.

The intention to republish is best shown by using a phrase in the codicil such as 'in all other respects I confirm my said will', but a mere reference to the will suffices. For example, in *Re Harvey* [1947] Ch 285, a testator made a will and five codicils. The last codicil did not contain any dispositions and did not expressly confirm any previous testamentary document. But it described itself as a codicil to the testator's will and reported the destruction of the second codicil. It was held that the will was republished by the last codicil. Vaisey J stated that 'a codicil described as a codicil to a particular will republishes that will' (p. 294).

5.6.2 The effect of republication

A republished will is deemed to have been made at the time of republication: s. 34 of the Wills Act 1837. The effect of republication was explained by Lord Russell in *Goonewardene v Goonewardene* [1931] AC 647, PC (at p. 650):

> ... the effect of confirming a will by codicil is to bring the will down to the date of the codicil, and to effect the same disposition of the testator's property as would have been effected if the testator had at the date of the codicil made a new will containing the same dispositions as in the original will but with the alterations introduced by the codicil.

The fact that a will is given a new starting-point can seriously affect the operation of the will, particularly as regards descriptions of persons and property.

5.6.2.1 Persons
The effect of s. 34 is that descriptions of persons in a will refer to those who satisfy the description *as at the time of republication*. In *Re Hardyman* [1925] Ch 287, the testatrix made a will in 1898 in which she bequeathed a legacy of £5,000 in trust for 'my cousin his children and his wife', but without referring to the wife's name. The wife died in 1901. Later that year the testatrix — who knew of the death of the cousin's wife — made a codicil which republished the will, and died soon afterwards. In 1903 the cousin remarried. The issue eventually arose whether the second wife was entitled. Romer J held that she took since she was the only person who could take under the description 'his wife' in the will as republished in the codicil. What if the will had not been republished? Then the phrase 'his wife' could only have applied to the first wife, in which case the gift to her would have lapsed.

5.6.2.2 Property
The rule that a republished will is deemed to have been made when it was republished must be considered in the light of s. 24 of the Wills Act 1837, under which a will speaks from death as regards property unless there is a contrary intention. Where a contrary intention is present it will normally be the

date of the will's execution that determines which property passes. If the will has been republished, it will be deemed to have been executed at the date of republication — the usual effect of s. 34. For example, in *Re Reeves* [1928] Ch 351, republication was held to pass an extension of a lease. The testator bequeathed to his daughter his 'present lease' in a property in Mayfair, which at that time had less than four years to run. On the expiry of the lease the testator obtained a renewal for a term of 12 years. Later he made a codicil which republished the will. It was held that since the republication brought the date of the will down to the date of republication, the daughter took the benefit of the renewed lease. *Re Champion* [1893] 1 Ch 101, CA, was similar.

5.6.2.3 Other consequences

The fact that a republished will is deemed to have been executed at the date of republication can substantially affect the application of a number of rules and principles of the law of succession. For example, under s. 15 of the Wills Act 1837, a gift to a witness to the will or his spouse is void (see 7.2.2). However, if the will is later republished without the participation of that witness/beneficiary, s. 15 does not apply and the gift is saved: *Anderson v Anderson* (1872) LR 13 Eq 381. Moreover, as regards the doctrine of incorporation, a document may be incorporated into a will, even though it came into existence after the will was executed, if the will was later republished and referred to the document as in existence: *In the Goods of Lady Truro* (1866) 1 P & D 201 (see 4.4.3).

What is the effect of republication on unattested alterations made in the will after its execution but prior to republication? Although *prima facie* republication might appear to validate the alteration, the presumption that unattested alterations were made after the will's execution will still apply: the alteration will be presumed to have been made after republication. But the presumption can be rebutted by evidence that the alteration was made prior to republication, as in *In the Goods of Heath* [1892] P 253: the testator left a legacy of £10,000 to Mary, one of his executors. After the execution of the will he made some unattested alterations including an interlineation giving a legacy of '£1,000 to each of my executors'. He later made a codicil which recited that he had given a legacy of £11,000 to Mary. It was held that the alteration was valid, though unattested, because the recital that £11,000 had been given to Mary showed that the interlineation had been made before the republication.

Where a gift in a will has been adeemed and replaced by a similar asset, it is unlikely that a subsequent republication will carry the new asset (for ademption see 7.2.6). In *Re Galway's WT* [1950] Ch 1, the testator devised certain lands, including 'the mines and minerals thereunder', to his eldest son. The lands were subsequently nationalised by the Coal Act 1938, the owner being given a right to compensation. He later made a codicil republishing the will and the issue arose whether the son was entitled to the compensation. It was held that he was not entitled since the testator could not be regarded as having intended — by republishing the will — to pass the compensation. Harman J emphasised that republication cannot operate to make good a legacy once adeemed, relying on *Drinkwater v Falconer* (1755) 2 Ves Sen 623; 28 ER 397. However, there are decisions which are arguably inconsistent with the rule that an adeemed gift cannot be saved by republication, e.g., *Re Harvey* (see 5.6.1.2). It was held in that case that a republished will could pass property which had in effect changed from realty to personalty (after the execution of the will) by the operation of the Law of Property Act 1925.

Republication of a will by a codicil does not republish an intermediate codicil: it can only be the document that has actually been republished that can have a new starting date under s. 34. In *Burton* v *Newbery* (1875) 1 Ch D 234, the testator bequeathed his residuary estate to be divided between 13 grandchildren. He then made a codicil similarly disposing of estate acquired after the execution of the will. Later he made a second codicil, described as a codicil to his will, but not referring to the first codicil. It was held that the second codicil republished the will but not the first codicil.

5.6.2.4 Contrary intention

There is case law authority to suggest that s. 34 will not operate if there is a contrary intention, that is, where it is clear that the testator did not intend that the republication should result in the will having a new starting-point for all purposes (although this exception is not found in s. 34). In *Re Moore* [1907] 1 IR 315, the testator left residuary estate in his will of January 1906 to 'the Presbyterian Orphan Society'. In August and September of that year he made two codicils containing minor alterations but otherwise confirming the will. He died two days after the execution of the second codicil. By statute, gifts to charity were invalidated if the testator died within three months of making the will. It was held that the will should be regarded as having been made in January 1906 and not at the date of republication. Barton J stated (at p. 318):

> Republication gives to the will a fresh starting-point, but it does not erase the old date. Nor does it . . . falsify the fact that the will contained a particular devise and was executed at a particular time. The authorities which have been cited lead me to the conclusion that the Courts have always treated the principle that republication makes the will speak as if it had been re-executed at the date of the codicil not as a rigid formula or technical rule, but as a useful and flexible instrument for effectuating a testator's intentions, by ascertaining them down to the latest date at which they have been expressed.

These remarks have been consistently approved in subsequent cases, e.g., *Re Hardyman* (above) and *Re Heath's WT* [1949] Ch 170. The remarks may be a fair summary of the approach of the court, but to describe the rule in s. 34 as 'a flexible instrument' and not as 'a technical rule' appears to diminish the force of the clear words of the statute. However, decisions such as *Re Moore* seem consistent with the testator's undoubted intentions: it would have been very harsh to have invalidated the charitable gift. Less clear is the decision in *Re Heath's WT* (above). The testator left property in his will of 1932 on trust for his daughter subject to certain restrictions. A statute enacted in 1935 made such restrictions void if imposed in any instrument executed after 31 December 1935. The testator executed two codicils in 1937 confirming the will. The court held that to regard the will as having been made in 1937 would have defeated the testator's intention to impose restrictions on his daughter: thus she was bound by them. This was a questionable decision since it was unclear what the testator's intentions were after 1932. The later codicils did not refer to the restrictions on the daughter. The court appears to have treated this as evidence that the testator's initial intention did not change, but such evidence can equally be said to suggest the contrary.

SIX
Construction of Wills

6.1 INTRODUCTION

'When I use a word', Humpty Dumpty said in a rather scornful tone, 'it means just what I choose it to mean, neither more nor less'. (Lewis Carroll, *Through the Looking Glass*, ch. 6)

Fortunately, most testators do not behave like Humpty Dumpty. But the immeasurable richness of the English language — with its vast vocabulary and variety of nuance — creates a minefield of potential problems for testators when drafting wills. The testator who makes a home-made will may well find it relatively uncomplicated to satisfy the required formalities to execute a valid will; but the drafting of the will — involving the need to appreciate the precise significance of the words used — is a more exacting task, requiring a certain level of expertise. For example, suppose that Arthur, intending that his wife should be sole beneficiary, makes a home-made will leaving her 'all my personal estate'. Arthur obviously did not appreciate the significance of the word 'personal', using it simply to denote his own estate. But a court might well hold that Arthur's will passes only personalty to his wife (see 6.2.3).

In trying to discover what the testator's intentions were in his choice of words, the court obviously lacks the chief witness — the testator. Consequently, there are a number of principles and rules of construction to aid the judges, but their task is fraught with difficulty: undoubtedly this is a difficult area of the law of succession, and a vast one. The text will focus on the essentials.

6.1.1 Jurisdiction

It will be remembered that jurisdiction over wills is shared primarily between the Family and the Chancery Divisions of the High Court (see 2.1.1.7). The Family Division's jurisdiction consists chiefly of probate business, whereas that of the Chancery Division is concerned largely with the construction of wills.

Hence they are often referred to as the 'Court of Probate' and the 'Court of Construction' respectively. However, the Chancery Division has jurisdiction over some probate matters — all contentious and solemn form probate — while the Family Division sometimes has to construe wills to decide whether they are admissible to probate. For example, the Family Division may need to construe a will where there is doubt whether it was made with *animus testandi*, or whether it revokes a prior will. In *Re Thomas* [1939] 2 All ER 567, the issue was whether a codicil should be admitted to probate. That depended on whether the codicil had any dispositive effect. Thus the Court of Probate had to construe the codicil for that purpose. Moreover, the Family Division may construe a will with the consent of the parties so as to minimise the depletion of the assets of a small estate: *In the Estate of Last* [1958] P 137. In such cases the Family Division combines the function of a court of probate with that of a court of construction; however, its decisions on matters of construction are not binding on the Chancery Division.

The division of jurisdiction over wills is largely the result of historical development. The desirability of maintaining the jurisdictional split is very questionable. There is much to be said for a system whereby one court decides all the issues arising from the making of a will, although there may be cases where the issues cannot be determined at the same time — for example, where an issue of construction becomes apparent only some time after the grant of probate.

6.1.2 Conflicting approaches

> In formulating rules for disputes about the meaning of a will, the law must hold the balance between giving effect to the testator's 'true' intentions on the one hand and enabling those concerned to rely on the words actually used in it on the other. These two aims may come into conflict with each other, and the longer the interval between the time when the will is made and the testator's death . . . the greater is the possibility that they may do so. (LRC Report No. 19, 1973, para. 3)

The construction of wills raises in an acute form the fundamental dichotomy in law between the need for certainty and the need for flexibility. The LRC Report No. 19 emphasises the need to hold the balance between the narrow and the broad approaches to construing wills. Pursuing a *via media* may seem an attractive solution, but it is also simplistic because sometimes there are only two plausible interpretations and thus there is no room for a convenient middle course. Consider, for example, Lord Denning's description (in *The Discipline of Law*, 1979) of Danckwerts LJ as 'a Chancery lawyer who was endowed with unusual common sense' (p. 27). This description could mean that in Lord Denning's view Dankwerts LJ had unusual common sense, or that *for a Chancery lawyer* he had unusual common sense. No third, middle-course interpretation seems plausible here.

All judges agree that their task is to interpret the words used by the testator in his will — it is his expressed meaning that they are concerned with, not his intended meaning. This follows from the requirement that a will should be 'in writing'. The conflict in approach stems largely from differing perceptions as to the means to achieve the goal.

6.1.2.1 The narrow approach

In the narrow approach a predominantly literal sense is taken of the words used by the testator; and there is a cautious attitude towards acceptance of evidence of the testator's 'true' intentions. The narrow approach is informed by the desire to achieve consistency and certainty in how testamentary provisions are construed by the court. This approach is entirely understandable and conforms to the traditional attitude of English law in striving for certainty in property matters so that parties and their legal advisers know where they stand. There is also inherent in this view that like cases should be treated equally, but it may be questioned whether equality of treatment demands identity of treatment.

The narrow approach to construction is traditional largely because it is Chancery that has had the primary task of construing wills. The Chancery judges of the Victorian era, steeped in a tradition of meticulous and lengthy consideration of property cases — allied to a rigid adherence to the doctrine of precedent — took a predominantly conservative view of their function as interpreters of wills. Occasionally judges have seemed oblivious of the clear intentions of the testator. The nadir was perhaps reached in *Lowe* v *Thomas* (1854) 5 De GM & G 315; 43 ER 891. The testatrix left 'the whole of my money' to her brother for life and on his death to the brother's two daughters, with ultimate remainder to the survivor. The estate included stocks and a small amount of cash. It was held that the bequest only passed the cash. Given the series of life interests in the bequest, the decision clearly thwarted the testatrix's intentions, as Turner LJ appeared readily to admit (at p. 892):

> It is not unlikely that it was the testatrix's intention to pass by the description 'the whole of my money' something more than what strictly and literally speaking would pass under the description of 'money', but probability is one thing and judicial certainty another.

Another dreadful decision was *Re Hodgson* [1936] Ch 203, where the testatrix made a will two days before her death leaving her 'money' to a named beneficiary. She had £800 in cash and £600 in savings certificates by her bedside. It was held that only the cash passed to the named beneficiary; the savings certificates passed to the Crown on intestacy as the testatrix left no next-of-kin. It was decisions such as these that prompted Lord Atkin to refer in *Perrin* v *Morgan* [1943] AC 399, at 415 to the 'ghosts of dissatisfied testators who ... wait on the other bank of the Styx to receive the judicial personages who have misconstrued their wills' (the Styx was a river in Greek mythology over which the shades of the dead were ferried). Although *Lowe* v *Thomas* and *Re Hodgson* would most probably be decided differently following *Perrin* v *Morgan* (see 6.2.2.1), they are symptomatic of strict, ultra-cautious Chancery attitudes. It may be that in more recent times Chancery judges have generally been prepared to follow a broader approach to construction. But highly questionable decisions still occur. Consider, for example, *Re Rowland* [1963] Ch 1, CA. A couple made mutual wills before going to the South Pacific. The wills contained gifts contingent on their deaths 'coinciding'. A small vessel in which they were sailing disappeared; after some days a body and some wreckage were found. A commission of inquiry concluded that the vessel had gone down suddenly and that all on board had drowned. Had the contingency expressed in the couple's will — that their deaths should coincide — occurred? The majority of the court (both Chancery judges) held that 'coinciding with' must be construed literally, in the sense of 'simultaneous'. As there was no proof that the couple had died simultaneously, the contingency which they had expressed had not occurred. This decision appears to have defied the intention of the couple, who most probably meant the phrase to cover exactly the situation that occurred, that is, dying together in the same accident or disaster. Russell LJ, however, explained (at pp. 18–19):

> . . . the testator's language does not fit the facts of the case, so far as they are known. To hold otherwise would not in my judgment be to construe the will at all: it would be the result of inserting in the will a phrase which the testator never used by guessing at what a man in his position would have wished had he directed his mind and pen to the facts as they now confront us. There is no jurisdiction in this Court to achieve a sensible result by such means.

6.1.2.2 The broad approach

The broad approach is characterised by a greater readiness to ascertain and to be guided by the intentions of the testator. And there is a lesser adherence to the strict, literal meaning of the words used if such meaning appears to be at odds with the testator's intentions. The broad approach is informed by a greater desire to achieve the most sensible result on the merits of each particular case, even at the cost of departure from alleged precedents. The supposition is that no one interpretation of a word can be expected to fit adequately the varying nuances of different cases. A classic exposition of this approach was given by Lord Atkin in *Perrin* v *Morgan* (above):

> . . . the construing court has to ascertain what was meant, being guided by the other provisions of the will and the other relevant circumstances, including the age and education of the testator, his relations to the beneficiary chosen, whether kinship or friendship, the provision for other beneficiaries, and other admissible circumstances. Weighing all these, the court must adopt what appears the most probable meaning. To decide on proven probabilities is not to guess but to adjudicate. If this is to decide according to the 'context', I am content, but I cannot agree that the court is precluded from looking outside the terms of the will. No will can be analysed *in vacuo*. There are material surroundings such as I have suggested in every case, and they have to be taken into account. The sole object is, of course, to ascertain from the will the testator's intentions. (at p. 414)

More recently it has been Lord Denning who has particularly championed
the broad approach, as demonstrated in several cases in the 1960s (for a full
account see Lord Denning, *The Discipline of Law*, ch. 3). In *Re Rowland* (above)
he refused to take the narrow view that 'coinciding with' meant 'simultaneous'.
In a superb dissenting judgment he stated (at p. 10):

> ... the whole object of construing a will is to find out the testator's intentions,
> so as to see that his property is disposed of in the way he wished. True it is
> that you must discover his intention from the words he used: but you must
> put upon his words the meaning which they bore to him ... And in order to
> discover the meaning which he intended, you will not get much help by going
> to a dictionary. It is very unlikely that he used a dictionary, and even less
> likely that he used the same one as you. What you should do is to place
> yourself as far as possible in his position, taking note of the facts and
> circumstances known to him at the time: and then say what he meant by his
> words.

6.2 GENERAL PRINCIPLES OF CONSTRUCTION

The law of construction is a mixture of general principles and specific rules. It
has been developed mainly by the courts, but with some help from Parliament.
To some extent the general principles can be regarded as broad guidelines to
the court rather than as strictly binding. Consequently, some judges will feel
that they have room for the exercise of a degree of discretion in achieving the
result they think is merited on the facts of the case. Moreover, there is no
universal agreement as to what constitutes a principle or a rule in this context.
Nevertheless, for the purposes of exposition, this broad classification will be
followed.

6.2.1 The court construes expressed intentions

Since a will must be made in writing, it follows that it is the function of the court
to construe the words used by the testator, and not to re-write a will or to
speculate what he might have intended to put in it. It is the intentions of the
testator as *expressed* in the words of the will that are the court's proper concern.

6.2.1.1 The case law
Because the expressed intentions principle is so fundamental, it is reiterated
time and again by the judges. For example, in *Perrin* v *Morgan* (above) Simon
LC stated (at p. 406):

> ... the fundamental rule in construing the language of a will is to put on the
> words used the meaning which, having regard to the terms of the will, the
> testator intended. The question is not, of course, what the testator meant to
> do when he made his will, but what the written words he uses mean in the
> particular case — what are the 'expressed intentions' of the testator.

In *Scale* v *Rawlings* [1892] AC 342, the testator gave three houses to his niece for life, and after her death '(she leaving no child or children)' the houses were to pass to two nephews. The niece died leaving children, and the question arose whether the testator had made an implied gift to her children. The House of Lords held that no such gift could be implied. Lord Watson stated (at pp. 344–5):

> We are not at liberty to speculate upon what the testator may have intended to do, or may have thought that he had actually done. We cannot give effect to any intention which is not expressed or plainly implied in the language of his will.

Abbott v *Middleton* (1858) 7 HLC 68; 11 ER 28 was a case where the testator left ambiguous provisions about the destination of remainders in an annuity following a life interest. Lord Wensleydale stated (at p. 46) that the principle in construing a will is to ascertain 'not what the testator meant, but what is the meaning of his words'. In *Re Bailey* [1951] Ch 407, CA, the issue was whether there was ambiguity in the way in which a conditional gift had been expressed. Jenkins LJ stated (at p. 421) that the court could not 'repair the imperfections' in the disposition of the estate:

> ... it is not the function of a court of construction to improve upon or perfect testamentary dispositions. The function of the court is to give effect to the dispositions actually made as appearing expressly or by necessary implication from the language of the will applied to the surrounding circumstances of the case.

6.2.1.2 Altering the will
Although the court cannot — as a general principle — re-write the testator's will, it has a very limited power to omit, substitute or insert words as part of the process of construction. The position was summarised by the LRC Report No. 19 (para. 12):

> This will be done only if two conditions are satisfied. First, the court must be left in no doubt not only that the words appearing in the will do not represent the testator's intention but also as to precisely what omission, substitution or insertion is to be made to carry out that intention. Second, the requisite certainty must be derived from the language of the will itself: extrinsic evidence does not appear to be admissible for this purpose.

Case law authority for this limited power can be found, for example, in *Re Whitrick* [1957] 2 All ER 467, CA. The testatrix left her whole estate to her husband, and then 'in the event of my husband ... and myself both dying at the same time' gave the estate to three relatives. The husband predeceased her. On her death the question arose whether the court should read words into her will to enable the relations to take. It was held that the words in the will did not express the contingency for which she intended to provide, namely either her husband dying in her lifetime or of both of them dying at the same time. Consequently, the appropriate words should be supplied. Jenkins LJ stated (at p. 469):

> The reading of words into a will as a matter of necessary implication is a measure which any court of construction should apply with the greatest caution.... The court cannot re-write the testamentary provisions in wills which come before it for construction. This type of treatment of an imperfect will is only legitimate where the court can collect from the four corners of the document that something has been omitted and, further, collect with sufficient precision the nature of the omission.

In *Re Cory* [1955] 2 All ER 630, the testator intended to give his daughters a power of appointment but failed to state the nature of the power. His will left property on trust for each daughter and after her death 'upon trust for all or such one or more exclusively of the others or other of the children or remoter issue of such daughter and in default of and subject to any such appointment in trust' for all her children in equal shares. Harman J held that the clause was imperfectly expressed in that it omitted operative words to confer a power of appointment. In the circumstances the judge felt it was justifiable for the will to be read as if the words 'as she shall appoint' were inserted after 'such daughter'. On the other hand, the court refused to supply words in *Re Follett* [1955] 2 All ER 22, CA. The testatrix granted a power of appointment to a beneficiary, but it was not clear whether this was a general or a special power: it was suggested that the testatrix had intended to grant a special power but had omitted the correct wording. It was held that the relevant words could not be inserted since it was not clear what had been omitted. Hence the will was construed as it stood, i.e. as creating a general power of appointment. *Re Follett* was distinguished in *Re Cory* on the ground that in the former case sense could be made of the will as it stood, whereas this was not possible in the latter.

In some circumstances a will can be altered (and words added thereby) in the process of rectification under s. 20 of the Administration of Justice Act 1982 — where there was a clerical error or a failure to understand the testator's instructions (see 3.2.6.5). A limited re-writing of the will is thereby possible, but it should be noted that the process of rectification is not the same as that of construction.

6.2.2 Words to be construed in their ordinary sense

Words are to be given their ordinary, natural meaning. This principle has been expressed in various ways. For example, in *Shore* v *Wilson* (1842) 9 Cl & F 355; 8 ER 450, Tindal CJ stated (at p. 532) that the general rule — where words were free from ambiguities — was that they should be construed 'according to the strict, plain, common meaning of the words themselves'. A fuller exposition of the principle was given by Lord Wensleydale in *Abbott* v *Middleton* (above):

... the rule is to read it [the will] in the ordinary and grammatical sense of the words, unless some obvious absurdity, or some repugnance or inconsistency with the declared intentions of the writer, to be extracted from the whole instrument, should follow from so reading it. Then the sense may be modified, extended, or abridged, so as to avoid these consequences, but no farther. (p. 46)

6.2.2.1 More than one ordinary meaning

What if a word has more than one ordinary meaning? The court will then try to determine which meaning was intended by the testator by considering the will as a whole in the light of any admissible extrinsic evidence. In *Perrin* v *Morgan* (above) the issue was the meaning of the word 'moneys'. A wealthy testatrix made a home-made will in which she left 'all moneys of which I die possessed' to named relations. The will also devised realty and bequeathed a small legacy to other named beneficiaries. The issue was whether the gift of 'moneys' passed all the net personalty, which consisted of cash at the bank, stocks and shares, rents due on her realty, income tax repayment due to her, certain dividends and household goods. The stocks and shares (valued at over £32,000) made up the vast bulk of the personal estate. It was held that the word 'money' did not have a fixed meaning; thus the court must choose from several meanings the one intended by the testator in the light of the context of the will and other relevant circumstances. Although 'money' had often been construed narrowly before (see 6.1.2.1), the House of Lords decided that the gift of 'moneys' included all the net personalty. In *Re Trundle* [1961] 1 All ER 103, the testator bequeathed to his godchildren 'any moneys that I have in the bank'. There was a gift of realty in the will to another beneficiary but no gift of residue. On his death the testator had a credit balance in his bank account, where he had also deposited other property, including National Savings Certificates, share certificates and a diamond ring. Uncashed travellers' cheques bought from the bank were found at his residence. It was held that the gift of 'any moneys that I have in the bank' was *prima facie* confined to the testator's bank account (but that included the travellers' cheques).

Perrin v *Morgan* and *Re Trundle* were applied in *Re Barnes's WT* [1972] 2 All ER 639, where the testatrix bequeathed 'any money I may leave' to certain relations and also left a gift of 'any other personal property'. The testatrix apparently had professional assistance in drafting the will, but seemingly not of the most expert kind given that a dispute arose as to which category of gift several of her assets fell into — a deposit account at a bank, a deposit in the Post Office Savings Bank, a share account with a building society, national development and premium savings bonds. It was held that all these assets passed as 'any money I may have'. Goulding J stated (at p. 644) that a judge should apply his own knowledge of the contemporary use of the English language 'in the light of such context and circumstances as may assist him'. What if the meaning of a word has changed — does 'contemporary' refer to the time when the judge decides the case, or when the will was made? It must be the latter: the judge's task is to construe the testator's meaning 'referable to the ordinary uses of the English language at the time when he is making his will' (*per* Lord Thankerton in *Perrin* v *Morgan*, at p. 417).

6.2.2.2 Secondary meaning

The principle that the ordinary meaning is to prevail is subject to two exceptions. When these exceptions apply, the court may prefer to construe the will according to the secondary sense of the words used.

(a) *The dictionary principle* A testator may use words to mean whatever he wishes them to mean (rather like Humpty Dumpty: see 6.1). But he runs the risk that the court will not construe them according to his meaning. To ensure that the words are construed in a secondary sense the testator needs to supply his own 'dictionary', i.e. some evidence in the will which (with the aid of any admissible extrinsic evidence) informs the court as to his true meaning. The dictionary may be along formal lines — for example, a definition clause in the will; but it may also consist of indications in the will from which the court can glean that the testator is using words in some secondary or unusual sense. Suppose, for example, that Arthur makes a will in which he leaves his wife 'the round table'. In construing the phrase the court would *prima facie* adopt the ordinary meaning of the words; but if there is an indication in Arthur's will that the phrase 'the round table' means his collection of porcelain knights, then the court would interpret the words in that sense. In *Re Lynch* [1943] 1 All ER 168, the testator appointed 'my wife Annie Ethel Lynch' to be one of the executors of his will, and left residuary estate 'to my wife during her widowhood', with remainders over in favour of his sons 'after the death or remarriage of my wife'. The testator was a widower who had been cohabiting for some years with Annie as man and wife. The question arose whether the gift to Annie was effective. It was held that the words 'wife' and 'remarriage' could not be construed in their ordinary sense. The testator had provided his own dictionary — drawn from the context of the will — so that it was clear that 'wife' described his cohabitant, and 'remarriage' meant marriage. In *Re Neville* [1925] Ch 44, the testator made a codicil which contained the provision 'I forgive all debts owing to me'. At his death the testator was owed money by certain friends and past employees to whom he had made personal loans. He had also loaned sums to a number of commercial companies and societies secured by mortgage. The question arose whether the testator had released these debts as well as the personal loans. The court held that 'debts' should be construed in a secondary sense as including only the latter particularly as the use of the word 'forgive' introduced a personal note into the matter. It was argued in this case that judges should be wary in adopting a secondary interpretation of a word because it could be difficult to draw the line as to when words should be construed in their primary or their secondary sense. Tomlin J's response was illuminating: 'Although I may not be able to say where day ends or night begins, I can say quite definitely that midnight is night and midday is day' (p. 54).

(b) *Ordinary meaning inappropriate* If, when a will is read in the light of the surrounding circumstances, the ordinary meaning does not make sense, the words may be construed in their secondary meaning (assuming they have one) if sense is thereby made of the testator's provisions. This exception is similar to but not identical with the dictionary principle, the difference being that the latter depends on there being a 'dictionary' in the will, whereas the former relies on extrinsic evidence of the surrounding circumstances. In *Thorn* v *Dickens* (see 5.2.1.2), a will reading 'All for mother' was construed as passing property to the testator's wife because of evidence that the testator commonly referred to his wife as 'mother'. In *Re Smalley* [1929] 2 Ch 112, CA, the testator left his wife and children and some years later went through a bigamous marriage with a widow, Eliza Ann Mercer. He later made a will in which he gave all his property to 'my wife Eliza Ann Smalley'. The estate was claimed by his lawful wife and by Eliza Ann. The court held that in the light of the surrounding circumstances 'wife' should be construed in its secondary sense of *reputed* wife.

6.2.2.3 The eccentric testator

Where there is no reason to depart from the ordinary meaning of a word, that meaning prevails even if the disposition of the estate appears to be strange or eccentric as a result. A testator is entitled to make eccentric provisions in his will. In *Gilmour* v *MacPhillamy* [1930] AC 712, PC, Lord Tomlin stated (at p. 716):

> In order to justify a departure from the natural and ordinary meaning of any word or phrase there must be found in the instrument containing it a context which necessitates or justifies such departure. It is not enough that the natural and ordinary meaning may produce results which to some minds appear capricious or fail to accord with a logical scheme of disposition.

Similarly, in *Re James's WT* [1962] Ch 226, Buckley J stated (at pp. 234–5) that a testator was entitled to be capricious or eccentric in making a will; and that the fact that its terms, when given their ordinary meaning, 'may produce odd results is not alone a ground for construing his language in some other sense which it is less apt to bear'. However, where the ordinary meaning principle is not applicable, and there is a choice between possible meanings, the court may adopt the meaning which leads to the least capricious consequences: *Abbott* v *Middleton*.

6.2.3 Technical words to be given technical meaning

> It is a rule in the judicial exposition of wills, that technical words, or words of known legal import, are to be considered as having been used in their technical sense, or, according to their strict acceptation, unless the context contain a plain indication to the contrary. (*per* Parke B in *Doe d Winter* v *Perratt* (1843) 6 M & G 314; 134 ER 914, at 925)

This principle applies even when the testator did not appreciate the significance of the words used. For example, in *Re Cook* [1948] Ch 212, the testatrix made a will in which the only dispositive part was a gift of 'all my personal estate whatsoever' to certain relations. Her estate consisted of two houses and a small amount of personalty. Did the realty pass under the gift of 'personal estate'? Harman J held that it did not (at p. 216):

The words 'all my personal estate' are words so well-known to lawyers that it must take a very strong context to make them include real estate. Testators can make black mean white if they make the dictionary sufficiently clear, but the testatrix has not done so. It may well be that she thought that 'personal estate' meant 'all my worldly goods'; I do not know. In the absence of something to show that the phrase ought not to be so construed, I must suppose that she used the term 'personal estate' in its ordinary meaning as a term of art.

Re Cook is a leading example of the operation of the technical words principle; it is also one of the decisions which calls into question the way in which judges construe wills in English law. For here was a case where the construction of the will was at odds with the testatrix's probable intentions (as the judge recognised). It is a vivid reminder of the dangers to laymen of making home-made wills without the necessary level of technical expertise.

6.2.3.1 Which words are 'technical'?

For the purposes of the rule, those words are construed technically which have a recognised specific meaning in English law, such as 'fee simple', or are terms of art in common use by lawyers, e.g., 'personal estate'. In *Re Harcourt* [1921] 2 Ch 491, a case which concerned *inter alia* a claim to a Sèvres china flower stand given to the Earl of Liverpool by Napoleon Bonaparte, Lord Sterndale MR justified the application of the principle to words that are 'terms of art' as follows (at p. 503):

> . . . when a testator has used words which have acquired a definite meaning in conveyancing and have for a long time been used in the drafting of wills and settlements and other like documents with that meaning, it requires a very strong case to justify their interpretation in a different sense.

It seems that the principle also applies to scientific terms with a technical meaning and words or symbols which have an ascertainable specialised meaning within the trade or profession to which the testator belonged. In *Goblet v Beechey* (1829) 3 Sim 24; 57 ER 910, an eminent sculptor bequeathed to one of his workmen various chattels used in his work, some of them described by technical names. The main issue was the meaning of the word 'mod' — did it refer to the sculptor's models (which were very valuable) or to his modelling tools (far less valuable)? Three eminent sculptors testified that in the statuary business 'mod' was a contraction for 'models', and the court adopted that construction. In *Kell v Charmer*, a will containing apparently meaningless symbols was construed with the help of extrinsic evidence showing that the testator (a jeweller) had used symbols well-known in the jewellery business (see 4.2.1). In *Re Gillson* [1949] Ch 99, CA, the testator (the owner of several thoroughbred horses) bequeathed 'all my bloodstock' to his trainer at Newmarket. The issue arose whether the gift passed a colt called Pink Flower — in which the testator owned half a share — and Colombo, a stallion in which he owned a fortieth share (for investment purposes). The ordinary meaning of bloodstock is 'thoroughbred or pedigree horses collectively', which would appear to exclude a horse in which the testator had only part ownership. But the court accepted that in the racing world 'bloodstock' includes partly-owned horses, and that the testator was familiar with this meaning. Accordingly, Pink Flower passed under the bequest, but not Colombo since the testator's interest was in the nature of a share in a syndicate rather than a share in a horse (which had never been at the testator's stud).

6.2.3.2 Contrary intention

Technical words should not be construed in their technical sense if that would thwart the testator's clear intention. If the words do not make sense (given the surrounding circumstances) when construed technically, but do make sense in a secondary, non-technical meaning, the court may adopt the latter. Similarly, the secondary sense prevails over the technical sense if the dictionary principle applies. In *Re Cook* (above) the realty would have passed under the gift of 'personal estate' if the testatrix had made it clear in her will that the phrase included her houses. In *Re Bailey* [1945] Ch 191, the testatrix made a will in hospital shortly before she died. She bequeathed several small pecuniary legacies to various beneficiaries, and appointed M.J. as 'my residuary legatee'. Her estate consisted of seven houses (worth a total of £3,500) and personalty valued at £279. Could M.J. take the undisposed-of realty? It was held that she could since there was sufficient context in the will and the surrounding circumstances to show that 'residuary legatee' should be construed as 'residuary beneficiary'. When the testatrix appointed M.J. her mind was directed to both her real and personal estate; and it was also thought significant that there was a considerable disparity between the values of the realty and personalty, the implication being presumably that the testatrix would not have intended M.J. to take only a small part of the estate. This decision can be readily justified on the merits, although the judgment gives the impression that the court was straining hard to find convincing reasons why a 'legatee' could inherit several houses. The distinction between *Re Bailey* and *Re Cook* is not obvious; one wonders why the court in the latter case did not find sufficient evidence of contrary intention to adopt a non-technical interpretation of 'personal estate'.

6.2.4 A will must be construed as a whole

The court must read the will as a whole in order to ascertain the testator's expressed intention. This principle is in reality little more than a gloss on the duty of the court to construe the testator's expressed meaning. In *Re Macandrew's WT* [1964] Ch 704, Ungoed-Thomas J stated (at p. 719) that the fundamental duty of the court was 'to ascertain the intention of the testator as expressed in his will as read as a whole'. And in *Higgins* v *Dawson* [1902] AC 1, Lord Halsbury expressed the principle thus (at pp. 3–4):

> ... where you are construing either a will or any other instrument, it is perfectly legitimate to look at the whole instrument — and, indeed, you must look at the whole instrument — to see the meaning of the whole

instrument, and you cannot rely upon one particular passage in it to the exclusion of what is relevant to the explanation of the particular clause that you are expounding.

If the testator's overriding intention is ascertainable from the will as a whole, it may prevail over the ordinary or technical meaning of words. For example, in *Key* v *Key* (1853) 4 De G M & G 73; 43 ER 435, the testator gave realty to Samuel Key for life charged with life annuities, and provided that 'in case the aforesaid annuitants, or any of them, shall survive the said Samuel Key' the property was to pass to Samuel's eldest son 'charged with the aforesaid annuities'. Despite the literal meaning of the provisions — that the son could take only if at least one annuitant survived Samuel — it was held that, reading the will as a whole, it was clear that the testator intended the son to take in any event after Samuel's death. Knight Bruce LJ stated (at p. 439):

> ... there are many cases upon the construction of documents in which the spirit is strong enough to overcome the letter; cases in which it is impossible for a reasonable being, upon a careful perusal of an instrument, not to be satisfied from its contents that a literal, a strict, or an ordinary interpretation given to particular passages, would disappoint and defeat the intention with which the instrument, read as a whole, persuades and convinces him that it was framed.

Since the court must ascertain the testator's meaning from the whole of the will, the testator's punctuation should be considered in construing the will. There is some inconsistency in the cases on this point, but the predominant trend is to regard punctuation as relevant. For example, in *Gauntlett* v *Carter* (1853) 17 Beav 586; 51 ER 1163, the testator devised freeholds 'situate in Bullen Court, Strand, and Maiden Lane' (in London) to named beneficiaries. The issue arose whether 'Strand' was part of the description of 'Bullen Court' (the latter being situated off the Strand), or whether the testator intended to pass property in the Strand, as well as in Bullen Court and Maiden Lane. The court held that the presence of commas before and after 'Strand' was 'a circumstance of importance', instrumental in the provision being construed as devising property at all three venues.

6.3   SPECIFIC RULES OF CONSTRUCTION

In construing wills the court applies a number of specific rules as well as general principles. For the purposes of exposition the specific rules can be classified according to their source — case law or statute.

6.3.1   Case law rules of construction

6.3.1.1   The 'golden' rule

There is one rule of construction, which to my mind is a golden rule, *viz.*, that when a testator has executed a will in solemn form you must assume that he did not intend to make it a solemn farce — that he did not intend to die intestate when he has gone through the form of making a will. You ought, if possible, to read the will so as to lead to a testacy, not an intestacy. This is a golden rule. (*per* Lord Esher MR in *Re Harrison* (1885) 30 Ch D 390, at 393–4)

This rule operates only when the words in question are capable of alternative meanings. Hence the rule does not apply where a particular meaning must prevail according to the general principles of construction, e.g., where a technical word must be construed in its technical sense. The traditional aversion of judges to intestacy appears to underpin the golden rule: the assumption is that because a person made a will he must have not wished to die intestate. But such an assumption cannot always be made: testators rarely appreciate the precise effect of the rules on intestacy. In any case there may be circumstances where a testator may have preferred to die intestate rather than have his estate distributed in some surprising way through a particular construction of his words: *Re Edwards* [1906] 1 Ch 570, CA.

The golden rule was formulated at a time when the intestacy rules probably did not reflect the wishes of the average testator. Given the reforms in the law of intestacy in the twentieth century, the justification for the rule has become less obvious. Its current status is uncertain: in reality it is little more than a general exhortation to the courts which hardly merits the description 'rule'. There is also some confusion in the description of the rule as 'golden' in that judges have occasionally referred to the principle that words must be construed *prima facie* in their ordinary, literal sense as 'the golden rule'.

6.3.1.2 The *falsa demonstratio* rule

Falsa demonstratio non nocet — 'a false description does not harm'. This rule (derived from Roman law) is concerned with incorrect descriptions of persons and property: a wrong description does not prevent a gift passing provided that there is sufficient evidence in the will, with the help of any admissible extrinsic evidence, as to the true intention of the testator. Suppose that Arthur makes a will in which he leaves his house in 'Camelot Way' to his best friend 'Lance Allott', and that it transpires that the correct address of his house is 'Camelot Drive' and that the intended beneficiary's name is Len Allott. Len will be able to claim the house, despite the incorrect descriptions, if there is sufficient evidence of Arthur's intentions.

The case law on the *falsa demonstratio* rule is rich and varied. A few examples must suffice. In *Ryall* v *Hannam* (1847) 10 Beav 536; 50 ER 688, the testator devised estate to 'Elizabeth Abbott a natural daughter of Elizabeth Abbott'. No such person answered to the description but the estate was claimed by John, the only illegitimate child of Elizabeth Abbott. Despite the misdescription as to name and sex, the estate passed to John. In *Re Mayell* [1913] 2 Ch 488, the testator devised his several houses in Trowbridge, Wiltshire. One devise was of two properties 'known as Nos 19 and 20, Castle Street'. He owned only one property in Castle Street (No. 39) but owned two in Thomas Street (Nos 19 and 20). It was held that the latter passed under the gift of 'Nos 19 and 20

Castle Street'. In *Re Gifford* [1944] Ch 186, a testatrix bequeathed in 1938 income derived from 'my war bonds'. She had no war bonds at the time but had purchased war bonds in 1920 which had been converted into consolidated stock. After the will was made she purchased national savings certificates and defence bonds. The court applied the *falsa demonstratio* rule and held that the consolidated stock passed under the gift of 'war bonds'. But the savings certificates and defence bonds did not pass because the *falsa demonstratio* rule does not apply to property which the testatrix did not possess — and did not contemplate possessing — when the will was made. Simonds J described the rule as follows (at p. 188):

> ... if, on consideration of the relevant parts of the will, one comes to the conclusion that the testatrix intended to pass something and can determine what that something is, then the fact that she has given it a wrong description will not prevent her will taking effect in regard to that which is wrongly described.

This formulation of the rule is wider than was originally the case. The previous version of the rule — traceable to the maxims of Lord Chancellor Bacon in the early seventeenth century — was that if the description consisted of more than one part, and one part was correct while the other was false, then the gift passed provided the correct part identified the person or property with sufficient certainty. It is clear that the rule is now wider, as demonstrated by *Re Gifford*. Indeed, the rule has been extended to cases where the description is *wholly* incorrect but the testator's intention was clear: *Re Price* [1932] 2 Ch 54.

What if the description, although incorrect as regards the intended beneficiary, exactly fits another claimant? In *NSPCC* v *Scottish NSPCC* [1915] AC 207, the testator, a Scotsman who had lived all his life in Scotland, bequeathed several legacies to Scottish charities. Among these legacies was one to 'the National Society for the Prevention of Cruelty to Children'. It was claimed by the society of that name (an English charity) and by the Scottish NSPCC. There was considerable extrinsic evidence to suggest that the testator intended the Scottish society to benefit, but much of it was held inadmissible, with the result that it was the NSPCC that was held entitled to take. Earl Loreburn stated (at p. 212):

> ... the accurate use of a name in a will creates a strong presumption against any rival who is not the possessor of the name mentioned in the will. It is a very strong presumption and one which cannot be overcome except in exceptional circumstances.

It is possible, however, that in such a case extrinsic evidence would now be more readily admissible by virtue of s. 21 of the Administration of Justice Act 1982 (see 6.4.3.3), or even that the remedy of rectification might apply on appropriate facts (see 3.2.6.5).

The *falsa demonstratio* rule does not apply where words of description can properly be read as words of restriction. Thus, if there is doubt whether such words impart a false description or restrict the generality of a gift, the court will apply the words restrictively. In *Morrell* v *Fisher* (1849) 4 Ex 591; 154 ER 1350, the testator devised 'all my lease-hold farm-house, homestead, lands, and tenements at Headington, containing about 170 acres, held under Magdalen College, Oxford, and now in the occupation of Thomas Burrows, junior, as tenant to me'. The issue was whether the gift passed two leaseholds (formerly belonging to the farm) which Thomas had never occupied. It was argued that the phrase 'now in the occupation of ...' should be rejected as a false description, but the court held that the words amounted to a restriction which prevailed since the testator had property to which they could properly apply. Thus the devise did not pass the two disputed leaseholds.

6.3.1.3   The *eiusdem generis* rule

This rule is concerned with the interpretation of words and phrases with a potentially wide meaning, e.g., 'effects', 'other goods', 'other property'. The rule is that if such general words are preceded by an enumeration of specific things, the meaning of the general words will be restricted so that they pass only property of the same class or type (*eiusdem generis*) as the things specifically mentioned. But, for the rule to apply, the specific things must be sufficiently alike to constitute a single class or type. In *Gibbs* v *Lawrence* (1862) 30 LJ Ch 171, the testator bequeathed 'all and singular my household furniture, plate, linen, china, pictures, and other goods, chattels and effects which shall be in or upon or about my dwelling-house and premises at the time of my decease' to his niece. The issue was whether this gift passed banknotes worth £460 found in his house after his death. It was held that since 'effects' had to be construed *eiusdem generis* with the items specifically enumerated, the money was not comprised in the bequest. The enumerated items did form a class as they were all articles 'that are of the kind which tend to the beneficial and comfortable occupation of the house in question' (p. 173). See also *Re Miller* (1889) 61 LT 365.

Since the application of the rule turns on whether the enumerated things form a class, the question arises — how many things must be enumerated? There must be sufficient enumeration for a class to be constituted in the opinion of the court. Most of the cases show the enumeration of several items of property; clearly reference to only one specific thing is insufficient. Thus in *Arnold* v *Arnold* (1835) 2 My & K 365; 39 ER 983, the rule was not applied to a gift of 'my wines and property in England' — the word 'property' was construed as passing the testator's property in England of every description. In *Swinfen* v *Swinfen* (1860) 29 Beav 207; 54 ER 606, the testator devised to his son's widow 'all my estate at Swinfen or thereto adjoining, also all furniture and other moveable goods here'. The question was whether livestock, farming implements and money (all at Swinfen) passed as 'other moveable goods'. The court refused to apply the *eiusdem generis* rule since the general words were preceded by only one particular word ('furniture'). Thus all the disputed items passed to the widow.

The *eiusdem generis* rule is more likely to be applied if there is an express gift of residue. If there is no gift of residue, the rule is less likely to apply since there is less justification in such a case to give the general words a narrow meaning. For example, in *Hodgson* v *Jex* (1876) 2 Ch D 122, the rule was held not to apply to a bequest of 'all my plate, linen, furniture, and other effects that may be in my possession at the time of my death'. There was no express residuary gift, and the court held that the whole of the residuary personalty (including money and jewellery) passed under the gift of 'other effects'. It may be that this decision reflected the court's desire to avoid an intestacy. The rule does not in any case apply if the testator has expressed a contrary intention.

What if general words *precede* the enumeration of specific words? The position is that the general words are not restricted to things *eiusdem generis*. In *Fisher* v *Hepburn* (1851) 14 Beav 626; 51 ER 425, a clause in the testator's will stated, 'And as to all the rest, residue, and remainder of my estate and effects, whatsoever and wheresoever, Canal shares, plate, linen, china, and furniture, I give, devise, and bequeath the same to my said wife'. It was held that the whole of the residuary personalty passed under this gift, the specific items being treated not as words of restriction but rather as words of enlargement (the object being to exclude nothing). It seems that it makes no difference if, following the general words, the specific words are prefaced by explanatory phrases, e.g., 'such as', 'consisting of', or 'namely'. In *Re Fleetwood* (1880) 15 Ch D 594, the testatrix devised her realty to JB and 'also all my personalty, such as cash, furniture, &c, to be applied as I have requested him to do'. It was held that the specific words did not cut down the phrase 'all my personalty'; hence the gift carried the entire personal estate.

6.3.1.4   Inconsistent provisions

If two parts of a will are inconsistent, the court may treat the later provisions as prevailing over the earlier. The rule (again derived from Roman law) is a rule of last resort, when the court cannot reconcile inconsistent provisions and despairs of resolving the dispute by any other means. The justification for the rule is that the later provision may be regarded as the latest expression of the testator's wishes, but this is hardly convincing. In reality the rule is somewhat arbitrary — it was described as a 'rule of thumb' in *Re Bywater* (1881) 18 Ch D 17, CA. Nevertheless, used with caution, and in appropriate circumstances, the rule can aid the court. In *Re Hammond* [1938] 3 All ER 308, the testator made several bequests to charitable institutions. Each bequest was stated in both words and figures to be £500, except one to 'Miss May's Mission' which read 'the sum of one hundred pounds (£500)'. Simmonds J applied the rule, so that the Mission was held entitled to £500. The judge stated (at p. 309) that the rule must 'give way to the context, but the context here justifies the view that the testator intended £500, and not £100'. Since the rule must give way to the context it follows that the earlier provision will prevail if that is consistent with the testator's intention. In *Re Bywater* (above), a testator bequeathed an annuity to his wife, payable when the daughters of his former wife reached the age of 21. Later in the same clause he directed that the first payment should be made within six months of his death. It was held that the earlier provision should prevail since it expressed the testator's intentions. The subsequent provision could not have the effect of altering the time of payment from that which the words of gift authorised.

Because the rule is one of last resort, and the justification for it is tenuous, the court will make every effort to reconcile the inconsistencies: *Re Potter's WT* [1944] Ch 70 (where the rule was described as a 'rule of despair'). Or the court may try to achieve a compromise where no reconciliation is strictly possible. This applies particularly where the same property is given to two (or more) persons in the same will. In *Re Alexander's WT* (1948) 64 TLR 308, the testatrix bequeathed her 'five row diamond bracelet' to a named legatee, and her 'diamond chain bracelet' to another legatee. She possessed only one diamond bracelet, a chain bracelet containing eight rows of diamonds. It was held that since the bracelet was divisible (without loss of value) each legatee should receive part of it.

The rule concerning inconsistent provisions does not apply where there are two residuary gifts to different beneficiaries in the same instrument. In such a case the earlier gift prevails, there being no property left to which the later one can apply. In *Re Gare* [1952] Ch 80, the testator left the 'residue of my estate' equally to St Peter's Church, Staines and Oxford University. In the last clause of the will he left all his estate 'not hereby otherwise disposed of unto my executors to deal with at their discretion'. It was held that the earlier gift carried the whole residue so that there was nothing on which the later one could operate. Again, the court will do its utmost to find consistency between the provisions.

Where an absolute gift of personalty has trusts imposed on it in the same instrument, and those trusts fail, the absolute gift takes effect free of those trusts. This is another variation of the inconsistent provisions rule, and often described as the rule in *Hancock v Watson*. It is clear that for this rule to operate there must be (i) an initial absolute gift, and (ii) failure of the imposed trusts. In *Hancock v Watson* [1902] AC 14, a testator divided the remainder in his residuary estate into five portions and bequeathed two of them to SD. The will then provided that the portions 'allotted' to SD should remain in trust for her life and after her death be held on other trusts. When SD died the question arose — the other trusts having failed — whether the two portions formed part of SD's estate. It was held that they did since the gift to SD had been absolute (shown by the use of the words 'allotted' and 'to SD I give . . .'). Lord Davey stated (at p. 22):

> . . . if you find an absolute gift to a legatee in the first instance, and trusts are engrafted or imposed on that absolute interest which fail, either from lapse or invalidity or any other reason, then the absolute gift takes effect so far as the trusts have failed to the exclusion of the residuary legatee or next-of-kin as the case may be . . . if the terms of the gift are ambiguous, you may seek assistance in construing it — in saying whether it is expressed as an absolute gift or not — from the other parts of the will, including the language of the engrafted trusts.

This rule is also known as the rule in *Lassence v Tierney* (1849) 1 Mac & G 551; 41 ER 1379 and seems to apply to realty as well as personalty: *Moryoseph v Moryoseph* [1920] 2 Ch 33.

6.3.2 The class-closing rules

6.3.2.1 Introduction
As with the rules discussed in 6.3.1, the class-closing rules were created by
the courts. But their importance justifies separate treatment. When a gift
is made to a class of persons, and the size of the class is capable of increasing
after the testator's death, the class-closing rules (sometimes referred to as 'the
rule in *Andrews* v *Partington*') determine when the class is to close. If
the class did not close, the property might not be distributed for possibly a
long time. For example, suppose that a testator leaves property to 'my
grandchildren'. When he dies he has two grandchildren alive, but others are
born after his death (perhaps many years after). At what point should the
class be regarded as closed, thus excluding grandchildren born after that
time? Protecting the interests of those who definitely qualify — they want early
vesting of the gift — should ideally be balanced against the interests of the
other members of the class who might qualify at a later stage. Why should they
be excluded just so that those already qualified might benefit earlier? Might
not the testator have intended that all his grandchildren, whenever born,
should be entitled? But there are other interests to be considered: the executors
would presumably prefer the size of the class to be determined at the earliest
time so that they can conveniently distribute the estate without undue
delay (hence the class-closing rules are often described as rules of
'convenience'). And there may be an economic argument for not allowing the
class to remain open indefinitely — the property might otherwise be tied up
for too long. Nevertheless, although there are serious arguments in justification
of the class-closing rules, the objection remains that they produce inequality
between members of the same class. Might not the application of the rules
fuel family strife?

The attitude of the judges to the class-closing rules has been diverse (see
J.H.C. Morris (1954) 70 LQR 61). Some have applied the rules with great
reluctance, regarding them as highly artificial and contrary to the testator's
probable intention. For example, in *Re Emmet's Estate* (1879) 13 Ch D 484,
Jessel MR described the rules (at p. 490) as 'not founded on any view of the
testator's intention'. The Court of Appeal in *Re Bleckly* [1951] Ch 740
castigated the rules as 'distasteful' and 'insensible' in origin (but nevertheless
still applied them). The judgment of Astbury J in *Re Chartres* [1927] 1 Ch 466
is particularly critical, referring to 'this so-called rule of convenience' which
when applied 'more or less defeats the intention of the testator'. He adds (at
p. 471):

> The principle of this rule is that the class to take is to be ascertained as
> soon as possible in order that the beneficiaries may know what their shares
> are and that the fund may be distributed. The rule is, of course, obviously
> convenient to those who take under it to the exclusion of others intended
> to benefit, but the irony of the rule is no doubt more apparent to those who
> are by its application excluded from taking what the testator intended them
> to take.

But the class-closing rules find occasional support. In *Re Henderson's Trusts* [1969] 3 All ER 769, CA, Russell LJ conceded that the rules may run counter to the testator's intentions but pertinently observed that if the testator 'were asked whether he meant an ageing class to be kept hanging about waiting for distribution of the capital in case an 80-year-old should perchance produce a whole string of additions to the class, he might say no' (p. 773). And in *Gimblett* v *Purton* (1871) LR 12 Eq 427, Malins VC commented (at p. 430):

> ... when I was a student at law, it struck me as unconscionable that the class of persons to take in cases of this nature should be ascertained at a particular period, and that those who came into existence after that period should be excluded; but experience has shewn me the sound sense of the rule, because the object of the law is to make property vest as early as possible, so that the persons to whom it is given may know what they have to expect, and make the fund available at the earliest period.

Although judicial opinion has been divided about the merits of the class-closing rules, they are too well established not to be followed. Even judges critical of the rules have been disinclined to consider other solutions — for example, early vesting for members eligible within the class on condition that a repayment is made if the class subsequently increases. It may be that the problems inherent in such alternatives point to the class-closing rules as being the least worst solution.

6.3.2.2 Class gifts
What is a class gift? It is a gift which is meant to be *shared* between persons answering a general description constituting a class. Thus the size of the gift to each member is determined by the number of persons in the class. In *Pearks* v *Moseley* (1880) 5 App Cas 714, Lord Selborne LC stated (at p. 723):

> A gift is said to be to a 'class' of persons, when it is to all those who shall come within a certain category or description defined by a general or collective formula, and who, if they take at all, are to take one divisible subject in certain proportionate shares.

Similarly, in *Kingsbury* v *Walter* [1901] AC 187, at 192, a class gift was defined as 'a gift to a class, consisting of persons who are included and comprehended under some general description and bear a certain relation to the testator' (*per* Lord Davey). Gifts can be made to individuals within a class, but such gifts are strictly not class gifts (which are gifts to a class, not to individuals). Thus, if a testator gives £1,000 'to each of my grandchildren', the gift is not a class gift; but a gift of £1,000 'to my grandchildren' would be.

Whether a gift is regarded as a class gift or as a gift to an individual is crucial in determining not only the size of each beneficiary's entitlement but also its destination in the event of lapse (i.e. where the beneficiary predeceases the testator). In the case of a gift to an individual, the rules on lapse operate (see 7.2.5), with the result that the property that would have passed to the beneficiary will normally fall into residue as a general rule. But in the case of a class gift, the share of any member who fails to take passes to the other members by *ius accrescendi* as a general rule.

A gift may be a class gift even though the testator names individuals within the class. In *Kingsbury* v *Walter* (above) the testator left all his shares in the *Daily Telegraph* to his wife for life, remainder to 'Elizabeth Jane Fowler and the child or children of my sister Emily Walter'. Elizabeth predeceased him. The question eventually arose whether Elizabeth's share lapsed or whether it went to the other members of the class. It was held that the share did not lapse since the testator had made a class gift (Elizabeth and the other beneficiaries were all nieces or nephews of the testator). The fact that Elizabeth was named did not prevent the gift from being a class gift.

6.3.2.3 Operation of the rules

The operation of the class-closing rules depends on whether the gift is immediate or postponed, and whether it is subject to any qualification imposed by the testator as to the time when the gift vests.

(a) *Immediate gift without qualification*: for example, 'to my grandchildren'. The rule is that if any member of the class is alive at the testator's death, the class closes at that time: *Viner* v *Francis* (1789) 2 Cox 190; 30 ER 88. All those alive (born or conceived) at the testator's death qualify as members of the class, but those conceived thereafter do not. However, if no members of the class are alive at the testator's death, the class stays open indefinitely: thus all those conceived thereafter will be entitled: *Shepherd* v *Ingram* (1764) Amb 448; 27 ER 296.

(b) *Postponed gift without qualification*: for example, 'to A for life, remainder to B's children'. The rule is that if any member of the class is alive when the postponement ends, the class closes at that time. Thus, if there is a child of B alive when A dies, the class closes at that time. But if no member of the class is alive when A dies, the class remains open indefinitely. In *Re Chartres* (above) Astbury J stated (at pp. 471–2):

> If the gift is *in futuro*, as for instance to A for life with remainder to B's children, the rule provides that only those children of B shall take who come into existence before A's death. Here again there is an exception that if there are no children of *in esse* before A's death, then the rule ceases to operate, and all subsequently born children take.

(c) *Immediate gift with qualification*: for example, 'to my grandchildren who attain the age of 21'. In *Andrews* v *Partington* (1791) 3 Bro CC 401; 29 ER 610, it was held that the rule in this situation is that if a member of the class has satisfied the qualification (i.e. attained 21 in the above example) when the testator dies, the class closes at that time; otherwise the class closes after the testator's death as soon as a member satisfies the qualification. Whenever the class closes, any members who are alive at that time will be entitled to take provided that they satisfy the qualification. For example, suppose that in the above scenario a grandchild has attained 21 when the testator dies. Not only is that grandchild entitled but also any grandchildren then alive may take on attaining 21. That the class-closing rules are sometimes referred to as 'the rule in *Andrews* v *Partington*' is puzzling since the decision was concerned only with the case of an immediate gift with qualification.

(d)   *Postponed gift with qualification*: for example, 'to A for life, remainder to my grandchildren who attain 21'. The class will close when the postponement ends (i.e. when A dies) provided that a member of the class has attained 21; otherwise the class will close as soon as a member attains 21 after A's death. Whenever the class closes, any members then alive will be entitled subject to attaining 21. In *Re Emmet's Estate* (see 6.3.2.1), the testator gave part of his property to Henry Emmet for life, remainder to the children of George Emmet on attaining 21 (or marrying under that age, in the case of daughters). When the eldest of George's children attained 21, there were five other children (all of whom lived to attain 21). It was held that these six children were entitled to share in the gift, but not a child conceived afterwards.

It should be noted that the effect of closing the class will be not only to exclude those coming into existence thereafter, but also to fix the minimum entitlement of those qualifying, which may increase if the shares of other members of the class lapse. For example, suppose that the testator leaves a gift to 'A for life, remainder to my grandchildren who attain 21', and that on A's death one grandchild (X) has attained 21 and two others are alive but under 21. X is entitled to a minimum one-third share, but it will increase to a half share if one of the other grandchildren fails to attain 21 (or to the whole of the gift if neither attains 21).

6.3.2.4   The effect of acceleration

What is the effect on a postponed gift if the preceding interest fails — for example, by lapse or disclaimer? As regards lapse, the class gift is accelerated, thus becoming an immediate gift. To illustrate: suppose that the testator makes a gift to 'A for life, remainder to my grandchildren'. If A then predeceased the testator, the class gift to the grandchildren would be accelerated — it would become an immediate gift. Thus the class would close if any grandchild was alive at the testator's death, otherwise it would remain open indefinitely.

What if, in the above example, A did not predecease the testator but disclaimed (or assigned) his life interest after the latter's death? The class gift to the grandchildren would be accelerated, but when should the class close — at the time of the disclaimer or when A dies? In *Re Davies* [1957] 3 All ER 52, it was held that the class closed at the date of disclaimer. However, in *Re Kebty-Fletcher's WT* [1969] 1 Ch 339 — where there was an assignment of a life interest rather than a disclaimer — it was held that the class remained open until the death of the beneficiary who had assigned his interest. Stamp J distinguished *Re Davies* on the ground that the latter was concerned with disclaimer, and stated (p. 344):

The release of a life interest in favour of children is one of the commonest features in the field of trusts and, so far as I am aware, it has never hitherto been suggested that such a release may have the dramatic effect now claimed of altering the membership of the class of children to take.

The decision in *Re Kebty-Fletcher's WT* turned partly on the judge's distaste for the possibility that the composition of a class could be determined by the unilateral act of the life tenant. The same reasoning was adopted in *Re Harker's WT* [1969] 3 All ER 1, where property was held upon trust for the testatrix's son for life, remainder to those of his children who attained 21. When the son surrendered his interest to his children (one aged over 21, the other two under 21) the question arose whether the class closed at that time or whether it remained opened during the son's life. It was held that the class remained open until the son died. Goff J was unable to distinguish between a disclaimer (*Re Davies*) and a surrender, but chose not to follow that case.

6.3.2.5   When the rules do not apply
There are a number of instances where the class-closing rules do not apply, apart from the situations mentioned previously (i.e. where the class stays open indefinitely). For example, class-closing rules obviously do not operate where a class is incapable of increasing: there is then no need to close the class. Thus the rules do not apply where a gift is made to the testator's children or to 'A for life, remainder to A's children'. Moreover, the class-closing rules do not apply to gifts of income to a class. In *Re Ward* [1965] Ch 856, the distinction was justified on the grounds that, whereas closing the class entitled to a gift of capital was based on the supposition that the testator would not wish a member to be denied his entitlement unduly, the same was not true of a gift of income — such a gift could be distributed from time to time among such members of the class then living. Each instalment of the income due is paid to the members of the class for the time being. In *Re Wenmoth's Estate* (1887) 37 Ch D 266, the testator made a gift of income to his grandchildren on their attaining 21. The question arose whether the gift was confined to (i) grandchildren alive at the testator's death, or (ii) those alive when the eldest attained 21, or (iii) all grandchildren, whenever born. The court held that all the grandchildren, whenever born, could take.

Since the class-closing rules are rules of construction, they are excluded if their application would be contrary to the testator's intention. This is potentially the most important of the exceptions to the operation of the rules. However, the significance of the exception is unclear since the rules themselves have often been judicially castigated as inconsistent with the testator's intentions (but yet applied). It seems that for the rules to be excluded, the contrary intention must be clearly proved, as was made clear by Lord Evershed MR in *Re Bleckly* (see 6.3.2.1) where he stated (at p. 750) that the class-closing rule must 'give way to the language of the will in question if the language is sufficiently clear to displace it'. A contrary intention may be shown where the testator sets aside a specified fund for claims of any members of the class born after his death: *Defflis* v *Goldschmidt* (1816) 19 Ves 566; 34 ER 626. Or where he specifically anticipates the problems that may arise from the closing of a class, or where he provides his own class closing date: *Re Tom's Settlement* [1987] 1 All ER 1081. In that case, concerning an *inter vivos* settlement, a fund of some £12m was created for the settlor's future grandchildren and great-grandchildren who attained 18. It was provided that at the 'closing date' (as defined by the settlement) each beneficiary would acquire an interest in possession in the fund. Since the class-closing date had been defined the normal rule in *Andrews* v *Partington* was excluded.

The choice of particular words or phrases by the testator, when describing the class, may indicate a contrary intention, but great care must be taken in this respect since the courts have engaged in some fine distinctions. In *Re Bleckly* (above) a gift on trust for 'all or any of the children or child of my son' who attain 21 was held insufficient to show a contrary intention — an understandable decision. Less obvious is why an apparently clear phrase, such as 'now born or who shall be born hereafter', is insufficient to exclude the rules, as was held in *Re Chapman's Settlement Trusts* [1978] 1 All ER 1122, CA. The explanation appears to be that such a phrase is merely a general reference to the future, lacking sufficient particularity — for example, it could be taken to refer merely to children born between the making of the will and the testator's death. On the other hand, in *Re Edmondson's WT* [1972] 1 All ER 444, CA, it was held that the phrase 'whenever born' did suffice to show a contrary intention. The testator gave his son a power of appointment over part of the testator's residuary estate. The son exercised it in favour of his grandchildren 'whenever born' on attaining 21. The court excluded the rule in *Andrews* v *Partington*, Russell LJ stating (at p. 449) that 'whenever born' was 'a particular reference to the future expressly unlimited in time and, therefore, readily to be distinguished as inconsistent with a time limitation such as is imposed by the rule'. The distinction between 'born hereafter' and 'whenever born' is one that may indeed be readily apparent to the finely-tuned legal brains populating the Chancery Division and the appeal courts, but is one that might well have escaped the testator.

6.3.3 Statutory rules of construction

6.3.3.1 A will speaks from death
Section 24 of the Wills Act 1837 provides:

> Every will shall be construed, with reference to the real estate and personal estate comprised in it, to speak and take effect as if it had been executed immediately before the death of the testator, unless a contrary intention shall appear by the will.

The fact that a will speaks from death (as regards property) is a consequence of the ambulatory nature of wills (see 2.1.1.2). All the property which satisfies the description of the gift as at the death of the testator passes, even if it was acquired after the making of the will. Suppose that Arthur leaves 'his horses' to his wife, and that he owned two horses when he made the will but acquired many more thereafter. His wife would be entitled to all the horses owned by him when he died. In *Lady Langdale* v *Briggs* (1855) 25 LJ Ch 100, the Earl of Oxford left all his freeholds to his eldest daughter for life, remainder to her sons. Later he acquired further freeholds; it was held that the after-acquired estates passed under the will.

Section 24 will not apply if a contrary intention appears 'by the will', i.e. the intention must be expressed in the instrument. The intention might be expressed directly by the testator by an appropriate phrase or clause, or it may be implied. Words that appear to indicate a particular time, such as 'where I *now* reside' or 'which I *presently* occupy', may suffice to show a contrary intention. But the use of such words can be ambiguous. Suppose, for example, that a testator leaves 'the house where I now live' to X. He later sells his house and buys another. Is X entitled to the later house? What did the testator mean by 'now' — did he mean to pass to X only the house in which he lived when the will was executed? From the inconsistent case law on this question it is possible to detect the following rule: the reference to the present (i.e. the time when the will was made) suffices to show a contrary intention if the reference is an essential part of the description of the subject-matter of the gift. For example, in *Re Whitby* [1944] Ch 210, CA, the testator left personal chattels to his niece but, by a later codicil, excluded 'all articles of jewellery and other chattels and effects belonging to me and which are now deposited for safe custody at the Manchester Safe Deposit Co.'. Later he deposited further articles in the safe deposit. The court held that the words used showed a contrary intention: thus only articles deposited when the later codicil was made were excluded. Lord Greene MR stated (at p. 215) that 'the testator was thinking of a particular time, namely, the date of his codicil, just as he was thinking of a particular place'. In *Re Edwards* (1890) 63 LT 481, the testator bequeathed his 'leasehold house and premises called the Anchor Inn, where I now reside'. The property was being reconstructed at the time with a view to separating two rooms from the inn. This was completed after the will was made, and the two rooms were let for use as a shop. The testator continued to reside at the inn until his death, the tenant occupying the shop. It was held that the shop passed under the gift.

In these cases the reference to time was treated as controlling the context of the gift's description. On the other hand, if the court considers that the reference to time is superfluous, or just an additional and non-essential part of the description, s. 24 will apply as no contrary intention will have been shown. Consider, for example, *Re Willis* [1911] 2 Ch 563: the testator devised 'all that my freehold house and premises situate at Oakleigh Park, Whetstone, in the county of Middlesex, and known as "Ankerwyke", and in which I now reside'. Later the testator acquired two adjoining plots of land, one of which was converted into a garden with tennis lawn. They were occupied as part of 'Ankerwyke'. It was held that 'in which I now reside' was merely an additional description of the property in the gift. Consequently, s. 24 applied so that the adjoining plots passed under the devise. In *Wagstaff* v *Wagstaff* (1869) LR 8 Eq 229, the testator made a gift of various parts of his estate and 'any other property that I may now possess'. The word 'now' was held to be superfluous: Lord Romilly MR stated (at p. 230) that the words 'I now possess' meant, on the facts, the same as 'I possess'.

Although each of these decisions may be justifiable on the facts, the impression gained is that the court has considerable flexibility in reaching the result it desires. In practice it will often be difficult for advisers to predict the probable interpretation of such words in a particular case.

What if the testator's interest in the property alters after the execution of the will? Section 24 will be excluded if it is clear that the testator intended to pass *only* the interest that he held when making the will. In *Re Fleming's WT* [1974] 3 All ER 323, the testator gave 'my leasehold house 54 Narcissus Road' Hampstead to a housing trust. Later he acquired the freehold in the property. Did the housing trust receive the leasehold or the freehold? It was held that the gift passed the testator's entire interest in the house since a mere reference in the will to the interest held by the testator at the date of his will was insufficient to disclose a contrary intention.

Section 24 appears to apply to all types of gift (for the classification of gifts see 7.1). As regards specific gifts, if the gift is generic — the subject-matter capable of fluctuating after the making of the will — s. 24 clearly applies. For example, if the testator leaves 'all my shares in British Petroleum', the legatee will be entitled to all the shares owned by the testator at his death (subject to any contrary intention). That may include shares acquired after the making of the will. In *Re Bancroft* [1928] Ch 577, the testator bequeathed to Sir Gerald du Maurier (the actor and impresario) 'all my rights to or in connection with the play "Diplomacy"'. Later the testator sold the film rights in the play for £1,500 but died before the assignment of the rights was executed. It was held that since no contrary intention appeared in the will, s. 24 applied. Thus the right to sue for specific performance of the contract passed under the bequest.

But if the specific right is particularised in such a way as to show that only the property existing at the time of making the will was intended to pass, a contrary intention is established. If the subject-matter of the gift ceases to exist, for example, or is disposed of, the gift fails through ademption. In *Re Gibson* (1866) LR 2 Eq 669, the testator bequeathed to his son 'my one thousand North British Railway preference shares'. He had at the time of making the will £1,000 North British Railway stock, but he later sold it and acquired other stocks and shares in the same company. It was held that the will expressed a sufficient contrary intention to exclude s. 24. Thus the gift comprised only the stock held at the time of the will's execution; the gift failed through ademption. In *Re Sikes* [1927] 1 Ch 364, the testatrix bequeathed 'my piano' but later sold the piano and bought another. It was held that the later piano did not pass under the bequest since the intention (in the court's view) was to give the particular piano in the testatrix's possession when she made the will, and no other. Although well-known, this case is unsatisfactory because of the very short judgment, in which the judge does not fully explain why he thought there was a contrary intention excluding s. 24. In *Re Evans* [1909] 1 Ch 784, the testator left to his wife his 'house and effects known as Cross Villa situated in Templeton in the county of Pembroke'. At the time of the will's execution he possessed some ground with a house on it, the premises being known as 'Cross Villa'. Later he erected two houses, named 'Ashgrove Villas', on the same ground (separated from the rest by a hedge). Was the wife entitled to the whole of the property known as 'Cross Villa' at the date of the will or, if s. 24 applied, only to the separated part answering that description at the testator's death? Joyce J held that s. 24 was excluded by a contrary intention:

> ... where there is such a peculiarity in the description of the subject of a gift as to shew that it was some object in existence at the date of the will that was intended to pass, it is considered that there is sufficient evidence of a contrary intention to exclude the application of the provisions of s. 24. (p. 786)

What is the effect of republication on the application of s. 24? Where s. 24 applies — that is, there is no contrary intention in the will — republication has *prima facie* no effect because the republished will speaks from death as regards property. But if there is a contrary intention, the will speaks from the date of execution, namely, the date of republication: s. 34 of the Wills Act 1837. The relationship of ss. 24 and 34, as illustrated in cases such as *Re Reeves* [1928] Ch 351, has already been considered (see 5.6.2.2).

Section 24 applies to property, not persons. Hence references in a will to beneficiaries are generally construed as applicable to persons alive at the will's execution. The general rule is illustrated by *Re Whorwood* (1887) 34 Ch D 446, CA: the testator bequeathed to 'Lord Sherborne and his heirs, my Oliver Cromwell cup ... for an heirloom' (the cup had been given by Cromwell to his son-in-law, General Ireton, who had given it to the Whorwood family). The person who was Lord Sherborne at the date of the will died two years later, predeceasing the testator. It was held that the bequest lapsed: on the true construction of the will the testator intended to benefit the person who was Lord Sherborne when the will was made and not the person who might be Lord Sherborne when the testator died (despite the phrases 'and his heirs' and 'for an heirloom'). In *Amyot v Dwarris* [1904] AC 268, PC, the testator devised 'Golden Grove' (a plantation in Jamaica) to 'the eldest son of my sister'. The sister had four sons — twins alive at the date of the will, and two sons born thereafter. The twins predeceased the testator. It was held that the gift operated in favour of the elder of her two sons living at the date of the will. Accordingly, an intestacy resulted.

The rule that descriptions of persons are construed as at the date of the will is subject to any contrary intention appearing in the will. In *Re Davidson* [1909] 1 Ch 567, CA, it was held that a gift to 'the Roman Catholic Archbishop of Westminster for the time being' meant the Archbishop at the time of the testator's death. Similarly, in *Re Daniels* (1918) 118 LT 435, a gift of £25,000 to 'the Lord Mayor of London for the time being' for charitable purposes was held to pass to the person who filled the office of Lord Mayor at the testator's death.

Where the general rule as to persons applies (i.e. there is no contrary intention in the will), the effect of republication will be to make the will apply to the persons answering the description at the date of republication: s. 34 of the Wills Act 1837, and see *Re Hardyman* (5.6.2.1).

6.3.3.2   General gift exercises a general power of appointment

Under s. 27 of the Wills Act 1837, a general gift by will of realty or personalty has the effect of exercising a power of appointment given to the testator to appoint property 'in any manner he may think proper'. It is clear that the section applies to a general but not to a special power of appointment. Nor does it apply to a 'hybrid' power, that is, a power to appoint generally but excepting certain specified persons. In *Re Byron's Settlement* [1891] 3 Ch 474, a widow settled property on her married daughter and gave her the power to appoint in favour of 'such person or persons (not being her said present husband, or any friend or relative of his)' as the daughter should choose. Eventually the daughter made a will containing a general gift of all her property in favour of her sister. It was held that since the power given to the testatrix was not a general power, it had not been exercised by the general gift in the will.

The gift need not be of the whole of the testator's estate, or of all of his realty or personalty. But the gift must be sufficiently wide to comprise the property subject to the power. A residuary gift may bring s. 27 into operation, as in *Clifford* v *Clifford* (1852) 9 Hare 675; 68 ER 684. The testatrix had a general power of appointment over a sum of £10,000. She devised her lands to A for life and gave A all the residue of her personal estate. It was held that the £10,000 passed under the residuary gift of personalty.

Section 27 is inapplicable if a contrary intention appears in the will. To prove such an intention there must be evidence from the will that the testator did not intend to exercise the power of appointment: *Re Jacob* [1907] 1 Ch 445.

6.3.3.3   Passing the fee

This rule of construction is not concerned (despite the name) with some arcane practice in the legal profession, or with a strange new ball game, but with devises made without words of limitation. Section 28 of the Wills Act 1837 provides:

> Where any real estate shall be devised to any person without any words of limitation, such devise shall be construed to pass the fee simple, or other the whole estate or interest which the testator had power to dispose of by will in such real estate, unless a contrary intention shall appear by the will.

Prior to the Act such a devise passed only a life interest, as a general rule. The courts are likely to be slow in finding a contrary intention under s. 28. For example, the mere fact that the will contains devises with words of limitation does not exclude s. 28: *Wisden* v *Wisden* (1854) 2 Sm & G 396; 65 ER 452. Section 28 has been applied to a devise of all the income of real property — such a devise passes the fee. In *Mannox* v *Greener* (1872) 14 Eq 456, the testator owned several properties. He made a gift to his children of 'all the income' of certain of the properties. It was held that the devise of the income passed the fee simple in them.

6.3.3.4   Presumption of absolute gift to spouse

Section 22 of the Administration of Justice Act 1982 provides:

Except where a contrary intention is shown it shall be presumed that if a testator devises or bequeaths property to his spouse in terms which in themselves would give an absolute interest to the spouse, but by the same instrument purports to give his issue an interest in the same property, the gift to the spouse is absolute notwithstanding the purported gift to the issue.

This section, which applies if a testator dies on or after 1 January 1983, deals with a situation commonly occurring in home-made wills — the testator gives property to his wife and provides that it should pass to their children on her death. The effect before the 1982 Act was that the wife might have received, probably unintentionally, only a life interest. This possibility was ended by s. 22 where an absolute interest is given to the spouse and an interest in the same property is purported to be given by the *same instrument* to *issue*. This reform was advocated by the Law Reform Committee (LRC Report No. 19, 1973):

... we favour a provision which would have the effect that any gift, however expressed, by which a testator leaves property to his wife in terms which, without more, would confer an absolute interest, and then to his issue ... should be presumed, unless a contrary intention appears, to be intended to take effect as an absolute gift to the widow. (para. 62)

6.3.3.5 Relationships
A number of statutes, of comparatively recent enactment, have affected the construction of words of relationship such as 'children'. The broad effect of these provisions has been to widen the interpretation of such words, thus increasing the number of potential claimants.

(a)   Illegitimate persons   The position depends on when the will was made. If the will was made before 1970, the rule in *Hill* v *Crook* (1873) LR 6 HL 265 applies whereby the term 'children' in a will *prima facie* means legitimate children. But there were two cases in which the *prima facie* interpretation could be departed from: (i) where it was impossible from the circumstances that any legitimate children could take; or (ii) where it was clear on the face of the will that the testator was including illegitimate children in the term 'children'. Although the rule in *Hill* v *Crook* was concerned specifically with the interpretation of 'children', the rule applies to words describing other relations, e.g., 'niece', as in *Re Fish* [1894] 2 Ch 83.

If the will was made after 1969 but before 4 April 1988, s. 15(1) of the Family Law Reform Act 1969 provides that any reference to the child or children of any person shall, unless the contrary intention appears, be construed as including a reference to any illegitimate child of that person. Moreover, any reference to a person or persons related in some other manner to any person shall be construed (subject to a contrary intention) as including a reference to anyone who would be so related if he, or some other person through whom the relationship is deduced, had been born legitimate.

Section 15(1) applies subject to any contrary intention appearing in the will. Thus a gift will exclude illegitimate children if that is the testator's expressed intention — for example, a gift to 'my legitimate children'. Moreover, s. 15(1) does not affect the construction of the word 'heir' or 'heirs', or any expression used to create an entailed interest: s. 15(2). And under s. 15(5), the rule in s. 15(1) does not affect the devolution of any property which devolves along with a dignity or title of honour. What if a will made before 1970 is republished by a post–1969 codicil? The normal effect of republication is to bring the date of the making of the will down to the day of republication, but s. 15(8) makes an exception. For the purposes of the application of s. 15(1), a will is treated as having been made before 1970 despite its subsequent republication.

If the will was made after 3 April 1988, the position is governed by the Family Law Reform Act 1987. Under s. 1, references to any relationship between two persons shall, unless the contrary intention appears, be construed 'without regard to whether or not the father and mother of either of them, or the father and mother of any person through whom the relationship is deduced, have or had been married to each other at any time'. This 'new' rule of construction was enacted following the recommendations of the Law Commission's *Second Report on Illegitimacy*, (Law Com. No. 157, 1986). There is little new in substance about the rule expressed in s. 1 — what is new is the language used. It describes illegitimacy without using the word 'illegitimate'. This is a laudable attempt to avoid the use of words indicative of stigma (or at least perceived as such). However, the word 'illegitimate' at least has the merit of being well-understood, a quality which arguably is absent in the rather convoluted terminology of s. 1. The 1987 Act *does* apply to the construction of 'heir' or 'heirs', and expressions creating entails: s. 19(2). However, it does not effect the inheritance of property devolving with a dignity or title of honour: s. 19(4). Moreover, a will made before 4 April 1988, but republished subsequently, is not treated as executed at the date of republication by reason of the republication alone: s. 19(7).

(b) *Legitimated persons* The only form of legitimation possible in English municipal law is by the subsequent marriage of the parents of the child. Under the Legitimacy Act 1926, the general rule was that the legitimated person could take the same benefit as if born legitimate, provided that the legitimation preceded the testator's death: s. 3(1).

For testators dying after 1975, the basic rule is similar. Under s. 5(3) of the Legitimacy Act 1976, 'a legitimated person, and any other person, shall be entitled to take any interest as if the legitimated person has been born legitimate'. If the parents of an illegitimate person marry after he dies, gifts taken by his spouse or issue are construed as if he had been legitimated by the marriage: s. 5(6). The rule of construction concerning legitimated persons has no effect on the inheritance of any dignity or title of honour (or property which devolves along with them). And the rule is displaced by 'any contrary intention': s. 5(1).

Where entitlement under a disposition depends on the date of birth of children, a legitimated child is regarded under s. 5(4) as if born at the date of legitimation. If two or more children were legitimated on the same date, they rank, as between themselves, in order of birth.

(c)   Adopted persons   Adoption was first introduced into English law by the Adoption of Children Act 1926. Under that Act gifts to 'children' or 'issue' did not include adopted children unless a contrary intention appeared in the will. The position was changed by the Adoption of Children Act 1949 which *included* adopted children under a gift to 'children' provided that the will was executed after the adoption order was made (and subject to any contrary intention). The current legislation, the Adoption Act 1976, applies to testators dying after 1975. Under s. 39, an adopted child is regarded as the lawful child of the adopted parents (or parent) but not of any other person. The rule applies even if the adoption order is made after the testator's death. It is subject, however, to 'any contrary indication', and does not affect succession to any dignity or title of honour (or any property devolving with them).

Where entitlement depends on the date of birth of children, an adopted child is regarded as born on the date of its adoption (i.e. the date of the adoption order). If two or more children were adopted on the same date, they are regarded as born on that date in the order of their actual births: s. 42.

6.4   EXTRINSIC EVIDENCE

6.4.1   Introduction

Cases invariably turn on the evidence before the court. As regards wills, evidence of the testator's intended meaning can be intrinsic, that is, contained in the will itself, or extrinsic — evidence from outside the will. Intrinsic evidence is obviously of primary importance as the clearest indication of the testator's meaning, e.g., where the testator includes his own 'dictionary' in the will. Extrinsic evidence is by definition less reliable, hence its admissibility has been a matter of some controversy. It could be argued that extrinsic evidence should never be admissible given that a will has to be in writing and that the function of the court is to construe the *expressed* meaning of the testator. But even a moment's reflection would suggest that such an extreme position is untenable since *some* extrinsic evidence is necessary to at least identify the intended beneficiaries and the subject-matter of the gift. The traditional approach of the courts — as evident in the so-called Wigram Rules (Sir James Wigram, *Admission of Extrinsic Evidence in the Aid of the Interpretation of Wills*, 5th edn, 1914) — has been rather cautious. However, s. 21 of the Administration of Justice Act 1982 has widened the potential admissibility of extrinsic evidence so that the position in English law is now closer to that in continental systems (where there are few restrictions).

It must be emphasised that there are limits to what can be achieved by extrinsic evidence. The function of such evidence is as an *aid to interpreting wills* — hence it cannot be used to re-write a will. In *Miller* v *Travers* (1832) 8 Bing 244; 131 ER 395, the testator devised 'all his freehold and real estates whatsoever, situate in the county of Limerick, and in the city of Limerick'. When he made his will he had a small estate in the city of Limerick but no realty in the county of Limerick. But he did have considerable estate in the county of

Clare (of which there was no mention in the will). It was argued that evidence should be admitted showing that the testator intended to pass the realty in Clare under the gift of realty in the county of Limerick. It was held that the evidence was not admissible since, if it were, that would make the will 'speak upon a subject on which it is altogether silent' and would amount to 'the making of a new devise for the testator' (p. 397).

Because a will cannot be re-written through the use of extrinsic evidence, it follows that total blanks in a will cannot be filled in by recourse to such evidence. In *Hunt* v *Hort* (1791) 3 BCC 311; 29 ER 554, the testatrix, having bequeathed certain pictures, wrote 'my other pictures to become the property of Lady   ' (leaving a blank after 'Lady'). She appointed a Lady Hort to be her executrix. It was held that Lady Hort's name could not be inserted even though extrinsic evidence suggested that she was intended to take the pictures. Nor can extrinsic evidence be used to give words a meaning which they are incapable of having. Moreover, extrinsic evidence can be used only where there is ambiguity or where the words are meaningless. In *Re Williams* [1985] 1 All ER 964, Nicholls J summarised the position (at p. 969):

> The evidence may assist by showing which of two or more possible meanings a testator was attaching to a particular word or phrase. 'My effects' and 'my money' are obvious examples. That meaning may be one which, without recourse to the extrinsic evidence, would not really have been apparent at all. So long as that meaning is one which the word or phrase read in its context is capable of bearing, then the court may conclude that, assisted by the extrinsic evidence, that is its correct construction. But if, however liberal may be the approach of the court, the meaning is one which the word or phrase cannot bear, I do not see how ... the court can declare that meaning to be the meaning of the word or phrase. Such a conclusion, varying or contradicting the language used, would amount to rewriting part of the will, and that is a result to be achieved, if at all, under the rectification provisions in s. 20.

An example of the rejection of extrinsic evidence because of the absence of ambiguity is *Higgins* v *Dawson* [1902] AC 1: the testator, having bequeathed a number of pecuniary legacies, gave 'all the residue and remainder' of certain mortgage debts owed to him to named beneficiaries, after payment of his debts, funeral and testamentary expenses. There was no general gift of residue. Extrinsic evidence showed that when the will was made there were virtually no assets other than the mortgage debts out of which the pecuniary legacies could be made. Consequently, it was argued that the mortgage debts should be charged with the payment of the legacies; but the House of Lords held that the extrinsic evidence was not admissible because there was no ambiguity in the will — the 'residue and remainder' of the mortgage debts had been charged only with the payment of debts and expenses (and not with payment of the pecuniary legacies). Following the enactment of s. 21 of the Administration of Justice Act 1982, this case would probably now be decided differently (see 6.4.3).

6.4.2   Types of extrinsic evidence

6.4.2.1   Direct and circumstantial evidence

It has been traditional to distinguish between two types of extrinsic evidence —
direct and circumstantial. Direct evidence consists of expressions by the
testator of his dispositive intentions — for example, statements made by him in
conversation about his will, or instructions given by him for drafting it.
Circumstantial evidence consists of evidence of such surrounding circumstances as may assist in interpreting the testator's words. Suppose that Arthur
leaves all his property to 'the Whitchurch Nursing Home', and that after his
death several nursing homes answering this description in the UK claim his
estate. The fact that Arthur had mentioned in conversation that he wanted 'the
Whitchurch Nursing Home in Cardiff' to benefit would constitute direct
extrinsic evidence of his intentions; the fact that he had always lived in
Whitchurch, Cardiff and had been a resident at the Whitchurch Nursing
Home, Cardiff would be circumstantial evidence.

Prior to the Administration of Justice Act 1982, the distinction was of
fundamental importance because the admissibility of direct evidence was far
more restricted than that of circumstantial evidence. The danger was perceived
to be that unrestricted use of direct evidence would threaten the basic principle
that a will must be made in writing. But following the 1982 Act the distinction
has lost much of its force.

6.4.2.2   The armchair principle

Circumstantial extrinsic evidence is admitted under the so-called 'armchair'
principle under which the court is entitled to know of the circumstances
surrounding the making of the will, as explained in *Boyes* v *Cook* (1880) 14 Ch
D 53, at 56, where the court held that it could place itself in the testator's
armchair 'and consider the circumstances by which he was surrounded when
he made his will' to assist it 'in arriving at his intention'. A fuller version of the
principle was formulated by Blackburn J in *Allgood* v *Blake* (1873) LR 8 Ex 160,
at 162:

> The general rule is that, in construing a will, the Court is entitled to put itself
> in the position of the testator, and to consider all material facts and
> circumstances known to the testator with reference to which he is to be taken
> to have used the words in the will, and then to declare what is the intention
> evidenced by the words used with reference to those facts and circumstances
> which were (or ought to have been) in the mind of the testator when he used
> those words.

The range of evidence admissible under the armchair rule is obviously very
wide. Such evidence often relates to the testator's relationship with the persons
claiming under his will. For example, in *Charter* v *Charter* (1874) LR 7 HL 364,
the testator left his farm to 'my son Forster Charter'. The testator had three
sons — Forster Charter (who had died before the will was made), William
Forster Charter and Charles Charter (both of whom survived the testator).

William became a butcher and settled 100 miles away, seeing his father only occasionally. Charles, however, lived with the testator and assisted him in managing the farm. It was held that such evidence was admissible to show which son was intended to take the farm (Charles) since the court had a right to ascertain all the facts known to the testator to determine whether there existed any person or thing to which the description in the will could be applied with sufficient certainty. Thus evidence of his relationship with any claimants was clearly relevant. In *Re Jeffery* [1914] 1 Ch 375, the testatrix left her residuary estate 'between my brother Walter Jeffrey his wife and their daughter'. The testatrix was survived by Walter, his wife and five daughters (all of whom had been alive when the will was made). Evidence was adduced that the testatrix was on extremely intimate terms with one of the daughters, Phoebe, but not with the others; moreover, that the testatrix had made an earlier will (later revoked) leaving her residuary estate to Walter and 'his daughter Phoebe'. It was held that such evidence was admissible to show that Phoebe was the intended beneficiary.

Another form of circumstantial evidence commonly admitted under the armchair rule relates to the testator's particular use of language, whether in describing beneficiaries or property. In *Parsons* v *Parsons* (1791) 1 Ves Jun 266; 30 ER 335, the testator left property to his brother Edward Parsons for life. When he made the will he had only one brother alive, Samuel Parsons. Evidence was admitted that the testator was in the habit of calling Samuel by the name of 'Edward' or 'Ned' — hence Samuel took. In *Thorn* v *Dickens* [1906] WN 54, extrinsic evidence was admitted to show that when the testator wrote 'all for mother' he intended his wife to take (he habitually referred to his wife as 'mother'). In *Kell* v *Charmer* (1856) 23 Beav 195; 53 ER 76, extrinsic evidence was admitted to show that 'i.x.x.' and 'o.x.x.' were symbols used by the testator in the jewellery business to denote £100 and £200 respectively. Similarly, extrinsic evidence is admissible to show which property the testator designated by a particular description up to the time of his death. For example, in *Castle* v *Fox* (1871) LR 11 Eq 542, the testator devised his mansion and estate called 'Cleeve Court' on trust for his wife for life. The issue was whether certain lands purchased by him after making the will, adjoining the Cleeve Court estate, were part of the devise. Evidence was admitted as to which property he regarded as answering the description 'Cleeve Court' before his death — as a result the after-acquired lands passed under the devise. In *Ricketts* v *Turquand* (1848) 1 HLC 472, the testator devised 'all my estate in Shropshire, called Ashford Hall'. The testator owned a mansion-house called Ashford Hall, adjacent lands and other realty in Shropshire. Evidence was admitted which showed that the testator regarded all his realty in Shropshire as the Ashford Hall estate.

6.4.3 Admissibility of extrinsic evidence after 1982

Section 21 of the Administration of Justice Act 1982 provides that extrinsic evidence, including evidence of the testator's intention, may be admitted to assist in the interpretation of the will:

(a)   in so far as any part of the will is meaningless;
(b)   in so far as the language used in any part of it is ambiguous on the face
of it;
(c)   in so far as evidence, other than evidence of the testator's intention,
shows that the language used in any part of it is ambiguous in the light of
surrounding circumstances.

This section, enacted following the recommendations of the LRC Report
No. 19 (1973), applies where the testator dies on or after 1 January 1983. The
broad effect of s. 21 is to widen the use of direct evidence so that the court is no
longer restricted as to the type of evidence that it can consider in the situations
stated in s. 21. A number of pre-1982 Act cases remain relevant to illustrate the
operation of s. 21.

6.4.3.1   Part of the will is meaningless
Part of a will is meaningless if the court is unable (without extrinsic evidence)
to give effective meaning to it. *Kell* v *Charmer* (above) provides a useful
illustration — the symbols 'i.x.x.' and 'o.x.x.' used in the jewellery trade were
meaningless (to the court). Circumstantial evidence was admitted to interpret
the symbols used. That evidence was sufficient to dispose of the matter. *Clayton*
v *Lord Nugent* (1844) 13 M & W 200; 153 ER 83 was a case which would be
decided differently following the 1982 Act. The testator made a will which was
described by the court as 'altogether unintelligible'. Various gifts were made to
beneficiaries designated not by name or initials but by capital letters bearing no
relation to the name, e.g., 'K', 'L', 'M', 'N' and so on. A card was found after
his death explaining to whom the letters referred. The card was held to be
inadmissible since it was direct extrinsic evidence (an expression of the
dispositive intentions of the testator). That evidence would now be admitted
under s. 21. Blanks presumably can have no meaning whatsoever. Extrinsic
evidence cannot be used to help fill in blanks because such evidence is
admissible under s. 21 to assist in the *interpretation* of the will. A blank space
cannot be *interpreted* — it is not so much 'meaningless' as incapable of bearing
any meaning.

6.4.3.2   Ambiguity on the face of the will
Direct and circumstantial extrinsic evidence is admissible to resolve an
ambiguity apparent on the face of the will from the language used (sometimes
referred to as 'patent ambiguity'). Ambiguity can arise because the words used
have more than one ordinary meaning ('money'), or because they have a
primary and a secondary meaning, or because the testator's words appear
equally applicable to two or more beneficiaries or items of property (equivoca-
tion). Consider, for example, *Doe d Gord* v *Needs* (1836) 2 M & W 129; 150 ER
698: the testator made various gifts of property including a gift to 'John Gord,
the son of George Gord', another to 'George Gord, the son of George Gord',
and another to 'George Gord, the son of Gord' (the despairing reader could be
forgiven at this point for exclaiming 'Oh God!'). The issue was which George

was to benefit under the last-mentioned gift — who was the 'son of Gord'? Evidence was allowed of the testator's declarations to show that he intended George, the son of George Gord to take. The case was probably wrongly decided at the time since direct evidence was not admissible to resolve patent ambiguity (such evidence is now admissible under s. 21).

6.4.3.3 Ambiguity in the light of surrounding circumstances
Where evidence — other than evidence of the testator's intention — shows that the language in the will is ambiguous in the light of surrounding circumstances, the ambiguity may be resolved by recourse to direct and circumstantial extrinsic evidence. Here we are concerned with latent ambiguity (not apparent on the face of the will). For example, suppose that the testator leaves 'my castle to my son'. There is nothing *patently* ambiguous in this gift; but if evidence shows that the testator has several sons or castles, latent ambiguity arises. In *Re Jackson* [1933] Ch 237, the testatrix left property to 'my nephew Arthur Murphy'. She was survived by three nephews called Arthur Murphy, one of whom was illegitimate. Evidence was admitted which showed that she was very close to the illegitimate nephew, to whom she always referred as 'nephew', and that he had been entrusted by her with the management of her affairs prior to her death. He was held entitled. It should be noted that the illegitimate nephew succeeded only because there was ambiguity (caused by there being two legitimate nephews). Had there been only one legitimate nephew, that nephew would have taken because at that time words of relationship were *prima facie* confined to legitimate relations (hence there would have been no ambiguity to let in extrinsic evidence). In *Watson v National Children's Home and Others* (1995), *The Times*, 31 October, the testator left property to the National Canine Defence League (amongst others) provided that the charity looked after his pets during the remainder of their natural lives. There was no pet alive when the testator died. The issue arose whether the charity could take the gift even though it was strictly unable to satisfy the condition. It was held that since the gift could be regarded as ambiguous in the light of the circumstances at the testator's death, extrinsic evidence was admissible to resolve the ambiguity. Hand-written instructions from the testator to his solicitor indicated that he wished to benefit the charity unless it refused to care for any pets which might survive him. Hence the charity was able to take the gift.

It should be noted that it is only the surrounding circumstances that can be relied on to reveal a latent ambiguity. Evidence of the testator's intentions cannot be used to *create* the ambiguity — s. 21 states as much — although it can be admitted to *resolve* the ambiguity revealed by the surrounding circumstances.

Would *NSPCC* v *Scottish NSPCC* (see 6.3.1.2) now be decided differently as the result of s. 21(c)? Certainly there was evidence that the gift to the NSPCC was ambiguous in the light of the surrounding circumstances. That would allow in evidence of the testator's intention (not admissible on the facts when the case was decided). The evidence of the testator's intention would probably suffice to enable the Scottish NSPCC to take. Nevertheless, it is arguable that the court might still be reluctant, despite the direct extrinsic evidence, to depart from the 'very strong' presumption (as described in the case) that the accurate use of a name in a will confers the gift on the beneficiary thus described rather than on an incorrectly described rival.

6.4.4 Admissibility of extrinsic evidence before 1983

Where the testator died before 1 January 1983 the position is governed entirely by case law. Since the law applicable in such cases is of obviously greatly diminished application, it will be dealt with briefly.

As a general rule, circumstantial extrinsic evidence is admissible under the armchair principle (as under s. 21), but direct extrinsic evidence is not. For example, in *Doe d Hiscocks* v *Hiscocks* (1839) 5 M & W 363; 151 ER 154, the testator devised lands to his son John Hiscocks for life, remainder to 'my grandson John Hiscocks', who was described as the 'eldest son' of the said John (the tenant for life). When the will was made the son John had an eldest son Simon and a second son John (who was his eldest son by his second marriage). There was direct extrinsic evidence which showed that it was Simon who was intended to take the remainder. The evidence consisted of the testator's instructions for the will and his declarations after its execution. The evidence was held inadmissible. There are, however, two exceptions to the general exclusion of direct evidence in pre-1982 cases. First, direct evidence is admissible to resolve a latent ambiguity (above). Secondly, such evidence can be admitted to rebut certain equitable presumptions concerning the effect of legacies on pre-existing obligations of the testator. These presumptions strictly are not rules of construction; they are concerned with the failure of gifts and will be considered later (see 7.2.8).

6.4.5 Failure to resolve the ambiguity

What is the position where the extrinsic evidence fails to resolve the ambiguity? The gift will normally fail for uncertainty, whereupon it will fall into residue or devolve on intestacy (where there is no effective residuary gift): *Asten* v *Asten* [1894] 3 Ch 260 (see 7.2.10.1). However, there may exist unusual circumstances where the court may find an alternative to failing the gift for uncertainty. Consider *Re Williams* [1985] 1 All ER 964: the testatrix's home-made will listed 25 names divided into three groups, which were unequal in size and comprised a mixture of next-of-kin, other relatives and three organisations. The will did not indicate the purpose of these groupings. However, the testatrix had written to her solicitors (before executing the will) explaining that she had divided her intended beneficiaries into three categories and wished that 'the first, for example, should receive, say, £2,000 each; the second £1,000, and the third £500'. What was the extent, if any, of the entitlement of the 25 beneficiaries? It was held that the letter was admissible as extrinsic evidence under s. 21(b) since there was an ambiguity on the face of the will (at least two possible meanings could be attached to the division into groups). However, the letter was of no assistance in resolving the ambiguity as it did not explain what the testatrix had meant by the divisions in the will. Nevertheless the rejection of the letter did not mean that the gifts necessarily failed; the court decided that the estate should be divided equally between the 25 beneficiaries.

SEVEN
Entitlement

This chapter considers, first, the various types of gift to which beneficiaries under a will may be entitled; and, secondly, the grounds on which there may be a failure of entitlement under the will (some of which apply also to intestacy).

7.1 THE CLASSIFICATION OF GIFTS

The basic classification of testamentary gifts is into legacies and devises. Legacies are gifts of personalty; devises comprise real estate. Legacies can be classified as specific, general, demonstrative, pecuniary or residuary. Devises are normally specific, but can be general or residuary. The classification of gifts is important since gifts differ in their legal consequences. For example, specific gifts can fail for ademption but not general gifts; on the other hand, general gifts abate before specific gifts (see 7.1.2).

7.1.1 Types of gift

7.1.1.1 Specific legacy
A specific legacy was defined by Lord Blackburn in *Robertson* v *Broadbent* (1883) 8 App Cas 812, at 820:

> ... something which a testator, identifying it by a sufficient description, and manifesting an intention that it should be enjoyed or taken in the state and condition indicated by that description, separates in favour of a particular legatee, from the general mass of his personal estate.

Thus a specific legacy is a gift of a particular part of the testator's personal estate, distinguished from the rest of the assets — for example, 'my British Airways shares to Alice' or 'my collection of teddy bears to Bruno'. The two essentials of a specific legacy are that the gift (i) must be part of the testator's property, and (ii) must be severed or distinguished from the totality of the estate. In *Bothamley* v *Sherson* (1875) LR 20 Eq 304, a gift of 'all my stock in the Midland Railway Company' was held to be specific, it being irrelevant that the gift would not be fully ascertained until the testator's death. Jessel MR stated the position as follows (at p. 309):

> It must be what has been sometimes called a severed or distinguished part. It must not be the whole, in the meaning of being the totality of the testator's property, or the totality of the general residue of his property after having given legacies out of it. But if it satisfy both conditions, that it is a part of the testator's property itself, and is a part as distinguished . . . from the whole, or from the whole of the residue, then it appears to me to satisfy everything that is required to treat it as a specific legacy.

7.1.1.2 General legacy

A general legacy is a gift of personalty which is not identified as a particular, distinguished part of the testator's estate, but is to be provided for the legatee out of the general estate. In *Bothamley* v *Sherson* Jessel MR described a general legacy thus (at pp. 308–9):

> A general bequest may or may not be a part of the testator's property. A man who gives £100 money or £100 stock may not have either the money or the stock, in which case the testator's executors must raise the money or buy the stock; or he may have money or stock sufficient to discharge the legacy, in which case the executors would probably discharge it out of the actual money or stock. But in the case of a general legacy it has no reference to the actual state of the testator's property, it being only supposed that the testator has sufficient property which on being realized will procure for the legatee that which is given to him. . . .'.

The use of words indicating possession — such as 'my' — normally indicates a specific rather than a general gift (though not conclusive in itself). For example, a gift of 'my 1,000 shares in British Airways' is specific; but a gift of '1,000 shares in British Airways' is general — there is no indication from the words used that the testator is referring to shares owned by him (he may be intending that they should be bought for the beneficiary). Even if the testator possesses the property in question when he makes the will, the absence of 'my' may be crucial: for example, in *Re Gage* [1934] Ch 536, a gift of 'the sum of £1,150 Five per Cent War loan 1929–1947 stock' was held to be a general gift even though the testator held that stock when the will was made. Similarly, in *Re Willcocks* [1921] 2 Ch 327, a gift of 948 Queensland 3½ per cent Inscribed Stock was held to be a general gift since there was no indication in the will that the testatrix was referring to property belonging to her (despite holding exactly that stock when making the will). In *Re O'Connor* [1948] Ch 628, the testator bequeathed by clause 5 of his will 'ten thousand preference shares of one pound each fully paid' in a hat-making business in which he had only 9,000 shares when he made the will (and at his death). The gift was held to be general since the testator did not use the word 'my' or any possessive word and because he never had 10,000 preference shares either at the date of his will or at the date of his death.

General legacies are not subject to ademption, unlike specific legacies. Consequently, litigation involving the classification of gifts is often concerned with beneficiaries trying to establish that a gift is general. To illustrate, suppose that the testator makes a will bequeathing property which he later sells. If the gift is specific, it will be adeemed by the sale — the legatee will take nothing; but if the gift is general, the beneficiary is entitled to its being paid out of the testator's general estate. Because of the liability of specific gifts to fail through ademption, the court leans in favour of a general legacy in cases of doubt. *Re Willcocks* and *Re O'Connor* (above) are both examples of this. In *Re Rose* [1949] Ch 78, Jenkins J stated (at p. 82) that 'the court leans against specific legacies, and is inclined, if it can, to construe a legacy as general rather than specific'; thus doubtful cases should be resolved 'in favour of the view that the legacy is general'.

7.1.1.3 Demonstrative legacy

A demonstrative legacy was described as a gift which is 'in its nature a general legacy, but where a particular fund is pointed out to satisfy it': *Ashburner v Macguire* (1786) 2 Bro CC 108; 29 ER 62, at 63. Thus a gift of '£1,000 from my account at Barclays Bank' is a demonstrative legacy (and a typical example of one). The intention of the testator is that the gift shall be *primarily* satisfied from the specified fund; if that fund is insufficient or ceases to exist, the deficit is to be taken from the general estate (as in the case of a general legacy). Demonstrative legacies are not subject to ademption.

In *Re Webster* [1937] 1 All ER 602, CA, the testator bequeathed to his son £3,000, payable 'out of the share of my capital and loans' in a specified family business in the meat trade. When the testator died his share was worth substantially less than £3,000. However, since the gift was meant to be paid primarily out of the business share, it was demonstrative; hence the son was entitled to have the deficit made good out of the testator's residuary estate (this would not have been possible if the gift were specific). Had the testator's intention been that the son's gift was payable *only* out of the business share, the gift could not have been held to be demonstrative.

7.1.1.4 Pecuniary legacy

A pecuniary legacy is simply a bequest of money. As such it may be specific, general or demonstrative, but in practice is most likely to be general (there is here some overlap in the classification of gifts). The term is defined by s. 55(1)(ix) of the Administration of Estates Act 1925 as including 'an annuity, a general legacy, a demonstrative legacy so far as it is not discharged out of designated property, and any other general direction by a testator for the payment of money'. In *Re Berkeley* [1967] 3 All ER 170, at 176, an annuity given by will was described as 'a series of legacies payable at intervals'. An annuity is normally payable from the date of the testator's death, so that if it is paid yearly, the first payment will be made a year after the testator's death (but it may be payable at other intervals if the will so directs). The duration of an annuity depends on the construction of the will; frequently it is for the lifetime of the annuitant. Annuities may be specific, general or demonstrative. Specific annuities may adeem, but general and demonstrative cannot.

7.1.1.5 Residuary legacy
A residuary legacy is à gift of the testator's general mass of personalty after the payment of any specific, general and demonstrative legacies, as well as any debts, liabilities and expenses charged on the personalty. It is more common, however, to make a residuary gift comprising both realty and personalty. Although it is not essential to include a residuary gift in order to make a valid will, it is highly desirable to do so because the possibility of property being left undisposed of — and thus passing on intestacy — is avoided.

7.1.1.6 Devises
Devises may be specific, general or residuary. Specific devises (the most common) consist of a gift of specified realty, which must be part of the testator's property and must be severed or distinguished from the totality of his estate, e.g., 'my house in Bristol'. A devise of 'all my land' would be general, whereas a gift of 'the rest of my land not otherwise disposed of by this will' would be residuary.

7.1.1.7 Testator's intention
The classification of gifts, whether legacies or devises, may depend on the testator's intention. If he intends a gift to be treated as belonging to a particular category, the court will take that into account. For example, in *Re Compton* [1914] 2 Ch 119, the testator made a specific gift of stocks, bonds and shares, describing it 'as a general and not as a specific legacy'. Sargant J stated (at p. 123) that 'the testator intended that these specific legacies should be treated, in respect of their legal consequences, as if they had been general legacies and not specific legacies'. Accordingly the legacies were regarded as general.

7.1.2 Consequences of classification

A number of important consequences follow from classifying gifts in one category rather than another, as has been seen already.

7.1.2.1 Ademption
A specific gift — whether a legacy or a devise — will fail by ademption if the subject-matter of the gift no longer exists as part of the testator's estate when he dies. The gift may have been adeemed, for example, because the property was disposed of by the testator or destroyed by whatever cause. The beneficiary of an adeemed specific gift takes nothing — he is not entitled to the proceeds, if any, resulting from the disposition of the property. General and demonstrative legacies do not fail by ademption. Ademption will be considered in more detail later (see 7.2.6).

7.1.2.2 Abatement

Abatement is the process whereby assets of the estate are consumed in the payment of the debts, liabilities and expenses on the testator's death. Part II of the First Schedule of the Administration of Estates Act 1925 prescribes the order in which assets will be so used. General legacies abate before specific gifts; hence in this respect it is advantageous to be a specific beneficiary. A demonstrative legacy is treated as a specific legacy to the extent that it can be paid out of the designated property; thus it will abate after a general legacy. A demonstrative legatee is therefore in a very advantageous position: his legacy is not subject to ademption and it abates after a general gift. However, in so far as a demonstrative legacy is *not* discharged out of the designated fund, it is regarded as a general legacy for the purposes of abatement. The statutory order may be varied by the testator if he shows in the will a clear intention to do so (see generally 10.2.3.6).

7.1.2.3 Income and interest

As a general rule, specific and residuary gifts carry all the income, profits and accretions (but not interest) from the date of the testator's death. On the other hand, general and demonstrative legacies carry simple interest at 6 per cent per annum (but not income, profits or accretions) from the date when they become payable. These rules are subject to the testator's contrary intention (see further 10.2.4.6).

7.1.2.4 Expenses

If expenses are incurred in preserving the subject-matter of a specific gift between the testator's death and the transfer to the beneficiary, they are the responsibility of the beneficiary. In *Re Pearce* [1909] 1 Ch 819, the testator bequeathed to his wife all his furniture and effects, horses, carriages, motor cars, yacht and jewellery, and gave the residue to his wife for life, remainder to Trinity College, Cambridge. After his death considerable expense was incurred in retaining staff to look after these various items of property (including the wages of the captain of the yacht). It was held that the wife had to pay for the expense. Eve J stated (at p. 821):

> . . . the specific legatee is entitled to the profits accrued due from the time of the testator's death. That being so, it seems to me to be right and fair that the specific legatee should be charged with the costs of the upkeep, care, and preservation of the specific legacy from the time of the death. . . .

The rule extends to the cost of delivering the property to the specific legatee. In *Re Scott* [1915] 1 Ch 592, CA — a case which attracted huge public interest due to the *dramatis personae* — the testator bequeathed his 'works of art' to Lady Sackville-West (the mother of Vita Sackville-West, the writer). These works included valuable tapestries which were attached to the walls of his luxurious house in Paris. Under French law a mutation duty (a form of inheritance tax) was payable on these items by the legatee. It was held that this duty must be borne by the legatee (including a penalty for late payment) as the gift of 'works of art' was specific. Presumably it is only reasonably incurred expenses for which the beneficiary is liable. If expense is incurred in preserving the subject-matter of non-specific gifts, it is regarded as part of the administration expenses.

7.2 FAILURE OF GIFTS

This section is concerned with the various grounds on which testamentary gifts can fail, despite the formal validity of the will. Some of the grounds are also applicable to intestacy. The treatment in this section is not exhaustive: for example, gifts can fail because they are in breach of the rules concerning perpetuities and accumulations, but this topic is outside the scope of this book. Moreover, a gift may fail if it was made as the result of a fraud on the testator (see 3.2.7.1). Gifts will fail through abatement or if the testator dies insolvent (dealt with mainly in Chapter 10). Before considering the various grounds of failure, the *effect* of failure requires attention — the case law will thereby be more readily understandable.

7.2.1 The effect of failure

The effect may vary according to the ground of failure, but the general rule is that a failed gift falls into residue, that is, it passes under the residuary gift in the will. This rule is subject to the testator's contrary intention: *Re Fraser* [1904] 1 Ch 726, CA. What if the failed gift is itself a residuary gift, or if there is no residuary gift? The property then passes on intestacy, subject to any contrary intention. An interest in an intestate estate may fail if the beneficiary disclaims or is prevented from taking by the forfeiture rule. The effect is as if that beneficiary did not exist. Thus, if the beneficiary is a spouse, the property passes to the children (if no children, then to the next class). If the beneficiary is a member of a class, then the 'failed' share passes to the other members of the class, if any; if none, then it passes to the next class entitled, and so forth.

The rules on the effect of failure are obviously different in the case of life interests. If the gift of a life interest fails, the doctrine of acceleration will normally apply — the interest in the remainder is accelerated. However, if the gift in remainder is only contingent, the acceleration will not occur until the contingency is satisfied.

7.2.2 Witnesses cannot benefit

Section 15 of the Wills Act 1837 provides that if a person witnesses a will to whom or to whose spouse any beneficial interest is given by the will, the gift is 'utterly null and void' but the witness shall be admitted to prove execution. This is a fundamental rule in the English law of succession but one that that is commonly misunderstood and misquoted. The rule is that a witness to a will cannot benefit under it, *not* that a beneficiary under a will cannot witness it. The importance of the rule is illustrated by the fact that a solicitor may be found negligent if he prepares a will which is witnessed by a beneficiary (or spouse): *Ross* v *Caunters* (see 4.5.2).

7.2.2.1   The purpose of s. 15
Why should a witness to a will not be able to take under it? Because ideally the witness should be a neutral, impartial participant in the execution of the will. One of the chief functions of the witness is to give evidence, when required, of due execution. How can such evidence have probative force if the witness has an interest in the upholding of the will? Moreover, if a witness were allowed to benefit, the possibility of fraud, undue influence and duress would thereby be increased, as emphasised in the case law. For example, in *In the Estate of Bravda* [1968] 2 All ER 217, CA, Russell LJ described s. 15 (at p. 224) as 'necessary to ensure reliable unbiased witnesses of due execution'. And in *Re Royce's WT* [1959] 3 All ER 278, CA, Lord Evershed MR stated that the object of the rule was to protect a testator 'who was in extremis, or otherwise weak and not capable of exercising judgment, from being imposed on by someone who came and presented him with a will for execution under which the person in question was himself substantially interested' (p. 281). The original rule was different. Under the Statute of Frauds 1677, a will could fail for lack of 'competent' witnesses. Incompetent witnesses included those who took an interest under the will. The effect of the Statute of Frauds was mitigated by the Wills Act 1752, which provided that the witness beneficiary would be regarded as a good witness (but would lose the gift). The rule was re-enacted with amendments by s. 15 of the Wills Act 1837.

7.2.2.2   The operation of s. 15
The rule applies where a benefit under the will is given to a witness or to the spouse of the witness. But it is only a spouse who was married to the witness at the time when the will was executed who loses the gift: *Thorpe* v *Bestwick* (1881) 6 QBD 311. Hence a gift to a fiancé or fiancée of the witness is not caught by s. 15. It seems that if the witness was married to the beneficiary when the will was executed, and the marriage was void, the gift should take effect (as the marriage is regarded as never having existed). It is otherwise if the marriage is voidable.

It is only beneficial gifts under the will that are caught by s. 15. Thus a gift to a witness in the capacity of a trustee takes effect: *Cresswell* v *Cresswell* (1868) LR 6 Eq 69. It appears to be irrelevant that the trustee may actually receive some benefit from the gift. In *Re Ray's WT* [1936] 2 All ER 93, the testatrix, a nun at a Franciscan convent, left all her property on trust for the convent to the person who at the time of her death should be the abbess. One of the witnesses later became abbess of the convent, and held that office when the testatrix died. It was argued that s. 15 was applicable since the witness would be benefited by the gift as a member of the convent. However, the gift was upheld since it was intended to benefit the community rather than an individual. A witness beneficiary (or spouse) must be entitled *under the will* in order for s. 15 to operate. Thus, if a gift is made in the will to A, subject to a secret trust in favour of B, the latter can take even if he witnessed the will. This is because B takes under the secret trust and not under the will: *Re Young* [1951] Ch 344.

Section 15 prevents only *witnesses* (and their spouses) from taking, and not those who signed the will in some other capacity or for some other purpose. Thus s. 15 will not apply where a person signed the will so as to record assent to the testator's provisions, as in *Kitcat* v *King* [1930] P 266; nor where the signature was added merely by way of identification of a beneficiary, as in *In the Goods of Sharman* (1869) 1 P & D 661 (see 4.2.6.2). But there is a rebuttable presumption that a person who signs the will (other than the testator) does so as an attesting witness: *Re Bravda* (above). The strength of the presumption varies according to the circumstances.

Section 15 applies to charging clauses in wills. These are clauses allowing executors to make a charge for their services (without such a clause the executor, being in a position of trust, could not charge). It is common, where solicitors and other professionals (such as banks) are appointed as executors, for a charging clause to be included in the will. But since such a clause is regarded as conferring a benefit, the executor should not witness the will if he wishes to charge. In *Re Pooley* (1889) 40 Ch D 1, CA, a will, appointing a solicitor as executor, contained a standard charging clause. It was witnessed by the solicitor, who therefore was unable to claim for his services. It was argued that the clause did not confer a gift but rather a right to payment for services rendered. The argument was rejected because 'the clause gives him a right which he would not otherwise have to charge for the work if he does it, and that, in my opinion, is a beneficial gift within the meaning of the section' (*per* Cotton LJ, at p. 4). However, a witness may enforce a charging clause if he had no beneficial interest under the will when it was executed, but was appointed as a trustee thereafter: *Re Royce's WT* (above), where Lord Evershed, MR stated that s. 15 did not disqualify 'someone who, at the time he attested the execution of a will, had no interest whatever under the will as it stood and only became interested under it by some later event or act' (p. 281). Payments made to an executor under a charging clause cannot be retained if the will containing the clause is later found to be invalid: *Gray* v *Richards Butler (a Firm)* (1996) *The Times*, 23 July.

What if a witness beneficiary is superfluous — that is, he is one of several witnesses, the will being valid without his attestation? It would be harsh to invalidate the gift in such a case, but that was the position before the Wills Act 1968: *Re Bravda* (above). However, under s. 1(1) of the Act, the attestation of a will by a beneficiary (or spouse) is disregarded if the will is duly executed without such attestation: there must be at least two witnesses to whom no benefit is given by the will. Suppose that a will is witnessed by three witnesses, A, B, and C. If A is given a benefit under the will, but B and C are not, A's gift takes effect.

What is the effect of subsequent codicils on the operation of s. 15? For example, suppose that the testator executes a will in which a gift is made to X, a witness. Later the testator makes a codicil which is not witnessed by X but which confirms the gift. Can X take? The basic rule — developed by the courts to avoid the drastic consequences of s. 15 — is that s. 15 does not apply if the beneficiary can take under a testamentary instrument that he did not witness. In *Re Trotter* [1899] 1 Ch 764, a solicitor witnessed a will which appointed him as executor and contained a charging clause. The testator later executed two codicils confirming the will in material respects. The solicitor witnessed the second codicil but not the first. It was held that he was entitled to the benefit of the charging clause: 'the legatee must be able to point to an instrument giving him his legacy not attested by himself before he can establish his right to his legacy' (per Byrne J, at p. 768). The same rule applies where a beneficiary under a will does not witness the will but witnesses a codicil confirming the will: *Gurney* v *Gurney* (1855) 3 Drew 208; 61 ER 882. In that case the testator left a share of his residue to X in a will which was not witnessed by X. Later the testator made a codicil which was witnessed by X and which revoked certain bequests (thus having the effect of swelling the residue). It was held that X could take his share of the residue even though he had witnessed an instrument which indirectly benefited him. This decision has been consistently followed as an authority for the rule that a witness to a codicil can take a benefit under an earlier will that he did not witness. But the fact that the beneficiary was thereby able to take an increased share is a rather dubious consequence of the application of the rule.

7.2.2.3 The effect of s. 15
What is the effect of s. 15? It renders a gift 'utterly null and void'. The will is treated as if the gift had not been made to the witness beneficiary; hence the subject-matter of the gift is undisposed of and passes on intestacy. In *Aplin* v *Stone* [1904] 1 Ch 543, a testator left a share in his freehold estate to his daughter or her children. The will was witnessed by the daughter's husband. The question was whether, as the daughter could not take, her children could take the substitutional gift to them. Swinfen Eady J held (at p. 548):

> . . . the proper way of dealing with these cases is first to construe the will, and ascertain what interests are given, and then to apply s. 15 of the Wills Act. I cannot, therefore, disregard the gift to Ellen [the daughter]. On the face of the will she takes absolutely in the events that have happened, and, her interest being rendered null and void by s. 15 of the Wills Act, there is an intestacy as to her share.

In *Re Doland's WT* [1970] Ch 267, the testator gave 2 per cent of his residuary estate to X, but X's spouse witnessed the will. There was a gift over if the trusts of any of the shares in the residuary estate 'should fail'. It was held that as the gift to X was null and void, there was no trust of that share which could be said to have failed. Thus the share was held to be undisposed of. Buckley J stated (at p. 276) that the nullified gift should not be disregarded 'if it is necessary to look at it for the purpose of ascertaining what is the nature of other gifts in the will, or in what event other gifts are intended to take effect'. However, as regards the conferring of any beneficial interest upon the witness (or spouse), 'the will has to be treated as though it did not contain that disposition at all'.

7.2.2.4 Reform?
Although the rule that a witness to a will cannot benefit under it is readily understandable, its consequences are somewhat drastic. The rule can operate

to deprive beneficiaries of gifts in circumstances beyond suspicion — it penalises the innocent as well as the fraudulent. This partly explains why the operation of the rule is circumscribed by a number of qualifications and exceptions, as seen already. In many jurisdictions the rule operates either in a restricted form or not at all (it was not part of Roman law). The Law Reform Committee, however, recommended in Report No. 22 that the rule be retained in its present form. But would it not be preferable to replace s. 15 by a *presumption* that a witness could not take a gift? The presumption would be rebuttable by evidence showing that there was no 'misconduct' on the part of the witness beneficiary. Admittedly such proof would be elusive, but at least the possibility would be there. Another idea might be to exclude s. 15 from applying to gifts below a percentage of the net estate (say 5 per cent, but the limit could vary according to the size of the estate). As for gifts exceeding the limit, the witness beneficiary would take unless a person with an interest in the estate objected. An objection would lead to an enquiry by the court, the onus being on the objector to show on a balance of probabilities that the beneficiary had misconducted himself in some relevant way (e.g., by exercising pressure on the testator).

7.2.3 Disclaimer

The law certainly is not so absurd as to force a man to take an estate against his will. *Prima facie*, every estate, whether given by will or otherwise, is supposed to be beneficial to the party to whom it is so given. Of that, however, he is the best judge, and if it turn out that the party to whom the gift is made does not consider it beneficial, the law will certainly, by some mode or other, allow him to renounce or refuse the gift. (*per* Abbott CJ in *Townson* v *Tickell* (1819) 3 B & A 31; 106 ER 575, at 576)

The general rule is that a beneficiary under a will or intestacy may disclaim his interest. A disclaimer can be retracted only if no one has altered his position in reliance on it. In *Re Cranstoun* [1949] Ch 523, the testatrix left her freehold property to the Home of Rest for Horses. Since the property was subject to a mortgage, and because the beneficiaries feared that they would be unable to maintain it, the gift was disclaimed. It took many years to wind up the testatrix's estate, at the end of which there was a considerable sum left in the residue. The beneficiaries were able to retract the disclaimer and take the residue since no one had altered his position.

7.2.3.1 Why disclaim?

At first sight it seems surprising that anyone might wish to disclaim a gift of property, but there could be a number of reasons for doing so. The most likely reason is to reduce tax liability (see 7.2.3.4). Or the beneficiary might wish to avoid onerous covenants or conditions attached to the property, or to avoid taking a hazardous or wasting asset. Suppose, for example, that Arthur devises his hotel, which is spectacularly perched on a cliff overlooking the North Sea. Unfortunately the cliff is being eroded by the sea and large cracks are appearing in the walls of the hotel. It would surprise no one if the beneficiary disclaimed such a *damnosa hereditas*. Sometimes a beneficiary might prefer to disclaim a gift where considerable expense would be incurred in safeguarding, maintaining or delivering the property. Moreover, there might be reasons of a personal nature for disclaiming. For example, the beneficiary might find it distasteful to accept a gift from the deceased; or acceptance might revive bad memories or feelings of guilt. In *Re Moss* (1977) 77 DLR (3d) 314, the testator left the residue of his estate to the Penticton Congregation of Jehovah's Witnesses (British Columbia). Five months before his death he was seen 'chewing tobacco' on the lawn of the premises used by the Congregation for their meetings, and was excommunicated for this 'distasteful deed'. The Elders of the Congregation decided to renounce the gift (but their precise reasons were not revealed).

7.2.3.2   The essential requirements of disclaimer
A disclaimer may be made in several ways. Often a deed is executed to that effect, but any form of writing is acceptable. Moreover, an oral disclaimer will suffice, as will implied disclaimer through conduct. A disclaimer is not possible once the beneficiary has unequivocally accepted the gift. In *Re Hodge* [1940] Ch 260, the testatrix left freeholds to her husband (the executor) subject to his paying £2 per week to her sister for her life; moreover, if he sold the property, he was to invest £2,000 for the sister and her children in lieu of the weekly payment. The husband paid the weekly sum for five years, but when he sold the property he tried to disclaim the investment provision. It was held that he could not disclaim as he had accepted the gift by his conduct. A joint beneficiary cannot disclaim since a joint gift can only be disclaimed by all the beneficiaries entitled. However, a joint beneficiary can *release* his interest to the other beneficiaries: *Re Schär* [1951] Ch 280.

What if the beneficiary wishes to disclaim only part of the gift? The general rule is that where property is given as one mass or aggregate thing (but consists of more than one asset) the beneficiary must take the whole gift or nothing — he cannot disclaim the onerous part and take the rest. In *Guthrie v Walrond* (1883) 22 Ch D 573, the testator gave his son 'all my estate and effects in the island of Mauritius absolutely'. The son wanted to disclaim an onerous lease relating to the Mauritius property but to accept the remainder of the gift. It was held that he must either take or disclaim the *whole* gift. However, where a beneficiary receives two or more *separate* gifts, he can accept one whilst disclaiming the other.

7.2.3.3   Disclaimer and intestacy
Entitlement under an intestacy, whether total or partial, may be disclaimed. The effect will be that the property will pass to other next-of-kin in the same class or, if none, to the next class entitled. In *Re Scott* [1975] 2 All ER 1033, Walton J stated (at p. 1045) that the effect of a disclaimer 'is not to throw the property onto the scrap heap' (i.e. to regard it as ownerless) but to pass the property to those next entitled under s. 46(1) of the Administration of Estates Act 1925. It can be argued that it is not possible to disclaim an interest on

intestacy because such an interest arises by way of automatic statutory entitlement. Whatever the technical merits of this argument, it lacks plausibility both in terms of principle and practicality. No one can effectively be forced to accept an interest against their will (or should be so forced).

7.2.3.4 Disclaimer and variation

Under the rule in Saunders v Vautier (1841) Cr & Ph 240; 41 ER 482, beneficiaries under a will or intestacy may agree to vary their entitlement provided that those affected all agree and are sui iuris (i.e. of full age and capacity). To this extent they can — in effect, if not in theory — re-write the will. Such a variation may entail the disclaimer of benefits, and the substitution of the agreed provisions. There are numerous reasons why a variation might be agreed. For example, one of the beneficiaries might be emigrating and thus be more interested in receiving money rather than the realty or the ponderous movables left to him. Or the testator might have divided his property equally between his children, but they agree that one amongst them is deserving of a larger share (perhaps because of special care shown to the testator).

The most common reason for agreeing a variation is to reduce tax liability, especially inheritance tax. Under s. 142 of the Inheritance Tax Act 1984, a beneficiary can vary or disclaim an interest under a will or intestacy. This might be useful in exploiting certain tax bands or reliefs under the Act. For example, if an exempt transferee is left property that qualifies for business or agricultural relief, it would be advantageous to agree a variation whereby the asset passes to a non-exempt transferee (for inheritance tax, see 10.2.6.3). Section 142 requires that the agreement should be made in writing within two years of the deceased's death, and that notice be given within six months of the written agreement to the Inland Revenue. Although it is normal to execute a deed of variation in such cases, it seems that it is not necessary to do so. In Crowden v Aldridge [1993] 3 All ER 603, the testator left £100 (out of an estate of £90,000) to his housekeeper, the residue to his 16 cousins. The gift to the housekeeper was somewhat ungenerous given that she had cared for the testator for 17 years and had been an employee of the family for over 50 years. The 16 cousins signed memoranda (mostly at the funeral) agreeing to vary the will so as to grant her a legacy of £5,000, the deceased's personal chattels and the freehold of his bungalow. The memoranda stated that each signatory was 'prepared to enter into a deed to formalise this gift'. Later, four of the cousins changed their minds and refused to sign the deed that had been prepared. It was held that the memoranda were binding. Although the decision is readily understandable on the merits of the case, it is dubious in principle in allowing informal memoranda, made at an emotional family occasion, to have potentially important consequences.

7.2.4 Divorce and annulment

7.2.4.1 Introduction

If a testator makes a will benefiting his spouse, what is the effect of a subsequent divorce or annulment on the provision for the spouse? Before 1983 neither had any effect. It is not surprising that the effect of divorce was not specifically recognised by the Wills Act 1837 since divorce was not generally available at that time. What *is* surprising, however, is that the substantial increase in the divorce rate in the twentieth century did not provoke reform until as late as 1982. For it is clear that the termination of marriage should have consequences for the operation of a prior will, as recognised in the LRC Report No. 22:

> The majority of us take the view that in almost all cases a will made during the subsistence of the marriage providing for quite a different division of the property will no longer be appropriate in the changed circumstances produced by the divorce.

The most sensible course for a testator whose marriage is subsequently terminated is to review his will and make any appropriate changes. But, following the trauma of marital breakdown and dissolution, it is hardly surprising that some divorcees fail to reconsider their wills. The Law Reform Committee recommended that a divorced spouse should be treated as having predeceased the testator subject to any contrary intention in the will (the same to apply to annulled marriages but not to judicial separation).

7.2.4.2   Section 18A of the Wills Act 1837
The recommendations of the Law Reform Committee were broadly enacted by s. 18(2) of the Administration of Justice Act 1982. A s. 18A was inserted into the Wills Act 1837, applicable to testators dying after 1982. Section 18A(1) provides that if, after a testator has made a will, a court dissolves or annuls his marriage or declares it void, any devise or bequest to the former spouse shall lapse, and the will shall take effect as if any appointment of the former spouse as an executor were omitted. This provision is subject to any contrary intention appearing by the will. Section 18A(2) maintains the right of a former spouse to apply for provision under the Inheritance (Provision for Family and Dependants) Act 1975. The change incorporated in s. 18A(1) makes such applications more likely. And s. 18A(3) provides that if a life interest lapses under s. 18A(1), the remainder is accelerated.

It was somewhat curious that although the Law Reform Committee recommended that the former spouse should be regarded as having *predeceased* the testator, s. 18A(1) states that the gift shall 'lapse'. The Court of Appeal in *Re Sinclair* [1985] 1 All ER 1066 considered the meaning of 'lapse'. The testator left all his estate to his wife and provided that if she predeceased him or failed to survive him by one month, the property was to pass to the Imperial Cancer Research Fund. The testator and his wife were divorced a few years later. On his death (the former spouse having survived him) the issue was whether the gift over to the charity took effect. It was held that 'lapse' in s. 18A(1) meant 'fail' and was not synonymous with 'predeceasing'. Since the wife had not predeceased the testator, the charity could not take: the property passed on intestacy. This was an unfortunate decision since the testator intended that his property should pass to his wife or, failing her, to the charity. He did not intend the property to pass on intestacy. Apart from being a very dubious decision on the merits of the case, *Re Sinclair* unfortunately overruled the eminently sensible decision in *Re Cherrington* [1984] 2 All ER 285, where Butler-Sloss J held that 'lapse' in s. 18A(1) comprised the notion of predeceasing.

The manifest difficulties stemming from *Re Sinclair* led the Law Commission to consider reform in *Family Law, The Effect of Divorce on Wills* (Law Com. No. 217, 1993). The Commission's view was that *Re Sinclair* revealed a serious defect in s. 18A(1) and that it was desirable 'to try to give effect to the presumed intention of the testator and deprive only the former spouse of any benefit that he or she might otherwise have received' (para. 3.7). Accordingly the Commission recommended that the lapse provision in s. 18A(1) should be replaced by one to the effect that any property which would have passed to the former spouse 'is to pass as if the former spouse had predeceased the testator' (para. 3.8).

7.2.4.3   Section 18A of the Wills Act 1837 (as amended)

The recommendations of the Law Commission were enacted by s. 3 of the Law Reform (Succession) Act 1995, which amended s. 18A(1) of the Wills Act 1837. The new s. 18A(1) — applicable to testators dying after 1995 — provides:

> (a)   provisions of the will appointing executors or trustees or conferring a power of appointment, if they appoint or confer the power on the former spouse, shall take effect as if the former spouse had died on the date on which the marriage is dissolved or annulled, and
> (b)   any property which, or an interest in which, is devised or bequeathed to the former spouse shall pass as if the former spouse had died on that date.

It can be seen that the approach in the amended s. 18A(1) — treating the former spouse as having predeceased the testator — follows that in *Re Cherrington* (above). However, the new provision does more than deem the former spouse to have predeceased the testator: it fixes the actual time when this is regarded as occurring, namely the date of the decree absolute. The Law Commission thought this was desirable when construing the effect of certain gifts, especially gifts in remainder:

> There could be problems in construing the effect of certain gifts unless the date upon which the former spouse is deemed to have died is specified. These might arise where the will defines the person or persons who are to benefit from a gift over, or with an interest in remainder after the spouse's life interest, by reference to the date upon which the spouse has died, as for example in a gift 'to such of our children as are living at the date of her death'. (para. 3.9)

Another novel feature of the amended s. 18A(1) is that it applies to the grant by will of a power of appointment to the spouse. It was argued that powers of appointment granted to the spouse should not be invalidated since the policy of the Act was to deprive a former spouse but no one else of a benefit under the will. But the Law Commission felt that for the sake of consistency, simplicity and clarity, all testamentary appointments involving the spouse should be ineffective, whether the spouse was a beneficiary or a grantee of the power. It should be noted that the amended s. 18A(1) does not deem the former spouse to have predeceased the testator for *all* purposes, but only for the purposes stated in the section.

If a guardian is appointed by will, the appointment is revoked if the person appointed was the spouse of the testator and the marriage was subsequently dissolved or annulled: s. 6 of the Children Act 1989, as amended by s. 4 of the Law Reform (Succession) Act 1995.

7.2.5   Lapse

7.2.5.1   The basic doctrine

In order to take a gift under a will the beneficiary must survive the testator. Until the testator's death the will, being ambulatory, has no effect. Thus if a beneficiary predeceases the testator, the gift lapses. The doctrine applies similarly in the case of gifts to corporate bodies that cease to exist before the testator's death: *Re Servers of the Blind League* [1960] 2 All ER 298. It should be noted that the normal rules as to the effect of failure apply to lapse: the lapsed gift falls into residue. But if there is no gift of residue, or if the lapsed gift is itself a residuary gift, the property comprised in the gift passes on intestacy.

A testator can avoid the consequences of the doctrine of lapse by making a substitutional gift. For example, it is quite common for the testator to provide that if the beneficiary predeceases him, the gift should pass to the beneficiary's children or personal representatives. But the consequences of lapse cannot be prevented simply by the testator declaring that lapse should not apply to his will. For example, in *Browne v Hope* (1872) LR 14 Eq 343, the testator's direction that residuary legacies were to vest from the date of the will's execution was held to be insufficient to prevent lapse. Wickens VC stated (at p. 347) that to prevent lapse the testator must do two things: 'he must, in clear words, exclude lapse; and he must clearly indicate who is to take in case the legatee should die in his lifetime.' Thus a declaration against lapse may be effective if the court can construe the will as providing a substitutional gift: *Re Ladd* [1932] 2 Ch 219.

The doctrine of lapse does not apply to general charitable gifts, class gifts or gifts to joint tenants. In the case of a charitable gift, if the charity ceases to exist before the testator's death, the gift will be applied *cy-près* provided that the testator showed a general charitable intent. As regards class gifts, lapse does not apply because strictly a person who predeceases the testator never becomes a member of the class. A class consists of persons who survive the testator or, if the gift is postponed, those who come into being before the period of distribution (see generally 6.3.2.2). Thus, if the testator leaves his property 'to the children of X', the property will be shared by those children of X who are alive when the testator dies. If a child of X predeceases the testator, there is no lapse as that child never qualified as a member of the class. As regards gifts to joint tenants, if one of the potential joint tenants predeceases the testator, his share is taken by the others by survivorship; thus the doctrine of lapse does not apply. However, lapse will apply if all the joint tenants predecease the testator.

7.2.5.2 Moral obligation

... if the Court finds, upon the construction of the will, that the testator clearly intended not to give a mere bounty to the legatee, but to discharge what he regarded as a moral obligation, whether it were legally binding or not, and if that obligation still exists at the testator's death, there is no necessary failure of the testator's object merely because the legatee dies in his lifetime; and therefore death in such a case does not cause a lapse (*per* Farwell J in *Stevens* v *King* [1904] 2 Ch 30, at 33).

This exception to the doctrine of lapse arises from the recognition by the testator in his will of a moral obligation on his part to the intended beneficiary. It apparently does not matter whether the obligation is legally enforceable or not: the rule has been applied to statute-barred debts. The precise scope of this exception is unclear. For example, what is meant by the requirement that the obligation must still exist at the testator's death? Must it exist objectively, or does it suffice that the testator believes it exists when he dies? Despite such uncertainties the rule appears to be established. It was applied (rather dubiously) in *Re Leach's WT* [1948] 1 All ER 383: the testatrix made a codicil reciting that her late son had at the time of his death owed £1,000 to X, and directed her executors to pay the sum to X (who later predeceased her). Since the judge was satisfied that there was sufficient evidence in the codicil of an intention to discharge a moral duty, it was held that the case came within the principle of *Stevens* v *King*, and thus the legacy was payable to X's estate. Nevertheless it is not clear why the judge was satisfied of the required intention. The recital of the son's debt was arguably the expression of a reason for the gift rather than evidence of a moral obligation felt by the testatrix.

7.2.5.3 Sections 32 and 33 of the Wills Act 1837

These statutory exceptions to the doctrine of lapse apply in certain circumstances where the predeceasing beneficiary leaves issue who survive the testator. The reason for these exceptions is that it is considered preferable for the gift to stay in the beneficiary's family in these cases rather than to lapse and fall into residue.

Section 32 provides that if real estate is devised to a beneficiary in tail, who predeceases the testator but leaves issue living at the testator's death capable of inheriting under the entail, 'such devise shall not lapse, but shall take effect as if the death of such person had happened immediately after the death of the testator, unless a contrary intention shall appear by the will'. This section applies also to entails of personalty: s. 130(1) of the Law of Property Act 1925. Section 32 has been repealed as from 1 January 1997 by the Trusts of Land and Appointment of Trustees Act 1996: an entailed interest cannot be granted by any instrument coming into operation after 1996 (sch. 1, para. 5(1)). But the section remains applicable to instruments operative before that date.

Section 33(1) of the Wills Act 1837 contains the most important exception to the doctrine of lapse. It provides:

Where —
    (a)   a will contains a devise or bequest to a child or remoter descendant of the testator; and
    (b)   the intended beneficiary dies before the testator, leaving issue; and
    (c)   issue of the intended beneficiary are living at the testator's death,
then, unless a contrary intention appears by the will, the devise or bequest shall take effect as a devise or bequest to the issue living at the testator's death.

The effect of s. 33 is to save the gift from lapse and pass it to the intended beneficiary's issue 'living at the testator's death'. That includes 'a person conceived before the testator's death and born living thereafter': s. 33(4)(b). The issue taking under s. 33 take stirpitally — they take the gift which their parent would have taken if the parent had survived the testator: s. 33(3). What if the testator makes a class gift to issue and a member of the class predeceases him? As seen already, the general rule is that the doctrine of lapse does not apply to class gifts. Thus, if the general rule were applied, the gift would pass to the surviving members of the class. However, s. 33(2) provides that the gift takes effect 'as if the class included the issue of its deceased member', subject to a contrary intention in the will.

Re Meredith [1924] 2 Ch 552 illustrates how a contrary intention in the will may exclude s. 33(1). The testator bequeathed a legacy of £100 to his son, leaving the residue of his estate to his five children (including the son). The son predeceased the testator, leaving two children. The gifts to the son were thus saved from lapse, but the testator, not realising this, made a codicil which referred to the supposed lapse and gave legacies of £100 to each of the son's children. The court held that the original gifts to the son were not saved from lapse by s. 33 because the testator had shown an intention that the two children should not take these gifts. The intention was discernible from reading the will and codicil together as one testamentary instrument.

Sections 32 and 33 apply if the testator dies after 1982, the current provisions having been enacted by the Administration of Justice Act 1982. The original s. 32 was similar to the current enactment, but the original s. 33 (still applicable to testators dying before 1983) was substantially different in several respects. The main difference was that the saved gift became an asset of the intended beneficiary's estate, to be distributed according to his will or intestacy. Thus his issue did not necessarily take (unlike the case with the current s. 33): *Re Pearson* [1920] 1 Ch 247. Moreover, the original s. 33 did not apply to class gifts; hence the issue of the intended beneficiary took nothing. Nor did the original s. 33 apply to gifts of interests that were determinable at or before the death of the testator's issue, such as life interests.

7.2.5.4 Presumption of order of death

The doctrine of lapse applies where the beneficiary predeceases the testator. Difficulties will obviously arise where the order of death of the testator and beneficiary is unclear — for example, where they perish together in the same accident or disaster. The technical term for two or more persons dying together — *commorientes* — is derived from Roman law. But it should be noted that uncertainty as to the order of death is not confined to situations where persons die together — there can be uncertainty (perhaps even more so) where persons die in opposite parts of the world.

Section 184 of the Law of Property Act 1925 provides a presumption of survivorship with regard to claims to property where the order of death is uncertain:

In all cases where … two or more persons have died in circumstances rendering it uncertain which of them survived the other or others, such deaths shall (subject to any order of the court), for all purposes affecting the title to property, be presumed to have occurred in order of seniority, and accordingly the younger shall be deemed to have survived the elder.

This presumption provides a clear if somewhat arbitrary rule, applicable 'for all purposes affecting the title to property'. Since the presumption is that deaths occurred 'in order of seniority', it cannot be applied if the court cannot determine who was the younger, who the elder. This could occur, for example, where birth certificates are not forthcoming and there is no other evidence of the parties' respective ages.

The presumption applies only if it is 'uncertain' who survived whom: if there is evidence pointing to survivorship, the estates of the deceased should be distributed accordingly. What does 'uncertain' mean in s. 184? In *Hickman* v *Peacey* [1945] AC 304, a small house in London was struck at the height of the Battle of Britain by a German high-explosive bomb which penetrated to the basement before exploding. Five persons were in the house at the time. They were all killed and buried in the debris. There was no evidence as to whether any of the deceased had survived the others. Two of them had made wills benefiting each other and some of the others. It was held by the House of Lords by a 3:2 majority (reversing the Court of Appeal) that s. 184 applied since it could not be proved that any person had survived the others. The argument was raised — which would have seriously limited the application of s. 184 — that the presumption should not apply because it could be inferred that the deaths had occurred simultaneously. Simon LC expressed this argument vividly in his dissenting judgment (at p. 316): 'A rule of racing which provided that, where the judge was uncertain which of two horses passed the winning post first, the younger horse should take the prize, would not prevent the sharing of the prize in a dead-heat.' But the majority view was that even if simultaneous death could be inferred on the facts, that would not remove uncertainty as to survivorship. Lord Macmillan stated (at pp. 323–5):

Can you say for certain which of these two dead persons died first? If you cannot say for certain, then you must presume the older to have died first. It is immaterial that the reason for your inability to say for certain which died first is either because you think they both died simultaneously or because you think they died consecutively but you do not know in what sequence ... Without resorting to fantastic or far-fetched conjectures it is perfectly possible that the blast of the explosion did not annihilate the whole of these five victims at the same instant. Thus, one of them may quite well have been out of the shelter in another part of the house at the moment of the impact of the shell and the blast, though by an infinitesimal interval, may have struck him sooner or later than the others. I simply do not know. Nobody can know ... I cannot accept the view that in the circumstances of this case there was no element of uncertainty, legal or other, on the cardinal issue.

Section 184 will not apply if there is proof of survivorship. Clearly the proof must suffice to render it not uncertain who survived whom, but what is the degree of proof necessary? There was some inconsistency on this issue in *Hickman* v *Peacey*: Lord Macmillan appears to require proof beyond all reasonable doubt, but Simon LC seems to have favoured a lesser degree of proof — 'evidence leading to a defined and warranted conclusion' (p. 318). In *Re Bate* [1947] 2 All ER 418, the court expressed preference for the view of Simon LC. A couple were found dead in a gas-filled kitchen. The husband's body was lying across his wife's. The level of carbon monoxide in her blood was lower. The court held on the facts that despite some indications that the wife died first there was insufficient evidence of survivorship. Thus s. 184 applied, and since the wife was the younger, she was presumed to have survived the husband. There was conflicting expert evidence as to the significance of the different levels of carbon monoxide in the blood of the two deceased. The conflict contributed to the judge's uncertainty as to survivorship. The Scottish case, *Lamb* v *Lord Advocate* 1976 SLT 151, held that survivorship could be established on a balance of probabilities (as regards the equivalent Scots provision).

What is the meaning of the phrase in parenthesis in s. 184, '(subject to any order of the court)'? In *Re Lindop* [1942] 2 All ER 46, a case concerning a married couple killed during an air raid in 1941 over Torquay, it was held that the words in question did not give the court a discretion to disregard the presumption where the court concluded that it would be unfair or unjust to apply it. Bennett J thought that the words simply emphasised that the presumption was rebuttable, but this appears to be based on a misconception of the operation of s. 184. The section lays down a presumption in cases where survivorship is uncertain. Thus the presumption cannot be applied if there is sufficient evidence of survivorship. It follows that the presumption is not rebuttable by evidence of survivorship because *there is nothing to rebut*. What else, then, can 'subject to any order of the court' mean? Possibly it allows the court to make an appropriate order if there is insufficient evidence of the order of seniority of the parties, or to make another order if fresh evidence emerges later.

Because s. 184 provides an arbitrary solution, and one which might not reflect the wishes of the testator had he directed his mind to the issue, survivorship clauses are commonly included in wills. A typical clause provides that the beneficiary can take only if he survives the testator by one month (or other period); and a substitutional gift would be made in case of failure to survive for the required time. However, particular care is required in drafting such clauses. It will be recalled that in *Re Rowland* (see 6.1.2.1) substitutional gifts were made by a couple in their wills in the event of their deaths 'coinciding'. The couple most probably had in mind the contingency of perishing together in the same accident, but the Court of Appeal held that since 'coinciding' meant dying simultaneously, and there was no proof that their deaths had been simultaneous, their survivorship clauses were inapplicable; hence their estates were distributed according to s. 184.

Where spouses die in circumstances rendering it uncertain which of them survived the other, and the elder spouse has died intestate, s. 184 shall have effect as respects the intestate 'as if the husband or wife had not survived the intestate': s. 46(3) Administration of Estates Act 1925. Without this exception the property of the intestate would have devolved according to his spouse's will or intestacy, and thus passed to that spouse's next-of-kin rather than to the intestate's side of the family. It should be remembered that in any case a person can no longer succeed on the intestacy of his or her spouse unless the survivor has survived the intestate's death for 28 days: s. 46(2A) of the Administration of Estates Act 1925 (as enacted by s. 1(1) of the Law Reform (Succession) Act 1995). This provision applies to intestates dying after 1995.

7.2.6   Ademption

7.2.6.1   The basic principles
A specific gift fails through ademption if the subject-matter of the gift ceases to be part of the testator's estate by the date of his death. Ademption may result from a variety of causes. For example, the property might be sold, given away or disposed of in some other way; or it might be converted or nationalised; or it might be lost or destroyed. Ademption bears a close similarity to lapse. In each case something ceases to exist before the testator's death: in lapse it is the beneficiary, whereas in ademption it is the subject-matter. A common example of ademption is where the testator sells the property which he had gifted in his will. In *Ashburner* v *Macguire* (1786) 2 Bro CC 108; 29 ER 62, the testator made a gift of 'my capital stock of £1,000 in the India Company's stock' to his son. He later sold the stock and thus the gift was adeemed. Moreover, the son was not entitled to the proceeds of the sale since the general rule is that the beneficiary of the adeemed gift cannot claim or trace the proceeds (if any) of the property which represents the former subject-matter of the gift.

The testator can prevent ademption by clearly expressing a contrary intention in the will and making a substitutional provision. For example, in *Re Lewis's WT* [1937] Ch 118, the testator bequeathed certain securities 'or the investments representing the same at my death if they shall have been converted into other holdings'. Later he redeemed one of the securities and placed the proceeds in bank deposit accounts. It was held that the gift had not been adeemed.

There is some authority to suggest that as a general rule a gift will not be adeemed if the property was disposed of without the testator's knowledge or consent. In *Jenkins* v *Jones* (1866) LR 2 Eq 323, a testator bequeathed farming stock to his son. The testator later became insane, incapable of managing his own affairs. His son converted the stock into money prior to the testator's death. It was held that the conversion had not adeemed the gift since it was done without the testator's knowledge and consent. And in *Re Jeffery* (1975) 53 DLR (3d) 650, Weatherston J stated (at p. 653) that 'where the subject-matter of a legacy is not in existence at the date of the testator's death because it has been disposed of without the knowledge of the testator or against his wishes or tortiously, then the legacy will not be adeemed'.

It is a basic principle that ademption can arise only through causes occurring before the testator's death. What then is the position where it is unclear whether the property was adeemed before the testator died? This scenario could easily arise where, for example, the testator and the specific gift perish together in an accident. Suppose that Arthur bequeaths his luxury vintage car, but that while driving it around the coast he accidentally drives over a precipitous cliff, with the result that both driver and car perish. Has the gift been adeemed? It seems that the gift will adeem if the property did not 'survive' Arthur. Thus the specific legatee will lose the gift if the evidence suggests that Arthur and the car perished together. In *Durrant* v *Friend* (1852) 5 DeG & S 343; 64 ER 1145, the testator bequeathed certain chattels and had them insured. He took some of them on a sea voyage but the ship was lost when returning from India. It was held that since the testator and the chattels 'perished together', the gift was adeemed and thus the legatee had no interest in the insurance proceeds. The decision was followed in *Re Mercer* [1944] 1 All ER 759 (rights to war damage insurance resulting from death and destruction caused by air-raid on York) and, more recently, in *Re Hunter* (1976) 58 DLR (3d) 175 where the testatrix, having devised her house and bequeathed the contents to certain beneficiaries, perished in a fire which totally destroyed the house and contents. As it was not clear whether the house and contents had survived her, it was held that the gifts adeemed. Thus the legatees were not entitled to the insurance proceeds.

7.2.6.2 Change in property

Suppose that the subject-matter of the gift undergoes some form of change prior to the testator's death — at what point can the gift be said to be adeemed? The principle was stated by Turner VC in *Oakes* v *Oakes* (1852) 9 Hare 666; 68 ER 680, at 683: 'The question is whether a testator has at the time of his death the same thing existing — it may be in a different shape — yet substantially the same thing.'

This test has been applied in numerous cases, especially those involving changes in companies and their assets. In *Re Slater* [1907] 1 Ch 665, CA, the testator bequeathed interest arising from money invested in the Lambeth Waterworks Company. Later the company was absorbed by the much larger

Metropolitan Water Board, and its shareholders were compensated by stock in the MWB. It was held that the gift of the interest was adeemed. The Metropolitan Water Board stock could not pass under the gift because it was not 'substantially the same thing' within the principle in *Oakes* v *Oakes* — the assets were now in a much larger concern operating over a much wider area. Cozens-Hardy MR stated (at p. 672):

> ... you have to ask yourself, Where is the thing which is given? If you cannot find it at the testator's death, it is no use trying to trace it unless you can trace it in this sense, that you find something which has been changed in name and form only, but which is substantially the same thing.

In *Re Clifford* [1912] 1 Ch 29, the testator bequeathed 23 shares belonging to him in a company (he held 104 £80 shares). Later the company altered its name and sub-divided each share into four new shares so that the testator held 416 £20 shares at his death. It was held that since the original 23 shares still substantially existed, though changed in name and form, there was no ademption. Similarly in *Re Leeming* [1912] 1 Ch 828, a gift of 'my ten shares in the Kirkstall Brewery Company' was not adeemed when the company issued substantially the same shares in place of the original holding, following the company's voluntary liquidation and reconstruction under the same name.

The principles in *Oakes* v *Oakes* and *Re Slater* are applicable *generally*, not just in the case of company takeovers and reorganisation. In *Re Dorman* [1994] 1 All ER 804, the testatrix gave a power of attorney to X to manage her affairs. Prior to the death of the testatrix, X closed the testatrix's deposit account at Barclays Bank plc and opened another account at the same bank to take advantage of a higher rate of interest. The issue was whether a gift of the money in the deposit account was adeemed by the acts of the attorney. It was held that there was no ademption since the change was not a substantial one — the arrangements under both accounts were similar — but a change in name and form only.

A change in the nature of the asset may be brought about by Act of Parliament. Whether the property is thereby adeemed depends again on whether there is a change in substance, or in name and form only. Moreover, the Act itself may exclude the operation of ademption. In *Re Jenkins* [1931] 2 Ch 218, the testator bequeathed his considerable holding in 'the Swansea Harbour Trust' upon certain trusts. The Great Western Railway Act 1923 converted holdings in the Swansea Harbour Trust into GWR stock and provided that any reference in a will to stock in the Swansea enterprise was to be deemed to be a reference to GWR stock. It was held that the gift was thereby saved from ademption. But compare *Re Galway's WT* [1950] Ch 1, where a gift was not saved because the Act in question did not exclude ademption (see 5.6.2.3). A number of cases of potential ademption arose following the conversion of jointly-held realty into an interest in the proceeds of sale by the Law of Property Act 1925, s. 35. In *Re Newman* [1930] 2 Ch 409, it was held that a specific devise was adeemed by the imposition of the trusts under the 1925 Act. But later cases distinguished *Re Newman* and held that a confirmatory codicil made after 1925 saves a pre–1926 undivided share of realty from ademption: see, for example, *Re Warren* [1932] 1 Ch 42 and *Re Harvey* [1947] Ch 285. The doctrine of conversion has now been abolished by s. 3 of the Trusts of Land and Appointment of Trustees Act 1996.

7.2.6.3 Contracts and options

What if a testator makes a specific gift in his will but later contracts to sell the property comprised in the gift? The gift is adeemed, whether or not the sale was completed prior to the testator's death. The beneficiary is thus not entitled to the proceeds of sale; but if the testator dies before completion, the beneficiary is entitled to the enjoyment of the property (and to any profits accruing) from the time of the testator's death until the time for completion: *Watts v Watts* (1873) LR 17 Eq 217, where the testator bequeathed his leaseholds to his sister but later agreed to sell them to the Great Western Railway Company. He died before the completion of the contract (which was effected by his executor). It was held that as the gift had been adeemed, the sister could not take the proceeds of sale but was entitled to the rents accruing between the testator's death and completion.

What if the will is made after the contract? Then the beneficiary is entitled to the testator's interest in the property, and is thus entitled to the proceeds of the contract. In *Re Calow* [1928] Ch 710, the testator entered a contract to sell his lands to the London County Council. Later he made a will devising the lands on trust for his sons. The completion of the sale occurred a few months after his death. It was held that the sons were entitled to the proceeds of sale since the circumstances showed that the testator intended to pass whatever interest he had in the property.

As regards options, the position is governed by the rule enunciated by Kenyon MR in *Lawes v Bennett* (1785) 1 Cox 167; 29 ER 1111, under which if an option is granted by a testator in his lifetime to buy property comprised in a specific gift, the exercise of the option after the testator's death adeems the gift. The rule is dubious for two reasons. First, whether the gift adeems or not depends on the whim of the party to whom the option was granted; and, secondly, the rule breaches the fundamental notion that ademption can arise only *prior* to the testator's death. Nevertheless, the rule appears to be well-established and has been consistently followed, although sometimes with reluctance. In *Re Carrington* [1932] 1 Ch 1, CA, the testator bequeathed shares in a company to various legatees, but many years later granted an option to purchase the shares to be exercised within one month of his death. On the exercise of the option within the time limit it was held that the gift was adeemed, but the court expressed its unease at applying the rule in *Lawes v Bennett*. Although the exercise of the option adeems the gift, the beneficiary is entitled in the interim to enjoy the property and take any accrued profits from the time of the testator's death: *Townley v Bedwell* (1808) 14 Ves 591; 33 ER 648. If the testator grants an option to buy property and later makes a will gifting the property, there is no ademption — the beneficiary is entitled to the purchase price on the exercise of the option. And the position is the same if the grant of the option was preceded by a will and the testator made a subsequent codicil (after the option or contemporaneous with it) confirming the will: *Re Pyle* [1895] 1 Ch 724.

In *Re Sweeting* [1988] 1 All ER 1016, the rule in *Lawes* v *Bennett* was held to apply to conditional contracts. The testator made specific gifts of plots of land ('the yard') adjoining his house. Shortly before his death he exchanged two contracts of sale, one for the house, the other for the yard, but died before either was completed. The contract for the yard provided that completion was conditional on the simultaneous completion of the contract for sale of the house, which in turn depended on the consent of the testator's wife (which she gave). After the testator's death both sales were completed and the issue arose whether the gifts of the yard were adeemed by the contract of sale (the proceeds thus falling into residue). It was held that the rule in *Lawes* v *Bennett* applied to conditional contracts; hence the gifts were adeemed.

7.2.6.4 Removal of chattels

Testators sometimes describe gifts of chattels by reference to a particular place or locality, e.g., 'all my furniture at Chatsworth House'. If the chattels are then removed from that place prior to the testator's death, is the gift thereby adeemed? The position depends on the significance of the venue and on the nature of the removal. If the place described in the gift is not a substantive part of the bequest, it is immaterial whether the chattels were removed or not (or for how long). But if the chattels are connected with a particular locality or the enjoyment of a particular house, the gift fails if there has been a permanent removal, but not if the removal has been temporary. Removal for the purposes of repair or a short loan is likely to be regarded as temporary, whereas removal for the purposes of long-term safekeeping or indefinite loan will probably be held to be permanent. In *Re Zouche* [1919] 2 Ch 178, the testatrix bequeathed various chattels 'at Parham House [her residence] at the time of my decease'. At the time of her death her estate included many valuable articles, including a superb collection of very rare books, e.g., the Mazarin Bible (*c.* 1456, the earliest book printed with moveable type). Many of the articles were in Parham House when she died, but a dispute arose as to some valuable plate which had been deposited with bankers for safe custody, and several rare books which had been loaned to the British Museum for exhibition. These items had been removed by her predecessor in title some years earlier. It was held that they did not pass under the bequest because the removal was not temporary — the plate was never removed from the bank, whilst the books appear to have been loaned indefinitely. In *Re Johnston* (1884) 26 Ch D 538, the testatrix bequeathed 'the whole contents of my said house, No. 9, Belgrave Square' (London). The issue was whether a box containing valuable jewellery was part of the gift. It was normally kept at the house but was deposited with bankers whenever the testatrix was away from London, as had occurred when the testatrix died. Chitty J held that the gift of the jewellery had not been adeemed by the removal: 'the usual locality of the goods in question was the house, and they were only removed for a temporary purpose. It is a very significant fact that the goods were in the house at the time the lady made her will' (p. 554).

The same rules have been applied to bank accounts. In *Re Heilbronner* [1953] 2 All ER 1016, the testator bequeathed 'my bank deposit at the Midland Bank' to his nurse. Shortly before his death the testator gave his executor a cheque for £100 drawn on his current account (he had never had a deposit account) to pay for various of the testator's expenses, and then instructed the bank to pay the executor the balance. It was held that the sum held by the executor when the testator died passed under the bequest to the nurse since it had been removed for a temporary purpose. This was certainly a generous decision, but justified on the merits of the case since the testator had clearly intended the nurse to benefit.

7.2.7 Election

7.2.7.1 Basis of the doctrine

> By the well-settled doctrine which is termed … the doctrine of 'election', where a deed or will professes to make a general disposition of property for the benefit of a person named in it, such person cannot accept a benefit under the instrument without at the same time conforming to all its provisions. (*per* Cairns LC in *Codrington* v *Codrington* (1875) LR 7 HL 854, at 861–2)

Election is an equitable doctrine which applies where the testator makes a gift to a beneficiary and by the same instrument gives property belonging to the beneficiary to a third party, often mistakenly thinking that it belongs to the testator. The beneficiary has three choices. First, he may disclaim the gift to him, in which case he preserves his own property but cannot derive any benefit from the disclaimed gift. Secondly, he may take *under* the will — that is, he complies with the testator's wishes by taking the gift meant for him and passing his own property to the third party. Thirdly, he may take *against* the will — that is, he takes the gift intended for him but does not pass his own property to the third party, in which case he must compensate the latter for the loss of the benefit. To illustrate: suppose that Arthur bequeaths his gold watch to Jack, and Jack's golf clubs to Jim. Jack can disclaim the watch and keep his golf clubs; or he can take the watch and give the golf clubs to Jim; or he can take the watch, keep the golf clubs but compensate Jim for their value. There is a failure of gift both in the first scenario — Jack's disclaimer — and in the third (Jim does not get the golf clubs, although he is entitled to compensation).

The doctrine of election should be distinguished from disclaimer. A beneficiary who disclaims does not *elect* in the technical sense; he renounces. Election strictly occurs where the beneficiary accepts his gift and elects whether to give his own property to the third party or to compensate him, as Jessel MR made clear in *Rogers* v *Jones* (1876) 3 Ch D 688, at 689:

> The doctrine of election is this — that if a person whose property a testator affects to give away takes other benefits under the same will, and at the same time elects to keep his own property, he must make compensation to the

person affected by his election to an extent not exceeding the benefits he receives.

The basis of the doctrine is that it would be unconscionable to allow the beneficiary to take his gift but not satisfy the testator's expressed wishes. Hence an obligation is imposed on his conscience to compensate the third party if the beneficiary chooses not to part with his own property. In *Re Mengel's WT* [1962] Ch 791, Buckley J described election (at p. 797) as 'a doctrine by which equity fastens on the conscience of the person who is put to his election and refuses to allow him to take the benefit of a disposition contained in the will ... except upon certain conditions'.

7.2.7.2 Requirements of the doctrine

There are several requirements to be satisfied in order for the doctrine of election to apply. First, it does not apply if a contrary intention appears in the will: *Re Vardon's Trusts* (1886) 31 Ch D 275, CA. Secondly, both gifts must be given in the same instrument. For this purpose a will and subsequent codicils are treated as one instrument. Thirdly, the testator must make an effective gift of his property — that is, property which he is competent to dispose of — to the beneficiary. Fourthly, the beneficiary's property must be freely alienable: he must be able to dispose of his property in favour of the designated third party. This requirement may be satisfied even though the beneficiary does not own the whole of the property that has been given away by the testator. In *Re Dicey* [1957] Ch 145, the doctrine was applied in the case of a gift by a testator of the beneficiary's half share in realty to a third party (since the half share could be assigned by the beneficiary). Fifthly, the property given to the beneficiary must be capable of being used to compensate the third party: *Re Gordon's WT* [1978] Ch 145, CA.

If any of the requirements are not satisfied, the doctrine of election is not applicable. Thus the beneficiary will be able to take the gift to him free of any obligation to the third party.

7.2.7.3 The process of election

The beneficiary may elect expressly or impliedly (by conduct). He is entitled to know the factors that could influence his decision, particularly the value of the property subject to the election. Indeed, as regards implied election, it has to be shown that the beneficiary knew the relevant facts. The beneficiary will be deemed to have elected *against* the will if he exceeds any time limit for election stipulated by the testator. Where an election is made *against* the will, the beneficiary loses the gift made to him by the testator up to the extent of the compensation required for the third party. The value of the compensation is determined as at the time of the testator's death, not when the beneficiary elects: *Re Hancock* [1905] 1 Ch 16.

7.2.8 Satisfaction

In certain circumstances equitable presumptions apply by which a legacy is deemed to have been given in satisfaction of a pre-existing obligation owed by the testator to the beneficiary, or in satisfaction of another legacy given by the same instrument. Thus the legacy 'fails' to the extent that it is regarded as simply satisfying the obligation or other legacy. Some of the presumptions could apply to devises, but it is legacies that are far more frequently involved. The presumptions are generally rebuttable by showing contrary intention, and this can be done by intrinsic or extrinsic evidence, including (in the latter case) direct evidence of the testator's declarations of his intention, even if he died before 1983 (see 6.4.4).

7.2.8.1   Satisfaction of a debt by a legacy
A debt will in certain circumstances be presumed to have been satisfied by a subsequent legacy. In order for the presumption to apply it must be shown that the debt preceded the will and that it was still owed at the date of the will's execution. The legacy must equal or exceed the debt; if it is less, the creditor-beneficiary is entitled to both. And the legacy must be at least as beneficial as the debt. Thus the presumption does not apply, for example, if the debt is secured but the legacy is not. Moreover, there must not be a substantial difference in the *nature* of the legacy and the debt. So a gift of land would not be held to be made in satisfaction of a money debt.

What if the testator pays off the debt prior to his death? The legacy is regarded as adeemed: *Re Fletcher* (1888) 38 Ch D 373, where the testator bequeathed £625 to his wife, the exact amount that he then owed her. Later he repaid the debt and drew a pen through the bequest (but did not effectively revoke it). It was held that the legacy had been adeemed by the payment of the debt.

7.2.8.2   Satisfaction of a legacy by another legacy
The presumption is that if a testator gives two general legacies of the same amount in the same instrument to the same legatee, the legacies are substitutional and not cumulative: the legatee can take only one legacy. However, even if the legacies are of the same amount, they are both payable if they are of a substantially different nature, or if they are expressed to be given from differing motives.

If the legacies are given in different instruments, the legatee *prima facie* takes both (for this purpose wills and codicils are regarded as separate instruments). But if the same motive is expressed in both instruments, the legatee can take only once — the 'double coincidence' (same amount, same motive) is too great for the legacies to be regarded as cumulative. In *Benyon* v *Benyon* (1810) 17 Ves 34; 34 ER 14, the testator bequeathed £100 to JB as an acknowledgment for his trouble as one of his executors. He later made a codicil in which he bequeathed the same amount to JB, and for the same reason. It was held that the legatee was entitled to one sum only: 'a legacy of the same sum, for the same cause, given by a codicil, is repetition, and not addition' (*per* Grant MR, at p. 17).

7.2.8.3   Satisfaction of a portion-debt by a legacy
If a testator bequeaths a legacy to a child or to someone to whom he stands *in loco parentis*, the legacy will be presumed in certain circumstances to be in

satisfaction of an obligation incurred by the testator to provide a portion for that person — 'equity leans against double portions'. What is a 'portion-debt'? A portion is a gift made to establish the child in life (who need not necessarily be a minor) or to make permanent provision for him. A portion-debt is the obligation to confer a portion on a person; it will often have been incurred under a covenant. The debt must still be existing when the testator dies.

The presumption that a portion-debt is satisfied by a legacy was apparently established in *Warren* v *Warren* (1783) 1 Bro CC 305; 28 ER 1149. In order for the presumption to apply the portion-debt must have been incurred before the will was executed. And the nature of the portion-debt and legacy must not be substantially different. Thus, if the portion-debt consists of a covenant to pay money, and the testator devises land, the child can take both since the presumption does not arise. Where the presumption does apply, the beneficiary is entitled to choose whether to take the legacy or to rely on the debt. He may prefer the latter option in some circumstances, even though the legacy is larger than the debt — for example, where there is a possibility that because of potential insufficiency of assets, the legacy might not be paid or might abate (debtors are paid before legatees in the administration of estates).

What if the legacy is less than the portion-debt? Unlike the case of the satisfaction of a debt by a legacy, a portion-debt can be *partially* satisfied, as occurred in *Warren* v *Warren* (above). To illustrate: suppose that the testator bequeaths a legacy to X of £5,000 to whom he owed £10,000 (not by way of portion-debt). X is entitled to the debt and the legacy since the presumption of satisfaction of a debt by a legacy does not apply. But if the £10,000 debt was a portion-debt, it is partially satisfied by the legacy. Thus X is not entitled to both.

7.2.8.4   Satisfaction of a legacy by a portion

If a testator makes a will bequeathing a legacy to a child (or someone treated as a child) and subsequently gives a portion to the legatee, or incurs an obligation to do so, the legacy is satisfied *pro tanto* by the portion. In effect, the legacy is partially or wholly adeemed — 'ademption' is sometimes used (rather than 'satisfaction') to describe this presumption. The presumption again results from equity's leaning against double portions, but it does not apply if there is a substantial difference in the nature of the legacy and the portion.

Neither of the presumptions concerning portions may be applied so as to benefit a stranger — that is, someone who is not a child (or treated as such) of the testator: *Meinertzagen* v *Walters* (1872) LR 7 Ch App 670.

Although all the presumptions concerning satisfaction are well-established, their status is somewhat fragile given the number of conditions attached and the ease with which they can be rebutted. Moreover, judges have frequently expressed disquiet at the consequences of these presumptions, the operation of which would sometimes have surprised the testator. This is particularly true of the presumptions arising from equity's leaning against double portions. Now that the notion of maintaining equality between children has been somewhat undermined by the ending of the requirement to account for advancements in intestacy, the future application of the presumptions concerning portions is unclear.

7.2.9 Public policy and forfeiture

A gift may fail if it was made for an illegal purpose or it contravenes public policy. For example, in *Thrupp* v *Collett* (1858) 26 Beav 125; 53 ER 844, the testator bequeathed £5,000 to his executors to be applied 'in purchasing and procuring the discharges of persons, who ... may be committed to prison for non-payment of fines, fees or expenses, under the game laws'. Romilly MR rejected the argument that the purpose of the bequest was charitable (the relief of prisoners) and held the bequest to be void as against public policy since the gift was 'obviously calculated to encourage offences prohibited by the Legislature' (p. 845).

7.2.9.1 Forfeiture: the basic rule

The most important rule of public policy in this context is that a person should not be able to profit from his crime. More specifically, the rule provides that a potential beneficiary forfeits his interest if he has unlawfully killed the testator or the intestate, as expressed by Kolbert J in *Jones* v *Roberts* [1995] 2 FLR 422, at 425:

> ... there is a long-standing and well-established rule of public policy, known as the forfeiture rule, which precludes a person who has unlawfully killed another from acquiring a benefit in consequence of the killing.

The forfeiture rule applies not only to interests under a will or intestacy, but also to a *donatio mortis causa*, nomination, trust, joint tenancy, or to the proceeds of an insurance policy: *Cleaver* v *Mutual Reserve Fund Life Association* [1892] 1 QB 147. Although the rule is concerned with 'unlawful killing', it has been confined so far to death caused by murder or manslaughter. There are other forms of unlawful killing, e.g., causing death by dangerous driving, but there appears to have been no reported case where the rule has been applied other than to murder and manslaughter. There have been *dicta*, however, in some cases to the effect that the rule should prevent a person from profiting from his *crime*. For example, in *Cleaver's* case, Fry LJ stated (at p. 156) that 'no system of jurisprudence can with reason include amongst the rights which it enforces rights directly resulting to the person asserting them from the crime of that person'. But this is too wide a formulation of the forfeiture rule on the current state of the authorities.

The cases are inconsistent as to whether the forfeiture rule applies to all types of manslaughter. The better view is that it does, apart perhaps from the so-called 'motor manslaughter' cases. The Court of Appeal in *In the Estate of Hall* [1914] P 1, held that the application of the forfeiture rule did not depend on the moral guilt of the killer and refused to distinguish between murder and manslaughter on the grounds of moral culpability. In *Re Giles* [1971] 3 All ER 1141, it was held that the forfeiture rule applied to a conviction for manslaughter on the grounds of diminished responsibility. A woman killed her husband (the testator) by a single blow with a domestic chamber-pot. A hospital order was made following her conviction. It was argued that the forfeiture rule should not apply where the conviction involved little or no moral culpability, but the argument was rejected and the court held that she was unable to take under the husband's estate. *Re Royse* [1984] 3 All ER 339, CA was similar — forfeiture applied in respect of a conviction (followed by a hospital order) of a wife for manslaughter of her husband on the grounds of diminished responsibility. Ackner LJ stated (at p. 341):

> It has not been, nor could it have been, disputed that the appellant, having been convicted of the manslaughter of her husband by stabbing him, was disqualified from taking any benefit under his will, or on his intestacy if he had died intestate, even though the sentence passed upon her was one of detention for hospital treatment . . . and was therefore a sentence designed to be remedial in nature and not by way of punishment.

A similar view was taken in *Jones* v *Roberts* (above). A man killed his parents by battering them with a hammer. He suffered from severe mental illness: he believed that his parents were controlled by the Russian Secret Service and were trying to poison him; that he was being persecuted by the IRA and the KGB; and that when he had had an operation for the removal of his appendix, a transmitter had been put in its place by the KGB. He was convicted of manslaughter on the grounds of diminished responsibility and was made subject to a hospital order. The issue was whether the son was entitled to succeed on his father's intestacy. It was argued on his behalf that public policy did not require the forfeiture rule to be applied in every case of manslaughter, but only where the claimant had been guilty of deliberate, intentional and unlawful violence (or threat of it). The court held that in *Re Royse* the forfeiture rule had been unequivocally stated as applying to manslaughter irrespective of the moral culpability of the claimant. Thus the son's claim was forfeited.

The rejected argument in *Jones* v *Roberts* was based principally on decisions in two earlier cases — *Gray* v *Barr* [1971] 2 QB 554, CA and *Re H* [1990] 1 FLR 441. In *Gray* v *Barr* — a claim to the proceeds of an insurance policy — it was held that the forfeiture rule did not apply to manslaughter unless the claimant had been guilty of deliberate, intentional and unlawful violence. On the facts the claimant was held in the civil proceedings to have been guilty of manslaughter involving such violence. Thus he forfeited his claim (even though he had been acquitted of manslaughter in the criminal proceedings). In *Re H* the test in *Gray* v *Barr* was applied where a husband killed his wife while he was suffering from hallucinations brought on by an unusual reaction to anti-depressant drugs. He was held entitled to the wife's estate under her will. This was a very questionable decision, the authority of which is greatly diminished because *Re Royse* was not cited. The *Re Royse* line of cases is not only more authoritative but also accords more satisfactorily with public policy. The principle that a person *prima facie* should not benefit as the result of his crime should be framed in the widest possible terms and should not depend on the questionable distinctions posited by the *Gray* v *Barr* test. However, such distinctions should be relevant when considering whether to allow relief from the operation of the forfeiture rule (see 7.2.9.3).

The forfeiture rule applies only if a person is guilty of murder or manslaughter; thus it does not apply where the killer is not guilty by reason of insanity. In *Re Houghton* [1915] 2 Ch 173, a man who while insane had killed his father and brother was held entitled to claim under the father's intestacy. Is a conviction for murder or manslaughter necessary in order for the forfeiture rule to apply? It might have been thought from first principles that a conviction was necessary because of the fundamental principle that a person is presumed innocent until proved guilty. However, such an approach would impose potentially awkward limitations on the forfeiture rule. Suppose, for example, that the evidence against the killer is overwhelming but that he commits suicide or dies before the conviction — would it be right if the forfeiture rule did not apply, thus allowing the killer's estate to benefit? It appears that a conviction is not necessary — the question is whether murder or manslaughter has occurred rather than whether a conviction has been obtained. It will be remembered that in *Gray* v *Barr* (above) the forfeiture rule was applied despite the claimant being acquitted of manslaughter. In *Re Sigsworth* [1935] Ch 89, the rule was applied where the killer committed suicide shortly after he had murdered his mother. In *Re Dellow's WT* [1964] 1 All 771, a husband and wife were found dead in a gas-filled room. Under s. 184 of the Law of Property Act 1925, the wife, being the younger, was presumed to have survived the husband. There was overwhelming evidence that the wife had killed her helpless, stroke-ridden husband and had committed suicide in the process. It was held that her estate could not benefit under the husband's will. *Re Callaway* [1956] Ch 559 was similar (see below).

7.2.9.2 The effect of forfeiture

Prior to 1870, the property of a person convicted of felonious killing was forfeited to the Crown. The Forfeiture Act 1870 ended the Crown's rights apart from its entitlement on intestacy to take the property as *bona vacantia*. The principal effect now of the forfeiture rule is to prevent the killer or his estate from benefiting under the victim's will or intestacy. A gift in a will to the killer falls into residue; if the gift is a residuary gift, or if there is no gift of residue, the property passes on intestacy (but with the killer disqualified from taking). Thus, where the testatrix gave the whole of her property to the killer, he was barred from taking not only under the will but also under the resulting intestacy: *Re Sigsworth* (above). The property passes to other members of the same class; if none, to the next class entitled on intestacy. In *Re Callaway* (above), the testatrix excluded her son from her will and left the whole of her estate to her daughter. Mother and daughter were found dead in a gas-filled room in circumstances suggesting that the daughter had turned on the gas, intending to kill them both. It was held that the property passed on the mother's intestacy to her son. The argument that the property passed to the Crown as *bona vacantia* was rejected, although Vaisey J clearly was not at ease with his decision: 'That the plaintiff [the son] should take the whole seems to me both illogical and unmeritorious. For why . . . should he be the person to profit by his sister's crime and the consequent frustration of his mother's testamentary intentions?' (p. 565).

Moreover, a person cannot benefit from the victim's estate if his title is dependent on that of the killer. Consider *In the Estate of Crippen* [1911] P 108: Mrs Crippen died intestate, murdered by her husband (one of the most sensational cases in English criminal history). Following his conviction and unsuccessful appeal, Crippen made a will leaving all his property to Ethel Le Neve (his alleged mistress) and appointing her his executrix. He was executed shortly afterwards. The issue was whether Miss Le Neve had any claim through Crippen's will to his wife's estate. It was held that she had not. Evans P stated (at p. 112):

> It is clear that the law is, that no person can obtain, or enforce, any rights resulting to him from his own crime; neither can his representative, claiming under him, obtain or enforce any such rights. The human mind revolts at the very idea that any other doctrine could be possible in our system of jurisprudence.

What if the killer and the victim were joint tenants of property? The effect of the forfeiture rule is that the joint tenancy is severed, thus creating a beneficial tenancy in common. Thus the killer *prima facie* cannot benefit through survivorship: *Re K* [1985] Ch 85.

7.2.9.3 The Forfeiture Act 1982
The Forfeiture Act 1982 was enacted in order to give the court discretion to modify the application of the forfeiture rule in cases of unlawful killing, except where the killer stands convicted of murder. The fact that the Act is stated to apply to 'unlawful killing' rather than *just* to manslaughter suggests that the forfeiture rule does apply to unlawful killing other than manslaughter (although this is not borne out by the current state of the authorities). References to persons who have unlawfully killed include those who have 'unlawfully aided, abetted, counselled or procured' the death of the victim: s. 1(2).

The central provision of the Act is s. 2(2), which attempts to define the circumstances in which the court's discretion to modify the effect of the rule can be exercised:

> The court shall not make an order under this section modifying the effect of the forfeiture rule in any case unless it is satisfied that, having regard to the conduct of the offender and of the deceased and to such other circumstances as appear to the court to be material, the justice of the case requires the effect of the rule to be so modified in that case.

It is uncommon for property legislation to refer to 'justice' as a determining factor in a court's decision. Presumably the intention was to allow the court a virtually unfettered discretion in modifying the effect of the forfeiture rule where appropriate. Clearly the degree of moral culpability of the killer is relevant, as is that of the victim — the court must have regard to 'the conduct of the offender and of the deceased.' In *Re K* (above), the testator was killed by his wife after she had been subjected to violence from him for many years. She was convicted of manslaughter and sentenced to probation. The issue was whether the forfeiture rule should be modified to enable her to take substantial benefits under the testator's will, and the matrimonial home (of which she had been the joint tenant) by survivorship. The court held that in the unusual circumstances of the case it would be unjust to deprive the wife of *any* of the benefits conferred on her by will or accruing to her by survivorship. Vinelott J stated (at p. 102):

> The widow ... was a loyal wife who suffered grave violence at the hands of the deceased. When she took hold of the gun and released the safety catch she was in a state of great distress and feared further violence. She must accept the blame for what happened but she should not, in my judgment, suffer the further punishment of being deprived of the provision which her husband made for her which was, it seems to me, wholly appropriate having regard to the fact that the widow gave up a worthwhile and satisfying career when she married him, to her conduct towards him to the very end of his life and to the fact that there were no other persons for whom he was under any moral duty to provide.

The judge held that the power to *modify* the effect of the forfeiture rule included granting total relief from its application. He concluded that that is what the draftsmen of the 1982 Act had intended. The Court of Appeal confirmed this interpretation: *Re K* [1985] 2 All ER 833. This was perhaps surprising given the natural meaning of 'modify', namely, to make partial changes. While the desire of the courts to have wide discretion in this area is readily understandable, their interpretation of 'modify' is very strained. It is regrettable that the draftsmen of the Act failed to employ a more appropriate word than 'modify' if they wished the Act to have the effect that *Re K* decided it has. Moreover, it would have been preferable if the 1982 Act had been given a more appropriate title (the Act is about relief from forfeiture).

Section 2(4)(a) lists the interests in property to which the power to modify applies: they include any beneficial interest in the deceased's share of a joint tenancy, or under the deceased's will, intestacy, nomination or *donatio mortis causa*. Moreover, the power applies to any beneficial interest which before the deceased's death 'was held on trust for any person': s. 2(4)(b). In *Re S (Deceased) (Forfeiture Rule)* [1996] 1 FLR 910, a husband who suffered from mental illness killed his wife during a violent attack, believing that she was having an affair. He was convicted of manslaughter on the ground of diminished responsibility. He applied under the Act for his benefits under his wife's life insurance policy to be held on trust for his son rather than be forfeited. It was held that the sum assured under the policy fell within s. 2(4)(b) and that the justice of the case required the effect of the forfeiture rule to be modified in the limited manner proposed. The case clarifies that modification may be ordered under the Act in favour of a third party.

Where a person is convicted of 'an offence of which unlawful killing is an element', the court has no power to modify unless proceedings are brought within three months of the conviction: s. 2(3). This provision applies where a conviction has been obtained; presumably it does not prevent modification in cases where there has been no conviction — for example, where the killer committed suicide before the trial. Where a person stands convicted of *murder*, the Forfeiture Act 1982 has no application: s. 5.

7.2.9.4   Forfeiture and the Inheritance Act

The Inheritance (Provision for Family and Dependants) Act 1975 allows certain persons to claim reasonable provision from the deceased's estate if such provision has not been made under the deceased's will or intestacy (see generally Chapter 8). Section 3 of the Forfeiture Act 1982 provides that a person to whom the forfeiture rule applies is not thereby precluded from applying under the Inheritance Act for provision from the estate of his victim. But the chances of success will probably be slim since the court must pay regard (under the 1975 Act) to the conduct of the applicant. Presumably the court would regard that killing the deceased was the ultimate form of misconduct by the applicant (although the conduct of the deceased would also be relevant). Moreover, if the deceased's will or intestacy would have resulted in reasonable provision for the killer but for the effect of the forfeiture rule, the application under the 1975 Act is bound to fail: *Re Royse* (see 7.2.9.1). In such a case the killer's only realistic option is to apply for relief from forfeiture under the 1982 Act.

7.2.10   Uncertainty

A testamentary gift fails if it is impossible to ascertain the subject-matter of the gift or who are the intended beneficiaries. The courts strive to uphold testamentary provisions whenever possible, generally preferring testacy to intestacy. However, if a gift remains uncertain despite the application of the rules of construction, the admissibility of evidence (internal and extrinsic) and the possibility of rectification, the gift must fail (with the normal consequences of failure).

7.2.10.1   Uncertainty of subject-matter

In *Peck* v *Halsey* (1726) 2 P Wms 387; 24 ER 780, a gift of 'some of my best linen' was held to be void since the testator failed to specify sufficiently how much linen could be taken and because the description 'best' was too uncertain. Either reason would have sufficed to invalidate the gift in the court's view. However, even if the amount given is *prima facie* uncertain, the gift might be upheld if the will enables the amount to be ascertained by the court. In particular, the use of the magic word 'reasonable' will usually save a gift from failure. In *Re Golay* [1965] 2 All ER 660, the testator directed that 'Tossy' (a female beneficiary) should receive 'a reasonable income' from certain properties. It was held that the provision was not void for uncertainty since it was capable of an objective meaning which the court could supply (the court was used to making objective assessments of what is reasonable). In *Talbot* v *Talbot* [1968] Ch 1, CA, an option given by will to purchase a farm at 'a reasonable valuation' was held not to be void for uncertainty. Similarly, a direction that trustees should retain 'any reasonable sum' sufficient to remunerate them for their trouble in executing the trusts under a will was upheld in the Irish case, *Jackson* v *Hamilton* (1846) 3 Jo & Lat 702. Compare, however, *Jubber* v *Jubber* (1839) 9 Sim 503; 59 ER 452, where a gift of 'a handsome gratuity' to be given to each executor was held to be void for uncertainty (the court is rather less used to interpreting 'handsome' than 'reasonable').

In *Asten* v *Asten* [1894] 3 Ch 260, the testator owned four houses in Sudeley Place, Colchester. In his will he made a separate gift to each of his four sons (in virtually identical terms) of 'All that newly built house, being No.   , Sudeley Place'. The number was omitted in each case. It was held that the gifts were void for uncertainty because the will showed that the testator intended to give a particular house to each of his sons but had failed to indicate which house each son was to take. Romer J stated (at p. 263):

> If a will shews that a testator intends to give a particular property to a legatee, and, owing to the testator having several properties answering the description in the will of the particular property given you are unable to say, either from the will itself or from extrinsic evidence, which of the several properties the testator referred to, then on principle the gift must fail for uncertainty. . . .

The gifts would not have failed for uncertainty in *Asten* v *Asten* if the testator had conferred, expressly or impliedly, a right of selection on the sons — for example, if he had given to each son 'one of my houses in Sudeley Place'. If the beneficiaries then fail to agree who takes what, the choice is to be exercised in turn, priority determined by the order in which they are named in the will; if they are not named, priority is determined by drawing lots (in accordance with the analogy of Roman law). In *Re Knapton* [1941] Ch 423, the testatrix, who owned several small houses, gave 'one house to each of my nephews and nieces and one to N.H. One to F.K. One to my sister. One to my brother'. It was held that the right of choice should go in the first place to the nephews and nieces and then to others in the order in which they were named. The choice among the nephews and nieces was to be determined by lot (in the event of disagreement). Cases such as this indicate the lengths to which courts will go to avoid failing gifts for uncertainty. However, although drawing lots may seem at first sight to be an unsophisticated way in which to determine property disputes, it has certain merits (as a method of last resort). Those who do badly will at least not be able to complain that the decision was wrong, or unfair, or that counsel failed to argue their case properly or that the judge was prejudiced against them.

7.2.10.2 Uncertainty of objects

A classic illustration of the failure of a gift for uncertainty is provided by *Re Stephenson* [1897] 1 Ch 75, CA. The testator left his residuary estate to certain cousins whom he specified as 'the children of the deceased son (named Bamber) of my father's sister'. The sister had three sons (all deceased), each of whom had the surname Bamber and each of whom had left several children surviving the testator. Since it could not be determined which Bamber the testator had in mind, the gift failed.

What if the testator does not choose the beneficiaries under his will himself but delegates this power to someone else? Does that invalidate his gifts for uncertainty? There are *dicta* to the effect that a testator cannot delegate his testamentary powers. For example, in *Chichester Diocesan Fund and Board of Finance* v *Simpson* [1944] AC 341, HL, Lord Macmillan stated (at p. 349): 'The choice of beneficiaries must be the testator's own choice. He cannot leave the disposal of his estate to others.' But a testator, in making a charitable gift, *can* delegate to his executors the choice of charitable objects. Moreover, a testator clearly delegates his testamentary powers when granting a power of appointment, whether general, special or hybrid. In *Re Beatty's WT* [1990] 3 All ER 844, the testatrix left an estate valued at £32,000,000 including a very valuable collection of paintings. She bequeathed her personal chattels and a legacy of £1,500,000 to her trustees to allocate 'among such person or persons as they think fit' subject to 'any wishes of mine of which they shall be aware'. The court upheld the gift and denied that there was a rule of law prohibiting the delegation of testamentary powers. The true principle appears to be that the testator cannot delegate *the right to make a will*, but, in making his will, he can in some circumstances delegate to others *the choice of beneficiaries*.

The rule that a testamentary gift can fail because of uncertainty of objects does not apply to charitable gifts provided that the testator has shown a general charitable intention. However, if the objects of the gift are not exclusively charitable, the exception does not apply — the gift can fail for uncertainty: *Chichester Diocesan Fund and Board of Finance* v *Simpson* (above) where a direction to executors to distribute property for such 'charitable or benevolent' objects as they might select failed for uncertainty.

7.2.11 Failure to satisfy conditions

7.2.11.1 The basic rules

A gift may fail if it has been made subject to a condition, and the condition has not been satisfied. Conditions are classified for this purpose as either precedent or subsequent. A condition precedent (sometimes termed 'suspensive') is a condition which has to be satisfied in order for the beneficiary to *take* the gift. For example, if Arthur leaves all his property to his son 'provided my son erects a monument in my memory', the condition is precedent: Arthur does not wish his son to take unless he erects an appropriate monument. The most common condition precedent in practice is the requirement that a beneficiary should have obtained a certain age. A condition subsequent, on the other hand, acts by way of defeasance: the beneficiary initially takes the gift, but loses it subsequently if he fails to satisfy the condition. So if Arthur leaves everything to his son 'provided that he does not join the Midshire Hunt', the condition is subsequent: the gift vests in the son, but divests if he breaches the condition.

Although the difference between conditions precedent and subsequent is clear in theory, it may sometimes be difficult in practice to determine to which category a condition belongs. The question is one of construction: the court must construe the testator's intentions as expressed in the will. However, where the condition requires that something be done which may take considerable time, the condition is more likely to be considered subsequent because of the law's preference for early vesting. Indeed, the courts generally prefer in cases of doubt to hold a condition to be subsequent: *Re Greenwood* [1903] 1 Ch 749, CA.

Why does it matter whether a condition is precedent or subsequent? First, the consequences of failure to satisfy the condition differ: if a condition precedent is not satisfied, the beneficiary receives no benefit at all; whereas in the case of a condition subsequent, the beneficiary takes the gift, but loses it — perhaps long afterwards — on breach of the condition. Secondly, different consequences follow when the condition itself fails. It might do so for a number of reasons. A condition is void, for example, if it is illegal, or contrary to public policy, or uncertain or impossible to perform. In *Watson v National Children's Home* (1995) *The Times*, 31 October a condition that an intended beneficiary should care for the testator's pets was held to be void for impossibility since the pets had predeceased the testator (see 6.4.3.3). The general rule is that if a condition precedent is void, the gift itself fails; thus the beneficiary cannot take (but may nevertheless benefit if the gift falls into residue or passes under intestacy). But if a condition subsequent is void, the beneficiary rejoices — the gift becomes unconditional, so that he cannot be divested of it. Thirdly, conditions subsequent must be expressed with greater precision than conditions precedent; thus the latter are less likely to fail for uncertainty.

7.2.11.2 Uncertain conditions

Uncertainty is the ground on which conditions are most likely to fail. As regards conditions precedent, the requirement of certainty is satisfied if the condition is sufficiently clear to enable the court to say of a particular person whether he, at least, satisfies the condition. In *Re Allen* [1953] Ch 810, CA, a gift conditional on the beneficiary being 'a member of the Church of England and an adherent to the doctrine of that Church' was held not to be void for uncertainty. Lord Evershed MR stated (at pp. 817–8):

> All that the claiming devisee has to do is at the relevant date to establish, if he can, that he satisfies the condition or qualification whatever be the appropriate test ... I am not persuaded that where a formula constitutes a condition precedent or a qualification it is right for the court to declare the condition or qualification void for uncertainty so as thereby to defeat all possible claimants to the gift unless the terms of the condition or qualification are such that it is impossible to give them any meaning at all, or such that they involve repugnancies or inconsistencies in the possible tests which they postulate, as distinct, for example, from mere problems of degree.

The approach in *Re Allen* has been consistently followed in subsequent cases. For example, in *Re Barlow's WT* [1979] 1 All ER 296, a testatrix gave an option to purchase paintings at a favourable price from her valuable collection to 'any member of my family and any friends of mine who may wish to do so'. It was held that this provision was not void for uncertainty — the expression 'friends' was sufficiently certain since it was possible to say that some claimants qualified, irrespective of how difficult it might be to decide whether others qualified; and 'family' meant on the facts those related by blood to the testatrix. In *Re Selby's WT* [1965] 3 All ER 386, the testator provided that no beneficiary under his will 'who shall have married, or who before, or on attaining a vested interest shall marry out of the Jewish faith shall take any interest or benefit under this my will'. The court held that the condition (held to be precedent) was not void for uncertainty since membership of the Jewish faith was a sufficiently defined concept to enable the court to determine in many instances whether a particular claimant satisfied the condition. On the other hand, in *Re Tarnpolsk* [1958] 3 All ER 479, gifts made to the testator's grandchildren on their marriage to 'a person of Jewish race' were held to be invalid since it was impossible to say whether or not a given person satisfied the condition.

As regards conditions subsequent, a greater degree of certainty is required in their delineation, as explained by Lord Cranworth in *Clavering* v *Ellison* (1859) 7 HL Cas 707; 11 ER 282, at 289:

> ... Where a vested estate is to be defeated by a condition on a contingency that is to happen afterwards, that condition must be such that the court can see from the beginning, precisely and distinctly, upon the happening of what event it was that the preceding vested estate was to determine.

Although a greater degree of precision is required for a condition subsequent than for a condition precedent, the court has the right to judge the degree of certainty 'with some measure of common sense and knowledge and without excessive astuteness to discover ambiguities': *per* Lord Wilberforce in *Blathwayt* v *Baron Cawley* [1976] AC 397, at 425, where a condition divesting any potential tenant for life if he became 'a Roman Catholic' was held not to fail for uncertainty. Similarly, in *Re Mills' WT* [1967] 2 All ER 193, a condition that beneficiaries should forfeit their gifts unless they were 'a member of the Church of England or of some Church abroad professing the same tenets' was upheld as sufficiently certain — the tenets of the Church of England are part of the law of England by virtue of the Act of Uniformity 1662.

Examples of conditions subsequent that have been held to fail for uncertainty are numerous: a few must suffice. In *Re Jones* [1953] Ch 125, a provision whereby a beneficiary was to forfeit half of her annuity payments if in the opinion of trustees she had a 'social or other relationship' with a certain named person was held to be void for uncertainty. *Clayton* v *Ramsden* [1943] AC 320 was concerned with a condition whereby a gift was forfeited if the beneficiary married a person 'not of Jewish parentage and of the Jewish faith'. The House of Lords was unanimous in holding that 'Jewish parentage' was too uncertain; and a majority thought similarly as regards 'the Jewish faith'. However, in *Re Tepper's WT* [1987] Ch 358, it was held that the phrase 'within the Jewish faith' (or 'outside') in a condition subsequent was not necessarily too uncertain. Extrinsic evidence of the relevant surrounding circumstances was admissible to show the meaning that the testator attributed to 'the Jewish faith' when making his will.

The difference in the degree of certainty required for conditions precedent and subsequent is clearly demonstrated by *Re Abraham's WT* [1969] 1 Ch 463: the testator's will contained a condition in clause 18 divesting a beneficiary of residuary estate in the event of his marrying 'a person who shall not profess the Jewish faith'. By clause 17 the beneficiary could take an additional gift if he married 'a person professing the Jewish faith'. The court held that the condition subsequent in clause 18 was void for uncertainty, but that the condition precedent in clause 17 was sufficiently certain. Thus the same phrase was sufficiently certain for one purpose but not for the other. Justifying his decision to uphold the condition precedent, Cross J stated (at p. 471):

In some cases, no doubt there may be difficulty in saying whether the person in question is professing the Jewish faith or not, and it is because of that possibility that the condition subsequent in clause 18 is void, but I do not think that the expression 'professing the Jewish faith' is meaningless. One can say of some persons that without a doubt they profess the Jewish faith. It would, for example, be absurd to say that one could not be sure whether the Chief Rabbi was a person professing the Jewish faith.

EIGHT

Family Provision and Testamentary Freedom

8.1 INTRODUCTION

To what extent should a testator be able to dispose of his property as he wishes? This is the fundamental issue in the law of succession, one that raises important and difficult questions. Does the testator owe a duty to provide for his family after his death, or for cohabitants and dependants? What legal force, if any, should be accorded to his wishes as to the disposal of his property? Can his property be said to be actually *his* after his death, or does it belong to someone else? Moreover, the issue is of considerable practical importance. The fact that English law provides a discretionary system under the Inheritance (Provision for Family and Dependants) Act 1975, whereby testators' wills (or the application of the intestacy rules) can be adjusted, is potentially conducive to litigation. But the importance of the 1975 Act cannot be measured alone by the amount of litigation thereby generated (which has actually not been as great as was feared). For the mere possibility of an application being made under the Act must be a vital negotiating factor in numerous disputes which never reach court.

8.1.1 The basic position

Under the 1975 Act, certain persons can apply for financial provision out of the deceased's estate on the grounds that the deceased's will or intestacy (or a combination of the two) does not make reasonable financial provision for the applicant. The persons entitled to apply are the deceased's surviving spouse, former spouses who have not remarried, children, children of the family, dependants, and cohabitants: s. 1(1). As a general rule, the surviving spouse can apply for 'such financial provision as it would be reasonable in all the circumstances of the case for a husband or wife to receive', whereas the other applicants apply for 'such financial provision as it would be reasonable in all the circumstances of the case for the applicant to receive for his maintenance': s. 1(2).

Applications must normally be made within six months from the date on which 'representation with respect to the estate of the deceased is first taken out': s. 4. The application proceeds in two stages. First, the court must consider whether reasonable financial provision has been made for the applicant. Secondly, if no such provision has been made, the court will determine whether (and in what manner) to exercise its powers.

The court has a wide range of orders that it can make, including lump sum and periodical payments orders: s. 2. The court must take a variety of factors into account in both stages of the application, including the financial resources and needs of the applicants and any beneficiaries of the deceased's estate: s. 3. Although the court *must* take such factors into account, the exercise of its powers under s. 2 will essentially be a matter for the court's *discretion* — there are no fixed rights of inheritance in English law.

The 1975 Act contains important measures aimed at preventing evasion of the Act. Dispositions made by the deceased less than six years before his death may be subject to the court's order if they were made 'with the intention of defeating an application for financial provision under this Act': s. 10. Moreover, the court may make an order in respect of any contract made by the deceased to leave a gift by will or pay or transfer money or other property out of his estate, if the contract was made with the intention of defeating applications under the Act: s. 11.

8.1.2 The fundamental issue: freedom or restriction?

It is at once obvious that absolute freedom of testation cannot be guaranteed by a legal system. There are bound to be some rules — and it is desirable that there are — which will restrict what a testator can do. For example, gifts made for illegal purposes are unlikely to be upheld in any rational legal system. The real question then is whether testamentary freedom should be restricted *apart from* such inevitable restrictions.

8.1.2.1 Allow testamentary freedom
The basic argument for testamentary freedom is that it is an essential incident of the ownership of property for a person to be able to dispose of his property on his death as he wishes — a natural continuation of an owner's freedom to deal with his property *inter vivos*. Some jurists of the seventeenth century (such as Locke and Grotius) regarded freedom of testation as inherent in Natural Law. Locke, for example, described men in the state of nature as having 'an uncontrollable liberty' to dispose of their possessions (*Civil Government*, Bk II, 2). This argument will undoubtedly strike a chord with many, reflecting that often-expressed sentiment — 'It's mine, so I can do with it what I like', or similar.

In his famous essay *On Liberty*, J.S. Mill argued that the only purpose for which power can be rightfully exercised over persons against their will is to prevent harm to others. In the context of Succession this principle would appear to justify testamentary freedom since restriction is permissible only to prevent harm, and making a will confers benefits, not harm. But this argument is unconvincing because the making of a will can clearly cause 'harm' in any natural sense of the word. Suppose, for example, that a testator has maintained his spouse and children during his life, but he leaves all his property (including the matrimonial home) to a charity. The effect of the will may be to leave his family destitute and homeless — the harm caused to them is obvious. Moreover, the provisions of a will may cause great disappointment among expectant beneficiaries, resulting sometimes in bitterness, acute family conflict, murder or even war. The fact that Julius Caesar named Octavian as his heir rather than Mark Antony probably contributed to the deterioration of relations and eventual civil war between Antony and Octavian. Wills have a considerable capacity for causing harm.

Do we not feel pleasure when we give presents to people? Of course we do. It can therefore be argued that any restriction on testamentary freedom reduces the potential for pleasure in giving. Furthermore, our security of mind in knowing that our wishes will be carried out on our death will arguably be all the less if the law allows restrictions on testamentary freedom. Then there is the argument that will-making enables a testator to exercise a measure of control over family and friends. The threat of being left out of the will may help to bring rebellious family members to heel, and to persuade friends of the need to remain on good terms with the testator. Restricting testamentary freedom would therefore lessen the testator's potential control and thus the value of his property as a bargaining counter. But the very distastefulness of the concept diminishes the validity of this argument.

Economic arguments can be suggested for allowing testamentary freedom. For example, such freedom may be seen as an incentive to the accumulation of wealth: there would be less incentive if the testator was restricted in his dispositions. Moreover, if testamentary freedom was restricted so that family members had a clear expectation in a share of the inheritance, they might work less hard as a result, thus reducing the total wealth of the country. Such arguments are not only dubious on economic grounds, but also take a simplistic view of what motivates people to work or accumulate wealth.

A more convincing argument is that no system of restricting testamentary freedom in order to protect the family is likely to do justice, because of the great variety in the potential circumstances affecting family members and other possible beneficiaries. It is, however, a defeatist argument in that it counsels against restricting testamentary freedom simply because an ideal, perfect system is unlikely to be achieved.

8.1.2.2 Restrict testamentary freedom

'Ownership dies with the man' stated the eighteenth-century jurist Montesquieu (*Esprit des Lois*, 1748). Montesquieu's observation is fundamental to an analysis of the issue of testamentary freedom. Although we commonly refer to 'the deceased's estate', it is obvious that a dead person cannot own property, and this is recognised in English law. Since he cannot own property after he dies, it is arguable that it is not his to give away following his death. This argument thus confronts the basic argument for testamentary freedom by denying that there can be any natural right to dispose of property freely on death. How can one dispose of what one does not own? But may it not be countered that when the testator made his will he *did* own the property? Yes, but then why should his wishes as to the disposal of his property *on his death* — when he no longer owns the property — carry any legal force? Developing this line of argument leads to the conclusion that will-making is a legal courtesy shown to the deceased as a matter of respect, and not some fundamental right. This conclusion accords with the history of will-making in English law and in other jurisdictions. The power of testation was severely limited for many centuries in English history. For much of the time the claims of the family of the deceased were regarded as paramount. The same was largely true of ancient societies: the claims of the family were generally preferred to the whims of individual testators. Indeed, unrestricted testation was hardly known in the ancient world. In Roman law, intestacy preceded testation, and when wills were first allowed they had to be made in a highly formal manner before an assembly of the people. So important were the rights of the family (the heirs on intestacy) that they could be overridden only in this manner.

The claims of the family are further strengthened when it is considered that the deceased's estate is often not the product of his efforts alone, but partly those of his family members, especially his spouse. The deceased should be regarded — for the purposes of this argument — as having been a co-owner rather than a sole owner, even if the strict legal position is different. The deceased's family can in any case be regarded as the natural successors to the property that the deceased owned before death, as the law of intestacy clearly recognises. Why should the family's claims be potentially overridden by an instrument (sometimes executed many years before death) allowed as a matter of courtesy?

There is another possible claimant to the property which the deceased owned prior to his death — the State. The claims of the State have been reflected in many systems, ancient and modern. They are particularly relevant in English law because of the type of feudal system that emerged after the Norman Conquest under which property was regarded as held of the Crown. The Crown's rights included escheat — succession to property when the deceased died without heirs. In modern law the Crown's rights are evident, for example, in the right to take *bona vacantia* on intestacy; and the State may take part of the deceased's estate through taxation. The fact that the State is a claimant to the deceased's estate diminishes the argument for testamentary freedom: the more plausible claimants there are, the weaker becomes the argument 'It's mine, so I can do what I like with it'.

Another argument for restricting testamentary freedom is that obligations which the deceased owed during his lifetime to his family may thereby continue to be satisfied. A spouse has a legal obligation during his lifetime to maintain his spouse and children. Should not that duty continue after death? Many would argue that it should, and that consequently there must be restrictions as to how that spouse disposes of his property in his will. But this argument — persuasive though it may be — must be regarded as an alternative rather than additional to the argument that a deceased owns no property. Those who argue for restricting testamentary freedom obviously cannot maintain both that the deceased owns no property and that his property must be used to maintain his family — the latter argument in effect concedes the former.

It can be argued that restricting testamentary freedom lessens the likelihood of disputes following the testator's death. By narrowing the testator's choice — presumably mainly in favour of the family — there is less risk that the testator will upset those close to him by leaving property, say, to a charity. The potential for harm (in the sense of bitterness among those close to the testator) inherent in unrestricted will-making would be reduced in a system of fixed or discretionary rights of inheritance — a compelling argument for restricting testamentary freedom.

The arguments propounded above for and against testamentary freedom are by no means exhaustive; for further discussion of most of them and others, see especially *Tyler's Family Provision*, 2nd edn., R.D. Oughton (ed.), 1984, Chapter 2.

8.1.2.3   Which form of restriction?

The arguments for restricting testamentary freedom appear more compelling. This conclusion is consistent with the experience of legal systems throughout the world. The overriding tendency is for family members (and sometimes others such as cohabitants and dependants) to be given fixed rights of inheritance or a right to ask the court to exercise its discretion to grant financial provision out of the estate. A balance is thereby achieved between respecting the testator's wishes and ensuring that family members and others receive adequate provision under the will. The argument for allowing unrestricted testamentary freedom has been lost. The more pertinent question is — what is the most satisfactory way to restrict testamentary freedom?

Civilian systems tend to apply a system of fixed rights of inheritance derived from the Roman concept of *legitima portio* ('rightful share'). In Roman law, family members could challenge a will on the ground that the testator had made inadequate provision for them, i.e., had left them less than their rightful share. In modern systems the concept of the *legitima portio* takes various forms and appears under various names — for example, *la réserve légale* in France; *ius relicti* or *legitim* in Scotland; *Pflichtheil* in Germany.

In those modern systems which have adopted the fixed rights approach there are two main variants — automatic fixed share and elective fixed share. In the former — applicable, for example, in French and Scots law — a claimant is automatically entitled to a fixed share of the estate. A part of the estate is in effect reserved for family members and is thus not subject to the testator's provisions. The size of the reserved share — the *réserve héréditaire* in French law — will usually vary according to the number of those entitled to it. In an elective fixed share system there is no automatic entitlement: claimants have to take steps to enforce their rights — normally by an application to the court — if the will fails to confer on them the share to which they are entitled. This system is similar to the one developed in classical Roman law and has been adopted, for example, in the Uniform Probate Code in the United States.

The preference in common law jurisdictions has generally been for the discretionary system, under which there is no fixed entitlement but instead claimants apply to the court for provision out of the deceased's estate at the discretion of the court. However, in order to achieve a measure of consistency in the exercise of the court's discretion, guidelines are usually laid down as to the principles that the court must follow and the factors that must be taken into account. This is the system that operates in English law.

What are the merits of these respective methods of restricting testamentary freedom? They are the familiar ones that apply in any comparison between fixed rights and discretion. A fixed rights system is more conducive to certainty, with the important consequence that those affected by the operation of the rules (as well as their advisers) will be better able to predict their entitlement. A discretionary system, on the other hand, will compensate for lack of certainty by its flexibility and greater potential for achieving the most desirable result in individual cases. In the 1970s the Law Commission considered the merits of each system (Working Paper No. 42, 1972; *First Report on Family Property*, Law Com. No. 52, 1973; *Second Report*, Law Com. No. 61, 1974). Although the Commission seemed initially attracted by the possibility of a limited fixed rights system, its eventual preference was for the discretionary system already *in situ* (but with important changes). This was consistent with a survey of public opinion by Todd and Jones, *Matrimonial Property*, 1972, which found a clear preference for the discretionary system. The Commission expressed its worries about fixed rights systems thus:

> Whatever the situation, the survivor would be entitled to a fixed proportion of the estate of the first to die. In some cases legal rights of inheritance would seem fair, in others they would not. In some cases the survivor may need to be provided for, in others he or she may be better off than the deceased. Legal rights could not be varied to suit the individual circumstances of each case. (Law Com. No. 52, 1973 para. 42)

8.1.3 The historical perspective

It has been seen in earlier chapters that testamentary freedom was severely limited for much of English legal history. The Anglo-Saxon will was rather like the earliest form of Roman will — an exceptional departure from the norms of succession. Throughout much of the medieval period land could not be disposed of by will. Even after 1540 — when the Statute of Wills allowed landowners to devise certain types of realty — there were important restrictions. For example, the right of dower gave the wife a life interest in one third of her husband's freeholds. As for personalty, it will be remembered that the basic position in early English law was that the spouse and children had a fixed entitlement in the deceased's estate, so that the testator could freely dispose only of the remainder. These fixed rights of inheritance gradually ceased to be enforced, but survived in some parts of the country until the eighteeth century. It was only in the century or so after the Dower Act 1833 that testators were substantially unrestricted.

In the 1920s there was considerable pressure for reform of the law to enable maintenance to be sought from a testator's estate. The precedent was cited of the Testators Family Maintenance Act 1900 (New Zealand), which enabled a testator's spouse and children to apply for provision on the ground that the will did not provide for the 'proper maintenance' of the applicant. But reform was frustrated, mainly through the opposition of the legal establishment, until the Inheritance (Family Provision) Act 1938, which enacted in effect the New Zealand model. The Act allowed applications to be made for provision by periodical payments or lump sums from the testator's estate on the ground that the will did not make reasonable provision for the maintenance of the applicant. The amount of provision that could be ordered by way of periodical payments was limited to a maximum of two thirds of the annual income of the net estate, and there were restrictions on the maximum that could be ordered by lump sum. The category of applicants was confined to spouses, unmarried daughters, infant sons (under 21) and children incapable of maintaining themselves by reason of disability. Objectors to the Act predicted that it would open the floodgates to litigation, but the predictions proved untrue. The 1938 Act was extended to intestacy by the Intestates' Estates Act 1952 and the category of applicants was widened by the Matrimonial Causes (Property and Maintenance) Act 1958 to include former spouses who had not re-married. The Family Provision Act 1966 removed the restrictions on the *quantum* of the provision that could be ordered and extended jurisdiction to the county courts (previously confined to the High Court).

The current legislation — the Inheritance (Provision for Family and Dependants) Act 1975 — was enacted following the recommendations made by the Law Commission in the *Second Report on Family Property* (Law Com. No. 61, 1974). The scope of the previous legislation was considerably extended. There were four main reforms. First, the surviving spouse was no longer confined to applying for maintenance but could now apply for such provision 'as it would be reasonable in all the circumstances of the case for a husband or wife to receive': s. 1(2)(a). Secondly, the categories of applicant were significantly widened to include persons not related to the deceased — namely, children of the family (persons treated by the deceased as his children) and dependants: s. 1(1)(d) and (e). Thirdly, the powers of the court were considerably extended as to the range of orders that it could make: s. 2. And fourthly, measures were enacted to restrict the deceased from evading the Act: ss. 10–12. More recently, the class of applicants was further extended to include cohabitants: s. 2(2) of the Law Reform (Succession) Act 1995.

8.2 APPLYING UNDER THE 1975 ACT

The 1975 Act applies if the deceased died on or after 1 April 1976 domiciled in England and Wales: s. 1(1). The Act does not apply in the case of persons dying domiciled in Scotland or Northern Ireland: Scotland has a fixed rights system, while Northern Ireland has adopted a discretionary system modelled on English legislation. A person is generally regarded as domiciled where he has his permanent home. The onus is on the applicant to show that the deceased died domiciled in England and Wales: *Mastaka v Midland Bank* [1941] Ch 192. There has been some criticism of the rule that jurisdiction is determined by the deceased's domicile, but the Law Commission felt that any alternative would be at least as problematic, and thus recommended no change (Law Com. No. 61, 1974, para. 262). It should be noted that the *applicant's* domicile is not relevant to applying under the Act.

8.2.1 Who can apply?

There are now six categories of applicant under the 1975 Act. Section 1(1), as originally enacted, contains the following five categories:

> (a) the wife or husband of the deceased;
> (b) a former wife or former husband of the deceased who has not remarried;
> (c) a child of the deceased;
> (d) any person (not being a child of the deceased) who, in the case of any marriage to which the deceased was at any time a party, was treated by the deceased as a child of the family in relation to that marriage;
> (e) any person (not being a person included in the foregoing paragraphs of this subsection) who immediately before the death of the deceased was being maintained, either wholly or partly, by the deceased.

In addition, s. 2 of the Law Reform (Succession) Act 1995 has inserted into s. 1(1) of the 1975 Act a new category — any person, other than a spouse or former spouse, who was living in the same household as the deceased, and as the husband or wife of the deceased, during the whole of the period of two years ending immediately before the date when the deceased died: s. 1(1)(ba). This category applies where the deceased died on or after 1 January 1996.

8.2.1.1 Wife or husband of the deceased
The onus is on the applicant to prove that he or she was the deceased's spouse when the deceased died: *Re Peete* [1952] 2 All ER 599. A party to a void marriage can apply within this category if that party entered into the marriage with the deceased in good faith, unless during the deceased's lifetime either (i) the marriage was dissolved or annulled, or (ii) that party entered into a later marriage: s. 25(4). A party to a voidable marriage can apply within this category if the marriage had not been dissolved or annulled before the deceased's death. A party to a polygamous marriage is a spouse for the purposes of s. 1(1)(a): *Re Sehota* [1978] 3 All ER 385, where the first wife of the deceased applied for provision out of his estate. He had left it all to his second wife, who opposed the application. It was held that the applicant (who was still married to the deceased when he died) was a 'wife' within s. 1(1)(a). Thus there may be

simultaneous applications from concurrent spouses — had Mr Sehota left all his property to charity, say, both wives could have applied. A spouse who was judicially separated from the deceased can apply within this category unless barred from doing so by s. 15 (below).

There were some indications in early cases following the 1938 Act that wives' applications might be more sympathetically considered than those of husbands, but this is no longer the case. In *Re Clayton* [1966] 2 All ER 370, it was held that the onus on a husband in seeking provision was no greater than that on a wife.

8.2.1.2   Former wife or husband of the deceased

Under s. 1(1)(b) of the 1975 Act, a former spouse may apply if he or she has not remarried. Section 25(1) defines a former spouse as a person whose marriage with the deceased was during the deceased's lifetime dissolved or annulled either by (i) a decree of divorce or nullity granted under the law of any part of the British Islands, or (ii) a divorce or annulment (outside the British Islands) recognised as valid by the law of England and Wales. A former spouse who has remarried does not qualify under s. 1(1)(b). For this purpose remarriage includes a marriage which is void or voidable: s. 25(5).

In the vast majority of divorces or annulments a financial settlement will have been agreed or imposed following the termination of the marriage. Often the parties feel that when they die they would not wish their ex-spouse to claim provision out of their estate. Accordingly, the court has the power — on the application of either party — to order that the other party should be disentitled from seeking an order under the 1975 Act following the death of the applicant: s. 15(1). The court can make the order — 'if it considers it just to do so' — on the grant of a decree of divorce, nullity or judicial separation or 'at any time thereafter'. However, the potential usefulness of s. 15(1) is questionable following the interpretation given to the phrase 'if it considers it just to do so' in *Whiting* v *Whiting* [1988] 2 All ER 275, CA. It was held that an application under s. 15(1) was unlikely to succeed without some evidence as to what the applicant's estate was likely to consist of and details of the persons whom the applicant considered to have a prior claim to the former spouse. The basis of the decision — that the court cannot decide what is 'just' without the relevant information — is readily understandable, but the effect is to restrict significantly the potential scope of s. 15(1). There is a case for omitting the phrase 'if it considers it just to do so' if the scope of s. 15(1) would thereby be widened.

Despite these doubts about the scope of s. 15, it was emphasised in *Cameron* v *Treasury Solicitor* [1996] 2 FLR 716, CA, that it was the practice to include a s. 15 restriction in clean break orders on the termination of marriage. However, the fact that such a restriction was not included, could not be regarded as improving the chances of a former spouse applying successfully.

8.2.1.3   Child of the deceased

A child of the deceased can apply under s. 1(1)(c). A 'child' includes an illegitimate child or a child *en ventre sa mère* at the deceased's death: s. 25(1). It also includes any child adopted by the deceased: Adoption Act 1976, s. 39. However, if a child of the deceased is adopted after the deceased's death, but before an application for provision is made by the child under the 1975 Act, the application must fail since the child is no longer 'a child of the deceased': *Re Collins* [1990] 2 All ER 47. A stepchild is not 'a child of the deceased' but may be a child of the family (below).

The age and marital status of a child are irrelevant to whether the child can apply under s. 1(1)(c). The original confinement of this category to infant sons and unmarried daughters was repealed by the 1975 Act. Regarding age, Booth J commented thus in *Re Callaghan* [1984] 3 All ER 790, at 793:

'Child', for the purposes of s. 1, clearly includes an adult child. One of the persons who may apply by virtue of s. 1(1)(c) is 'a child of the deceased', and it cannot be suggested that in that context 'child' must be limited to a minor or dependent child. In s. 1(1)(c) 'child' relates to the relationship between the deceased and the applicant.

8.2.1.4 Child of the family

Under s. 1(1)(d) any person (not being a child of the deceased) may apply who was treated by the deceased as a child of the family in relation to any marriage to which the deceased was at any time a party. This category obviously includes stepchildren of the deceased, but not every stepchild will necessarily qualify: the test is whether the applicant was treated by the deceased as a child of the family (there may be stepchildren who are not treated thus). As in the case of children, applicants under s. 1(1)(d) can be of adult age: *Re Callaghan* (above).

The concept of treating a person as a child of the family is derived from matrimonial law. It seems that there must be evidence of some behaviour of a parental nature by the deceased towards the applicant. In *Re Callaghan*, the applicant was a married man aged 47 with a family of his own. He applied for provision out of the estate of his stepfather, who had died intestate. The deceased had lived for many years with the applicant's mother before eventually marrying her. Throughout all this time — before and after the marriage — the deceased treated the applicant as his own son. The applicant's children regarded the deceased as their grandfather. During the deceased's last illness the applicant and his wife looked after him. It was held that the applicant had clearly been treated by the deceased as a child of the family. He was awarded a lump sum of £15,000 (out of an estate worth about £31,000). On the issue of treatment Booth J stated (at pp. 793–4):

In this case the acknowledgment by the deceased of his own role of grandfather to the plaintiff's children, the confidences as to his property and financial affairs which he placed in the plaintiff and his dependence on the plaintiff to care for him in his last illness are examples of the deceased's treatment of the plaintiff as a child, albeit an adult child, of the family. All these things are part of the privileges and duties of two persons who, in regard to each other, stand in the relationship of parent and child; it is the existence of that relationship that enables the plaintiff to apply under s. 1(1)(d) of the Act.

In *Re Leach* [1985] 2 All ER 754, CA, the applicant (aged 55) applied for provision out of her stepmother's intestate estate. The applicant never lived with the stepmother and the evidence suggested that the latter's treatment of the applicant as a child of the family had occurred partly after the applicant's father had died. It was argued that such treatment was irrelevant since s. 1(1)(d) requires that the treatment be in relation to a *marriage* to which the deceased was a party (whereas the treatment occurred after the marriage's termination). It was held that the phrase 'in relation to that marriage' in s. 1(1)(d) did not mean 'during the subsistence of that marriage'. Hence the treatment of the applicant by the deceased after the death of the other spouse was relevant, as long as it was referable to, or stemmed from, the marriage. The applicant was eligible to apply on the basis that the deceased had expressly or impliedly assumed the position of a parent towards the applicant, with the attendant responsibilities and privileges of that relationship. But mere displays of affection, kindness or hospitality towards the applicant were in themselves insufficient. However, provided that the appropriate treatment had occurred, it was not necessary that it should have continued up to the deceased's death. The applicant was awarded £19,000 out of the net estate (worth about £34,000). It should be noted that in both *Re Leach* and *Re Callaghan* the court regarded it as significant that the deceased's estate was largely derived from the other spouse (i.e. the parent of the applicant).

8.2.1.5 Dependant of the deceased

Under s. 1(1)(e), an application may be brought by any person 'who immediately before the death of the deceased was being maintained either wholly or partly by the deceased'. This category was introduced by the 1975 Act and was regarded as the most controversial reform in that Act (for comment see especially Naresh (1980) 96 LQR 534; Cadwallader [1980] Conv 44; Green (1988) 51 MLR 187). Some feared that, by including persons who might be outside the deceased's family, the floodgates to litigation would be opened. Concern was expressed that cohabitants would be able to apply and thus diminish the benefit that the deceased's family would receive under a will or intestacy. As often, the fears proved exaggerated. Indeed, the first important reported case concerned two elderly sisters living together: *Re Wilkinson* [1978] 1 All ER 221. The case illustrated *inter alia* that s. 1(1)(e) could apply to family members (other than those falling within the other categories in s. 1(1)). The rationale of s. 1(1)(e) was that the maintenance of a person by the deceased during the latter's lifetime could result in an obligation that the maintenance be continued after the deceased's death. This approach, it will be remembered, reflects one of the major arguments for restricting testamentary freedom.

To qualify under s. 1(1)(e) it must be shown that (i) the applicant was being maintained (wholly or partly) by the deceased, and (ii) that this was being done immediately before the death of the deceased.

(a) 'Maintained' by the deceased   What does 'maintained' mean? Section 1(3) provides:

> ... a person shall be treated as being maintained by the deceased, either wholly or partly, as the case may be, if the deceased, otherwise than for full valuable consideration, was making a substantial contribution in money or money's worth towards the reasonable needs of that person.

The contribution must be in money or 'money's worth'. This phrase obviously covers things that can be valued in money, e.g., accommodation. The contribution must have been towards 'the reasonable needs' of that person. It seems that there is no universal objective standard applicable to decide this question. Reasonable needs will vary from person to person, and the court is likely to take into account what the applicant has been accustomed to (as occurs in maintenance awards in matrimonial proceedings). The contribution must have been 'substantial'; whether it was depends on what were the reasonable needs of the applicant. In *Re Viner* [1978] CLY 3091, the deceased had paid £5 a week for six months before his death to the applicant, an elderly widowed sister living in very poor financial circumstances. The deceased had left most of his estate (worth about £44,000) to a woman who had been his partner in his private company. It was held that the applicant had been maintained by the deceased — he had made a substantial contribution to her reasonable needs. She was awarded a lump sum of £2,000.

Under s. 1(3) the contribution must have been made 'otherwise than for full valuable consideration'. Marriage or a promise of marriage does not constitute 'valuable consideration': s. 25(1). The purpose of excluding applicants who were maintained in return for full valuable consideration is presumably to restrict the s. 1(1)(e) category to those who can show dependency on the deceased. It is curious that the word 'dependant' is not used in s. 1(1)(e) although the category is clearly concerned with dependants (and the word appears in the Act's title). The need for an applicant to show dependency on the deceased, and thus not to give full valuable consideration, may involve the court in the potentially difficult task of having to weigh the respective contributions of the applicant and the deceased. Suppose, for example, that Arthur is a sick, elderly widower who invites his sister, Ethel, to come to live with him so that she can act as his nurse and companion. Ethel does so, receiving free accommodation. Arthur is undoubtedly maintaining her within s. 1(3), but is Ethel providing 'full valuable consideration'? If she is, she cannot apply under s. 1(1)(e). The paradox is that the more that the applicant contributes, the less the likelihood of the applicant satisfying s. 1(1)(e). In *Re Wilkinson* (above) the applicant went to live with the deceased, her sister, who was suffering from severe arthritis. The applicant received free board and accommodation. She looked after the deceased and acted as her companion virtually on a full-time basis. They shared the light housework and cooking. It was held that since the services provided by the applicant did not amount to full valuable consideration, she fell within s. 1(1)(e). The issue was raised whether the full valuable consideration must arise under a contract. Arnold J held that the applicant's services had to be valued whether they were contracted or not. Perhaps he was reluctant to confine 'full valuable consideration' to contractual services because to do so would have widened the potential scope of s. 1(1)(e) in the first test case concerning this category.

The approach in *Re Wilkinson* was followed in subsequent decisions, although the difficulties in evaluating the contributions of the parties were clearly recognised by the courts. For example, in *Jelley* v *Iliffe* [1981] 2 All ER 29, CA, Griffiths LJ stated (at p. 38):

> ... the object of Parliament in creating this extra class of persons who may claim benefit from an estate was to provide relief for persons of whom it could truly be said that they were wholly or partially dependent on the deceased. It cannot be an exact exercise of evaluating services in pounds and pence. By way of example, if a man was living with a woman as his wife and providing the house and all the money for their living expenses she would clearly be dependent on him, and it would not be right to deprive her of her claim by arguing that she was in fact performing the services that a housekeeper would perform and it would cost more to employ a housekeeper than was spent on her and indeed perhaps more than the deceased had available to spend on her. Each case will have to be looked at carefully on its own facts to see whether common sense leads to the conclusion that the applicant can fairly be regarded as a dependant.

In *Bishop* v *Plumley* [1991] 1 All ER 236, CA, the applicant and deceased cohabited as man and wife (though both were married to other people) for about 10 years. They pooled their resources and for most of the period lived in a cottage rented from Oxford University. But in the 10 months prior to his death they lived in the deceased's house, which he had bought with the proceeds of an inheritance. During the last three years of his life he suffered from angina and received exceptionally devoted care from the applicant. In his will (made 10 years before his death) the deceased left all his property to his two children by his marriage. It was held at first instance that the benefits given by the applicant to the deceased as he became more ill equalled those received by the applicant (free accommodation for the last 10 months of the deceased's life). Therefore the application must fail since the applicant had given full valuable consideration. The Court of Appeal reversed the decision, holding that the provision of a secure home for the applicant for 10 months was a substantial contribution which was not equalled by the applicant's exceptional care of the deceased. Butler-Sloss LJ stated (at p. 242):

> Counsel for the beneficiaries [the deceased's children] argues that on her own evidence the applicant gave services which were out of the ordinary, and by this exceptional care she was giving him full valuable consideration. I do not consider that her evidence that she did everything for him over a period of years can be assessed in isolation from the mutuality of the relationship. If a man or a woman living as man and wife with a partner gives the other extra devoted care and attention, particularly when the partner is in poor health, is

he or she to be in a less advantageous position on an application under the
Act than one who may be less loving and give less attention to the partner? I
do not accept that this could have been the intention of Parliament in passing
this legislation.

Bishop v *Plumley* was a most welcome decision. By excluding from the
evaluation process things done by the applicant arising from 'the mutuality of
the relationship' — or diminishing their significance — the decision appears to
avoid the problems arising from *Re Wilkinson*. In effect *Bishop* v *Plumley*
interprets 'full valuable consideration' in s. 1(3) more narrowly than *Re
Wilkinson*, thus enabling a potentially greater number of persons to qualify
under s. 1(1)(e).

(b) 'Immediately before' the deceased's death The cases show that 'immediately before' must not be construed literally. In *Re Beaumont* [1980] 1 All ER 266,
Megarry VC considered various hypothetical scenarios to test the meaning of
the phrase 'immediately before'. In one, the applicant had been entirely
maintained by the deceased but had fallen ill and had entered a State hospital.
The deceased died while the applicant was in hospital. Could the applicant be
said to have been maintained by the deceased 'immediately before' the latter's
death? The judge suggested a broad, common-sense approach. The 'gaze of the
court' was not to be confined to whatever was the state of maintenance existing
at the precise moment immediately before the deceased's death:

> If at the moment before the death of the deceased there is some settled basis
> or arrangement between the parties as regards maintenance, then I think that
> s. 1 should be applied to this rather than to any *de facto* variation in the actual
> maintenance that may happen to exist at that moment.

This approach was subsequently confirmed by the Court of Appeal in *Jelley* v
Iliffe (above) and has been consistently followed. It is clear that if there is no
evidence of a settled pattern of dependence immediately before the deceased's
death, the application cannot proceed. In *Kourkgy* v *Lusher* (1983) 4 FLR 65,
the applicant had been the deceased's mistress for over 10 years. They
cohabited intermittently and bought property to which the deceased contributed. The deceased throughout this time remained in contact with his wife
(they ran a chiropody practice) and returned to the matrimonial home on a
regular basis. Shortly before his death he went on holiday with his wife, telling
her that he was returning to her permanently. On returning from holiday he
resumed cohabitation with his wife but died soon afterwards. It was held that
the deceased's failure to resume cohabitation with the applicant, coupled with
the indications that he was not going back to her, meant that he was not
maintaining her 'immediately before' his death.

(c) Assumption of responsibility for maintenance Is there anything else that an
applicant must prove — besides being maintained by the deceased immediately
before the deceased's death — in order to qualify under s. 1(1(e)? Megarry VC

emphasised in *Re Beaumont* (above) the relevance of s. 3(4), which provides that where an application is made under s. 1(1)(e) the court shall have regard to 'the extent to which and the basis upon which the deceased assumed responsibility for the maintenance of the applicant'. The judge concluded that this meant that an applicant could not proceed under s. 1(1)(e) unless it could be shown that the deceased had assumed maintenance for the applicant (the mere fact of maintenance was insufficient). In this case the applicant and deceased had cohabited as man and wife for some 36 years in the deceased's bungalow, pooling their resources and sharing in the household and living expenses. It was held that the applicant could not proceed under s. 1(1)(e) because there was no evidence that the deceased had ever assumed responsibility for his maintenance. This was an unfortunate decision which seriously restricted the operation of the s. 1(1)(e) category, but the Court of Appeal in *Jelley* v *Iliffe* (above) overruled *Re Beaumont* on this point, holding that it could be presumed from the fact that the deceased was maintaining the applicant that the deceased had assumed responsibility for maintaining him. Griffiths LJ stated (at p. 39):

> In practice the evidence of the applicant will reveal the relationship with the deceased and if it also shows an arrangement subsisting at the time of death under which the deceased was making a substantial contribution in money or money's worth to the reasonable needs of the applicant it will, as a general rule, be proper to draw the inference that the deceased has undertaken to maintain the applicant and thus 'assumed responsibility for the maintenance' within the meaning of s. 3(4). It should not be necessary to search for any other overt act to demonstrate the 'assumption of responsibility'. If such an overt act were necessary I suspect that most claims intended to be covered by the 1975 Act would fail.

The facts of *Jelley* v *Iliffe* were similar to those of *Re Beaumont* — cohabitation (for eight years) as man and wife in deceased's home, with pooling of resources and sharing of expenses. It was held that the applicant could proceed under s. 1(1)(e) since it could be presumed that the deceased had assumed responsibility for his maintenance.

8.2.1.6   Cohabitant of the deceased

If the deceased died on or after 1 January 1996, a person may apply for provision if he or she lived in the same household as the deceased, and as their husband or wife, during the whole of the period of two years ending immediately before the date when the deceased died: s. 1(1)(ba). This category was enacted by s. 2 of the Law Reform (Succession) Act 1995 following the recommendations of the Law Commission's Report, *Distribution on Intestacy* (Law Com. No. 187, 1989). This reform — enabling cohabitants to apply even though unable to show the dependence on the deceased required under s. 1(1)(e) — was an important step in the increasing recognition of cohabitants' rights.

Cohabitants are defined by the same formula as used in the Fatal Accidents Act 1976 for loss suffered as the result of death. Under s. 1(1)(ba), the applicant must satisfy three requirements: that he or she was living (i) in the same household as the deceased, (ii) as the husband or wife of the deceased, and (iii) that such living occurred during the whole of the period of two years immediately before the deceased's death. It is likely that 'household' will have the same meaning as it does in matrimonial law, referring to a 'state of affairs' rather than a place. A household exists as long as there is some element of communal living between the parties as man and wife. The phrase 'immediately before' will presumably be given the broad interpretation adopted in *Re Beaumont* as regards the same words in s. 1(1)(e). The word 'whole' will very probably be interpreted in similar vein. It is unlikely that every interruption (however short) to the period of living in the same household as the deceased would be fatal to qualifying under s. 1(1)(ba).

8.2.1.7 Close relations of the deceased

Should the 1975 Act be extended to other categories of applicant? The obvious candidates are the close relations of the deceased such as parents and siblings. Under the current law such relations have no *locus standi* under the Act unless they were dependants of the deceased within s. 1(1)(e). Would it be restricting testamentary freedom unacceptably to allow such relations to apply? Consider this plausible scenario. Arthur makes a will leaving all his considerable estate to a charity. He is survived by only one relation, Edith, his sister, who is in impoverished financial circumstances. They were close but he had not maintained her prior to his death. Under the current law Edith cannot apply under the 1975 Act. It may be that Arthur had very good reasons for not leaving Edith anything in his will. If so, this may make all the difference. But should not the matter at least be capable of being tested in court rather than there being a blanket exclusion of such cases, as occurs now? A case can certainly be made out for extending the Act to parents and siblings in appropriate circumstances.

8.2.1.8 Right to apply is a personal right

Whatever the category of applicant, the court can make an order only if the applicant is alive. In *Whyte* v *Ticehurst* [1986] 2 All ER 158, the testator devised his home to a charity subject to the wife's right to remain there during her lifetime. After his death she applied under the 1975 Act but died before any order was made. It was held that since the right to apply under s. 1(1)(a) was personal to the surviving spouse, her personal representatives could not carry on her action for the benefit of her estate. The same principle was applied in *Re Bramwell* [1988] 2 FLR 263.

8.2.2 Which courts have jurisdiction?

Applications under the 1975 Act can be made either to the High Court or to the county court. As regards the High Court, both the Family Division and the Chancery Division have jurisdiction. The 1975 Act does not indicate which

Division is appropriate in any particular case — the choice is the applicant's. Nevertheless, there may be certain aspects to an application which would make one Division more suitable than another. For example, if an order has been granted in former matrimonial proceedings involving the deceased, the Family Division may be the more appropriate forum. But the Chancery Division would be more convenient if the application raises difficult questions of interpretation of a will or administration of the deceased's estate. Whichever Division is involved, it appears that most applications are heard in chambers rather than in open court.

The county courts now have unlimited jurisdiction, but the High Court and County Courts Jurisdiction Order 1991 indicates that claims in excess of £50,000 should be tried in the High Court. Claims worth less than £25,000 should be heard in the county court unless the case is complex or raises issues of public interest.

Costs are in the court's discretion (the 1975 Act is silent on the matter). In practice it appears that if an application is successful, the costs of all the parties are likely to be borne by the estate. If the application fails, the applicant is likely to be responsible for the costs of all the parties. However, the court might relieve the applicant of part of his burden the more meritorious the claim or larger the estate. Costs may also be influenced by any reasonable offer of a settlement made by the defendants. An applicant who rejects a reasonable offer and then fails is very likely to be penalised in costs. Legal aid is available to both applicants and defendants, but the Legal Aid Fund may have a charge against the successful party.

8.2.3 When must the applicant apply?

Section 4 of the 1975 Act states:

> An application for an order under section 2 of this Act shall not, except with the permission of the court, be made after the end of the period of six months from the date on which representation with respect to the estate of the deceased is first taken out.

Section 4 attempts to strike a balance between the need to distribute the deceased's estate promptly and the need to ensure that potential applicants have a reasonable period in which to learn of the deceased's death and decide whether to apply. Also, the period will allow some time for negotiations between potential applicants and the beneficiaries of the estate. Accordingly, personal representatives should not distribute the estate within the six-month period if there is any possibility of an application being made (they may incur personal liability as a result). However, once the period has elapsed they may safely distribute the estate, and cannot be held personally liable for doing so: s. 20(1).

There are two main issues under s. 4: what is meant by representation 'first taken out', and when will the permission of the court be granted for a late application?

8.2.3.1 Representation first taken out

Suppose that following the deceased's death it is assumed that he died intestate and a grant of administration is made as a consequence. A valid will is later discovered. Does the period run from the original grant of administration or from the later grant of probate? In *Re Freeman* [1984] 3 All ER 906, probate was granted of a will in which the testator had provided for his cohabitant and his parents. Over three years later the grant of probate was revoked because the will was shown to have been invalidly executed. Letters of administration were granted to the deceased's mother. The cohabitant applied under the 1975 Act some eight months after the grant to the mother. It was held that 'representation' in s. 4 means valid or effective representation. Hence the period ran from the grant of administration to the mother. The position would have been the same in the converse circumstances — valid will discovered after previously assumed intestacy — or where probate of a will is revoked because of the discovery of a later will. But if the same will receives common form probate and (later) solemn form probate, the period runs from the earlier grant: *Re Miller* [1968] 3 All ER 844 (for the different forms of probate see 10.2.1.5).

8.2.3.2 Permission for late applications

Section 4 rightly gives the court a discretion to allow late applications, but does not indicate how such discretion is to be exercised. The leading case is *Re Salmon* [1980] 3 All ER 532, where the application was made over five months after the time limit had expired. The fault for the delay was wholly on the applicant's side (caused by her solicitors). Megarry VC disallowed the application but hinted strongly that an action for negligence against the solicitors would lie. He laid down the following six guidelines as to how the court's discretion should be exercised (at pp. 537–8):

> First, the discretion is unfettered. No restrictions or requirements of any kind are laid down in the Act. The discretion is thus plainly one that is to be exercised judicially, and in accordance with what is just and proper. Second, I think that the onus lies on the plaintiff to establish sufficient grounds for taking the case out of the general rule, and depriving those who are protected by it of its benefits ... a third point is that it must be material to consider how promptly and in what circumstances the applicant has sought the permission of the court after the time limit has expired ... The whole of the circumstances must be looked at, and not least the reasons for delay, and also the promptitude with which, by letter before action or otherwise, the claimant gave warning to the defendants of the proposed application.... This leads to a fourth point ... I think that it is obviously material whether or not negotiations have been commenced within the time limit; for if they have, and time has run out while they are proceeding, this is likely to encourage the court to extend the time ... Fifth, I think that it is also relevant to consider whether or not the estate has been distributed before a claim under the Act has been made or notified ... Sixth, I think that it is relevant to consider whether a refusal to extend the time would leave the claimant without redress against anybody.

The criteria enumerated in *Re Salmon* were not intended to be exhaustive and have since been augmented. In *Re Dennis* [1981] 2 All ER 140, the applicant applied some 18 months late in respect of his millionaire father's estate, seeking to secure provision in order to satisfy the applicant's large debt to the Inland Revenue. Since children can apply for provision only by way of maintenance, the court did not regard the applicant as having an arguable case. The applicant was refused permission to apply out of time, the court emphasising that in such applications it was relevant to consider the merits of the application. The more meritorious it was, the greater the chance of the court granting permission. Another case where the merits of the application proved to be a crucial factor — this time in favour of the applicant — was *Stock v Brown* [1994] 1 FLR 840. An elderly widow was left a life interest in her husband's investments and the former matrimonial home. She accepted these benefits, but some years later interest rates fell sharply with the result that the widow no longer had enough to live on. She applied for provision out of the estate nearly six years out of time. The court exercised its discretion to allow the application to proceed. The burden on the applicant was a heavy one when the time limit had been exceeded as grossly as in this case. But in her favour was the perception of the court that her application was a meritorious one, that she had not received independent legal advice when her husband had died, that the interests of the other beneficiaries would not be prejudiced by a late application, and that extraneous events outside her control (the collapse of interest rates) had triggered her application. The particular emphasis placed by the court on the last-mentioned factor — uncontrollable extraneous events — was a novel feature of *Stock v Brown*. The facts of *Escritt v Escritt* (1982) 3 FLR 280, CA, were similar in that the applicant changed her mind and applied several years after the time limit had elapsed (because of her deteriorating health and financial position). But the court took the view that it should not permit the applicant to make the claim irrespective of the length of time that had elapsed, given that she had decided not to apply with full understanding of her position. The two cases can be reconciled on the ground that in *Stock v Brown* the applicant had not had independent legal advice and thus had not made a conscious decision not to apply with full understanding of her legal position.

What if the applicant is a child below the age of majority — does the court need to show special consideration in such a case in exercising its discretion to grant leave? In *Re C* [1995] 2 FLR 24, the applicant was the eight-year-old daughter of the deceased. He left his substantial estate to his sister subject to a power in trustees to appoint (in the two years following his death) in favour of a potentially wide class of beneficiaries, including the applicant (but the trustees did not appoint in her favour). The mother took no steps for some 30 months to claim under the 1975 Act on the child's behalf. Wilson J stated (at p. 28) that 'it would be wrong to discern any general principle in favour of granting permission to a minor child. In relation to permission, Parliament has chosen not to distinguish between the minor child and any other claimant'. Nevertheless, leave to apply out of time was granted because of the merits of the application — the prospects of success were substantial — the fact that there had not yet been any distribution of the estate, and because the child would be without an effective remedy as a result of another's fault if permission was refused.

8.2.4   The ground of the application

On what grounds can an application be brought under the 1975 Act? Section 1(1) provides that a person may apply:

> ... on the ground that the disposition of the deceased's estate effected by his will or the law relating to intestacy, or the combination of his will and that law, is not such as to make reasonable financial provision for the applicant.

The central question then is whether reasonable financial provision has been made for the applicant. This is the first stage in the court's consideration of the application (assuming the applicant has *locus standi*). If the applicant shows that reasonable provision was not made for him, the court will proceed to the second stage — deciding what provision to make. In both stages the court must take into account the general and specific factors contained in s. 3 (see 8.4). The test when deciding (in the first stage) whether reasonable provision was made for the applicant is objective, as emphasised in *Re Goodwin* [1968] 3 All ER 12, by Megarry J (at p. 15):

> The question is simply whether the will or the disposition has made reasonable provision, and not whether it was unreasonable on the part of the deceased to have made no provision or no larger provision for the dependant ... the question is not subjective but objective. It is not whether the testator stands convicted of unreasonableness, but whether the provision in fact made is reasonable.

Prior to the 1975 Act all applicants were subject to the same standard of provision, namely, whether they had received such provision as was reasonable for their maintenance. But the 1975 Act introduced a different standard of provision for the surviving spouse of the deceased. Thus there are two standards of provision under the Act — the surviving spouse standard, and the maintenance standard (for all other applicants).

8.2.4.1   The surviving spouse standard
Under s. 1(2)(a), 'reasonable financial provision' as regards a surviving spouse means:

> ... such financial provision as it would be reasonable in all the circumstances of the case for a husband or wife to receive, whether or not that provision is required for his or her maintenance.

The rationale of s. 1(2)(a) is that the spouse should be able to claim not just maintenance but a share of the family assets comparable to the position of a spouse on divorce. Consequently, s. 3(2) provides that the court shall have regard to 'the provision which the applicant might reasonably have expected to receive if on the day on which the deceased died the marriage, instead of being terminated by death, had been terminated by a decree of divorce'. Thus decisions in matrimonial law as to a spouse's entitlement on divorce are relevant to applications under the 1975 Act. A very general *starting-point* in assessing entitlement on divorce is to award a spouse at least one third to one half of the couple's capital assets and joint earnings: *Wachtel* v *Wachtel* [1973] 1 All ER 829, CA. In applications under the 1975 Act the courts have taken heed of this general approach — as they must — as regards the capital assets (the question of joint earnings obviously does not arise after the deceased's death). However, there has been some inconsistency in the cases as to how much emphasis should be placed on the imaginary divorce guideline. In *Moody* v *Stevenson* [1992] 2 All ER 524, CA, the deceased left all her estate (valued at about £45,000) to her stepdaughter. It consisted principally of the house in which the deceased had lived with her husband, the applicant. She had left him nothing in her will because she considered that he had adequate resources of his own. In the last few years of her life the deceased became senile and had to live in a nursing home, her husband continuing to live in the matrimonial home. The applicant was aged 81, had savings of £6,000 and lived on his pension. The stepdaughter, aged 55, lived alone in council accommodation and was entirely dependent on State benefits. She took out a summons for possession of the house, while the husband applied under the 1975 Act. The court directed that the applicant should be able to continue living in the house as long as he was willing and able to do so. Waite J, referring to the imaginary divorce guideline, stated (at p. 533) that 'the acceptable minimum posthumous provision for a surviving spouse should correspond as closely as possible to the inchoate rights enjoyed by that spouse in the deceased's lifetime by virtue of his or her prospective entitlement under the matrimonial law'.

But consider the 'Oxbridge' cases — *Re Besterman* [1984] 2 All ER 656, CA, and *Re Bunning* [1984] 3 All ER 1. In *Re Besterman*, the testator was a millionaire as well as a distinguished academic, a rare combination. In his will he left his wife personal chattels and a life interest in War Stock producing an income of £3,500 a year. He left the vast bulk of his estate to Oxford University. The widow first secured an interim order, including £75,000 to enable her to buy a smaller house and vacate the luxurious matrimonial home. The trial judge increased the provision to produce aggregate capital of £259,000. The Court of Appeal increased the overall sum to £378,000, made up as follows: house — £75,000; War Loan — £28,000; capital — £275,000. Oliver LJ thought that 'the *Wachtel* proportion' could be 'a useful cross-check' (p. 671), although the main consideration was what was reasonable in all the circumstances: the divorce guideline was only one of the several factors which the court had to consider. In *Re Bunning*, the testator left most of his estate (worth £237,000) to Cambridge University, making no provision for his wife. During the marriage he had given her substantial gifts (worth nearly £100,000). She left him a few years before his death. She applied under the 1975 Act and the court awarded her £60,000. The decision illustrates that the divorce analogy cannot always be applied with precision. The judge thought that on divorce the wife would have been awarded £36,000. Why then was she awarded £60,000? Because on divorce the court would have had to take into account the husband's future needs (a factor no longer applicable in an application under the 1975 Act). This is a point of fundamental importance. The analogy between divorce and death is not really close since on divorce the needs of *both* spouses have to be taken into account.

In *Re Krubert* [1996] 3 WLR 959, the Court of Appeal emphasised this difference and expressed a clear preference for the approach taken in *Re Besterman* rather than *Moody* v *Stevenson*; namely, that the court did not have to take as its starting point what the applicant would have received on divorce. The applicant, a widow aged nearly 90, was left pesonal chattels, £10,000 absolutely, and a life interest in the matrimonial home in her husband's will (the home had been held in his sole name). The remainder (valued at £100,000) was left to his brother and sister who lived in Czechoslovakia. The trial judge, applying *Moody* v *Stevenson*, took as his starting point the provision that the applicant would have received on divorce and awarded her the whole estate absolutely save for payments of £7,000 to each of the siblings. The Court of Appeal thought that the judge had erred in awarding the applicant an absolute interest in the house. The court directed that she should take an absolute interest in the whole of the estate except for the house, in which she was to retain her life interest. Cazalet J commented (at p. 966–7):

> One unsatisfactory aspect of placing too much emphasis on the award which would have been made on the hypothetical divorce is that, where the spouses are living together at the date of death, such an approach may well, in what may be described as small asset cases, produce financial provision below reasonable financial provision within the meaning of the Act of 1975. This is because the funds available cannot provide satisfactorily for two homes as opposed to one and support the couple living apart. However, because the court in claims under the Act is concerned with one spouse and not two, as contrasted with the divorce situation, the entitlement which the deceased would have received or obtained on divorce can be brought into consideration as potentially available to ensure that reasonable financial provision for an applicant under the Act is made available.

In cases such as *Re Besterman*, *Re Bunning* and *Re Krubert* there were no substantial calls on the estate of the deceased apart from that of the applicant. In many cases, however, the court will have a more difficult task, having to balance the needs of several parties. For example, in *Kusminow* v *Barclays Bank* [1989] Fam Law 66, the deceased left his entire estate (valued at £100,000) to his nephew and niece, who both lived in impoverished conditions in the Soviet Union. An application was brought by his wife, who was elderly and arthritic. She had left the deceased a year before he died and was living in rented accommodation. The court held that the applicant was entitled to a sufficient capital sum to ensure her future, but that her needs had to be balanced against the obvious needs of the beneficiaries. The applicant was awarded a lump sum of £45,000.

The surviving spouse standard under s. 1(2)(a) is not applicable to a judicially separated spouse. However, the court has the discretion to apply that standard provided that (i) the deceased died within 12 months of the granting of a decree of judicial separation, and (ii) the court had not made an order for financial provision in matrimonial proceedings by the time of the deceased's death: s. 14. This section applies also to former spouses who have not remarried. It enables the court to deal more satisfactorily with cases where the deceased dies shortly after a decree before the surviving spouse has been able to obtain a financial settlement in matrimonial proceedings. In the case of judicial separation, s. 14 does not apply unless the decree was in force and the separation was continuing when the deceased died: s. 14(2).

8.2.4.2 The maintenance standard

As regards all applicants other than the surviving spouse (and the exceptional cases in s. 14) 'reasonable financial provision' means 'such financial provision as it would be reasonable in all the circumstances of the case for the applicant to receive for his maintenance'.

(a) What is meant by 'maintenance'? The Act does not define the term but s. 1(3) defines 'being maintained', for the purposes of s. 1(1)(e) in terms of a substantial contribution to the reasonable needs of the applicant (see 8.2.1.5). One might reasonably expect some correlation between the meanings of 'being maintained' and 'maintenance', especially as the terms appear in close proximity in the Act. The case law on the meaning of 'maintenance' shows some inconsistency. In *Re Christie* [1979] 1 All ER 546, the court held that the term referred to 'the applicant's way of life and well-being, his health, financial security' (p. 550). However, this interpretation was regarded as too wide by the Court of Appeal in *Re Coventry* [1979] 3 All ER 815, where Goff LJ commented (at pp. 819–20):

> What is proper maintenance must in all cases depend on all the facts and circumstances of the particular case being considered at the time, but I think it is clear on the one hand that one must not put too limited a meaning on it; it does not mean just enough to enable a person to get by, on the other hand, it does not mean anything which may be regarded as reasonably desirable for his general benefit or welfare.

In *Re Dennis* (see 8.2.3.2), the applicant, the son of a rich father, was described by the judge as 'a spendthrift drifter who has spent substantial periods of his life depending on, and dissipating, moneys provided by other people' (p. 143). A major issue was whether he could seek an order under the Act in order to pay a large tax debt incurred from the lifetime gifts made to him. It was held that provision for the payment of this debt could not be regarded as maintenance. Browne-Wilkinson J stated (at pp. 145–6):

> ... the word 'maintenance' connotes only payments which, directly or indirectly, enable the applicant in the future to discharge the cost of his daily

living at whatever standard of living is appropriate to him. The provision that is to be made is to meet recurring expenses, being expenses of living of an income nature.

However, the judge recognised the possibility that maintenance could include the payment of debts in some cases — for example, to enable the applicant to continue to carry on a profit-making business or profession. *Re Dennis* was applied in *Re Goodchild* [1996] 1 All ER 670, where the applicant, the son of the deceased, had substantial business debts. The court thought that provision was appropriate to relieve him of his financial difficulties and referred the matter back to the parties for final settlement. In *Re Abram* [1996] 2 FLR 379, the court declined to make a capital provision for an applicant who had entered a voluntary arrangement under the Insolvency Act 1996. Under the arrangement, any capital sum received by the applicant from the deceased's estate was payable to his creditors. The court was prepared, however, to order a settlement whereby the applicant could receive income from the estate for his maintenance (see 8.3.1.4).

Can provision be sought for payment of a mortgage debt? In *Re Jennings* [1994] 3 All ER 27, CA, it was held that although the discharge of a mortgage could be regarded as desirable for the applicant's general benefit, it did not enable him to discharge the cost of daily living at the standard appropriate to him. The court considered *Re Callaghan* (see 8.2.1.4), where an order was made enabling the applicant to buy his council house at an advantageous price without the burden of taking on a mortgage. That case was distinguished in *Re Jennings* (where the applicant was much more financially secure) on the ground that the applicant in *Re Callaghan* 'had a need which enabled him to say that the provision was reasonably required for his maintenance' (*per* Nourse LJ, at p. 37). The decision in *Re Callaghan* was consistent with remarks in *Re Dennis* to the effect that provision could be ordered by way of a lump sum to enable an applicant to buy a house, thus relieving him of income expenditure.

A recurring element in the court's interpretation of 'maintenance' has been the emphasis on the standard of living 'appropriate' to the applicant. In several cases the courts have quoted with approval a *dictum* from the Canadian decision *Re Duranceau* [1952] 3 DLR 714, at 720:

Is the provision sufficient to enable the dependant to live neither luxuriously nor miserably, but decently and comfortably according to his or her station in life?

The problem with this approach is that there is doubt as to whether 'station in life' refers purely to material circumstances or to other considerations (status, for example, or birth). Moreover, a person's 'station in life' is not necessarily immutable: should the court consider the applicant's latest circumstances rather than the previous life-style? In the case of former spouses and cohabitants, the length of the relationship may be a critical factor. In *Malone* v *Harrison* [1979] 1 WLR 1353, the applicant became the mistress of the deceased, a successful businessman, and for 12 years was wholly maintained by him in a lavish life-style (expensive holidays, luxurious flats, gifts of cars and shares). She had previously lived in a council flat in an underprivileged area in Birmingham, and had worked as a telephonist and receptionist at a low salary. In ordering provision for her, the court took into account the life-style to which she had become accustomed. The provision made — a lump sum of £19,000 out of an estate valued at £480,000 — seems *prima facie* distinctly ungenerous, but was considered sufficient to enable her to maintain a reasonable life-style. She was still young and had received considerable assets from the deceased during his lifetime. He had several other calls on his estate, and had in any case always made it clear to the applicant that he would not make provision for her in his will.

(b) Former spouses The fact that all the categories of applicant — apart from the surviving spouse — are limited to applying for maintenance has diverse consequences. For example, former spouses will not normally have a realistic claim. This is because in the vast majority of divorces, the maintenance issue will already have been settled in the matrimonial proceedings. In *Re Fullard* [1981] 2 All ER 796, the Court of Appeal commented that there would be few cases — in view of the court's powers in matrimonial proceedings — in which it would be possible for a former spouse to show that reasonable financial provision had not been made. Nevertheless, the court indicated the circumstances (not exhaustive) in which an application from a former spouse might succeed:

> Where there has been a long period of time since the dissolution of the marriage in circumstances in which a continuing obligation to support the ex-spouse has been established by an order of the court, by consent or otherwise, under which periodical payments have been, and continue to be, made up to the date of the death. There may be circumstances . . . where the death itself unlocks a substantial capital sum of which the testator should have been aware, and from which, had he made a will at the time immediately before his death, he ought, within the criteria of the 1975 Act, have made some provision. There may be other incidents of further accretion of wealth, but I doubt that the mere fact of accretion of wealth after the dissolution of the marriage would of itself justify an application. (*per* Purchas J, at p. 804)

A former wife succeeded in *Re Crawford* (1983) 4 FLR 273. Following a divorce after a long marriage, the deceased agreed to pay the applicant one third of his gross salary by way of maintenance. He continued to be responsible for these payments for over 11 years until he died, although there was a long period when he defaulted. The applicant's financial resources were 'extremely slim' when the deceased died (he made no provision for her in his will). His surviving wife and children were well provided for by the will and through other benefits. The court awarded a lump sum of £35,000 to the applicant (potential value of the estate was about £65,000). In *Re Farrow* [1987] 1 FLR 205, a former wife succeeded mainly because the deceased died less than a year after being ordered (in the matrimonial proceedings) to make periodical payments to her. She had benefited from the periodical payments for only a short time. But in *Cameron* v *Treasury Solicitor* (see 8.2.1.2), a former wife failed in an application in respect of an intestate estate (valued at £7,677) which had passed to the Crown as *bona vacantia*. There were no special circumstances to demonstrate that the lack of provision for her was unreasonable. The estate could not be treated as a windfall to be distributed to a person because she was in need and in ill health.

(c)   Children   Restricting children of the deceased to maintenance out of the estate is very questionable. Unlike the surviving spouse, the deceased's child cannot apply for a share of the estate simply because of the relationship between child and parent. In this respect the child in English law is in a substantially inferior position compared to his counterpart on the continent (where fixed rights of inheritance are the norm). Should children not be treated on more of an equal footing with the surviving spouse, especially now that remarriage has become more common?

The general attitude of the courts to applications by adult children is that proof of impoverished circumstances is not sufficient. It appears that unless the applicant proves a moral obligation on the part of the parent to provide for him, or some special circumstances, the application will fail. In *Re Coventry* [1979] 2 All ER 408, Oliver J stated (at p. 410) that applications for maintenance by 'able-bodied and comparatively young men in employment and able to maintain themselves must be relatively rare' and need to be approached 'with a degree of circumspection'. The deceased died intestate leaving an estate of £7,000 which passed entirely to his elderly wife. She had left him many years before, and was living on a pension in a council flat. The applicant was their son, aged 46, who was working as a self-employed chauffeur and living in his parents' home (in which the widow had a one third interest). The applicant was in difficult financial circumstances, part of his income being required for payment of maintenance to his wife following the breakdown of their marriage. His application failed; being a blood relation and in necessitous circumstances was insufficient to entitle him to any provision. Oliver J stated (at p. 418):

> ... it always has to be borne in mind that the 1975 Act, so far as it relates to applicants other than spouses, is an Act whose purpose is limited to the provision of reasonable maintenance. It is not the purpose of the Act to provide legacies or rewards for meritorious conduct. Subject to the court's powers under the 1975 Act and to fiscal demands, an Englishman still remains at liberty at his death to dispose of his own property in whatever way he pleases or, if he chooses to do so, to leave that disposition to be regulated by the laws of intestate succession.... The court has no *carte blanche* to reform the deceased's dispositions or those which statute makes of his estate to accord with what the court itself might have thought would be sensible if it had been in the deceased's position.... There must, as it seems to me, be established some sort of moral claim by the applicant to be maintained by the deceased or at the expense of his estate beyond the mere fact of a blood

relationship, some reason why it can be said that, in the circumstances, it is unreasonable that no or no greater provision was in fact made.

These remarks will be regretted by those who think that a person owes some obligation to provide for his family after his death, whether adult children or not. Does not a moral obligation arise from the very fact of being a parent? Nevertheless, the decision in *Re Coventry* was entirely justifiable on the facts. A contest over a small estate between an able-bodied adult son in employment and his elderly mother living in difficult financial circumstances was, inevitably, no contest. Would it have made any difference if the estate had been large, or if the son had been the only surviving relative and the deceased had left the estate to charity? Not according to Oliver J — he made it clear that his decision did not depend on the priority of the mother's needs but rather on the son's failure to satisfy the court that he had any claim at all. The decision was confirmed on appeal: *Re Coventry* [1979] 3 All ER 815.

The need for an adult applicant under s. 1(1)(c) to show a moral obligation on the parent or some special reason for maintaining the child has been consistently emphasised in cases before and after *Re Coventry*. For example, in *Re Andrews* [1955] 3 All ER 248, a daughter failed in her application because the court held that her father ceased to owe her a moral obligation when she left home many years previously to live with a married man. Given that the applicant was now incapable of maintaining herself by reason of physical disability, the decision was extremely harsh on the facts. In *Williams* v *Johns* [1988] 2 FLR 475, the applicant, who had led a highly eventful life, applied for provision out of her adoptive mother's estate (the entire estate, worth £36,000, was left to the deceased's son). The relationship between the applicant and her adoptive parents had been a very difficult one. She had caused them considerable distress through her delinquent activities and drugs offences (including growing cannabis in her window-box), but they continued to support her financially when she became an adult. Placed with the deceased's will was a statement that the deceased had never received the affection she had hoped for from her daughter and that she felt no moral obligation towards her. The applicant failed because she was unable to show that the deceased owed her an obligation. Judge Micklem stated (at p. 488):

> ... it seems to me the cases say that, although she is unemployed and necessitous, that is not enough; she has to show something in the nature of an obligation. It has been called a 'moral obligation'; some reason why it would be reasonable for the testatrix, her mother, to make provision for her. ...

The emphasis placed by the courts on moral obligation in applications by adult children is surprising given that the legislation does not require (and never has) that any such obligation should be proved. Admittedly, under s. 3(1)(d) the court must consider 'any obligations and responsibilities which the deceased had towards any applicant' (see 8.4.2.4). But this is no more than a general directive to the court to take account of certain factors. It was not intended to be a statutory *precondition* for an application succeeding.

There have been some reported cases of successful applications by adult children. For example, in *Millward* v *Shenton* [1972] 2 All ER 1025, CA, a son, who was unable to earn his own living by reason of illness and was entirely dependent on State assistance, succeeded in obtaining virtually the whole of his mother's estate, worth about £3,000, which she had left to a cancer charity. In *Re Debenham* [1986] 1 FLR 404, the applicant was a daughter (aged 58) who was unemployed, epileptic and dependent on State assistance. Her mother left her only £200 out of an estate valued at about £172,000 (the bulk of which was bequeathed to charity). There was some evidence that the applicant had been an unwanted child — she was brought up mostly by her grandparents. It was held that as the applicant was epileptic, any mother, however aloof, might have felt some obligation to help her. The court awarded the applicant a lump sum of £3,000 for immediate needs and an annuity of £4,500 for future needs. It was felt that a substantial capital payment was inappropriate because of the age and life expectancy of the applicant. It will be remembered that in *Goodchild* v *Goodchild*, it was held that the deceased had a moral obligation to benefit his son arising from the fact that the deceased and his wife had each made a will in favour of the son, and the wife believed that the deceased would not depart from his will (see 2.1.3.6). In *Re Abram* [1996] 2 FLR 379 the testatrix left the bulk of her large estate to charity, excluding her son, her only child, from benefiting (she had previously made a will substantially in his favour). From the age of 17 he had worked in the family business — run by his mother — for minimal wages, but when he was 34 he left because he was unable to support his own family. It was then that his mother revoked her earlier will and disinherited him. Although they were later reconciled, she did not alter her later will. The son went into business but it failed. His application under the 1975 Act succeeded. The court found that there were special circumstances in this case which made the lack of provision for him by his mother unreasonable: he had worked for many years at a minimal wage for a business which he expected would one day be his, and he had then been forced to leave it mainly because of his mother's treatment of him. The court ordered a settlement of half the estate for the son's life.

In the two leading cases on applications by children of the family under s. 1(1)(d) — *Re Callaghan* and *Re Leach* — adult stepchildren succeeded (see 8.2.1.4). Paradoxically, it may be that stepchildren are more likely to succeed than the children of the deceased. This is because the applicant under s. 1(1)(d) must show that the deceased 'treated' him as a child of the family — that requires proof of conduct towards the stepchild from which a moral obligation or other special circumstances might be more easily inferred than in the case of a child (where there may be nothing beyond the 'mere' blood-tie). If this is a plausible assessment of the case law, it further illustrates the generally parsimonious attitude shown by the courts to applications by adult children.

8.3   POWERS OF COURT TO MAKE ORDERS

Under the 1975 Act the court has power to make a wide range of orders, similar to those available in matrimonial proceedings on divorce.

8.3.1   Section 2 orders

The court has power to make one or more of the orders specified in s. 2(1) of the Act 'if it is satisfied that the disposition of the deceased's estate effected by his will or the law relating to intestacy, or the combination of his will and that law, is not such as to make reasonable financial provision for the applicant'. Here again we have a reminder that a 1975 Act application proceeds in two stages. First, the court considers whether reasonable financial provision has been made for the applicant. Secondly, if no such provision has been made, the court considers which orders (if any) to make. There are six orders specified in s. 2(1).

8.3.1.1   Periodical payments: s. 2(1)(a)

The court may order out of the net estate of the deceased 'such periodical payments and for such term as may be specified in the order'. The court thus has a discretion as to the *quantum* and the length of the order. Under s. 2(2), the order may provide for:

(a)   payments of a specified amount; or
(b)   payments equal to the whole income of the net estate, or a specified portion thereof; or
(c)   payments equal to the whole of the income of such part of the net estate as the court directs to be set aside or appropriated.

Or the order may provide for the amount of the payments or any of them 'to be determined in any other way the court thinks fit'. It should be noted that under (c) the court may set aside a specific part of the net estate for the purpose of making payments out of the income. This is similar to the powers of the court to secure periodical payments in matrimonial proceedings.

The court may order periodical payments to be made for the term specified in the order. This allows the court a complete discretion in the matter, except that an order in favour of a former spouse or judicially separated spouse is automatically ended by the remarriage of that spouse: s. 19(2). This exception does not apply to surviving spouses or, it seems, cohabitants: subsequent marriage does not *automatically* terminate an order (but may be a ground for variation or termination: s. 6, see 8.3.1.8). An order for periodical payments will often be ordered to run from the deceased's death, but the court may order otherwise — for example, from the date of the court's judgment.

8.3.1.2   Lump sum orders: s. 2(1)(b)

The court may order the payment out of the net estate 'of a lump sum of such amount as may be so specified'. Lump sum orders may be made whatever the size of the estate, but they will be particularly appropriate if the estate is too small to bear periodical payments. Moreover, they are potentially useful in aiding the administration of the estate since they may dispose of an application once and for all: lump sums cannot be varied. In *Re Besterman* (see 8.2.4.1), Oliver LJ drew particular attention (at p. 670) to the fact that such orders are not variable:

I also think that the absence, which is inherent in a lump sum order, of an opportunity to return to the court does mean that, in assessing the lump sum, the court must take rather greater account than might otherwise be the case of contingencies and inflation.

The court may order a lump sum to be paid by instalments: s. 7(1). Such an order may subsequently be varied as to the number of instalments payable, the amount of any *instalment* and the date of payment s. 7(2). But the *amount* of the order cannot be varied.

8.3.1.3   Transfer of property: s. 2(1)(c)

The court may make 'an order for the transfer to the applicant of such property comprised in that estate [the net estate] as may be so specified'. This is an important power in practice — a necessary adjunct to the other powers of the court. For example, if the applicant establishes a need to be housed (such as the surviving spouse or cohabitant), it will be this power which will enable the deceased's home to be transferred to the applicant. Also, the power can be useful in order to avoid an improvident realisation of assets in the net estate. It seems that 'property' in s. 2(1)(c) is to be given a wide meaning. It includes, for example, 'any chose in action': s. 25(1). An order under s. 2(1)(c) cannot be varied.

8.3.1.4   Settlement of property: s. 2(1)(d)

The court may make 'an order for the settlement for the benefit of the applicant' of such property comprised in the net estate as may be specified. The settlement ordered may take various forms but it cannot be subsequently varied. A settlement of property may be particularly appropriate where the applicant is a minor, or where future contingencies need to be addressed. The court may confer on the trustees of the settlement such powers as appear to be 'necessary or expedient': s. 2(4). In *Re Abram* (above) the court ordered a settlement whereby half the estate was settled on the applicant for life on protective trusts so that if he became bankrupt or tried to dispose of his interest, the life interest would be replaced by a discretionary trust for him and his family.

8.3.1.5   Acquisition of property: s. 2(1)(e)

The court may order the acquisition of specified property out of assets from the net estate, and its transfer or settlement to the applicant 'for his benefit'. This power will be useful, for example, if the applicant needs a home, but a smaller one than that comprised in the net estate; or where the estate does not include any home. An order under s. 2(1)(e) cannot be varied.

8.3.1.6   Variation of settlements: s. 2(1)(f)

The court can make an order varying

... any ante-nuptial or post-nuptial settlement (including such a settlement made by will) made on the parties to a marriage to which the deceased was one of the parties, the variation being for the benefit of the surviving party to that marriage, or any child of that marriage, or any person who was treated by the deceased as a child of the family in relation to that marriage.

The Act does not define 'ante-nuptial or post-nuptial settlement', but the power under s. 2(1)(f) is similar to that exercisable in matrimonial proceedings. The matrimonial courts have interpreted the term as including any financial arrangement of a continuing nature which makes provision for spouses in their capacity as spouses. For example, in *Brooks v Brooks* [1995] 3 All ER 257, HL, it was held that a pension scheme in a family company, under which the spouses were entitled to benefit, could be regarded as a nuptial settlement and thus could be varied on divorce. An order for variation can be made only for the benefit of spouses, children, or children of the family, and not for dependants and cohabitants. The order cannot be varied.

8.3.1.7   Who bears the loss?

If an order is made under s. 2, it follows that one or more beneficiaries under the will or intestacy are bound to have their entitlement adversely affected. Section 2(4) enables the court to make 'such consequential and supplemental provisions as the court thinks necessary or expedient for the purpose of giving effect to the order or for the purpose of securing that the order operates fairly as between one beneficiary of the estate of the deceased and another'. More specifically, s. 2(4) enables the court to:

(a)   order any person holding property from the net estate to transfer it or make such payment as may be specified;

(b)   vary the disposition of the estate affected by the deceased's will or intestacy 'in such manner as the court thinks fair and reasonable having regard to the provisions of the order and all the circumstances of the case';

(c)   confer on trustees of any property which is the subject of an order such powers as appear to be 'necessary and expedient'.

In *Re Preston* [1969] 2 All ER 961, the testator, anticipating a possible successful application by his estranged wife, directed that the beneficiaries under his will should bear the burden of any subsequent order in certain proportions. The court made an order in favour of the wife, apportioned the burden quite differently, and held that it had the discretion not only to apportion unequally between different classes of beneficiaries, but even between members of the same class, exonerating some at the expense of others. All the beneficiaries were parties to the action. This is significant because the court is very unlikely to diminish the entitlement of a beneficiary unless he is a party to the action. This was emphasised in *Re Bunning* (see 8.2.4.1), where it will be remembered that a wife was awarded £60,000 from an estate that was bequeathed mostly to Cambridge University. The other beneficiaries were the Royal Society for the Protection of Birds and a number of individual legatees (most of whom were not parties to the action). The burden of the wife's award was imposed almost entirely on Cambridge University, the court remarking

that it would have been wrong to impose it on those who were not parties to the
action.

8.3.1.8 Variation of orders

Section 6 of the 1975 Act gives the court extensive powers of varying periodical
payment orders. No other orders are capable of variation (but *instalments* in
lump sum orders can be varied, see 8.3.1.2). Variation includes discharging an
order, or suspending (or reviving) any of the order's provisions. Moreover, the
court's powers include making:

(a) a new periodical payments order;
(b) a lump sum order; or
(c) a transfer of property order: s. 6(2).

It should be noted that although lump sum and transfer orders cannot be
varied, such orders can be *made* on an application to vary a periodical payments
order. The court may of course alter the duration of the previous order or the
circumstances in which it is to terminate. The Act does not specify the grounds
on which a variation may be sought, but usually it is because there has been a
change in circumstances such as the remarriage of an applicant. The court
must pay regard 'to all the circumstances of the case, including any change in
any of the matters to which the court was required to have regard' (the factors
in s. 3) when making the order sought to be varied: s. 6(7).

Who can apply for a variation order? Under s. 6(5), any of the following may
apply:

(a) any person who by virtue of s. 1(1) has applied for a s. 2 order (or would
be entitled to apply but for the time limit in s. 4);
(b) the deceased's personal representative;
(c) the trustees of any relevant property; and
(d) any beneficiary of the deceased's estate.

It should be noted that an applicant under s. 1(1) who failed to obtain an order
may nevertheless apply for variation under s. 6. However, since variation can
be sought only if an order has been made by the court, it follows that the failed
applicant cannot have *locus standi* unless someone else has obtained an order.

8.3.2 Interim orders: s. 5

'The whole purpose of an interim order is to hold the situation as reasonably as
possible pending final determination' (*per* Ormrod LJ in *Barnsley* v *Ward*,
(unreported) 18 January 1980, but noted in *Tyler's Family Provision*, 2nd edn.,
p. 330). Interim orders enable the court to give immediate financial assistance
to an applicant for a s. 2 order, prior to the hearing of the application. Under
s. 5(1), the court may order from the net estate 'such sum or sums and (if more
than one) at such intervals as the court thinks reasonable'. Thus the court can
order lump sum and periodical payments; both may be appropriate in some

cases. In *Re Besterman* (see 8.2.4.1), the widow was made an interim order consisting of a £75,000 lump sum to enable her to move to a smaller property, and £15,000 income per annum. The order may be made 'subject to such conditions or restrictions, if any, as the court may impose': s. 5(1). For example, the court might require the applicant to repay any sums paid under the interim order if the application fails. Or the court might provide that sums paid under an interim order shall be treated as having been paid on account of any payments resulting from the final order: s. 5(4). An unusual condition was imposed in *Barnsley* v *Ward* (above) where the applicant had to give an undertaking to seek reasonable employment. In making a s. 5 order the court must have regard to the factors specified in s. 3 'so far as the urgency of the case admits': s. 5(3). An interim order can be varied.

When can the court make an interim order? Section 5(1) provides that the order can be made if it appears to the court:

> (a)   that the applicant is in immediate need of financial assistance, but it is not yet possible to determine what order (if any) should be made under that section [s. 2]; and
> (b)   that property forming part of the net estate of the deceased is or can be made available to meet the need of the applicant.

'Immediate need' can arise in various ways, but often will involve the payment of mortgage instalments or rent, or having to move out of the matrimonial home (as in *Re Besterman*). As regards s. 5(1)(b), an interim order is unlikely to be made unless there is ready money in the net estate, or property which can easily be sold so as to provide the necessary sums. Apart from satisfying the court about the matters specified in s. 5(1)(a) and (b), the applicant must satisfy the court 'that it is right in the circumstances to exercise the court's discretion and make an order in the manner sought' (*per* Templeman LJ in *Barnsley* v *Ward* (*Tyler's Family Provision*, p. 328)).

8.3.3   The net estate

The meaning of 'net estate' in the 1975 Act is of crucial importance since orders under s. 2 (and interim orders) can only be made out of the net estate. The term is defined by s. 25(1) which specifies five categories of property as constituting net estate.

8.3.3.1   Property disposable by will
Under s. 25(1), net estate includes '(a) all property of which the deceased had power to dispose by his will (otherwise than by virtue of a special power of appointment) less the amount of his funeral, testamentary and administration expenses, debts and liabilities, including any inheritance tax payable out of his estate on his death'. A person who is not of full age and capacity shall be treated as having the power to dispose by will of all property of which he would have had power to dispose by will if he had been of full age and capacity: s. 25(2).

Paragraph (a), although of wide ambit, does not necessarily include benefits payable under life insurance policies or occupational pension schemes, two of the most important likely assets in practice. Everything turns on the type of policy or scheme in question. The proceeds of a life insurance policy are net estate if they are payable directly to the deceased's estate under the terms of the policy. If the proceeds do not fall directly into the deceased's estate, but, for example, pass under a trust in favour of a particular beneficiary, such proceeds are not net estate. As regards occupational pension schemes, death benefits will be regarded as net estate if under the scheme such benefits pass directly into the deceased's estate, but not if they are payable directly to a particular beneficiary.

8.3.3.2 *Inter vivos* general powers of appointment

Paragraph (b) of the meaning of 'net estate' in s. 25(1) comprises 'any property in respect of which the deceased held a general power of appointment (not being a power exercisable by will) which has not been exercised'. Had the property been subject to a general power of appointment exercisable by will, it would have been regarded as net estate under paragraph (a).

8.3.3.3 Net estate under s. 8

Paragraph (c) of the definition in s. 25(1) refers to property treated as net estate by virtue of s. 8(1) or (2) of the 1975 Act. Section 8(1) is concerned with statutory nominations. If the deceased had 'in accordance with the provisions of any enactment nominated any person to receive any sum of money or other property on his death and that nomination is in force at the time of his death' that property is treated as net estate (less any inheritance tax payable thereon). It will be recalled that a number of statutes authorise persons who hold funds in certain bodies to dispose of their holding, usually by written nomination, up to a specified limit (see further 9.2.1.1).

It appears that non-statutory nominations are excluded from the definition of net estate. Such nominations are most likely to occur in certain types of pension schemes under which employees are given the power to nominate the persons to whom they wish the pension to be paid on their deaths. Case law tends to confirm that property passing under such nominations is unlikely to be regarded as net estate. In *Jessop* v *Jessop* [1992] 1 FLR 591, CA, it was held that a nomination under a pension fund held at the discretion of trustees was not net estate. Similarly, in *Re Cairnes* (1983) 4 FLR 225, it was held that death benefits payable under an occupational pension scheme were not part of the deceased's net estate. The deceased had nominated the benefits in favour of his wife, and had not cancelled the nomination despite subsequent divorce. It seems that the court treated the fact that nominations could be made only with the consent of the trustees of the scheme as material, thus implying that some non-statutory nominations might fall within the definition of net estate.

Section 8(2) deals with *donatio mortis causa* — a gift made in contemplation of death (see generally 9.2.2). Such gifts are made *inter vivos* but are conditional on the contemplated death occurring. They pass immediate *control* of the property to the donee. Under s. 8(2), any property received by any person as a *donatio mortis causa* made by a deceased person is treated as net estate (less any inheritance tax payable thereon).

8.3.3.4 Joint tenancies: s. 9
Paragraph (d) of the definition in s. 25(1) refers to property treated as net estate by virtue of s. 9. The deceased's severable share in property held on a joint tenancy *may* be treated as part of the deceased's net estate: the court 'may order that the deceased's severable share of that property, at the value thereof immediately before his death, shall, to such extent as appears to the court to be just in all the circumstances of the case, be treated for the purposes of this Act as part of the net estate of the deceased'. When a joint tenant dies his interest normally passes to the other joint tenant by survivorship — a basic principle of English property law. But s. 9 allows the court to disregard this principle, where appropriate, and to regard the deceased's severable share as part of his net estate. Section 9 was clearly a radical departure from the basic principle, which may explain why the severable share is not *automatically* treated as net estate. The section was enacted on the recommendation of the Law Commission, whose particular concern was the common scenario where the principal asset of a married couple is the jointly-owned matrimonial home. Unless the severable share was treated as net estate, there might be no property available to worthy applicants:

> ... if one of the spouses dies and the power of the court to make an order for family provision is limited to making provision out of the estate of the deceased, no part of the value of the house will be available for such provision. In some cases the result might be that no property at all was available for an order for the maintenance of the children of other dependants of the deceased. (Law. Com. Report No. 61, 1974, para. 139)

A court can consider whether to order that a severable share of a joint tenancy be treated as net estate only if the application for the order under s. 2 was made within six months from the date when representation with respect to the estate of the deceased was first taken out. The court has no power to extend the time limit. The intention is to protect the surviving joint tenant against undue delay.

If property was held by the deceased by tenancy in common, his interest is net estate by virtue of paragraph (a) (see 8.3.3.1). Thus, before s. 9 was enacted, whether property was held by tenancy in common or joint tenancy was of fundamental importance in evaluating the deceased's net estate. It was partly to avoid the differing consequences of these forms of co-ownership that the Law Commission recommended the enactment of s. 9.

Section 9 applies where the deceased was entitled to a joint tenancy of 'any property'. Thus personalty is included as well as realty; and the provision applies to choses in action (such as the credit balance in a bank account): s. 9(4). In *Re Crawford* (1983) 4 FLR 273, the applicant received provision from the deceased's share of a bank account that had been held jointly with the deceased's surviving wife. Where the deceased's home was subject to a joint tenancy, the court will be slow to make any order under s. 9 if the surviving spouse continues to live in the home (otherwise the survivor's occupation of the home is likely to be substantially affected). This was one of the reasons why in *Kourkgy* v *Lusher* (see 8.2.1.5) the applicant, the former mistress of the deceased, failed to secure an order — the bulk of the estate consisted of the matrimonial home occupied by the deceased's widow as surviving joint tenant. But if the occupant of the home is not going to be forced out, the court is much more likely to make an order under s. 9. In *Jessop* v *Jessop* (see 8.3.3.3) the deceased led a double life, cohabiting with a mistress and keeping in regular contact with his wife and children (the wife knew nothing about the mistress until the deceased died). The deceased became a joint tenant of the property where he cohabited with his mistress. He died intestate, his estate valued at £2,500. His wife, aged 72, was living in needy circumstances in rented accommodation. She applied for provision and was awarded £10,000. The court ordered that the deceased's severable share of the joint tenancy should be treated as part of his net estate to the extent of £10,000, and that the respondent (the mistress) should pay that sum to the wife. The respondent had sufficient capital to do that and was not required to sell her home.

At what value is the deceased's severable share to be assessed under s. 9? It is 'at the value thereof immediately before his death': s. 9(1). In *Powell* v *Osbourne* [1993] 1 FLR 1001, it was held at first instance that the value of a life insurance policy immediately before the deceased's death was effectively zero since the policy had been in force for only two months and had no surrender value. However, the Court of Appeal explained that the requirement that the value was to be determined immediately before death reflected the fact that it was the last moment when the deceased could have severed the joint tenancy. But in order to value the severable share the court had to have regard to the imminence of death. Accordingly, where the value of the property depended on death — as in the case of a life insurance policy — the value immediately before death would be the same as the value upon death.

Where an order is made under s. 9, no one is liable 'for anything done by him before the order was made': s. 9(3). This provision appears to apply to the surviving joint tenant — he can dispose of the property before the order (although the property or its proceeds would be subject to tracing). And the exclusion of liability clearly applies, for example, to a bank which pays the balance of a joint account to the surviving account holder.

8.3.3.5   Dispositions or contracts: ss. 10 and 11

A radical feature of the 1975 Act was the enactment of anti-evasion measures whereby certain dispositions (s. 10) or contracts (s. 11) made by the deceased with the intention of defeating applications for financial provision could be subsequently policed by the court (see generally 8.5). Power is given to the court to order the recovery of property passing under such dispositions or contracts; and such property is treated as net estate by paragraph (e) of the definition in s. 25(1).

8.4 MATTERS TO BE CONSIDERED

8.4.1 Introduction

Section 3 specifies the 'matters' which the court must take into account in applications for an order under the 1975 Act. These matters are factors or guidelines which aid the court in both stages of the application, namely, to determine:

(a) whether reasonable financial provision has been made for the applicant; and
(b) which orders the court should make, if any, if it is shown that reasonable financial provision has not been made.

The matters specified in s. 3 fall into two categories — the general and the particular. The general matters are relevant to all applications, whereas the particular matters apply in addition to particular categories of applicant. No indication is given as to the relative importance of the various factors. Any attempt to do so would admittedly be fraught with difficulty; but the absence of any weighting makes the court's task harder and its decisions less predictable.

In considering the matters specified in s. 3, 'the court shall take into account the facts as known to the court at the date of the hearing': s. 3(5). Thus the court must have regard to facts which arise after the deceased's death. This reinforces the fundamental principle that the test of reasonable provision is not whether the deceased acted reasonably or not, but whether reasonable provision was made for the applicant. A testator might well have acted reasonably, but facts may arise after his death which make the provision for the applicant unreasonable. In *Re Goodwin* (see 8.2.4), the testator's gift to his wife of his residuary estate was less beneficial than he had hoped as it became apparent after his death that a debtor of his estate (his son) was unlikely to repay a debt because of illness. The court awarded the wife increased provision, taking into account (as it must) the developments after the deceased's death. However, the court's duty is satisfied provided that it has taken into account the relevant facts: it need not necessarily be influenced by such facts in making its decision. In *Rajabally* v *Rajabally* [1987] 2 FLR 390, the testator left his house equally between his wife and three sons. She applied on the ground that this left her without proper security as she owned only a part-share. At the hearing the sons gave assurances that they would not enforce their rights; consequently, no order was made. The Court of Appeal held that although the trial judge had to take into account the circumstances existing at the time of the hearing, the decision that reasonable provision had been made should not have been based on unenforceable assurances given at the hearing (too much weight had been given to them).

8.4.2 General matters

Section 3(1) directs the court to have regard in all applications to the following matters:

(a)   the financial resources and financial needs which the applicant has or is likely to have in the foreseeable future;
(b)   the financial resources and financial needs which any other applicant for an order under section 2 of this Act has or is likely to have in the foreseeable future;
(c)   the financial resources and financial needs which any beneficiary of the estate of the deceased has or is likely to have in the foreseeable future;
(d)   any obligations and responsibilities which the deceased had towards any applicant for an order under the said section 2 or towards any beneficiary of the estate of the deceased;
(e)   the size and nature of the net estate of the deceased;
(f)   any physical or mental disability of any applicant for an order under the said section 2 or any beneficiary of the estate of the deceased;
(g)   any other matter, including the conduct of the applicant or any other person, which in the circumstances of the case the court may consider relevant.

8.4.2.1 Financial resources and needs of applicant

The court must have regard to the financial resources and financial needs which the applicant has or is likely to have in the foreseeable future. In considering 'financial resources' the court must take into account earning capacity; in considering 'financial needs' the court must take into account financial obligations and responsibilities: s. 3(6). In *Re Ducksbury* [1966] 2 All ER 374, the applicant's actual earnings were rather meagre because she wanted to study art and thus could work only part-time. The court took account of the fact that her potential earnings were far greater than her actual earnings, and accordingly awarded her a lesser amount of provision than if she had no choice as to her employment.

A person's financial resources include earned and unearned income, pensions, allowances, and capital assets such as realty, chattels, investments, awards of damages in litigation and money in bank and building society accounts. State aid must be taken into account, but it does not prevent the court from considering whether reasonable provision has been made. In *Re Collins* [1990] 2 All ER 47, it was argued by the Official Solicitor that it could not be said that there was a failure to provide reasonable provision (on intestacy) since the applicant was receiving support from the Department of Social Security. Hollings J responded: 'I do not consider that the fact of support from the DSS precludes consideration of whether the intestacy has or has not made reasonable financial provision for her' (p. 51). In *Re E* [1966] 2 All ER 44, an application by a widow in receipt of a State pension failed, but the decision turned on the fact that the estate was very small. In such a case the court felt that it was reasonable not to make provision for an applicant if the only effect of making provision would be to relieve the State from paying welfare benefits, leaving the applicant little better off.

The consideration of future resources is limited to those that the applicant 'is likely to have in the foreseeable future'. Should the possibility of inheriting under a will or intestacy be taken into account? There appears to be no reported case under the 1975 Act dealing with this issue, but the court is likely to adopt the approach of the matrimonial courts in divorce cases — that the possibility of inheriting should be taken into account only if there is a likelihood of it materialising in the foreseeable future: *Michael* v *Michael* [1986] 2 FLR 389.

As regards financial needs, both present and future, the issue of accommodation will always be central to the court's decision. For example, the court will be slow to make any order which results in the applicant having to vacate settled accommodation, especially if the applicant is elderly and there is no suitable alternative. In *Harrington* v *Gill* [1983] 4 FLR 265, the applicant had lived for several years with the deceased in his home and had been maintained by him. She had a right to occupy a council flat but surrendered it after the deceased's death. The applicant, aged 77 when the deceased died, had capital of about £1,400 and received a State pension. The deceased's entire estate (worth £65,000) passed on his intestacy to his daughter, a married lady in her forties in a reasonably comfortable financial position. The trial judge awarded the applicant a lump sum of £5,000 and the income from £5,000 for life, but ordered her to vacate the home since she could be expected to find a smaller place to live in. The Court of Appeal ordered the home to be settled on the applicant for life (remainder to the daughter) in addition to the sums awarded at first instance. Dunn LJ explained the decision (at p. 271):

> It is said, as it is so often said in these cases, that if the plaintiff were allowed to stay in the house the defendant would be kept out of her money. Having regard to the plaintiff's age, in the natural course of events one would expect that would only be a temporary postponement and, putting myself as far as I can into the position of a reasonable man in this deceased's circumstances, I think that he would have wanted her, after the time that they had spent together, to remain in this house for her lifetime . . .

The accommodation needs of an applicant do not necessitate entitlement to an absolute interest in property. In *Davis* v *Davis* [1993] 1 FLR 54, the testator left his residuary estate to trustees, his wife having a life interest in the proceeds. After the testator's death the trustees bought a house for the widow's occupation for life. She applied for a transfer to herself of the freehold of the purchased house, arguing that the will did not make reasonable provision for her in that it failed to make any capital provision for her. The Court of Appeal held that reasonable provision had been made, in the light of the action taken by the trustees after the deceased's death, since the applicant was rehoused and given an adequate level of maintenance.

8.4.2.2 Financial resources and needs of any other applicant

Under s. 3(1)(b), the court must consider the financial resources and financial needs which any other applicant has or is likely to have in the foreseeable future. This provision directs the court to consider an application not in isolation but balanced against competing claims from other applicants. The meaning of 'resources', 'needs' and 'foreseeable future' is the same as in s. 3(1)(a) and s. 3(1)(c).

8.4.2.3 Financial resources and needs of any beneficiary

Under s. 3(1)(c), the court must consider the financial resources and financial needs which any beneficiary of the estate has or is likely to have in the foreseeable future. A 'beneficiary' is anyone entitled to a beneficial interest under the deceased's will or intestacy (or combination of the two). Again, the court must balance the resources and needs of the beneficiaries against those of the applicants. It is when the court is involved in such balancing that the lack of guidance in the Act as to how to weight the various factors becomes especially problematic.

8.4.2.4 Deceased's obligations and responsibilities

Under s. 3(1)(d), the court must consider any obligations and responsibilities which the deceased had towards any applicant or beneficiary. This includes not only legal obligations — such as the duty of maintenance imposed on parents and spouses in matrimonial law — but also moral obligations recognised by the court. We have seen that the existence or otherwise of a moral obligation is of crucial importance in applications by children. Indeed, it is likely to be an important factor in all non-spouse applications.

In *Re Jennings* [1994] 3 All ER 27, the Court of Appeal held that as a general rule it was only obligations which the deceased had immediately before his death which had to be considered. It was not possible to construe s. 3(1)(d) as including legal obligations which the deceased had during his child's minority but failed to discharge. The applicant, a successful businessman in his late forties, applied for provision out of his father's estate, worth £300,000, which was left to remote relatives and certain friends and charities. The applicant's parents had divorced soon after his birth; thereafter the father never had any contact with him and never made any financial provision for him or the mother. The decision that the application should fail was regrettable: the concept that obligations which were owed but never satisfied should lapse through passage of time is highly questionable.

8.4.2.5 Size and nature of the estate

Section 3(1)(e) provides that the court must consider the size and nature of the net estate of the deceased. In *Re Clayton* [1966] 2 All ER 370, it was emphasised that the legislation places 'no bottom limit to the value of the estate in respect of which an application can be made' and that 'the smallness of the estate neither excludes jurisdiction nor full consideration' (*per* Ungoed-Thomas J, at p. 371). Nevertheless, the judge thought that smallness of the estate was significant in three particular respects. First, the court is more likely to find that provision for the applicant is reasonable if the only effect of making an order would be to relieve the State: see *Re E*, at 8.4.2.1. Secondly, the smallness of the estate may affect the extent to which it can effectively contribute to the applicant's maintenance (where that standard is applicable). This will largely depend on the applicant's resources and needs. Thirdly, the costs of an application must be borne in mind. In *Re Coventry* [1979] 3 All ER 815 and in *Re Fullard* [1981] 2 All ER 796, the Court of Appeal emphasised that applications in small estates should be discouraged because the costs may consume much of the estate (for the same reason appeals should be discouraged). The court may well award costs against an applicant in such cases: *Brill v Proud* (1984) 14 Fam Law 59, CA.

What is a 'small' estate? Not surprisingly the courts have eschewed laying down guidelines. Obviously there cannot be an immutable yardstick because of the changing value of money. In *Re Coventry*, £12,000 was considered to be a small estate. At that time (the late 1970s) the average house price in England was about £18,000. It is suggested that any estate which is valued substantially below the average house price is likely to be regarded as small.

As regards the 'nature' of the estate, the court should consider the effect of realising particular assets. Suppose, for example, that there are several deserving claimants and beneficiaries, but that the estate consists principally of a house. The court will have to consider the desirability of making orders which result in the division of the house or in its sale. The source of the deceased's assets may prove relevant. For example, in *Re Sivyer* [1967] 3 All ER 429, the deceased's estate passed entirely to his third wife under his intestacy. The applicant was his daughter by his second wife. The principal asset was the proceeds of a house which had been bought mainly out of savings owned by the applicant's mother, the deceased's second wife. In making an order for the applicant the court was heavily influenced by the fact that the deceased's estate was derived primarily from the contribution of the applicant's mother. A similar approach was taken in the applications by stepchildren in *Re Callaghan* and *Re Leach* (see 8.2.1.4).

8.4.2.6   Disability of applicant or beneficiary

Under s. 3(1)(f), the court must consider any physical or mental disability of any applicant or beneficiary. Since the financial resources and needs which have to be considered under s. 3(1)(a)–(c) are inevitably affected by a person's disability, it might be concluded that s. 3(1)(f) adds little. However, the disability of an adult child is more likely to persuade the court that the deceased owed the applicant a moral obligation: *Millward v Shenton* and *Re Debenham* (see 8.2.4.2). If the disabled person is receiving State aid, the court must take that into account. In *Re Watkins* [1949] 1 All ER 695, it was held that the fact that the applicant was detained in a mental hospital and provided for by the State could be regarded as justifying only a limited provision in the testator's will. However, that does not preclude the court from taking the view that the deceased can reasonably be expected to have made provision for the applicant beyond the basic level available from the State, except where the estate is small: *Re E* (above).

8.4.2.7 Any other matter

Section 3(1)(g) provides that the court must have regard to 'any other matter' considered to be relevant, including the conduct of the applicant or any other person. It was held in *Re Jennings* (above) that the phrase excludes the matters listed in s. 3(1)(a)–(f). What if the deceased stated reasons explaining the distribution of his estate? Need the court consider them? If they are considered relevant, such reasons must be taken into account as 'any other matter'. However, it will be in the court's discretion as to how much weight to attach to them. For example, in *Williams* v *Johns* the deceased's statement that she had never received the affection she had hoped for from her daughter was considered by the court but does not appear to have been regarded as significant in the decision (see 8.2.4.2). If a reason is shown to be spurious, it will be disregarded. In *Re Clarke* [1968] 1 All ER 451, the testator left most of his property to his mother and made only a small provision for his wife, stating that the latter had reneged on an agreement that they should live with his mother. The statement was disregarded since it was shown to be totally misleading as to the arrangement actually reached. If a testator wishes to state a reason for excluding a person from his will (or leaving him less than might be expected) it is best to do so in the will.

The phrase 'any other matter' specifically includes the conduct of applicants or of 'any other person'. Thus the conduct of the deceased and the beneficiaries is relevant. As with all the factors listed in s. 3, it is not clear what weight should be given to conduct. Regarding applications by *spouses*, it is arguable that conduct should be a significant factor only if it would be wrong to discount it. This is because in matrimonial proceedings for ancillary relief conduct is relevant only if it would be 'inequitable to disregard it' (s. 25 of the Matrimonial Causes Act 1973), and the 1975 Act attempts to assimilate the position of spouse applicants with those of divorced spouses. *Re Snoek* (1983) 13 Fam Law 18 provides an example of abnormal conduct. The applicant was left nothing in her husband's will, all of his estate passing to his children. The evidence suggested that the marriage deteriorated because of her uncontrollable temper and frequent outbursts of violence directed at the testator, described as 'atrocious and vicious behaviour'. The court made an order for her, but emphasised that the provision would have been substantially higher but for her abnormally bad behaviour.

Should good conduct be taken into account as it is in matrimonial proceedings? It would seem so: the reference to 'conduct' in s. 3(1)(g) presumably includes good conduct as well as misconduct.

8.4.3 Particular matters

In addition to the general matters specified in s. 3(1), the court must have regard to a number of particular matters affecting each category of applicant. These particular matters are similar to the factors which courts have to consider in matrimonial proceedings.

8.4.3.1   Spouses and former spouses

Section 3(2) provides that in the case of applications by a spouse or former spouse the court must have regard to:

> (a)   the age of the applicant and the duration of the marriage;
> (b)   the contribution made by the applicant to the welfare of the family of the deceased, including any contribution made by looking after the home or caring for the family . . .

These factors are identical to those applicable in matrimonial proceedings under the Matrimonial Causes Act 1973. Age is relevant principally to the extent that it affects employment and remarriage prospects. As for duration of marriage, an applicant married for a substantial number of years is generally in a stronger position than one married for only a short period, other things being equal, as illustrated in matrimonial cases: *Leadbeater* v *Leadbeater* [1985] FLR 789. The contribution made to the welfare of the family (s. 3(2)(b)) may take various forms but specifically includes non-financial contributions. The rationale is that spouses should not be prevented from having an arguable claim to family assets simply because they made no direct financial contribution to the welfare of the family.

Section 3(2) provides further that in the case of an application by a spouse under s. 1(1)(a) the court shall have regard to 'the provision which the applicant might reasonably have expected to receive if on the day on which the deceased died the marriage, instead of being terminated by death, had been terminated by a decree of divorce'. This is the imaginary divorce guideline, which has already been discussed (see 8.2.4.1).

8.4.3.2   Cohabitants

Under s. 3(2A) of the 1975 Act — inserted by the Law Reform (Succession) Act 1995 — the court must consider in an application by a cohabitant under s. 1(1)(ba):

> (a)   the age of the applicant and the length of the period during which the applicant lived as the husband or wife of the deceased and in the same household as the deceased;
> (b)   the contribution made by the applicant to the welfare of the family of the deceased, including any contribution made by looking after the home or caring for the family.

The increasing recognition given to the rights of cohabitants is demonstrated not only by the fact that cohabitants can apply — even if not maintained by the deceased — but also by the application of factors identical to those in the case of spouses (age, length of marriage, contribution to family welfare). But the standard of provision applicable is the maintenance standard, not the surviving spouse standard.

8.4.3.3 Children and children of the family

Section 3(3) provides that in applications made by children of the deceased (s. 1(1)(c)) and by children treated by the deceased as children of the family (s. 1(1)(d)), the court must consider 'the manner in which the applicant was being or in which he might expect to be educated or trained'. This factor has prompted little discussion in the case law, but clearly it will be relevant to consider the educational background and aspirations of the applicant and the deceased. There may be circumstances in which a child 'might expect' to be educated privately, for example. Since children can apply for provision only by way of maintenance, it follows that maintenance is regarded under the Act as including the costs of education.

Section 3(3) requires additional factors to be considered in applications by children of the family. The court must have regard:

(a) to whether the deceased had assumed any responsibility for the applicant's maintenance and, if so, to the extent to which and the basis upon which the deceased assumed that responsibility and to the length of time for which the deceased discharged that responsibility;

(b) to whether in assuming and discharging that responsibility the deceased did so knowing that the applicant was not his own child;

(c) to the liability of any other person to maintain the applicant.

These factors are the same as those applying in matrimonial proceedings. Section 3(3)(c) refers principally to the parents of the applicant: their liability to maintain the applicant is of obvious importance both in deciding whether reasonable provision has been made for the applicant and, if not, which order the court should make.

8.4.3.4 Dependants

Section 3(4) provides that in an application by a dependant under s. 1(1)(e), the court must consider 'the extent to which and the basis upon which the deceased assumed responsibility for the maintenance of the applicant and to the length of time for which the deceased discharged that responsibility'. It will be recalled that *Jelley* v *Iliffe* [1981] 2 All ER 29, CA, held that the assumption of responsibility could generally be presumed from the fact of maintenance (see 8.2.1.5). In *Rhodes* v *Dean* [1996] 7 CL 593, CA, the court found that the deceased's responsibility towards the applicant involved accommodation only and did not include living expenses. This was obviously pertinent to the extent to which and the basis upon which the deceased could be said to have assumed responsibility for the applicant's maintenance. On the facts the application failed.

8.5 ANTI-AVOIDANCE PROVISIONS

The anti-avoidance provisions of the 1975 Act were as radical a measure as any introduced by that Act. There were no comparable provisions under the previous legislation. The deceased could avoid the 1938 Act by reducing his net estate through *inter vivos* dispositions or contracts binding his estate on his death. The Law Commission's view (Law Com. No. 61, 1974, para. 191) was that it was 'a matter of overriding importance to ensure that family provision laws are effective'. The provisions enacted by the 1975 Act are concerned with dispositions and contracts intended to defeat an application for financial provision under the Act.

8.5.1 Dispositions: s. 10

Under s. 10(2), the court can order the donee of a disposition by the deceased to provide, for the purpose of making provision under the Act, 'such sum of money or other property as may be specified in the order' (such property will then be regarded as 'net estate' under s. 25). For such an order to be made the court must be satisfied of the following:

(a) that, less than six years before the date of the death of the deceased, the deceased with the intention of defeating an application for financial provision under this Act made a disposition, and

(b) that full valuable consideration for that disposition was not given by the person to whom or for the benefit of whom the disposition was made (in this section referred to as 'the donee') or by any other person, and

(c) that the exercise of the powers conferred by this section would facilitate the making of financial provision for the applicant under this Act.

8.5.1.1 Which provisions?

A disposition under s. 10 includes any payment of money (including payment of a premium under a policy of assurance); also any conveyance, assurance, gift of property, appointment (other than one made under a special power of appointment): s. 10(7). In *Clifford v Tanner* [1987] CLY 3881, CA, the deceased transferred his own home to his daughter, who covenanted to allow him and his wife to live there for life. A few years later the deceased released his daughter from her covenant. It was held that the release was a disposition within s. 10. The benefit of the covenant was of obvious value; hence the release was a disposal of an asset, 'a gift of property'. But 'disposition' in s. 10(7) does not include any provisions in a will, any statutory nomination, and any *donatio mortis causa*.

8.5.1.2 The required intention

What does 'the intention of defeating an application for financial provision under this Act' mean in s. 10(2)(a)? Suppose that Arthur makes *inter vivos* dispositions — intending to reduce his net estate and avoid his will being challenged — but he has never heard of the 1975 Act. Can he be said to have an intention of defeating an application under 'this Act'? On a literal interpretation of s. 10(2)(a) it would seem that he could not have had the required intention; but that would be nonsensical because it would undermine the efficacy of the anti-avoidance measures (few laymen will presumably know of the 1975 Act). Fortunately, the courts have taken the sensible approach. In *Re Kennedy* [1980] CLY 2820, it was held that it was not essential to show that the deceased knew of the provisions of the Act when he made a disposition. But there had to be evidence that he intended to defeat possible claims against his estate made after his death. In *Re Dawkins* [1986] 2 FLR 360, the testator left his wife £8,000 and a life interest in the matrimonial home. Some 15 months before his death he transferred the home to his daughter for £100 (there was evidence that his relationship with his wife had deteriorated). His wife received nothing under his will as he died insolvent. The court ordered the daughter, who had raised £27,000 by selling the house, to pay the wife £10,000. The court was satisfied that the testator had an intention to defeat claims against his estate even if this was not the sole motive for the transfer of the house.

8.5.1.3 Consideration and other matters

Full valuable consideration for the disposition must not have been given by the donee or any other person in order for s. 10 to apply. In *Re Dawkins* (above) it was considered that £100 was not full valuable consideration for a transfer of a house. Under s. 25(1), 'valuable consideration' does not include marriage or a promise of marriage. When the court decides whether and in what manner to exercise its powers under s. 10, it must consider 'the circumstances in which any disposition was made and any valuable consideration which was given therefor, the relationship, if any, of the donee to the deceased, the conduct and financial resources of the donee and all the other circumstances of the case': s. 10(6). Regarding the conduct of the donee, the court is presumably more likely to make an order under s. 10 where the donee's conduct is questionable — for example, if he co-operates with the deceased's attempts to evade the family provision legislation.

8.5.1.4 Position of the donee

The court can order the donee to provide such sum of money or other property as may be specified: s. 10(2). However, s. 10(3) and (4) afford the donee some protection: he cannot be ordered to provide more than the value of the money or the property he received under the disposition. Moreover, s. 10(5) allows a donee to challenge other dispositions made by the deceased. The court may then make orders relating to those dispositions provided that the requirements in s. 10(2) are satisfied.

8.5.2 Contracts: s. 11

Before the 1975 Act, if a person made a contract to leave property by will, that created a contract debt in favour of the intended beneficiary of the contract, resulting in a reduction of the net estate. Section 11 changes the position. The court has power to direct the donee under the contract to provide such sum of money or other property as may be specified 'if any money has been paid or any other property has been transferred to or for the benefit of the donee in accordance with the contract': s. 11(2)(i). Moreover, if money or property has not been paid or transferred in accordance with the contract, the court may order the personal representatives not to make payment except such as may be specified: s. 11(2)(ii).

8.5.2.1 Requirements of s. 11

The court may exercise its powers under s. 11 provided that it is satisfied of the following:

(a) that the deceased made a contract by which he agreed to leave by his will a sum of money or other property to any person or by which he agreed that a sum of money or other property would be paid or transferred to any person out of his estate, and

(b) that the deceased made that contract with the intention of defeating an application for financial provision under this Act, and

(c) that when the contract was made full valuable consideration for that contract was not given or promised by the person with whom or for the benefit of whom the contract was made (in this section referred to as 'the donee') or by any other person, and

(d) that the exercise of the powers conferred by this section would facilitate the making of financial provision for the applicant under this Act . . . (s. 11(2))

The required intention under s. 11(2)(b) is expressed identically to the provision regarding dispositions; thus it is certain that the interpretation of the requirement will be the same as in *Re Kennedy* and *Re Dawkins* above. But unlike the case with dispositions, the intention of defeating an application under the Act can be sometimes *presumed* in the case of contracts. If no valuable consideration was given or promised by any person for a contract, it shall be presumed (unless the contrary is shown) that the deceased made the contract with the intention of defeating an application: s. 12(2). A contract without valuable consideration is *prima facie* more dubious than a disposition made without consideration; hence the difference in the position regarding presumed intention.

In determining whether to exercise its powers under s. 11 — and in what manner — the court must consider 'the circumstances in which the contract was made, the relationship, if any, of the donee to the deceased, the conduct and financial resources of the donee and all the other circumstances of the case': s. 11(4). The court can exercise its powers only to the extent that the value of the property given, or to be given, under the contract exceeds the value of any valuable consideration (the value of the property is that at the date of the hearing): s. 11(3).

8.5.2.2 No time limit

Unlike the case with dispositions, there is no time limit applicable to contracts. In theory s. 11 applies to any contracts, whenever made before the deceased's death, provided that the requirements of s. 11(2) are satisfied. Why this difference between dispositions and contracts? The rationale was explained by the Law Commission (Law Com. No. 61, 1974, para. 237):

In the case of a disposition *inter vivos,* the donor is immediately divesting himself of property and this must in most cases have a restraining effect upon him. In the case of contracts of the kind with which we are concerned there is no similar disincentive, because the deceased remains in full enjoyment of his property during his lifetime. We think that any rule rendering such contracts immune from challenge if made more than a specified period before death might be a positive encouragement to make them. Accordingly we do not recommend any such rule.

8.5.3 Common matters

Apart from the matters already mentioned, there are a number of other provisions common to both dispositions and contracts. In each case the court has the power to give such consequential directions as it thinks fit 'for giving effect to the order or for securing a fair adjustment of the rights of the persons affected thereby': s. 12(3). In each case the court may make an order against the donee's personal representatives, but not in respect of any property of the donee which has been already distributed by them: s. 12(4). In each case the court may make an order against any trustees who held property under the disposition or contract, but only to the extent of the value of the assets held by them at the date of the order: s. 13(1). In each case personal representatives (s. 12(4)) and trustees (s. 13(2)) are not liable for having distributed property on the ground that they should have taken into account the possibility of an application under ss. 10 and 11.

NINE

Alternative Succession

This chapter is concerned with the various ways in which succession to property may occur on death, other than by intestacy or by a will executed under s. 9 of the Wills Act 1837. The subject-matter can be divided for the purposes of exposition broadly into two categories: (i) alternative wills, and (ii) alternative entitlement.

9.1 ALTERNATIVE WILLS

9.1.1 Privileged wills

Certain persons are allowed by reason of their occupation to make wills which need not conform to the formalities required under s. 9 of the Wills Act. Such wills can be made orally as well as in writing, and need not be witnessed. The privilege is allowed to three categories of testator:

(a)   soldiers in actual military service;
(b)   mariners or seamen at sea;
(c)   members of Her Majesty's naval or marine forces in actual military service.

9.1.1.1   Why the privilege?
Prior to 1677, wills of personalty could be made, as a general rule, by oral declaration without any form being necessary. The Statute of Frauds 1677 insisted on certain formalities being followed, but exempted soldiers and seamen from the new requirements. Thus they could make wills of personalty in the same informal manner as before 1677. The privilege was confirmed by the Wills Act 1837 and now applies to realty as well as personalty.

The reason for allowing the privilege was that soldiers and seamen are likely by reason of their occupation to be outside the routine of civilian life and thus have less opportunity and fewer facilities to make a properly executed will, as emphasised by Henn Collins J in *Re Gibson* [1941] 2 All ER 91, at 92: 'The foundation of the rule is that a man is parted from civil surroundings.' The concept of allowing soldiers to make privileged wills may have been derived from Roman law. The Roman soldier was entitled to make an informal will *in expeditione* (while on campaign) because he was *inops consili* (bereft of advice). In *Drummond v Parish* (1843) 3 Curt 522; 163 ER 812, Fust J traced the privilege of making a soldier's will back to Julius Caesar, and suggested that resort should be had to Roman law in order to interpret the English statutes. But the position in English law shows important differences. For example, the English privileged will does not lapse after the end of military service (the Roman will lapsed after a year from discharge from the army). In any case, the original justification for privileged wills — being parted from civil surroundings — became somewhat obscured in time. This was largely due to the changing nature of warfare and military service. The soldier of 1677 could expect lengthy periods away abroad and was hardly a target for the enemy except when actually fighting in a particular locale. Modern warfare has inevitably necessitated some widening of the circumstances in which a privileged will can be made.

Should the privilege be retained? It could be argued that the privilege is an anachronism, originally allowed in circumstances which no longer apply. Soldiers and seamen are far more literate now than in 1677, far more easily able to obtain legal advice, and likely to be away for far shorter periods. The Army encourages soldiers to make wills (in the usual form under s. 9 of the Wills Act 1837) and the same is true of the other services. Moreover, it is arguable that by allowing the privilege to persons in certain occupations, an arbitrary division results whereby certain other possibly deserving categories are excluded (this argument could be used both in favour of expanding or abolishing the categories entitled to make privileged wills). Why should the privilege not be allowed to others engaged for lengthy periods in work 'parted from civil surroundings' — for example, scientists on polar expeditions? The Law Reform Committee considered the abolition of the privilege but in Report No. 22 (1980) recommended retention:

> ... even if not many privileged wills are submitted for probate at present, circumstances can be envisaged when the privilege may again be needed. The Ministry for Defence, for example, was strongly in favour of its retention unaltered for this reason. They also pointed out that, even in peacetime, there were occasional cases of servicemen making privileged wills in the course of certain military operations, giving as an example a case where a soldier in Northern Ireland was fatally injured by terrorists and gave oral instructions as to the disposal of his property. (para. 2.21)

Nevertheless, there is much to be said for restricting the present scope of the privilege. Such wills are, after all, an exception to the fundamental requirement that wills should be made in writing, signed by the testator and duly attested. There are good reasons for insisting on such minimum formalities, not least because they reduce the potential for argument about whether a will was made and what its contents are. It follows that if an exception is to be allowed, then it should be carefully circumscribed. Certainly in some of the cases it is difficult to justify why the privilege was allowed. Given the infrequency of privileged wills, it might be preferable to treat each on an *ad hoc* basis, requiring it to be shown that the testator had no reasonable opportunity to make a will in the normal form under s. 9.

9.1.1.2   Soldier in actual military service

Under s. 11 of the Wills Act 1837, a privileged will may be made by 'any soldier being in actual military service'. The term now includes a member of the Royal Air Force: Wills (Soldiers and Sailors) Act 1918. The required status has to be satisfied at the time of the making of the will; hence it is irrelevant whether or not the testator was in actual military service when he died.

(a)   Soldier   The judges have generally shied away from defining the meaning of 'soldier', being mostly content to decide in individual cases whether the testator has qualified as such. It is clear, however, that the word connotes more than just those engaged in fighting — it includes, for example, doctors, nurses, and chaplains serving with the forces. In *In the Estate of Rowson* [1944] 2 All ER 36, it was held that a member of the Women's Royal Auxiliary Air Force serving in the balloon command was privileged. Civilians who work with the armed forces are 'soldiers': *In the Estate of Stanley* [1916] P 192, where a nurse serving under contract to the War Office on hospital ships was held to be entitled to the privilege. A civilian engineer employed by the United States Army in the South Pacific was held to be a soldier, despite being issued with a certificate describing him as a 'Noncombatant': *In the Application of White* [1975] 2 NSWLR 125, where being a soldier was equated with being subject to military law (which the engineer was).

Although the vast majority of the cases have concerned members of the British Armed Forces, it appears that this is not a prerequisite of being regarded as a soldier under s. 11. The privilege has been applied, for example, to a surgeon in the military service of the East India Company: *In the Goods of Donaldson* (1840) 2 Curt 386; 163 ER 448. However, it is doubtful whether the privilege applies to mercenary soldiers.

(b)   Actual military service   The testator must be in actual military service when the will is made. Clearly the legislature did not intend that every soldier should be entitled to make a privileged will, only those in actual military service. What does 'actual military service' entail? Consider *Re Wingham* [1949] P 187, CA: the testator joined the Royal Air Force during the Second World War and was sent to Saskatchewan, Canada to complete his training. There he made an unattested will and died a few months later in an aircraft accident. The court unanimously held that the testator was entitled to make a privileged will. Bucknill LJ stated (at pp. 191–2):

I do not think the test is whether the airman was in danger from enemy action at the time when the will is made ... In my opinion the tests are: (a) was the testator 'on military service'? (b) was such service 'active'? In my opinion the adjective 'active' in this connexion confines military service to such service as is directly concerned with operations in a war which is or has been in progress or is imminent.

Applying these tests Bucknill LJ found that the testator was on active service when the will was made since *inter alia* he was at any time liable to be ordered to some area to take part in active warfare. Cohen LJ gave a similar judgment, but Denning LJ perhaps went further than his colleagues:

Doubtful cases may arise in peacetime when a soldier is in, or is about to be sent to, a disturbed area or an isolated post, where he may be involved in military operations. As to these cases, all I say is that, in case of doubt, the serving soldier should be given the benefit of the privilege.

While one can readily understand the concern for soldiers engaged in military operations — whether in peacetime or otherwise — the application to doubtful cases of what is an exception to a fundamental rule in the law of succession is questionable. Nevertheless it would have been harsh to deny the privilege in *Re Jones* [1981] 1 All ER 1, the facts of which raised one of the 'doubtful' scenarios envisaged by Lord Denning (military operations in 'a disturbed area' in peacetime). The testator was a soldier serving in Northern Ireland in 1978 'at a time of armed and clandestine insurrection against the government'. His unit was stationed there at the request of the civil authorities to assist in the maintenance of law and order. He was shot (by an unknown gunman) while on patrol and died the following day. On the way to hospital he told the other members of his patrol, 'If I don't make it, make sure Anne gets all my stuff' (Anne was his fiancée). He had previously made a written will in favour of his mother. It was held that whether the soldier was in actual military service when he made the oral will in Anne's favour depended on the nature of the activities of the deceased and the unit to which he was attached. The fact that a state of war did not exist, or that the enemy was not a uniformed force engaged in regular warfare, was irrelevant. On the facts the testator was held to be clearly in actual military service. It was this case in particular which led to the recommendation by the Ministry of Defence to the Law Reform Committee that privileged wills should not be abolished (above). That peacekeeping operations at times of insurrection and civil order may amount to actual military service was made clear in *In the Goods of Tweedale* (1874) LR 3 P & D 204, where an officer with the Bengal Cavalry was held to be privileged when engaged in quelling disturbances in a region of India. A similar decision was reached in *In the Will of Anderson* (1958) 75 WN (NSW) 334 regarding an Australian soldier engaged in suppressing terrorist activity in Malaya in 1956.

A soldier can be in actual military service even though no military operations have occurred provided that they are believed to be imminent, as is clear from the test laid down by Bucknill LJ in *Re Wingham* (above). It seems that receiving orders to join a unit in such circumstances will suffice. In *Re Rippon* [1943] P 61, the testator, an officer in the Territorial Army, made a will in August 1939 after being ordered to rejoin his artillery battery, but before the Territorial Army was embodied and mobilised. It was held that he had been on actual military service when he made his will. Just as actual military service can begin before the commencement of military operations, so it can continue long after they have ceased, as was demonstrated in *Re Colman* [1958] 2 All ER 35: a soldier on leave in England in 1954 from the British Army of the Rhine was held to be entitled to make a privileged will since he was part of an army of occupation *in situ* as the result of hostilities in the Second World War.

9.1.1.3 Mariner or seaman at sea
Section 11 of the Wills Act 1837 allows 'any mariner or seaman being at sea' to make a privileged will.

(a) Mariner or seaman The term 'mariner or seaman' includes not only members of the merchant navy and Royal Navy but also anyone serving in essentially a civilian capacity in the merchant navy. Thus in *In the Estate of Knibbs* [1962] 2 All ER 829, a barman on a liner was held to be entitled to make a privileged will, although in the event he failed to make one (see 3.2.2). Similarly, in *In the Goods of Hale* [1915] 2 IR 362, a typist regularly employed on ocean-going liners was held to be a 'seaman'. She worked for the Cunard Steamship Company primarily on the Liverpool-New York crossing, and was one of the victims when the *Lusitania* was sunk by a German submarine in May 1915 (one of the most notorious incidents in the early months of the First World War). In doubtful cases it is important to focus on the rationale of allowing the privilege, namely the removal from normal civilian life of certain persons *by reason of their occupation*. Thus a lone round-the-world yachtsman is probably not to be regarded as a 'seaman' unless his sailing can be regarded as his occupation (rather than just as a hobby). But a pilot working a boat on the tidal portion of the river Mersey (part of the Manchester Ship Canal) may be a 'seaman' — this possibility was raised in *Hodson v Barnes* (1926) 43 TLR 71 (see 4.2.1).

(b) At sea What is the meaning of 'at sea'? The term has been interpreted widely. Maritime service on lakes, rivers and canals can generally be considered as being 'at sea'. For example, in *In the Goods of Austen* (1853) 2 Rob 611; 163 ER 1431, a codicil made by Admiral Austen while on a naval expedition on the Rangoon river was held to be privileged. However, each case will turn on its facts: presumably some stretches of water will be considered not to be compatible with maritime service (because of their small size or because they are not navigable).

What if the will is made on board the ship while it is docked — is the testator 'at sea'? Certainly, even it seems if the ship is permanently docked: *In the Goods of M'Murdo* (1867) 1 P & D 540. But can a seaman be said to be 'at sea' if he makes a will on land? Sarah Hale, the testatrix in *In the Goods of Hale* (above) actually made her will in the Liverpool offices of Cunard after

receiving notification of her next voyage. It was held that the will had been
written when Sarah was preparing for the voyage; hence she was 'at sea' (the
analogy can be made with soldiers receiving call-up orders, as in *Re Rippon* (see
above). In *Re Newland's Estate* [1952] 1 All ER 841, the testator, an apprentice
in the merchant navy, made a will while he was on shore leave (his ship was
being refitted in Liverpool). He was held to be entitled to make a privileged will,
the judge inferring from the facts that the testator had received instructions to
rejoin his ship for the next voyage. Compare, however, *Re Rapley's Estate*
[1983] 3 All ER 248, where the facts were similar except that the testator had
been discharged from his previous ship and had not yet been instructed to join
another ship when he made his will. If such a distinction seems over-fine,
it has at least the merit of being reasonably easy to apply. Moreover, it can be
said in favour of the decision in *Re Rapley's Estate* that to have allowed the
privilege would have rendered the term 'at sea' almost meaningless. Finlay J,
QC stated (at p. 254):

> The cases have gone very far to extend the meaning of 'at sea' to include
> those who are in a state of preparation for going to sea, being under orders to
> do so, but to go beyond that and to extend the ambit of the section to cover
> the case where a mariner or seaman is on furlough or leave, knows well that
> he may at any time be instructed to join another ship but has not at the
> moment received such instructions is, I think, to extend the operation of the
> section beyond the circumstances which were no doubt in the contemplation
> of the legislature. . . .

9.1.1.4 Royal naval personnel in actual military service
Under s. 2 of the Wills (Soldiers and Sailors) Act 1918, any member of Her
Majesty's naval or marine forces may make a privileged will, though not at sea,
if he is 'so circumstanced that if he were a soldier he would be in actual military
service'. Fighting naval men are thus placed in the same position as soldiers.
For example, where an officer in the Royal Navy made an oral will at a railway
station in England, having received orders to join his ship in Cape Town, it was
held that he was entitled to make a valid privileged will: *In the Estate of
Yates* [1919] P 93.

9.1.1.5 Formalities
Privileged wills can be made without any formalities. Writing is not required —
an oral will is perfectly valid. Nor are witnesses or attestation required; but in
practice it is difficult to see how an oral will can be upheld unless there is some
evidence from a witness as to what the testator said. In many cases of privileged
wills the testator in fact attempted to make a properly executed written will but
failed to satisfy the requirements of s. 9 of the Wills Act 1837 — hence it was
necessary in such cases to argue that the testator was entitled to the privilege.
If, on the other hand, the testator succeeds in executing a will that satisfies s. 9,
it obviously matters not whether he was privileged or not. Since witnesses are
not required (in theory) for a privileged will, it is irrelevant whether or not a

witness is a beneficiary. The witness can keep the benefit — s. 15 of the Wills Act 1837 does not apply. In *Re Limond* [1915] 2 Ch 240, the testator was mortally wounded by a 'fanatic' while serving with the Punjab Infantry in frontier operations in India. Before he died he dictated a will to his brother-in-law, whom he made his residuary legatee. The will was signed by the testator and attested by his brother-in-law and another officer. It was held that since the will was privileged, s. 15 did not apply: the brother-in-law could take.

It may be thought that since no form is required to make a privileged will, such a will is in some sense 'inferior' compared to one properly executed under s. 9. But that is not the position: a privileged will counts as a fully valid will. Consequently, it will revoke *any* prior will to the extent of any inconsistency. Moreover, once made, a privileged will endures in the same way as one executed under s. 9. It does not lapse by virtue of the testator ceasing to be privileged. In *Re Booth* [1926] P 118, it was argued that the rule of Roman law that a soldier's will lapsed following discharge from service was part of English law. The argument was rejected: a privileged will remains operative until revoked. Furthermore, a privileged will can serve the same functions as an ordinary will.

Although no particular formalities need be satisfied to make a privileged will, the testator must have *animus testandi*, as in the case of an ordinary will. Some of the leading cases on *animus testandi* — for example, *Re Knibbs, Re Stable* — were concerned with privileged wills (see 3.2.2).

9.1.1.6 Minors
It will be recalled that under s. 7 of the Wills Act 1837, a valid will cannot be made by a person under 18 years of age. But privileged testators are not subject to that provision: soldiers and seamen who are minors — it is possible to join the Armed Forces or the merchant navy while under 18 — can make a privileged will by virtue of s. 1 of the Wills (Soldiers and Sailors) Act 1918. Minors can revoke privileged wills, as well as making them, but what if a minor ceases to be privileged after making a will? Under s. 3(3) of the Family Law Reform Act 1969, a privileged will may be revoked by a minor even though he is no longer entitled to make such a will.

9.1.1.7 Revocation
A privileged will revokes any prior will (whether privileged or not) and can itself be revoked by any of the methods of revocation under ss. 18 and 20 of the Wills Act 1837. For example, in *In the Estate of Wardrop* [1917] P 54 it was held that wills made by soldiers and sailors were revoked by the subsequent marriage of the testator. But what is the position regarding the methods of revocation by privileged testators? Clearly they can revoke any prior will by any of the methods under ss. 18 and 20. In addition, a privileged testator can revoke any prior will by an informal writing declaring an intention to revoke: *In the Estate of Gossage* [1921] P 194, CA. The testator made a properly executed will, having received orders to proceed with his unit to South Africa. The will was handed in a sealed envelope to his fiancée, the residuary legatee. Later, having

been informed about the fiancée's conduct, the testator wrote to her requesting that she hand the will to his sister (which she did). Later still he wrote an unattested letter to his sister asking her to burn the will. It was held that this letter revoked the will since it contained a clear intention to revoke it. The decision is justifiable on the ground that since a person can make a privileged will without any formalities, he should be able to revoke any will in similar fashion. It would seem to follow that an oral statement, such as 'I revoke my prior will', should suffice as an express revocation (although no reported case appears to have dealt with this point).

If a person, whilst privileged, alters a privileged will, he can do so without having to satisfy the alteration formalities under s. 21 of the Wills Act 1837; moreover, a presumption arises in such cases that the alteration was made whilst the testator was still privileged: *In the Goods of Tweedale* (1874) 3 P & D 204. On principle, a person should be able, whilst privileged, to alter *any* will informally (whether the will was privileged or not).

9.1.2 Statutory wills

A statutory will is a will executed on behalf of a mental patient under the Mental Health Act 1983. Under s. 96 the Court of Protection (the Chancery Division) can authorise the execution of a will, 'making any provision . . . which could be made by a will executed by the patient if he were not mentally disordered'. However, a statutory will cannot dispose of immovable property outside England and Wales. A person can become a patient under the 1983 Act if he is incapable of managing his affairs, and the Court can authorise a will if it has reason to believe that the patient is incapable of making a valid will: s. 96(4). *Re Davey* [1980] 3 All ER 342, provides a somewhat dramatic illustration of the exercise of this power. A 92-year-old testatrix, Olive, made a will (soon after entering a nursing home) in which she benefited a large number of relatives. A few weeks later she went through a marriage ceremony at a register office with an employee at the home (aged 48) in suspicious circumstances. The effect of the marriage was to revoke the will. Soon afterwards Olive was placed under the Court of Protection (but not literally) and a statutory will was quickly executed on her behalf in the same terms as the earlier will. The husband was not given notice of the proceedings, speed being thought to be of the essence given Olive's poor state of health. It was held that in the circumstances the Court was entitled not to notify the husband. If he was unhappy about the execution of the statutory will, he could apply for a fresh one to be made or, if Olive died, he could claim for reasonable financial provision under the Inheritance (Provision for Family and Dependants) Act 1975.

9.1.2.1 Formalities
The Court of Protection empowers 'the authorised person' (usually the receiver put in charge of the patient's affairs) to execute the will. Under s. 97(1), the will shall be expressed to be signed by the patient acting by the authorised person, and shall be —

(a)   signed by the authorised person with the name of the patient, and with his own name, in the presence of two or more witnesses present at the same time, and

(b)   attested and subscribed by those witnesses in the presence of the authorised person, and

(c)   sealed with the official seal of the Court of Protection.

9.1.2.2   Exercise of the jurisdiction

What guidelines are there as to the content of a statutory will? The Act authorises any provisions which the patient could have made 'if he were not mentally disordered', but this guidance is not especially illuminating. However, in *Re D (J)* [1982] 2 All ER 37, the court laid down several important principles to aid the making of a statutory will. A testatrix made a will devising her house to one of her daughters (A) and leaving the residuary estate to the testatrix's five children. She sold the house (thus adeeming the devise) and bought another one, but insisted on moving in with A. The expense of looking after the testatrix was borne by A and her husband. Eventually the testatrix became a patient under the Court of Protection and A applied for a statutory codicil to be made for the testatrix. There was disagreement between the five children as to how the estate (worth £50,000 inclusive of £22,000 from the sale of the new house) should be disposed of in the will, although it was conceded that A was entitled to the greatest share. It was held that A should receive £15,000 and that the residue should be divided equally between all five children. Megarry VC enumerated five principles (partly based on previous cases), but described them as not 'exhaustive or very precise'. First, it is to be assumed that the patient is having a brief lucid interval at the time when the will is made; secondly, that during the lucid interval the patient has a full knowledge of the past, and a full realisation that as soon as the will is executed the patient will relapse into the actual mental state that previously existed, with the prognosis as it actually is; thirdly, that it is the actual patient who has to be considered and not a hypothetical patient (thus a subjective rather than an objective approach needs to be adopted); fourthly, that during the hypothetical lucid interval the patient is to be envisaged as being advised by competent solicitors who know, for example, about lapse and ademption, and who will draw attention to matters which the testator should bear in mind. The fifth principle was expressed thus (at p. 43):

> ... in all normal cases the patient is to be envisaged as taking a broad brush to the claims on his bounty, rather than an accountant's pen. There will be nothing like a balance sheet or profit and loss account. There may be many to whom the patient feels morally indebted; and some of that moral indebtedness may be readily expressible in terms of money, and some of it may not.

The third principle enumerated above — that it is the actual patient who must be considered — may require modification in certain circumstances. In *Re C (a patient)* [1991] 3 All ER 866, a statutory will was made on behalf of an elderly patient who enjoyed *(inter alia)* music, the sound of birds and the smell of flowers, but who had never been capable of managing her own affairs and who had lived at a hospital since an early age. Adopting a subjective approach would obviously have been inappropriate — the patient had never had a sufficient mind of her own to guide the court. She had inherited an estate of £1,600,000 from her parents. She had several relations, but they had shown little or no interest in her; the only persons to take an interest in the patient were the staff and other patients at the hospital, and a member of a voluntary organisation which befriended mental patients. The court held that it should be assumed that the patient was 'a normal decent person, acting in accordance with contemporary standards of morality' (p. 870). A person in that position would feel an obligation to recognise the community (as well as her family) since she had spent virtually the whole of her life in the care of the community. The court ordered immediate gifts of £100,000 to a charity connected with the hospital and £400,000 to the next-of-kin; and it directed that a will be executed for the patient dividing the residuary estate between the charity and the family in equal shares.

Under s. 95 of the Mental Health Act 1983 *inter vivos* dispositions may be authorised by the Court of Protection on behalf of a patient, as occurred in *Re S (Gifts By Mental Patient)* [1997] 1 FLR 96. An elderly spinster who has been in care for virtually all her life was entitled to a large estate for greater than her current and prospective needs. The Court authorised the making of *inter vivos* gifts under s. 95, and a statutory will under s. 96, in the proportions of 25% to charity and 75% to her next-of-kin.

9.1.3 Foreign and international wills

9.1.3.1 Foreign wills
A person may succeed to property under a will made abroad. The position is governed by the rules on succession of the English Conflict of Laws, a subject essentially outside the scope of this book. Hence only a brief outline of the position will be attempted (for a fuller account see Theobald, *Wills*, 15th edn, 1993, chapter 1).

A fundamental distinction must be drawn between movables and immovables. The distinction is not the same as that between realty and personalty because *all* interests in land are regarded as interests in immovables. The general position is that succession to movables is governed by the law of the testator's domicile, whereas succession to immovables is governed by the *lex situs* (the law of the country where the immovables are situated). As regards formalities, however, the Wills Act 1963 prescribes special rules. Under s. 1, a will is treated as properly executed 'if its execution conformed to the internal law in force in the territory where it was executed, or in the territory where, at the time of its execution or of the testator's death, he was domiciled or had his habitual residence, or in a state of which, at either of those times, he was a national'. In addition, a will is valid — as regards immovables — 'if its execution conformed to the internal law in force in the territory where the property was situated': s. 2(1)(b). Moreover, if a will was executed on board a vessel or aircraft, it will be regarded as properly executed if the execution conformed to 'the internal law in force in the territory with which, having regard to its registration (if any) and other relevant circumstances, the vessel or aircraft may be taken to have been most closely connected'.

As regards capacity to make a will, it appears that in the case of movables capacity is governed by the law of the testator's domicile at the date of the will's execution; in the case of immovables capacity is governed by the *lex situs*. Where questions as to 'essential validity' arise — for example, whether certain gifts are valid or whether family members are entitled to fixed rights of inheritance — the matter is governed by the law of the testator's domicile at his death as regards movables; in the case of immovables the relevant law is the *lex situs*. Where problems of construction arise, the general rule is that the will should be construed according to the law intended by the testator, which is presumed to be the law of his domicile when the will was executed. The presumption is subject to any contrary intention appearing in the will.

9.1.3.2 International wills

The Washington Convention on the Form of an International Will 1973 agreed on the form of a will which would be regarded as valid — in any country that ratified the Convention — irrespective of the nationality, domicile or residence of the testator, or the place of the will's execution or the location of the testator's assets. Sections 27 and 28 of the Administration of Justice Act 1982 provide for the incorporation of the international will into the law of the United Kingdom. The provisions will be made operative on a date to be fixed by statutory instrument (apparently not fixed as yet).

The requirements of an international will are essentially an amalgam of the English formalities under s. 9 of the Wills Act 1837 and the continental notarial will. The main difference from the s. 9 will is the need for an 'authorised person' (a solicitor or notary public) whose function is to be present at the execution of the will and to issue a certificate that the formalities have been carried out. The grant of the certificate is conclusive as to the satisfaction of the formalities unless evidence is adduced to the contrary. The chief requirements of the international will are that the will must be in writing; the testator must declare that the document is his will, and that he knows the contents, in the presence of the authorised person and at least two witnesses; the testator must sign or acknowledge his signature in their presence; the witnesses and the authorised person must then attest the will in the presence of the testator; all the signatures (including the testator's) must be placed at the end of the will. Of course, even if a will fails to satisfy the form required of an international will, it may nevertheless be operative as a will under s. 9 or as a foreign will within the English Conflict of Laws rules.

9.2 ALTERNATIVE ENTITLEMENT

This section is concerned with the miscellaneous ways in which succession on death may occur other than by will or intestacy.

9.2.1   Nominations

A nomination is a written direction, by a person with an interest in certain funds or investments, to the body holding the relevant funds to transfer them (or an interest in them) to the nominee. Nominations can be classified as statutory or non-statutory.

9.2.1.1   Statutory nominations

Originally, statutory nominations were conceived as a form of poor man's will, enabling holders of funds in certain bodies to dispose of their interests, normally within a maximum limit, without the necessity for making a will. The bodies included Trustee Savings Banks, the National Savings Bank, friendly societies, industrial and provident societies and trade unions. The legal nature of nominations was expounded by Lord Mersey in *Eccles Provident Industrial Co-operative Society Ltd* v *Griffiths* [1912] AC 483. He stated (at p. 490) that the object of the statutory power of nomination with which the case was concerned was to give 'the poorer members of a society' the power to make provision for the disposal of a small sum without the expense of making a will or having that part of their estate administered. He continued:

> Once made the nomination takes effect, not by creating any charge or trust in favour of the nominee as against the nominator ... but by giving to the nominee a right as against the society, in the event of the death of the member without having revoked the nomination, to require the society to transfer the property in accordance with the nomination. Until death the property is the property of the member, and all benefits accruing in respect of it during his lifetime are his also.

The current maximum limit on nominations is £5,000: Administration of Estates (Small Payments) (Increase of Limit) Order 1984. The formal requirements for nominations vary according to the rules of the particular fund-holder. Nominations must always be in writing; it is usual for an attesting witness to be required and for the nomination to be kept at an office of the relevant body. In *Pearman* v *Charlton* (1928) 44 TLR 517, a nomination of a sum in a Post Office Savings Bank account was held invalid because of breach of the statutory regulations. The nomination had to be signed in the presence of the witness, but there was no evidence that it had been (despite the appearance of the witness's name on the relevant form). Like a will, a nomination is ambulatory and revocable. The nominator may revoke the nomination by complying with the requirements of the relevant statute. But a nomination cannot be revoked by a subsequent will or codicil; this is an important point to be remembered in practice, especially as there is a danger that nominations can easily be forgotten about. However, the marriage of the nominator does revoke a prior nomination. What if the nominee predeceases the nominator? The rule is that the nomination lapses — the assets remain part of the nominator's estate and do not pass to the nominee's estate: *Re Barnes* [1940] 1 Ch 267.

It can thus be seen that nominations, although differing from wills, do have certain testamentary characteristics. Indeed, if a nomination is executed like a will but fails to satisfy the necessary statutory formalities (for a nomination), it may nevertheless take effect as a will: *In the Goods of Baxter* [1903] P 12, where the deceased nominated the whole of his assets in favour of his nephew (amounting to over £120). The nomination was invalid since the maximum limit was £100. However, the court held that the nomination could be admitted as a will since it satisfied s. 9 of the Wills Act 1837. Nominations that exceed the maximum are now generally treated as valid up to the limit.

9.2.1.2 Non-statutory nominations

Non-statutory nominations — described as 'odd creatures' by Megarry J in *Re Danish Bacon Co. Ltd; Christensen v Arnett* [1971] 1 All ER 486 — are often used to dispose of assets in pension schemes or the proceeds of life insurance policies. As these assets frequently constitute a sizeable fund on the death of the deceased, the importance of such nominations is obvious. In some pension schemes entitlement on death is fixed by the terms of the scheme. In a contributory pension scheme the trustees will normally have the power to dispose of the fund on the deceased's death in their discretion, but in practice will be guided by his nomination (if any) as to whom the benefits should be paid. There is an important difference from the way in which statutory nominations operate. There the deceased's directions are binding (assuming that the nomination is executed correctly) since they deal with assets to which he is beneficially entitled. But in the case of a non-statutory nomination the deceased's direction is simply the expression of a wish to trustees as to how to distribute the assets (which they will normally implement).

In *Re Danish Bacon Co. Ltd v Arnett*, it was argued that a nomination under an employer's pension scheme was essentially a testamentary disposition and therefore should be executed like a will. It was held, however, that the nomination operated by reason of the rules of the pension scheme and not as a testamentary disposition by the deceased. Hence it did not have to be executed in accordance with s. 9 of the Wills Act 1837. The decision was followed by the Privy Council in *Baird v Baird* [1990] 2 All ER 300, where the deceased nominated his brother as beneficiary of a pension scheme to which the nominator contributed as an employee of Texaco Trinidad Inc. Later the nominator married but did not vary the nomination. On his death his widow argued that the nomination was invalid since it had not been executed like a will. The argument was rejected — the brother took the pension benefits. This case illustrates another important difference between statutory and non-statutory nominations: the former are revoked by subsequent marriage, the latter are not.

9.2.2 *Donatio mortis causa*

9.2.2.1 Introduction

A *donatio mortis causa* in English law is a gift made in contemplation of death. The gift is made in the donor's lifetime but operates fully only on death. Thus such gifts are hybrid in character: they are like *inter vivos* gifts because they are made *inter vivos*, but they are testamentary in the sense of operating on death, as explained by Buckley J in *Re Beaumont* [1902] 1 Ch 889, at 892:

> A *donatio mortis causa* is a singular form of gift. It may be said to be of an amphibious nature, being a gift which is neither entirely *inter vivos* nor testamentary. It is an act *inter vivos* by which the donee is to have the absolute title to the subject of the gift not at once but if the donor dies.

The most likely scenario for a *donatio mortis causa* is where the donor is seriously ill and is either unwilling or unable to make a will. The concept appears to date in English law from the early-eighteenth century and was largely borrowed from Roman law. In *Sen* v *Headley* [1991] 2 All ER 636, CA, Nourse LJ stated (at 639) that there were three general requirements for a valid *donatio mortis causa*:

> First, the gift must be made in contemplation, although not necessarily in expectation, of impending death. Secondly, the gift must be made upon the condition that it is absolute and perfected only on the donor's death, being revocable until that event occurs and ineffective if it does not. Thirdly, there must be a delivery of the subject-matter of the gift, or the essential indicia of title thereto, which amounts to a parting with dominion and not mere physical possession over the subject-matter of the gift.

9.2.2.2 Contemplation of death

It is insufficient to contemplate death sometime in the future — the donor must be considering the probability of death in the near future. In *Re Craven's Estate* [1937] Ch 423, the donor instructed her son to put certain moneys and securities in her bank in Monaco into his own name. She wished the property to be his in the event of her death, and had in mind a pending operation which might prove fatal (which it did). It was held that a valid *donatio mortis causa* had been made. Farwell J held that the donor must be contemplating 'death within the near future, what may be called death for some reason believed to be impending' (p. 426). However, it is not necessary that the donor should be contemplating death immediately or that he should be on his deathbed.

What if the donor dies from a cause other than that contemplated? In *Wilkes* v *Allington* [1931] 2 Ch 104, the donor transferred the mortgage deeds of a farm to his nieces. He was at that time suffering from cancer, had refused to undergo an operation and considered himself as 'a man under sentence of death'. A month later he caught a chill on a bus journey and died of pneumonia. It was held that the gift was valid. It was not necessary that the donor should have died from the same cause that he was contemplating when he made the gift, provided that he was still contemplating death when he died. But suppose that the donor's belief in impending death is mistaken — for example, the donor believes that he is dying from an incurable disease when that is not the case. Or suppose that the donor has a phobia about flying and makes a *donatio mortis causa* before travelling by aeroplane. Is the gift made in contemplation of death in these circumstances? In principle what should matter is the donor's actual state of mind when making the gift and not whether the donor's belief was mistaken or irrational. There is an absence of clear authority on this issue. In *Thompson* v *Mechan* [1958] OR 357 (Ontario), the court applied an objective test of contemplation of death. A purported *donatio mortis causa* was made by a businessman shortly before boarding a flight in Toronto for Winnipeg. Although he thought that air travel was very perilous, the court held that he had not made a *donatio mortis causa* since he could not be considered to be in peril 'from a cause that exists only in his fancy or imagination and where in fact, he is exposed to no more than the ordinary risks that affect mankind in ordinary and natural movements and pursuits' (*per* Roach JA at p. 365). For a different approach see *Re Miller* (1961) 105 Sol Jo 207.

What if the *donatio* is made in contemplation of the donor's suicide? In *Re Dudman* [1925] Ch 553, the donor gave her brother envelopes containing money and letters. One of the letters showed clear evidence of an intention to commit suicide. The donor committed suicide shortly afterwards. The court followed an Irish decision, *Agnew* v *Belfast Banking Co.* [1896] 2 IR 204, which had held that contemplation of suicide was insufficient. These decisions were reached at a time when suicide was a crime and it was felt that a gift arising through contemplation of a crime could not be valid. However, since the Suicide Act 1961 it is no longer a crime to commit suicide; thus there no longer seems any objection in principle to the making of a *donatio mortis causa* through contemplation of suicide. Moreover, it has been held that where the donor makes the gift in contemplation of death from illness (but not suicide) the gift is valid even if the donor later kills himself: *Mills* v *Shields* [1948] IR 367.

9.2.2.3   Gift intended to be conditional on death

The donor must intend the gift to be conditional on his death. Thus there is no *donatio mortis causa* if his intention is to make an immediate *inter vivos* gift or a gift at some time in the future. Until death the gift is fully revocable; moreover, if the condition is not satisfied, the property reverts to the donor. Suppose that Arthur has an irresistible compulsion to climb the Eiger mountain. Fearing — as a novice climber — that he will perish in the attempt, he makes a gift in contemplation of death. Once he safely negotiates the mountain, the gift is of no effect — Arthur's survival of the peril from which he feared death results in the gift being revoked. Thus, if Arthur is killed in a road accident whilst driving back to his hotel, the gift does not take effect — Arthur was no longer contemplating death when he died. But if the donor dies whilst contemplating death, albeit from a different cause than the one contemplated, the gift takes effect: *Wilkes* v *Allington* (above).

The intention that the gift is conditional on death will often be expressed by the donor, but it can be implied from the circumstances. For example, in *Gardner* v *Parker* (1818) 3 Madd 184; 56 ER 478, the donor, who was seriously ill and confined to bed, gave the donee (with whom he was on intimate terms) a bond for £1,800 saying 'There, take that and keep it'. It was held that it could be inferred that the donor's intention was that the bond should be held as a gift only if he died. Can the gift be regarded as conditional on death if the donor thinks his imminent death is certain? In principle, even if the donor believes imminent death to be certain, that does not preclude him from having the intention that the gift should take effect only when he dies. If the 'certain death' argument had been adopted by the English courts, the number of cases in which a *donatio mortis causa* was held to be valid would have been greatly diminished (because in many of them the donor believed death was certain).

9.2.2.4 Delivery of the subject-matter
The donor must deliver the subject-matter of the gift to the donee. This requirement involves both an intention and an act on the part of the donor.

(a) Intention The donor must intend to part with dominion over the property comprised in the gift. Parting with dominion consists of enabling the donee to take control of the property. In *Reddel* v *Dobree* (1839) 10 Sim 244; 59 ER 607, the donor's health was deteriorating. After visiting a physician he delivered a locked cash-box to the donee and told her to obtain the key for the box after his death from his son. He added that the box contained money for her and her sister 'after I am gone' and asked her to bring the box to him every three months while he was alive. It was held that there was no valid *donatio mortis causa* since the donor clearly did not intend to part with control over the cash-box. In *Wildish* v *Fowler* (1892) 8 TLR 457, HL, the donor, 'a very nervous man and particularly apprehensive of sudden death', was taken ill at his lodgings. While his landlady was helping him to undress he gave her a small parcel, saying 'Take care of this'. She locked up the parcel in a book-case belonging to the donor. After the donor's death the parcel was found to contain money totalling over £1,600. Previously, the donor had given her a present of cash sufficient to buy two houses. The court held that there was no *donatio mortis causa* of the parcel — there were no words of gift and the landlady had acted merely as an 'attendant' for the purposes of safekeeping the property. A similar decision was reached in *Trimmer* v *Danby* (1856) 25 LJ Ch 424, which concerned the estate of J.M.W. Turner, the greatest of all English painters. Turner gave Hannah Danby, his housekeeper for some 40 years, the key to a box containing money bonds, five of which were intended for her. It was argued that this constituted a valid *donatio mortis causa* in her favour. Kindersley VC held that the key was given to her 'in the character of her being the housekeeper . . . for the purpose of taking care of it for his benefit' and 'not in the character of beneficial owner of the property' (p. 426).

(b) Delivery It is essential that the delivery is made in the lifetime of the donor: *Bunn* v *Markham* (1816) 7 Taunt 224; 129 ER 90, where a direction that parcels containing money should be delivered to the donees after the donor's death was held to be insufficient. The delivery must be of the property comprised in the gift, or of the means of controlling it. For example, the delivery of the only keys to a box, locker or chest will suffice. In *Re Lillingston* [1952] 2 All ER 184, the donor, a permanent resident at a hotel, was

nursed by the hotel manageress, Edith. She handed Edith the key to a trunk in her bedroom, saying that she wanted Edith to have all her jewellery, and that the trunk contained the key to her safe deposit at Harrods, which contained a key to a city safe containing more jewellery. Edith was told that she could obtain the jewellery from the deposits after the donor's death; and the donor said 'Keep the key, it is now yours'. It was held that there had been a valid *donatio mortis causa* of all the jewellery in the trunk and in the Harrods and city safes. Wynn-Parry J stated (at p. 191) that 'it does not matter in how many boxes the subject of a gift may be contained or that each, except the last, contains a key which opens the next, so long as the scope of the gift is made clear'. In *Re Mustapha* (1891) 8 TLR 160, the donor, fearing that he was dying, said to one of his daughters, 'Lulu, dear, take my purse and keys'. Lulu did so, whereupon the donor said 'That is right; put them in your pocket; take the bonds; all is yours'. The keys were to a wardrobe which contained the key of a safe in which were found very valuable bonds. It was held that a valid *donatio mortis causa* had been made in Lulu's favour.

What if the donor gives the donee keys to the property but retains other keys to the same property? In *Re Craven's Estate* (see 9.2.2.2) the view was taken that the retention of a key by a donor could indicate that the donee was not given exclusive control over the property. Consider, however, *Woodard v Woodard* [1995] 3 All ER 980, CA: the donor was in hospital suffering from leukaemia. His car was in the possession of his son. Shortly before the donor's death, he told the son 'You can keep the keys, I won't be driving it any more'. The son did not have the car's registration document and it was not clear whether the donor had retained another set of keys. Nevertheless it was held that there was a sufficient intention to part with dominion, because even if the donor had a second set of keys, he was very unlikely to use the car again in the circumstances. And it was irrelevant that the son already had possession of the car and a set of keys, since the words of gift 'can operate to change the nature of the possession from possession as bailee to possession as donee' (p. 984).

As regards the delivery of choses in action, the position depends on the type involved. If the chose in action is transferable by delivery (for example banknotes or the bonds in *Re Mustapha*) the normal rule applies — that is, there must be actual delivery of the property or of the means of controlling it. Where, however, the chose in action is not transferable by delivery, there must either be a legal transfer of the property, or the delivery of some document which constitutes the essential *indicia* of title. In *Birch v Treasury Solicitor* [1951] Ch 298, CA, the donor, a frail elderly woman, was severely injured in an accident and died a month later. While in hospital she was regularly visited by a married couple, her closest friends (she had no blood relations). On one visit she told the wife to collect from her flat a black bag containing several bank books. The donor made it clear that she wanted the couple to have the money in the banks 'if anything happens to me'. The issue was whether a valid *donatio mortis causa* had been made of the moneys in certain accounts identified respectively by a Post Office Savings Bank book, a Barclays Bank deposit pass book, and a Westminster Bank deposit account book. It was held that the gift of the passbooks constituted a *donatio mortis causa* in each case since they were essential evidence of title without which money could not be withdrawn from the accounts.

How is delivery to be effected in a *donatio mortis causa* of land? In *Sen* v *Headley* (see 9.2.2.1), it was held that a freehold house could be gifted by delivery of title deeds. The case was concerned with unregistered land (for which title deeds are the essential *indicia* to title). The Court of Appeal did not specifically express an opinion about registered land, although it appears to have laid down the *general* rule that land can be the subject of a *donatio mortis causa*. It would surely be anomalous to make a distinction in this respect between registered and unregistered land. Thus it seems that the delivery of a land certificate would suffice for registered land.

What if the delivery is made without the intention to part with dominion, but that intention is later manifested? The position is that although there must be proof of delivery and intention, they need not coincide. In *Cain* v *Moon* [1896] 2 QB 283, the donor gave her mother a deposit note for safekeeping. Later, when seriously ill, she said to the mother 'The bank-note is for you if I die'. The issue arose whether the earlier delivery — made when the donor was not contemplating death — sufficed for a valid *donatio mortis causa*, or whether a re-delivery should have taken place. It was held that the earlier delivery was sufficient.

9.2.2.5 Which property?

Most property is capable of being the subject-matter of a *donatio mortis causa*, but not all. As regards land, certain *obiter* remarks by Lord Eldon in *Duffield* v *Elwes* (1827) 1 Bli NS 497; 4 ER 959, HL, can be construed as suggesting that there cannot be a *donatio mortis causa* of land, although it is doubtful whether they accurately represented the position in English law at the time. The position has been clarified by *Sen* v *Headley* (above) where it was held that a *donatio mortis causa* of land is possible. The donor, the owner of a substantial freehold house in London, was diagnosed as having an inoperable cancer. He was visited regularly in hospital by the donee, a woman with whom he had a very close relationship. The donor told her that the house and contents were hers, and that the title deeds were kept in a steel box in the house to which she had the keys (they were probably slipped into her handbag by the donor on a previous visit). The donor died intestate soon afterwards. The donee subsequently found the box, opened it and took possession of the deeds. It was held by the Court of Appeal (reversing the first instance decision) that a valid *donatio mortis causa* of the house had been made to the donee as there had been a delivery of the essential *indicia* of title to the house — the title deeds. It was also held that s. 53(1) of the Law of Property Act 1925 — which requires that the transfer of equitable interests in land should be in writing — had no application since a *donatio mortis causa* created an implied or constructive trust: hence it fell within s. 53(2), under which writing is not required in the case of such trusts.

As regards personalty, chattels are generally capable of being the subject-matter of a *donatio mortis causa* as are cheques, promissory notes and negotiable instruments drawn in favour of the donor, even though not endorsed by him: *Veal* v *Veal* (1859) 27 Beav 303; 54 ER 118. But a gift of a cheque or promissory note drawn by the donor himself cannot constitute a *donatio mortis causa*, as a general rule, since it does not constitute a gift of property. Bank deposits can be the subject-matter of a *donatio mortis causa* by delivery of the passbook provided that it is the essential evidence of title: *Birch* v *Treasury Solicitor* (above). But since bank accounts are now normally held on computer, it seems that a *donatio* of such funds is not possible. It is still usual, however, for passbooks to be issued for accounts held in building societies. If the passbook is regarded as the essential evidence of title, a *donatio mortis causa* can be made of funds held in a building society. It seems that passbooks are generally so regarded.

9.2.2.6 Effect of a *donatio mortis causa*

Like a will, a *donatio mortis causa* is revocable until the donor dies. Revocation can be express, as where the donor resumes dominion over the property or informs the donee that the gift is revoked. However, it seems that the gift cannot be revoked by a subsequent will: *Jones* v *Selby* (1710) Prec Ch 300; 24 ER 143. Where the donor recovers from the illness or survives the event from which he was contemplating death, the gift is automatically revoked. If the donee predeceases the donor, the gift lapses: *Tate* v *Hilbert* (1793) 2 Ves Jun 111; 30 ER 548.

A valid *donatio mortis causa* may vest full title in the donee — for example, where the donor does everything that would be necessary to make a valid *inter vivos* gift. But in many cases, especially where choses in action are involved, a valid *donatio mortis causa* does not necessarily suffice to transfer the title in the property to the donee. In these circumstances the donor's personal representatives hold the legal title on trust for the donee and can be compelled to perfect the gift: *Re Wasserberg* [1915] 1 Ch 195. But if the donor has failed to make an effective *donatio mortis causa* — having attempted to do so — the personal representatives are not compelled to perfect the gift to the donee. The gift may still take effect, however, under the rule in *Strong* v *Bird* (see 9.2.3).

9.2.2.7 The need for *donatio mortis causa?*

In *Sen* v *Headley*, Nourse LJ described the 'doctrine' of *donatio mortis causa* as 'anomalous' and stated that every such gift is 'a circumvention of the Wills Act 1837' (p. 647). Similar sentiments have been expressed in other cases, and yet — despite the admitted anomaly — the courts have extended the scope of *donatio mortis causa* in cases such as *Birch* v *Treasury Solicitor* and *Sen* v *Headley*. In defence of the concept it may be argued that in some circumstances making a *donatio* is the only convenient method open to the deceased to dispose of property. As has been seen, many of the cases have concerned donors who were dying, or were very seriously ill, for whom making a will could have presented serious difficulty. Would it be right to remove from such persons the opportunity to make a disposition of their property? On the other hand, why allow a circumvention of the Wills Act 1837 to persons who, because they are dying, may be less able to make considered, rational decisions about the destination of their estate? At least the formalities for making a will help to focus the mind of the testator on what he is doing; but that can hardly be said of making a *donatio mortis causa* — not much time or effort need be expended on handing over some keys or saying 'There, take that and keep it' as in *Gardner* v *Parker* (see 9.2.2.3). Those opposed to the concept of *donatio mortis causa* must have been perturbed that in *Sen* v *Headley* a house was held to have been validly transferred through a few words uttered in hospital by a dying man.

Is there a sensible compromise to be sought between these opposing views? The complete abolition of *donatio mortis causa* cannot be justified: it would remove the only practical opportunity for some persons of disposing of their property. Assuming retention, can some limitations be imposed beyond the existing conditions? There is no convincing reason for limiting such gifts to personalty, as was made clear in *Sen* v *Headley*. A more sensible limitation would be to introduce a presumption against a *donatio mortis causa* unless it could be shown that the donor had no reasonable alternative method of disposing of the property comprised in the gift. Another possibility would be to introduce an upper limit on the value of property that could be transferred by *donatio mortis causa*.

9.2.3   The rule in *Strong* v *Bird*

9.2.3.1   The basic rule
The rule in *Strong* v *Bird* (1874) LR 18 Eq 315 is that a donee of an incomplete gift acquires full title to it if he becomes an executor of the donor's estate. By operation of law the previously imperfect gift is converted to a perfect one. The rule was stated in full by Neville J in *Re Stewart* [1908] 2 Ch 251, at 254:

> ... where a testator has expressed the intention of making a gift of personal estate belonging to him to one who upon his death becomes his executor, the intention continuing unchanged, the executor is entitled to hold the property for his own benefit. The reasoning by which the conclusion is reached is of a double character — first, that the vesting of the property in the executor at the testator's death completes the imperfect gift made in the lifetime, and, secondly, that the intention of the testator to give the beneficial interest to the executor is sufficient to countervail the equity of beneficiaries under the will, the testator having vested the legal estate in the executor.

In *Re Stewart* the donor bought some bonds shortly before his death which he intended to give to his wife. He handed his wife an envelope, saying 'I have bought these bonds for you'. However, the letter contained not the bonds (they had not yet been delivered to him) but some documents relating to the purchase; hence the wife received no interest in them by the attempted gift. However, as one of the proving executors of the donor's will, she was held entitled to the bonds under the rule in *Strong* v *Bird*. Although the case was concerned with personalty, it seems that the rule does apply to imperfect gifts of land.

Strong v *Bird* was concerned with the release of a debt. Bird borrowed a large sum of money from his stepmother who was then living in his house at a rent. They agreed that the loan to him should be repaid through deductions in the stepmother's rent; but after two payments of the reduced rent the stepmother expressly forgave the balance of the debt. However, this did not amount to a valid release at law since there was no consideration (nor was her promise made under seal). But as she appointed Bird as her executor, it was held on her death that he was entitled to the benefit of the release. Although he was still a debtor of the estate, he was also an executor in whom legal title to the debt had vested. He could not be expected to pay the amount owed since the donor had a continuing intention until her death to forgive him the balance of the debt. The rule in *Strong* v *Bird* is laudable in its desire to give effect to the donor's clear intention. But the manner of achieving that end is somewhat dubious. There is no convincing reason — other than expediency — why the fact that a person is appointed as an executor should perfect a gift made to him in a different capacity, i.e. donee. The office of executor is mostly fiduciary in character: why should the attainment of that office convert an imperfect donee into one with full beneficial (as opposed to fiduciary) title?

9.2.3.2 The donor's intention

The donor must have a present intention of giving when making the gift. Thus it is insufficient if the donor merely intends to give at some time in the future or by will (but it seems that an incomplete *donatio mortis causa* could be perfected under the rule in *Strong* v *Bird*). Moreover, the intention to give must continue unchanged until the donor's death. In *Re Freeland* [1952] Ch 110, CA, the donor owned a Hillman car which had been immobilised for some years and was not in roadworthy condition. When she heard that her friend, Hilda, needed a car she told Hilda that she could have the Hillman when it was made roadworthy. The car remained in the donor's garage until it was repaired; but it was then lent to May, another of the donor's friends, with Hilda's permission. It remained in May's possession until the donor's death. Under the donor's will, Hilda and May were appointed as her executrices. It was held that Hilda was not entitled to the car. The rule in *Strong* v *Bird* had no application since the donor merely had an intention to make a gift in the future (when the car was roadworthy). Moreover, the loan of the car to May was fatal to Hilda's claim that there was a continuing intention to make an immediate gift. Jenkins LJ stated (at p. 121):

> ... the principle in *Strong* v *Bird* is directed to perfecting gifts complete in all respects, except as regards the legal formalities necessary for the proper transfer of title to the particular property in question ... there can be no room for its application in a case where there is an intention to give, but the gift is not completed because the intending donor desires first of all to apply the subject-matter of the contemplated or promised gift to some other purpose.

9.2.3.3 Vesting of property

The rule in *Strong* v *Bird* concerns property vesting in the donee as executor. Although the donee in that case was a sole executor, the rule clearly applies where the donee is one of several executors. There is an absence of clear authority as to whether the rule applies only if the executor-donee obtains probate. In principle, probate should not be essential since the executor derives title from the will, not the probate.

What if the donee is appointed as an administrator? In *Re James* [1935] Ch 449, the donor handed over the furniture and title deeds of a certain house and premises, which he had inherited from his father, to his father's housekeeper. The donor later died intestate, and the housekeeper was appointed administratrix. It was held that the housekeeper was entitled to the property comprised in the gift under the rule in *Strong* v *Bird*. However, *Re James* was queried in *Re Gonin* [1979] Ch 16 by Walton J, who perceived a material distinction between executors and administrators as regards the application of the rule, namely that administrators were 'selected by law' and not by 'the will of the testator' (p. 35).

9.2.4   Joint tenancy and survivorship

The law on co-ownership is outside the scope of this book, so the basic rules will be stated in outline only. If property is held under a joint tenancy and one of the joint tenants dies, his interest accrues automatically to the surviving joint tenant(s). The survivor succeeds by the *ius accrescendi* — the right of survivorship. Succession by this method is of enormous importance in practice because of the frequency with which certain assets, such as houses and bank accounts, are held jointly by a married couple or cohabitants. It follows from the basic rules that a joint tenant cannot dispose of his interest by will; nor do the intestacy rules apply. The position is quite different in the case of a tenancy in common — the share of a tenant in common passes under his will or intestacy.

The operation of these rules is subject to two important factors. First, it is possible for a joint tenant to sever the tenancy, thus converting it into a tenancy in common. This can be easily done, for example, by notice to the other tenants. But a joint tenant cannot sever the tenancy by attempting to dispose of his interest in his will. Secondly, the tenant's legal and equitable interests in the tenancy may differ. All co-owners must be joint tenants at law, but the equitable interest may be held either by joint tenancy or by a tenancy in common. On the tenant's death, the legal joint tenancy passes to the other joint tenants by survivorship, but the equitable tenancy in common (if any) will be held by his personal representatives and will devolve along with the rest of his estate.

A legal joint tenancy is created where property is acquired by co-owners. There is a common law presumption that the equitable interest is to be held on joint tenancy as well. However, the presumption may be rebutted by the surrounding circumstances or by 'words of severance' in the instrument creating the tenancy, such as 'equally' or 'between', i.e. words showing the intention that the tenants should take separate rather than joint shares. Moreover, in certain situations equity will presume a tenancy in common — for example, where co-purchasers of property make unequal contributions to the purchase money.

TEN
Administration

The law of administration comprises a vast mass of technical rules and procedures. Much of it does not easily lend itself to textbook exposition and analysis but is best learned and appreciated in actual practice. It is in many respects a separate world from the main bulk of the law of succession. Indeed, it is arguable that it should not be regarded as part of that law but should be treated as a subject in its own right. Nevertheless, *some* appreciation of the way in which estates are administered is important in order to obtain a sufficiently broad understanding of Succession. This chapter focuses on the basic essentials of what is a highly detailed area of law.

There are two central questions:

(a) Who administers the deceased's estate?
(b) What does administration entail?

The material in this chapter will be divided accordingly. Briefly, it is the deceased's personal representatives who administer the estate, either executors or administrators. Executors are the representatives appointed by the testator (usually) to administer his estate. Administrators, on the other hand, are appointed by the court. This occurs where the deceased died intestate or, less frequently, where there was a will but no proving executor. The administration of the estate entails principally the obtaining of a grant of representation — probate in the case of a will, letters of administration in an intestacy — collecting and managing the assets of the estate, paying the debts and liabilities and distributing the net estate according to the testator's will or the rules of intestacy.

10.1 PERSONAL REPRESENTATIVES

10.1.1 Executors

10.1.1.1 The appointment of executors
The vast majority of executors are appointed expressly in the will by an appropriate clause which names or identifies them as executors. It is sensible

practice to state the address and occupation of an executor. The appointment should be clearly expressed otherwise it may fail for uncertainty, as in *In the Goods of Blackwell* (1877) 2 PD 72: the testator appointed 'one of my sisters my sole executrix' but failed to indicate which of his three sisters was the intended appointee. He was survived by only one of them, but nevertheless the appointment was held void for uncertainty.

An executor may be appointed conditionally — for example, the testator might specify that the executor should have attained a particular age. Or the appointment may be qualified in some respects, as where the testator specifies that the executor is to act only during a particular period, or in respect of particular assets of the estate, or as a literary executor in relation to the deceased's literary works. The testator can appoint substitute executors, but it is important to specify the circumstances that will make the substitution operative. The testator in *In the Goods of Foster* (1871) LR 2 P & D 304 was not specific enough, with the result that litigation ensued. He appointed his wife sole executrix and 'in default of her' he appointed two further executors. On the wife's death (she had previously obtained probate) the issue arose whether the substitution operated only in the event of her not acting at all, in which case the substitution was inoperative. It was held that the substitution took effect since it was intended to operate on her death.

Even if the testator fails to appoint an executor expressly, he may be regarded as having appointed impliedly in certain circumstances. An executor appointed impliedly is often referred to as an executor according to 'the tenor of the will' (for those who have heard of 'the three tenors' it should be explained that none of them is 'the tenor' — in this context 'the tenor' means the overall meaning of the testator's provisions). What is required for an executor to be impliedly appointed? There must be a clear intention on the part of the testator that a named or identified person should act as executor — that is, carry out the essential duties of an executor. Consider *In the Goods of Adamson* (1875) LR 3 P & D 253, where the testator requested that his beneficiaries should pay his 'just debts and funeral expenses'. It was held that they were executors according to the tenor, and that the essential duties of an executor were 'to collect the assets of the deceased, to pay his funeral expenses and debts, and to discharge the legacies' (p. 254). It seems that it is sufficient if the testator directs that *some* of the essential duties should be performed by a particular person. In *In the Estate of Fawcett* [1941] P 85, the testatrix executed a home-made will in which she made a number of small gifts and concluded 'All else to be sold and proceeds after debts, etc., Barclays Bank will do this . . .'. It was held that the phrase 'Barclay's Bank will do this' constituted an implied appointment. The court regarded it as significant that she had appointed the bank as executor under a previous will (in which case it seems that the tenor of the will might be gleaned from more than just the will in question). However, it is insufficient to show that a person has been made sole beneficiary: *Re Pryse* [1904] P 301, CA. Nor does it suffice merely to request that a person acts as trustee if there is nothing to indicate that the trustee should be involved in administering the estate: *Re Punchard* (1872) LR 2 P & D 369. On the other hand, the phrase 'I nominate as trustees to carry out this will' was held to amount to an implied appointment of the nominated trustees: *In the Goods of Russell* [1892] P 380, where the President stated (at p. 381) '... where the direction is to carry out the general provisions of the will, and not to execute a specific trust, the trustees are executors according to the tenor'.

There are special circumstances in which the court may appoint executors, although it has no *general* power to do so. For example, if a life or minority interest arises under the deceased's will or intestacy, and there is only one personal representative (other than a trust corporation), the court has power to appoint additional personal representatives to act — while the life or minority interest subsists — until the estate is fully administered: s. 114(4) of the Supreme Court Act 1981. Moreover, under s. 50 of the Administration of Justice Act 1985, the court has power to appoint 'a substituted personal representative' to act in place of any existing personal representatives.

10.1.1.2 The chain of representation

An executor of a sole or last surviving executor of a testator is the executor of the testator (s. 7(1) of the Administration of Estates Act 1925)

The rationale of the chain of representation is to ensure a degree of continuity in administration of estates. The chain applies as follows: suppose that A is the sole or last surviving executor under T's will, and has obtained probate but dies before the administration of T's estate has been completed. If A himself has an executor, B, who obtains probate of A's will, then B becomes an executor of T's will as well — B represents A. This avoids the expense, delay and inconvenience of having to appoint another personal representative to complete the administration of T's estate. The chain could be extended to C, B's executor, if B died without completing administration — 'So long as the chain of such representation is unbroken, the last executor in the chain is the executor of every preceding testator': s. 7(2).

In order for the chain of representation to operate several conditions must be satisfied. Using the preceding example, A must have obtained probate of T's will, must have been the sole or last surviving executor when he (A) died, and must have died without completing the administration. Moreover, B must have obtained probate of A's will. Section 7(3) provides that the chain of representation is broken by:

(a)   an intestacy; or
(b)   the failure of a testator to appoint an executor; or
(c)   the failure to obtain probate of a will;

but is not broken by a temporary grant of administration if probate is subsequently granted. What if the chain of representation is broken? Then a grant of administration *de bonis non administratis* with the will annexed will be necessary in the case of each estate where administration has not been completed (see 10.2.1.6).

If an executor of an estate does not wish to act as an executor by representation of another estate, he must renounce probate of *both* estates. The executor cannot pick and choose which executorship to accept: he must accept both or renounce both. The Law Reform Committee recommended in its Report, *The Powers and Duties of Trustees* (LRC Report No. 23, 1982, para. 7.5) that 'a person who finds himself the executor of more than one estate through a chain of representation should be able to renounce in part provided that he has not inter-meddled in the affairs of those estates he wants nothing to do with'. This recommendation has not been enacted to date.

10.1.1.3 Number of executors

There is no restriction on the number of executors that may be appointed, but probate will not be granted to more than four executors 'in respect of the same part of the estate of a deceased person': s. 114(1) of the Supreme Court Act 1981. If more than four executors have been appointed in respect of the same part of the deceased's estate, and they cannot agree as to which of them is to take a grant of probate, the matter can be resolved by a district judge or registrar: r. 27(6) of the Non-Contentious Probate Rules (NCPR) 1987. Probate may be granted to a lone executor, although the court has power to appoint additional personal representatives if a minority or life interest arises under the will: s. 114(4) of the Supreme Court Act 1981. Analysis of the wills sampled by Finch *et al.*, *Wills, Inheritance, and Families*, 1996 (see 1.1.2) shows that just over half the testators in the sample appointed only one executor and that only 5 per cent appointed more than two.

10.1.1.4 Capacity to act as executor

The basic rule is that anyone can be appointed as executor by the testator, but that probate will not be granted to a minor or to a person incapable of managing his affairs because of mental or physical incapacity. Once a minor reaches 18 years of age or a previously incapacitated person becomes capable of managing his affairs, a grant of probate can be made. As regards corporations, the general position is that a corporation cannot act (unless it is a trust corporation) except through a nominee, and then only if empowered to do so by its memorandum of association. A trust corporation may act as executor in its own name, alone or jointly: s. 115(1) of the Supreme Court Act 1981. If a partnership is appointed as executor — usually a solicitor's firm — it is the individual partners that are considered to have been appointed. In *Re Horgan* [1971] P 50, the court approved a clause for appointing solicitors' firms (now commonly referred to as 'the *Horgan* clause'). The clause appoints the partners *at the testator's death* of the particular firm or *of its successors*. Analysis by Finch *et al.*, 1996 suggests that testators appoint professional executors (usually solicitors) in about a quarter of all wills.

Because of the relative paucity of the rules on capacity, there is little restriction as to the appointment of executors. For example, the fact that a person is insolvent or has a criminal record is not a bar to obtaining probate. This is somewhat curious given the considerable responsibilities that an executor has, and the trust that is placed in him. However, under s. 116(1) of the Supreme Court Act 1981, the court can pass over an executor and appoint an administrator if 'by reason of any special circumstances' it appears 'necessary or expedient' to do so. The court has a discretion to appoint 'such person as it thinks expedient'. In *Re S* [1968] P 302, the testator appointed his wife as his executrix. Later she was sentenced to life imprisonment for his manslaughter. Not surprisingly, she was passed over as executrix, administration being granted to the victim's daughters. *In the Estate of Biggs* [1966] P 118 was rather different in that there was little, if any, element of wrong-doing on the part of the executors, an elderly and infirm couple who were implacably opposed to seeking probate (the husband was even prepared to undergo imprisonment for disobeying a court order that he should take out probate). Their attitude made it inevitable that they should be passed over. But the court is unlikely to pass over an executor if the purpose of an application under s. 116(1) is in effect to restrict the executor's enjoyment of the estate to which he is beneficially entitled: *In the Goods of Edwards-Taylor* [1951] P 24 (large estate, allegedly immature executor-beneficiary).

10.1.1.5   Acceptance, renunciation and retirement

One who is appointed an executor may renounce (*per* Best CJ in *Douglas* v *Forrest* (1828) 4 Bing 686; 130 ER 933, at 940)

An executor is free to accept or renounce the office to which he has been appointed. However, the executor can be forced to make a decision whether to accept or renounce: the court can issue a citation under s. 112 of the Supreme Court Act 1981 to force a decision. Anyone may apply for the citation to be issued who would be entitled to a grant of administration should the executor renounce. If the executor does not appear to the citation, 'his rights in respect of the executorship shall wholly cease': s. 5 of the Administration of Estates Act 1925. However, no action can be brought for loss resulting from neglect to take out probate: *Re Stevens* [1898] 1 Ch 162, where the executors did not obtain probate until nearly seven years after the testator's death, and consequently paid a higher rate of interest than originally necessary to creditors of the estate. They were held not liable to account for the loss to the estate.

An executor accepts either by obtaining probate or by intermeddling, that is, behaving as an executor typically does — for example, by gathering the testator's assets or paying his debts. In *Long and Feaver* v *Symes and Hannam* (1832) 3 Hagg Ecc 771; 162 ER 1339, the executors advertised in a local newspaper for claims against the estate but failed to apply for probate. It was held that they had accepted the office by intermeddling, Nicholl J stating (at p. 1341) that 'nothing can be a more strong intermeddling than the insertion of such an advertisement'. However, not all acts typically performed by executors will necessarily constitute intermeddling. Everything turns on the intention with which they were done. Thus, if the executor's acts were done out of necessity, humanity or charity, rather than with the intention of accepting the office, they will not constitute intermeddling. If an executor has intermeddled but has not sought probate, he may be cited by anyone interested in the estate. The court may order the executor to take out probate within a specified period, or the reluctant executor might be passed over under s. 116 of the Supreme Court Act 1981.

To renounce the office, an executor must sign a written renunciation, which is then filed in the probate registry. As a general rule the executor must renounce the *whole* of the executorship: he cannot accept in part, renounce in part. It will be recalled that this rule may be particularly inconvenient when the chain of representation operates (above). An executor may renounce only if he has not accepted the office: thus, if he has intermeddled, he may not renounce but must seek probate. The effect of renunciation is that the executor's rights of executorship wholly cease: s. 5 of the Administration of Estates Act 1925.

What if the executor, having renounced, changes his mind? The renunciation can be retracted only with the leave of the court, which is unlikely to be granted unless the retraction is considered to be for the benefit of the estate. In *In the Goods of Stiles* [1898] P 12, one of two executors renounced but was allowed to retract when the other executor (a solicitor) absconded after obtaining probate. But leave was refused in *In the Goods of Gill* (1873) LR 3 P & D 113, where the renunciation was based on erroneous advice given to the executor that acceptance would prove onerous for him. The effect of a retraction is that 'the probate shall take effect and be deemed always to have taken effect without prejudice to the previous acts and dealings of and notices to any other personal representative who has previously proved the will or taken out letters of administration': s. 6 of the Administration of Estates Act 1925.

An executor has no *right* to retire from office. But he may do so with the leave of the court under s. 50 of the Administration of Justice Act 1985, which allows the court to appoint a substituted personal representative in his place. Leave of the court is unlikely to be given unless good cause is shown (such as ill-health or unreasonable burdens imposed by the office). It should be noted that an executor cannot rid himself of the office by assigning it (since it is an office of personal trust): *Re Skinner* [1958] 3 All ER 273. But an executor may appoint a person to act for him for a maximum of 12 months by power of attorney.

10.1.1.6 Executor *de son tort*

There are many cases in the books where a person has assumed to have authority when in truth he has none. It has always been held that he is accountable just as if he had in fact the authority which he assumed. The classic instance is the executor *de son tort*. If a person intermeddles with the assets of an estate in such a way as to denote an assumption of the authority of an executor, he is accountable just as if he were an executor (*per* Lord Denning MR in *Phipps* v *Boardman* [1965] Ch 992, CA, at 1017–18)

An executor *de son tort* is someone who intermeddles with the deceased's property without authority. The intermeddling involves him in potential liability to creditors and beneficiaries of the estate, and to the lawful personal representatives. The term can be used in relation to intestate estates — the intermeddler is still described as an executor *de son tort.*

The acts which constitute a person an executor *de son tort* are those which are typically performed by executors. In *Pollard* v *Jackson* (1994) 67 P & CR 327, CA, the deceased granted a tenancy on the ground floor of his home to the defendant. Following the deceased's death no one took out a grant to his estate for over 12 years. The defendant, who remained on the premises, eventually became very concerned about the squalid state of the upper part of the premises. Eventually he burnt some clothes ('old rags, old cloth, crawling things') and other rubbish which had accumulated in the upper part. Did he thereby become an executor *de son tort*? It was held that he had not done anything which might be regarded as characteristic of an executor — the burning of the rubbish was simply a sensible attempt to avoid a health hazard. Nor did continuing as tenant on the ground floor or later taking possession of the upper floor as a squatter make the defendant an executor *de son tort.* In *IRC* v *Stype Investments (Jersey) Ltd* [1982] 3 All ER 419, CA, a company in Jersey was held to be an executor *de son tort* for directing that the proceeds of sale (£20m) of a large estate in England belonging to Sir Charles Clore, a leading industrialist, should be paid into the company's account in Jersey. The transfer of the right to the £20m from the personal representatives constituted in England to those constituted in Jersey amounted to an intermeddling with the English estate. The company was thus liable to account for the capital transfer tax due on the £20m.

The position of the executor *de son tort* is governed by s. 28 of the Administration of Estates Act 1925:

> If any person, to the defrauding of creditors or without full valuable consideration, obtains, receives or holds any real or personal estate of a deceased person or effects the release of any debt or liability due to the estate of the deceased, he shall be charged as executor in his own wrong to the extent of the real and personal estate received or coming to his hands, or the debt or liability released, after deducting —
>
> (a)   any debt for valuable consideration and without fraud due to him from the deceased person at the time of his death; and
>
> (b)   any payment made by him which might properly be made by a personal representative.

An executor *de son tort* is liable for the assets with which he has intermeddled. But he may deduct debts due to him and payments made by him which might properly have been made by a personal representative (e.g., the discharge of debts owed by the estate). Moreover, he owes no duty — unlike a personal representative — to gather in the assets of the estate. He is liable, however, for the payment of inheritance tax on assets with which he has intermeddled: ss. 199–200 of the Inheritance Tax Act 1984. In practice it is the liability for inheritance tax that is perhaps the most significant aspect of the position of the executor *de son tort.*

A person may become an executor *de son tort* quite innocently — without any obvious 'wrong' on his part. For example, in *New York Breweries* v *Attorney-General* [1899] AC 62, an English company transferred shares owned by a domiciled American to his American executors, at their request, who had obtained probate in New York but not in England. It was held that as a result the company was an executor *de son tort* and was thus liable to account for the estate duty payable on the deceased's English estate.

10.1.2 Administrators

An administrator is a personal representative appointed by the court by a grant of letters of administration. The essential difference from an executor is that the administrator is the appointee of the court, not of the testator. The most frequent situation when an administrator is appointed is where the testator dies wholly intestate; however, they are also appointed when there is a will but no proving executor. Because there may be a number of potentially suitable appointees, an order of priority is necessary as regards entitlement to a grant of administration.

10.1.2.1 Total intestacy
The order of priority to a grant of letters of administration in a total intestacy (known as simple administration) is specified by the NCPR 1987, r. 22(1):

(a)   the surviving husband or wife;
(b)   the children of the deceased and the issue of any deceased child who died before the deceased;
(c)   the father and mother of the deceased;
(d)   brothers and sisters of the whole blood and the issue of any deceased brother or sister of the whole blood who died before the deceased;
(e)   brothers and sisters of the half blood and the issue of any deceased brother or sister of the half blood who died before the deceased;
(f)   grandparents;
(g)   uncles and aunts of the whole blood and the issue of any deceased uncle or aunt of the whole blood who died before the deceased;
(h)   uncles and aunts of the half blood and the issue of any deceased uncle or aunt of the half blood who died before the deceased.

In default of any person having a beneficial interest in the estate, the Treasury Solicitor is entitled to a grant if he claims *bona vacantia* on behalf of the Crown: r. 22(2). If all persons entitled to a grant have been cleared off, a grant may be made to a creditor of the deceased or to any person who may have a beneficial interest in the event of an accretion to the estate: r. 22(3).

This order of priority naturally follows the order of entitlement under the intestacy rules. As a general rule, the personal representative of any person in the specified classes has the same right to a grant as the person whom he represents: r. 22(4). If a person wishes to apply for a grant of simple administration, but there are others with a prior right, they must be 'cleared off'. The process of clearing off is not as sinister as it sounds: it involves the applicant establishing that all those with a prior entitlement have either renounced, or been passed over, or have been cited but have not entered an appearance.

What if there are two or more persons entitled in the same degree and a grant to all of them is inappropriate? According to r. 27(5), administration shall be granted to a person of full age in preference to a guardian of a minor, and to a living person in preference to the personal representative of a deceased person. Apart from these guidelines the court has a discretion as to whom to make the grant, but will obviously favour the person who is most likely to administer the estate in the most beneficial way. The court often prefers to appoint the person with the largest interest or who has the support of those with the largest interests. In *Budd* v *Silver* (1813) 2 Phill 115; 161 ER 1094, two cousins, Budd and Silver, of the intestate were equally entitled to a grant but neither wished to act jointly with the other. Administration was granted to Budd partly because 'the majority of interests' were in his favour, and partly because Silver's son might have a claim against the estate (thus Silver would have a potential conflict of interests as administrator). The court does not appear to have attached much, if any, significance to the argument that Silver was 'a person of superior situation in life' (being an alderman of the city of Winchester) whereas Budd was 'only a small shopkeeper'.

10.1.2.2   Where there is a will
If the deceased leaves a will, but there is no executor who obtains probate, the court will grant letters of administration with the will annexed in accordance with the order of priority specified by the NCPR 1987, r. 20:

(a)   the executor;

(b)   any residuary legatee or devisee holding in trust for any other person;

(c)   any other residuary legatee or devisee (including one for life), or, where the residue is not wholly disposed of by the will, any person entitled to share in the undisposed of residue (including the Treasury Solicitor when claiming *bona vacantia* on behalf of the Crown), provided that —

(i)   unless a district judge or registrar otherwise directs, a residuary legatee or devisee whose legacy or devise is vested in interest shall be preferred to one entitled on the happening of a contingency, and

(ii)   where the residue is not in terms wholly disposed of, the district judge or registrar may, if he is satisfied that the testator has nevertheless disposed of the whole or substantially the whole of the known estate, allow a grant to be made to any legatee or devisee entitled to, or to share in, the estate so disposed of, without regard to the persons entitled to share in any residue not disposed of by the will;

(d)   the personal representative of any residuary legatee or devisee (but not one for life, or one holding in trust for any other person), or of any person entitled to share in any residue not disposed of by the will;

(e)   any other legatee or devisee (including one for life or one holding in trust for any other person) or any creditor of the deceased, provided that, unless a district judge or registrar otherwise directs, a legatee or devisee whose legacy or devise is vested in interest shall be preferred to one entitled on the happening of a contingency;

(f)   the personal representative of any other legatee or devisee (but not one for life or one holding in trust for any other person) or of any creditor of the deceased.

The order indicates that if there is no proving executor, it is the residuary beneficiary (if any) holding in trust who has the prior right to administration with the will annexed. This is because such a beneficiary is the closest in function to an executor. The rest of the order appears to be based on the degree of entitlement to the testator's estate. The rules as to clearing off and determining entitlement between applicants of the same degree are the same as under r. 22 (above).

10.1.2.3   Appointment of administrators

The rules on the capacity and number of administrators, passing over, acceptance, renunciation and retirement are either identical or very similar to those applicable to executors. As regards the number of administrators, the position is the same as for executors (see 10.1.1.3), except in the case of a minority or life interest. Any grant of administration in such a case shall normally be made to a trust corporation or to *not less than two individuals*: s. 114(2) of the Supreme Court Act 1981 (whereas probate *may* be granted in such cases to a *lone* executor).

The rules governing the capacity and passing over of administrators are identical to those applicable to executors (see 10.1.1.4). So the court may pass over a person *prima facie* entitled to a grant of administration if it appears necessary or expedient to do so: s. 116(1) of the Supreme Court Act 1981. For example, in *In the Goods of Ardern* [1898] P 147, the deceased's husband was passed over as administrator because it was found that he was a dissipated man of drunken habits and was mismanaging a public house (part of the estate) in such a way as to imperil the licence and lessen the value of the property.

The position of an administrator as regards acceptance, renunciation and retirement is very similar to that of the executor (see 10.1.1.5). The only significant difference is that for an administrator to accept the office he must take a grant of letters of administration: intermeddling with assets does not constitute acceptance.

10.2   ADMINISTERING THE ESTATE

The principal duties of personal representatives are to obtain a grant of representation, to collect and manage the assets of the estate, to ascertain and pay the deceased's debts and liabilities, and to distribute the net estate in accordance with the provisions of the will or the law of intestacy (or a combination of the two). Section 44 of the Administration of Estates Act 1925 provides that 'a personal representative is not bound to distribute the estate of the deceased before the expiration of one year from the death'. Thus personal representatives have at least one year — the so-called 'executor's year' — from the date of the deceased's death before they can be called on to distribute the estate. This should normally allow sufficient time to obtain a grant, collect the assets and pay the debts. The amount of time taken for administration will inevitably vary with the circumstances, particularly the nature of the estate. The majority of estates are likely to be fairly uncomplicated to administer, with administration completed within a year.

10.2.1   Obtaining a grant

10.2.1.1   Position before grant

A testator's estate vests on his death in his executor. An intestate's estate, on the other hand, vests in the Public Trustee until the grant of administration: s. 9(1) of the Administration of Estates Act 1925, as enacted by s. 14 of the Law of Property (Miscellaneous Provisions) Act 1994. If a testator left a will but there is no executor able to obtain probate, the estate likewise vests in the Public Trustee: s. 9(2). Once letters of administration are granted the deceased's property vests in the administrator, whereas a grant of probate confirms that the estate vested in the executor on the deceased's death (but such confirmation is essential — it is the indispensable proof of the executor's title).

To what extent can personal representatives act before a grant of representation? The basic principle is that since an executor derives title from the will, whereas an administrator obtains authority from the grant of letters of administration, an executor can act before a grant, but an administrator cannot. An executor may in theory do anything that is incidental to his office apart from acts which require a grant of probate as proof of title: *Re Stevens* [1897] 1 Ch 422. He may gather the deceased's assets, commence managing them, pay debts and distribute the net estate. In practice, however, the executor is likely to find that the lack of a grant of probate severely restricts what he can do. For example, if he tries to collect debts owed to the estate, he may find that the debtor is unwilling to pay without proof of the executor's authority. The executor may commence an action, but will be unable to maintain it to judgment without a grant of probate. What if the executor dies before obtaining probate? In *Re Stevens*, it was held that acts done before probate 'stand firm and good'. For example, if the executor collected assets or paid debts and legacies, such acts are valid and binding on the estate.

As regards administrators, the general rule is that a person entitled to administration cannot act in that capacity prior to a grant of administration. Thus, an administrator cannot commence an action before a grant. In *Ingall* v *Moran* [1944] KB 160, the deceased died intestate in a road accident caused by the negligence of a Canadian soldier. The victim's father commenced an action 'as administrator' (prior to obtaining a grant) for damages in respect of the son's death. The Court of Appeal held that the action was incompetent since it was commenced without authority (it was irrelevant that the father obtained a grant some two months afterwards). The decision was followed in *Finnegan* v *Cementation Co. Ltd* [1953] 1 QB 688, CA: an action for damages was commenced by the widow of the deceased (killed in a construction accident in

Eire). She obtained a grant of administration in Eire but omitted to do so in England. The action failed because she purported to sue as 'administratrix' but had no title to do so in England.

However, some acts by an intending administrator before a grant of administration can be validated through 'the doctrine of relation back'. In such cases the grant of administration is regarded (exceptionally) as relating back to the deceased's death, that is, as taking effect from that time. 'It is clear that the title of administrator, though it does not exist until the grant of administration, relates back to the time of the death of the intestate' (*per* Parke B in *Foster* v *Bates* (1843) 12 M & W 226; 152 ER 1180, at 1183). The purpose of this doctrine is to protect the estate against damage in the period between the deceased's death and the grant. In these circumstances the acts of the intending administrator will be regarded as valid provided that they benefited the estate. The test of benefit is objective. In *Mills* v *Anderson* [1984] 2 All ER 538, the deceased died in a collision with a tractor while riding his moped. His father obtained a grant of administration, having earlier accepted an offer (which later transpired to be unfavourable) from the defendant's insurers in settlement of potential claims. The issue was whether the administrator was bound by the settlement. It was held that it was not binding — the doctrine of relation back did not apply — because it was not objectively beneficial to the estate even though the administrator thought it was.

In *Fred Long and Sons Ltd* v *Burgess* [1949] 2 All ER 484, CA, a contractual tenant of a house to which the Rent Restrictions Acts applied died intestate. The landlords started an action for possession against her sons who had continued to live there after her death. On obtaining a grant of administration, one of the sons contended that her estate (including the tenancy) was vested in him as from the date of her death by reason of relation back, and that consequently he was protected by the Acts as a person deriving title under the original tenant. It was held that the doctrine of relation back could not be used to give the administrator title to something which had been extinguished: 'The doctrine of relation back cannot breathe new life into a corpse' (*per* Asquith LJ, at p. 488). It was emphasised that the doctrine applies only for the limited purpose of protecting the estate.

10.2.1.2 Applying for a grant

Section 105 of the Supreme Court Act 1981 provides that applications for grants of probate or administration and for the revocation of grants may be made to:

(a) the Principal Registry of the Family Division; or
(b) a district probate registry.

Jurisdiction over probate business (used in its wide sense to include administration) is split between the Family Division and the Chancery Division of the High Court. The Family Division deals with non-contentious or common form probate; the vast bulk of probate business is non-contentious. The Chancery Division deals with contentious or solemn form probate (see 10.2.1.5). However, even where there is contentious business, any subsequent grant is made by the Family Division (since it has sole jurisdiction over making grants). Contentious business may be dealt with by county courts if the value of the deceased's estate is less than £30,000.

As a general rule, a will is admissible to probate only if it contains a disposition of property. The normal basis of the court's jurisdiction to make a grant, whether of probate or administration, is that the deceased left property situated in England or Wales. But the court does have the discretion to make a grant even in the absence of such property. For example, in *In the Estate of Wayland* [1951] 2 All ER 1041, probate was granted in respect of the deceased's Belgian wills even though they only disposed of property in Belgium (see 5.2.1.1). Such grants are likely to be exceptional, particularly in view of the comments of Ormrod J in *Aldrich* v *Attorney-General* [1968] P 281, where he stated (at p. 295) that it appeared to be 'contrary to principle for this court to make a grant of representation in the estate of a person domiciled in some other country who died leaving no assets within the jurisdiction of this court'.

When can a grant of representation be issued? No grant of probate or of administration with the will annexed shall issue within seven days of the death of the deceased, and no grant of administration shall issue within 14 days thereof (except with leave of a district judge or registrar): NCPR 1987, r. 6(2). There is no maximum time limit within which a grant must be issued — sometimes a grant is not issued until many years after the deceased's death, e.g., *Pollard* v *Jackson* (see 10.1.1.6). However, delay in applying for a grant increases the likelihood of the potential applicant being cited.

In order to apply for a grant the personal representatives must have delivered to the Inland Revenue an account of the nature and value of the deceased's estate (unless it does not exceed £125,000) and must have paid the inheritance tax payable, if any. Sometimes the value will not be ascertainable for some time, in which case a provisional assessment is made (which must later be amended if found to be incorrect). The account must be delivered within 12 months from the end of the month in which the deceased died, but in practice it will be among the earliest acts of the personal representatives since a grant cannot be applied for otherwise. They will often have to borrow to pay tax because until a grant of representation is made they may find it difficult to realise the deceased's assets.

A number of documents have to be lodged with the registrar in an application for a grant. An application must be supported by an oath by the applicant: NCPR 1987, r. 8(1). The oath is a sworn affidavit concerning, for example, the deceased's death and domicile, whether he died testate or intestate, the entitlement of the applicant to a grant, and the value of the estate. Moreover, the applicant swears to administer the estate dutifully (the duties are specified in the oath form). In an application for a grant of administration, the oath must state 'in what manner all persons having a prior right to a grant have been cleared off and whether any minority or life interest arises under the will or intestacy': NCPR 1987, r. 8(4). The applicant must also lodge a receipted Inland Revenue Account if inheritance tax is payable on the value of the estate, and any will or codicils in respect of which a grant is sought. It is the original will and codicils that need to be lodged, but if the original cannot be produced (e.g., because it is lost or destroyed) the registrar may accept a copy or other evidence of the contents. The applicant will also have to lodge such other papers as the registrar or district judge may require. For example, if there is some doubt as to the will's execution, the applicant will probably be required to submit an affidavit of due execution from the attesting witnesses. Or if the will is in poor physical condition or appears to have been torn, burnt or otherwise tampered with, an affidavit 'of plight and condition' may be necessary specifying the state in which the will was found. Moreover, an affidavit may be required if there is doubt whether the testator knew and approved of the will's contents, or where he was blind or illiterate, or where there is evidence, for example, of improperly authenticated alterations.

A grant of representation is not essential in all cases. Under the Administration of Estates (Small Payments) Act 1965, payments may be made and assets transferred by certain bodies to the deceased's estate without the necessity for a grant up to a specified maximum amount (currently £5,000). The Act applies predominantly to various registered societies and public employers.

10.2.1.3   Caveats and citations

In *Moran* v *Place* [1896] P 214, Lindley LJ described a caveat as follows (at pp. 216–7):

> It is a notice to the registrar or officer of the Court not to let anything be done by anybody in the matter of the will, or the goods of the deceased, without notice to the person who lodges the caveat.... When a caveat has been entered the person who wishes to prove the will has to warn the person who entered the caveat, and if such person, i.e. the caveator, intends to make any real objection, he enters an appearance.

Anyone who wishes to show cause against the sealing (i.e. issuing) of a grant may enter a caveat in any registry of the Family Division of the High Court. No grant can be issued by a registrar or judge with knowledge of an effective caveat until the caveat is removed or ceases to be effective. A caveat is intended to allow the caveator time to decide whether to oppose the grant. A caveat expires after six months but may be extended for further periods. An applicant for a grant may issue a 'warning' to the caveator — a notice requiring him either to enter an appearance within eight days setting out his interest or, if he has no contrary interest but wishes to show cause against the sealing of the grant, to issue a summons for directions within eight days: NCPR 1987, r. 44(5) and (6). Failure to comply with the warning results in the caveat ceasing to be effective (thus enabling the grant to be sealed). It also ceases to be effective if the caveator has used the procedure in a vexatious manner: *Re Hancock* (1978) CLY 1443, where a caveator entered a series of caveats in the course of a bitter dispute with the National Trust. If the caveator appears, no grant can be sealed (except to the caveator) without an order of the court for the withdrawal of the caveat.

A citation is an instrument issued by the court, following an application by a person interested in the estate (the citor), stating that a matter is before the court and requiring the person cited to enter an appearance (normally within eight days) and possibly to take other steps specified by the court. Citation is used particularly to force personal representatives to decide whether to accept office (see 10.1.1.5) and to encourage them to take out probate or to propound a will. Citing to propound a will occurs where the citor doubts the validity of an unproved will: failure to appear by the person cited enables the citor to apply for a grant on the basis that the will is invalid; similarly where the former appears but fails to proceed to propound the will with reasonable diligence: NCPR 1987, r. 48(2).

10.2.1.4 Omission of words from probate

Suppose that Arthur makes a will leaving his estate to charity and nothing to his family. In his will he writes diatribes against his family in language too offensive to be repeated here. Can such words be omitted from probate? The general rule is that the court may exclude words which have no testamentary value if they are offensive, libellous or blasphemous. Consider *In the Estate of T* (1961) 105 SJ 325: the testator stated in his will 'I have made no provision whatsoever for my wife because of her utterly unjust and despicable behaviour towards me, my family, my friends and my employees, which has caused me the greatest unhappiness. . . .' In a motion to exclude the offending passage (and others) it was held that the testator went too far in using the phrase 'utterly unjust and despicable' — those words were omitted. The court remarked, however, that it was one of its duties to preserve a testator's right of disposing of his property in words he considered appropriate, subject to the qualification that he must not use words which had no testamentary relevance and which were offensive, libellous, or blasphemous. Words may be excluded even if they are not aimed at any individuals. For example, in *In the Goods of Bowker* [1932] P 93, passages relating solely to the mode of disposal of the testator's remains were omitted since they were 'offensive, objectionable and repugnant' to the testator's family. And in *In the Estate of Heywood* [1916] P 47, parts of the will of an officer killed in the early months of the First World War were omitted at the request of the military authorities (the passages had no testamentary value). Words may also be omitted on grounds such as the lack of capacity or knowledge and approval of the testator (Chapter 3). Where the court does omit words, they are normally omitted from the probate copy rather than from the will itself.

10.2.1.5 Forms of probate

The primary classification of the forms of probate relates to the methods of proving a will. It may be proved in two ways — in common form or in solemn form. A will is proved in solemn form if its validity is contested in a probate action and the court pronounces for it. If a will is admitted to probate without the court pronouncing for its validity, it is said to have been proved in common form.

Proving a will in common form is essentially a paper exercise consisting of a written application to a probate registry, with appropriate affidavits, and the registrar's decision (usually a formality). Common form probate is aptly named because the majority of wills are proved in this manner. Such probate may be challenged, however, by interested persons — those who are adversely affected (e.g., those entitled on intestacy). It appears that lapse of time is not a bar to an action to revoke common form probate. In *Re Flynn* [1982] 1 All ER 882, it was stated that an action to revoke a grant of probate (or administration) would be struck out only if the action was frivolous, vexatious or an abuse of the court's process, and not because of mere passage of time. Nor does acquiescence by an interested party in a common form grant, or the acceptance of a legacy under a will proved in that manner, prevent a challenge: *Bell* v *Armstrong* (1822) 1 Add 365; 162 ER 129. Because of the possibility that the validity of a will proved in common form may be challenged, perhaps years later, it is advisable that personal representatives should seek solemn form probate if there are serious doubts as to the will's validity.

Where solemn form probate is obtained, the validity of the will cannot later be challenged by anyone who was a party to the action, unless he had no opportunity to appear and oppose the proceedings (e.g., through unavoidable accident) in which case the court has discretion to allow that party to proceed: *Re Barraclough* [1965] 2 All ER 311. Nor may the will be challenged by persons who are privy to the solemn form proceedings — namely those who are *sui iuris*, and aware both of the proceedings and their interest in them: *Newell* v *Weeks* (1814) 2 Phill 224; 161 ER 1126. However, even parties and privies are not bound by a solemn form grant if it was obtained by fraud or if a later will is discovered.

There are several instances of 'special' grants of probate, that is, grants that are made in special circumstances, or limited in some respects, or applicable to a particular type of property. For example, a grant of 'double probate' is possible where several executors have been appointed but not all have taken out a grant. If power is reserved to those without a grant to apply for one, a successful later application will result in a grant of double probate. Grants of probate may be limited in various ways — 'in any way the court thinks fit': s. 113(1) of the Supreme Court Act 1981. A grant may be limited, for example, to a particular part of the estate (as in the case of a literary executor), or for a particular period of time or until the occurrence of some specified event. Where a grant is limited to particular assets, the *later* grant of probate of the remainder of the estate is termed probate *caeterorum* ('of the rest'). If a grant of the general assets was made first, it is termed a grant 'save and except'. Where an original grant is made determinable on the passage of time or on the occurrence of an event, another grant may be made — a cessate grant — when the original grant terminates. A settled land grant to the trustees of the settlement is necessary if the estate contains settled land vested in the deceased on his death: s. 22 of the Administration of Estates Act 1925. A 'save and except' grant is normally made to the general executor in respect of the rest of the estate. Section 22 applies only if the land continued to be settled land after the testator's death. Thus, if the settlement ended on death, a general executor has title to sell the previously settled land: *Re Bridgett and Hayes' Contract* [1928] Ch 163. The need for settled land grants will gradually diminish as a result of the phasing out of settled land by the Trusts of Land and Appointment of Trustees Act 1996.

10.2.1.6 Forms of administration

The two basic forms of administration — simple administration and administration with the will annexed — have been considered previously. In addition, various other grants of administration are possible, for limited purposes or in special circumstances. Section 113(1) of the Supreme Court Act 1981 applies to administration as well as probate. Moreover, several forms of special or limited grant apply to both types of personal representatives. For example, a grant of administration limited to settled land can be made; cessate grants of administration are possible, as also grants of administration *caeterorum*.

Some grants are confined to administrators. A grant *de bonis non administratis* ('concerning goods not administered') — usually referred to as a grant *de bonis non* — is made when the sole or last surviving personal representative has died without completing administration, and the chain of representation has been broken. The grant enables the administration to be completed. Also, a grant *de bonis non* is appropriate if representation has been revoked and administration was incomplete. For example, in *In the Goods of Galbraith* [1951] P 422, such a grant was made following the revocation of probate granted to two elderly executors who were unable, due to mental and physical infirmity, to continue administering a complicated estate (shares in Argentine companies). A similar grant was made in *In the Goods of Loveday* [1900] P 154, where a grant to an administratrix was revoked following her disappearance. Jeune P stated (at p. 156):

> ... the real object which the Court must always keep in view is the due and proper administration of the estate and the interests of the parties beneficially entitled thereto; and I can see no good reason why the Court should not take fresh action in regard to an estate where it is made clear that its previous grant has turned out abortive or inefficient.

To whom is a grant of administration *de bonis non* made? The order of priority depends on whether the personal representative who failed to complete administration was an executor or an administrator. In the latter case priority follows the rules applicable to simple administration contained in the NCPR 1987, r. 22 (see 10.1.2.1). If an executor fails to complete administration, priority is determined by the rules applicable to administration with the will annexed (NCPR 1987, r. 20, see 10.1.2.2).

Since a minor cannot obtain a grant of representation, a grant of administration may be necessary during minority. Under the NCPR 1987, r. 32, where a person to whom a grant would otherwise be made is a minor, administration for his use and benefit is granted to a parent with parental responsibility for him, or to a guardian of the minor, or to any person appointed by a district judge or registrar to obtain administration for the use and benefit of the minor. However, where the minor is sole executor and has no interest in the residuary estate of the deceased, administration is granted to the person entitled to the residuary estate. Grants under r. 32 terminate when the minor attains the age of 18, and he is then entitled to a grant of probate or administration himself.

A person who would otherwise be entitled to a grant, but is unable to manage his affairs by reason of mental incapacity, cannot obtain a grant. Administration may be granted for his use and benefit during his incapacity provided that anyone equally entitled with the incapable person has been cleared off: NCPR 1987, r. 35. The order of priority is:

(a) the person authorised by the Court of Protection to apply for a grant;
(b) if no person is so authorised, to the attorney (under a registered enduring power of attorney) of the incapable person;
(c) if there is no such attorney entitled to act (or if he renounces), to the person entitled to the deceased's residuary estate.

If it is proved that the mental incapacity has ceased, the grant terminates and a cessate grant can be made to the formerly incapable person.

What if a person entitled to a grant is absent from the jurisdiction? Formerly a grant *durante absentia* ('during absence') could be made, but this jurisdiction has been subsumed under s. 116 of the Supreme Court Act 1981 which gives the court a wide discretion to appoint an administrator to replace the one entitled. Such absence is clearly a ground for the exercise of the powers under s. 116.

Where action is necessary to collect and preserve the deceased's assets before a general grant is obtained, a grant *ad colligenda bona* ('for collecting property') can be made to any suitable person. Such grants are normally made only when the assets of the deceased require urgent attention — for example, if they are perishable or wasting assets. The grantee is given powers solely for the purpose of collecting and preserving the estate (although wider powers may be specifically conferred). A grant *ad colligenda bona* was made in *In the Goods of Bolton* [1899] P 186: the deceased, a newsagent in London, died intestate survived by next-of-kin living in South America. It was imperative to sell the deceased's business quickly since it would become valueless if the shop was closed. As communications with the next-of-kin were problematic, the court made a grant to the deceased's landlord who had been requested by the deceased to manage his affairs.

Where any proceedings are pending concerning the validity of a will or the administration of an estate, the court may grant administration if expedient to do so to an administrator pending suit (*pendente lite*): s. 117(1) of the Supreme Court Act 1981. Such an administrator has the powers of a general administrator, but is subject to the 'immediate control' of the court and must act under its direction; no distribution of the estate shall be made without the court's leave: s. 117(2). The purpose of a grant pending suit is to ensure that the estate is properly administered during the proceedings: the grant ceases when the proceedings terminate. The parties may agree that the grant should be made to one of them or someone else interested in the estate; otherwise it will usually be made to someone neutral. Where the estate needs to be represented in legal proceedings, but there is no personal representative to do so, a grant *ad litem* ('for the suit') may be made. The grant is limited for the purpose of representing the estate, and terminates when the litigation is completed.

10.2.1.7 Revocation of grants
Section 121(1) of the Supreme Court Act 1981 provides:

Where it appears to the High Court that a grant either ought not to have been made or contains an error, the court may call in the grant and, if satisfied that it would be revoked at the instance of a party interested, may revoke it.

The court has a wide discretion under s. 121: it can revoke grants for a variety of reasons. For example, the original grant may have been wrongly made because the grantee lacked capacity to take a grant, or a will is found after a grant, or where there was some substantial procedural irregularity. Moreover, events subsequent to the making of the grant may provide grounds for revocation, such as the onset of mental or physical disability. If a sole representative or all the remaining representatives become incapable, a grant *de bonis non* is appropriate: *In the Goods of Galbraith* (above). Revocation will be appropriate if a grantee, for example, has convincing reasons for being relieved from his office, or is in serious breach of his duties. In *Hewson* v *Shelley* [1914] 2 Ch 13, CA, the deceased died apparently intestate and his widow was granted simple administration. However, a will was found some 11 years later appointing executors. Consequently, the grant to the widow was revoked and probate was granted to the executors. But the sale of assets by the widow prior to revocation was held to give valid title' to a purchaser who bought them in good faith. In *In the Estate of Shaw* [1905] P 92, probate was granted to three executors, one of whom was later struck with paralysis affecting her mental and physical capacity. The court revoked the grant and made a fresh grant to the other executors, reserving power to the affected executor to take probate if she recovered. A remarkable case of revocation occurred in *In the Goods of Napier* (1809) 1 Phill 83; 161 ER 921: probate was granted to the executor of a testator who was believed to have been killed at Corunna during the Peninsular War. The grant was revoked when it transpired that the 'deceased' was alive — he appeared personally in the revocation proceedings!

What are the consequences of a revocation of a grant of representation? The position of the personal representative whose grant has been revoked needs to be considered, as does the position of those affected by his acts in the course of administration. Section 27(1) of the Administration of Estates Act 1925 provides:

Every person making or permitting to be made any payment or disposition in good faith under a representation shall be indemnified and protected in so doing, notwithstanding any defect or circumstance whatsoever affecting the validity of the representation.

A person is indemnified under s. 27(1) provided that he has acted 'in good faith'. Thus, if the personal representative continues acting despite being aware of doubts about the validity of his grant, he will be liable: *Woolley* v *Clark* (1822) 5 B & Ald, 744; 106 ER 1363. A personal representative may reimburse himself for payments or dispositions properly made by him: s. 27(2). If payments or dispositions were made in good faith *to* a personal representative (for example, by a debtor of the estate), they are regarded as a valid discharge to the person making them: s. 27(2). But payments made by an executor to himself under a charging clause in a will later found to be invalid cannot be retained: *Gray* v *Richards Butler (a Firm)* (1996), *The Times*, 23 July.

Purchasers from personal representatives are specifically protected by s. 37 of the Administration of Estates Act 1925, which provides that any conveyance of any interest in real or personal property made to a purchaser by a grantee is valid despite any subsequent revocation or variation of the grant of representation. 'Conveyance' is construed widely under the Act, but must consist at least of an 'instrument': s. 55(I)(iii). This would appear to exclude most purchasers of personalty, but presumably they are protected under the principle of *Hewson* v *Shelley* (above). For s. 37 to apply, the purchaser must have obtained the interest in good faith and for valuable consideration. Purchasers are also protected by s. 204(1) of the Law of Property Act 1925, which provides that an 'order of the court' shall not, as against a purchaser, be invalidated on the ground of irregularity, whether he had notice of the irregularity or not.

10.2.2 Collecting and managing the assets

Section 25 of the Administration of Estates Act 1925 provides that it is the duty of a personal representative to 'collect and get in the real and personal estate of the deceased and administer it according to law'. This requires the personal representative to take control of the estate and to preserve and manage it for the overriding purpose of paying off the debts and distributing the net estate in accordance with the provisions of the will or the law of intestacy.

10.2.2.1 Devolution of property

Under s. 1(1) of the Administration of Estates Act 1925, real estate (including leaseholds) to which the deceased was entitled for an interest not ceasing on his death devolves on his personal representatives. Personalty devolves at common law on the personal representatives. Causes of action vested in the deceased at his death survive for the benefit of the estate by virtue of s. 1 of the Law Reform (Miscellaneous Provisions) Act 1934, but actions for defamation are specifically excluded. Any damages recovered in a surviving cause of action devolve as part of the deceased's estate, but damages awarded in an action under the Fatal Accidents Act 1976 do not since they are received by his dependants. Contracts made by the deceased may generally be enforced by and against the estate (but not contracts for personal services). The wide scope of the rules on devolution is illustrated by *Rickless* v *United Artists* [1987] 1 All ER 679, CA, where it was held that the executors of the estate of Peter Sellers had the right to refuse permission for the distribution of a film — 'The Trail of the Pink Panther' — consisting largely of discarded material from the earlier 'Panther' films. The actor's right to refuse permission devolved on his executors.

When does the deceased's estate devolve on the personal representatives? It will be recalled that it vests in an executor automatically on the deceased's death; but in the case of an administrator, the vesting occurs when the grant of administration is made (see 10.2.1.1).

10.2.2.2 Collecting and preserving the assets

Personal representatives have a duty — which must be exercised with due care — to take control of and preserve the assets of the estate. They will be liable for loss caused to the estate by their failure to do so. Obviously they must secure any *indicia* of the title to the assets such as building society passbooks and title deeds. Moreover, they must seek payment of debts due to the estate, but have wide powers under s. 15 of the Trustee Act 1925 to 'compromise, compound, abandon, submit to arbitration, or otherwise settle any debt'. They will not be liable for any loss resulting from any act done by them in good faith. If necessary, they should bring legal proceedings to recover the debt. In *Re Brogden* (1888) 38 Ch D 546, CA, it was held, however, that executors could be excused from not taking action to enforce payment of a debt if they had a well-founded belief that such action would be fruitless. Personal representatives may be required to 'exhibit on oath in the court a full inventory of the estate and when so required render an account of the administration of the estate to the court': s. 25 of the Administration of Estates Act 1925. Anyone with an interest in the estate can apply to the court for such an inventory and account to be ordered.

What is the position regarding insurance? Personal representatives *may* insure 'any personal property against loss or damage' to any amount (but not exceeding three quarters of its value): s. 19 of the Trustee Act 1925, as amended by the Trusts of Land and Appointment of Trustees Act 1996, sch. 3, para. 3(4). It appears that, as regards realty, s. 6(1) of the 1996 Act enables the property to be insured to its full value since trustees of land have 'all the powers of an absolute owner' (the provision applies to personal representatives). However, it seems that personal representatives are not under a duty to insure unless instructed to do so in the will. In *Bailey* v *Gould* (1840) 4 Y & C Ex 221; 160 ER 987, the executors of the deceased, a silk manufacturer, failed to continue the insurance on his factory following his death, although they insured other property belonging to the estate. They were held not liable for the loss resulting from the factory burning down.

10.2.2.3 Managing the estate

Wide powers of management are granted to personal representatives by statute. They have, as regards trusts of land, 'all the functions conferred on them by Part I of the Trusts of Land and Appointment of Trustees Act 1996': s. 39(1)(ii) of the Administration of Estates Act 1925, as amended by sch. 3, para. 6(2) of the 1996 Act. Personal representatives are given a very wide discretion by the 1996 Act: for the purpose of exercising their functions they have 'all the powers of an absolute owner' in relation to the land subject to the trust: s. 6(1). This incorporates, *inter alia*, the various specific powers that a tenant for life has under the Settled Land Act 1925 for maintaining and realising the estate. Section 6(3) gives the specific power to purchase a legal estate in any land in England or Wales. In exercising the powers conferred by s. 6 the personal representatives 'shall have regard to the rights of the beneficiaries': s. 6(5). The powers may be restricted or excluded by provision in the will: s. 8(1). Under s. 9(1), the personal representatives may delegate, by power of attorney, any of their functions which relate to the land to any beneficiary 'of full age and beneficially entitled to an interest in possession in land'. Thus it will be possible for the right to realise the estate — by sale, for example — to be delegated. The beneficiary will be liable for the exercise of the delegated function as if he were a trustee: s. 9(7). The personal representatives are liable for any act or default of the beneficiary if they 'did not exercise reasonable care in deciding to delegate the function': s. 9(8). It should be noted that the above provisions of the 1996 Act apply to personal representatives 'with appropriate modifications and without prejudice to the functions of personal representatives for the purposes of administration': s. 18(1).

The Trustee Investments Act 1961 gives personal representatives the same powers of investment as are conferred on trustees. They are empowered to invest in certain authorised investments for the purposes of administration, and must seek competent advice in doing so. If wider powers of investment are desired than the ones authorised by the Act, the will should be drafted accordingly.

The power to manage is obviously confined to acts done for the purposes of administration. Consequently personal representatives may incur liability for acting outside their powers. However, a purchaser is protected if he did not know that a disposition to him was not made in the course of administration. Even if he did know, he may be protected by s. 36(8) of the 1925 Act, which provides that a conveyance of a legal estate by a personal representative 'shall not be invalidated by reason only that the purchaser may have notice that all the debts, liabilities, funeral and testamentary or administration expenses, duties, and legacies of the deceased have been discharged or provided for'. But the purchaser must have acted in good faith, so that he will not be protected by s. 38(6) if he knew that the disposition was a breach of duty by the personal representative.

10.2.2.4 Carrying on a business

What is the position of personal representatives if the deceased had carried on a business prior to his death? The business devolves on the personal representatives as part of the deceased's assets. They have no *general* authority to carry on the business, but can do so for the limited purpose of properly realising the estate. This may involve maintaining the business so as to ensure that it is sold as a going concern. For this purpose the business will not normally be continued substantially beyond the executor's year, but circumstances may justify a longer period.

Moreover, personal representatives may carry on a business if expressly or impliedly authorised to do so in the will. Express authority should be stated in unequivocal terms: 'to authorise executors to carry on a trade ... there ought to be the most distinct and positive authority and direction given by the will itself for that purpose' (*per* Langdale MR in *Kirkman* v *Booth* (1848) 11 Beav 273; 50 ER 821, at 824). Where a testator empowers personal representatives to postpone the sale of his estate, he thereby gives them implied authority to continue the business during the period of postponement: *Re Crowther* [1895] 2 Ch 56.

Any profits or assets acquired in continuing a business after the deceased's death accrue to the estate: *Mosely* v *Rendell* (1871) LR 6QB 338, where the wife of the deceased, a coachbuilder employed by the defendant, carried out substantial repairs on the defendant's coaches after the deceased's death in her capacity as administratrix. The money owed by the defendant was held to be an asset of the deceased's estate, thus enabling an action for its recovery to be brought by the administratrix. Regarding liabilities incurred by the personal representatives, the basic rule is that they are *personally* liable for such debts and thus may be sued by the business creditor: *Ex parte Garland* (1804) 10 Ves 110; 32 ER 786. However, they are entitled to an indemnity from the estate in two instances. First, the indemnity applies if the personal representatives had authority to continue the business — where they acted in the course of proper realisation of the estate or under the authority expressed in the will. If they acted for the purposes of realising the estate, the indemnity has priority over the claims of creditors and beneficiaries of the estate. But if they acted because authorised to do so by the will, the indemnity is exercisable only against beneficiaries (and is confined to the assets which were authorised by the will for use): *Dowse* v *Gorton* [1891] AC 190. Secondly, even if personal representatives lack authority to continue a business, they can claim an indemnity for properly incurred liabilities in priority to any creditor who assented to their acts. In *Re Oxley* [1914] 1 Ch 604, it was held (at p. 616) that there had to be proof of 'active affirmative assent': mere 'standing by with knowledge and doing nothing' was insufficient. Where personal representatives have incurred a liability in carrying on a business but are entitled to an indemnity, a business creditor is entitled to seek payment from the deceased's assets by subrogation, that is, taking the representative's place: *Re Johnson* (1880) 15 Ch D 548.

10.2.3   Paying the debts

10.2.3.1   Introduction

... it is the duty of the executors as a matter of the due administration of the estate to pay the debts of their testator with due diligence having regard to the assets in their hands which are properly applicable for that purpose, and, in determining whether due diligence has been shown, regard must be had to all the circumstances of the case.... The duty is owed, not only to creditors, but also to beneficiaries, for the ultimate object of administration of an estate is to place the beneficiaries in possession of their interest, and that object cannot be fully achieved unless all debts are satisfied. (*per* Uthwatt J in *Re Tankard* [1941] 3 All ER 458, at 463)

The general rule is that personal representatives are liable to pay debts up to the extent of the assets. If the estate is insolvent, an order of priority of debts is necessary to determine which debts will be paid. Regarding solvent estates, a different problem may arise: the assets, though sufficient to pay the debts, may be insufficient to satisfy the legacies. It will then be necessary to determine how the burden of the debts is to be borne by the assets. If there is any doubt whether an estate is solvent, it should be administered as if it were insolvent until all the debts are paid, otherwise the personal representatives may be liable for *devastavit* (see 10.2.5.5) if it later transpires that the estate was indeed insolvent. However, if they pay a debt in good faith, having no reason to believe that the estate is insolvent, they are not liable to creditors of the *same class* as the paid creditor should it transpire that the estate is insolvent: s. 10(2) of the Administration of Estates Act 1971. In practice personal representatives will usually, but not necessarily, pay the debts within 'the executor's year'. Their *duty*, however, is to pay with due diligence. In *Re Tankard*, the executors did not pay most of the debts until well after a year had elapsed from the testator's death. They had delayed realising certain assets with which to pay the debts (as they were entitled to by the will). When they eventually sold the assets, their value had dropped. It was held that the executors were not liable to the beneficiaries for the loss since they acted diligently within the provisions of the will.

10.2.3.2 Ascertaining the debts

Personal representatives take on all the debts and liabilities of the deceased that survive his death. For example, they must perform his contractual obligations (other than contracts for personal service) and are liable for any causes of action subsisting against the estate under the Law Reform (Miscellaneous Provisions) Act 1934. They should plead any justifiable defences otherwise they may be liable for *devastavit*. The same applies as regards debts — personal representatives should contest any claim where an appropriate defence can be raised. Exceptionally, they need not plead limitation: they have discretion to pay a statute-barred debt: *Stahlschmidt* v *Lett* (1853) 1 Sm & Giff 415; 65 ER 182.

Personal representatives are liable for debts even if they had no notice of them when they distributed the estate, provided there were sufficient assets: *Norman* v *Baldry* (1834) 6 Sim 621; 58 ER 726, where the executors were held liable for a bond — executed by the testator many years previously on his marriage — of which they had no notice. However, liability for unknown debts can be avoided if personal representatives advertise for claims against the estate in accordance with s. 27 of the Trustee Act 1925. The advertisement gives notice of the intention to distribute the estate and requires interested persons to inform the personal representatives of any claims. Notice must be given in the *London Gazette*, and in a newspaper circulating in the district in which land comprised in the estate is situated, and by such notices as would have been directed by the court 'in any special case' (e.g., notices outside the jurisdiction): s. 27(1). The effect of advertising is that personal representatives can distribute the estate (when the notice expires) without liability for claims of which they were then unaware: s. 27(2). However, if a creditor materialises later, he may seek payment by following the distributed assets where appropriate.

Apart from advertising under s. 27, personal representatives may always seek the directions of the court and its leave to distribute the estate on the footing that all the debts have been ascertained. This is particularly advisable if there are serious doubts or complications in determining the creditors or future contingent liabilities. For example, in *Re Gess* [1942] Ch 37, the administrators of the estate of a Polish national — who had died intestate in England — advertised for claims under s. 27 but were unable to do so in Poland because of the German occupation at the outbreak of the Second World War. They were given leave to distribute the estate on the footing that all the debts had been ascertained. Such leave protects the personal representatives but does not prevent a creditor from following the distributed assets.

10.2.3.3 Ascertaining the assets

Section 32(1) of the Administration of Estates Act 1925 states that the assets which may be used for the payment of debts and liabilities are the real and personal estate (whether legal or equitable) of the deceased to the extent of his beneficial interest therein, and the estate which the deceased disposes of by will under a general power. Thus property held in trust by the deceased does not constitute assets under s. 32(1) — for example, the proceeds of an insurance policy paid for by the deceased but held by him as trustee for another: *Re Webb* [1941] Ch 225. Neither does property appointed under a special power constitute assets. But the definition in s. 32(1) is not exhaustive. For example, in *Re Korvine's Trust* [1921] 1 Ch 343, it was held that the subject-matter of a *donatio mortis causa* is available — in the last resort — for the payment of the donor's debts upon a deficiency of assets. Moreover, various assets which were never in the deceased's hands, but which vest in his estate after his death, constitute assets for the payment of debts — for example, business profits, renewed leases, income and accretions derived from the deceased's property, such as 'the lambs born to the testator's sheep after his death': *Re Tong* [1930] 2 Ch 400, at 404.

10.2.3.4 Insolvent estates

... the estate of a deceased person is insolvent if, when realised, it will be insufficient to meet in full all the debts and other liabilities to which it is subject. (s. 421(4) of the Insolvency Act 1986)

Whether an estate is insolvent or not is a question of fact (the court may direct an inquiry to determine the matter). The law applicable to insolvent estates is contained largely in the Insolvency Act 1986 and the Administration of Insolvent Estates of Deceased Persons Order 1986 (henceforth 'the 1986 Order'). An insolvent estate can be administered in three ways:

(a) by the personal representatives out of court;
(b) by the Chancery Division following an administration action; or
(c) in bankruptcy, following an insolvency administration order, in which case the estate is administered by the trustee in bankruptcy.

One important effect of an insolvency administration order is that assets held by persons with whom the deceased had certain dealings may be used for paying debts by virtue of special bankruptcy rules (e.g., extortionate credit transactions entered into by the deceased: s. 343 of the Insolvency Act 1986).

Whichever method of administration is adopted, the rules governing the priority of debts are the same, and cannot be varied by the deceased. Personal representatives may be liable for *devastavit* if they fail to follow the statutory order and instead pay a debt in an inferior class in preference to a superior debt of which they have notice. If there are two or more creditors of the same class, personal representatives have a general duty to pay the debts *pari passu* ('on an equal footing'): the creditors must be paid equally in proportion to the respective debts. To illustrate: suppose that there are three creditors of equal class — A is owed £3,000, B £2,000, C £1,000 — and that the remaining assets total £3,000. A is entitled to £1, 500, B to £1,000 and C to £500. What if the personal representative is himself an equal-ranking creditor? He is subject to the same rules — he cannot pay himself in priority to other creditors of the same class but must pay them all (including himself) *pari passu*. Before 1972, personal representatives could pay themselves in full first (the right of 'retainer') and could prefer one creditor to another in the same class (the right of 'preference'), but these rights were abolished by s. 10(1) of the Administration of Estates Act 1971.

The priority of debts in insolvent estates is specified by the 1986 Order. The debts must be paid in a strict *order*, that is, all the debts of one class must be paid before any debts of an inferior class. Suppose, for example, that there are 100 creditors, all of whom are of the same class apart from Arthur, who is in a superior class. If the debt owed to Arthur exhausts the remaining assets, only he will be paid. The order of priority is as follows:

(a) *Secured creditors*. If a debt is secured on the deceased's property — for example, by a mortgage or lien — the creditor can resort to the security if his debt is not paid. To that extent he has precedence over any unsecured creditor. The secured creditor has various options: for example, he may realise his security and prove for the balance of the debt; or, if the security is adequate, he may rely on it alone and not prove for the debt; or (less likely) he may surrender the security and prove for the whole debt. When a secured creditor proves for the balance (or the whole debt) he ranks equally with unsecured creditors *in that respect*.

(b) *Specially preferred debts*. These are debts which are given special preference by statute. This category includes certain debts of deceased servicemen, property of a Friendly Society held by the deceased as an officer of that society, and expenses arising in the administration of a voluntary arrangement under the Insolvency Act 1986.

(c) *Bankruptcy expenses*. These are the expenses which are incurred — mainly by the trustee in bankruptcy — if the estate is administered in bankruptcy.

(d) *Funeral, testamentary and administration expenses*. When a person dies, funeral arrangements are made with an undertaker, usually by a member of the deceased's family (who will often be a personal representative). The general rule is that reasonable funeral expenses are recoverable from the estate — to the extent of the assets available — by the person (whether the personal representative or someone else) who incurs them by arranging the funeral with the undertaker. If the expenses incurred are unreasonable, the excess spent cannot be recovered.

What are reasonable funeral expenses? The question is one of fact and is dependent entirely on the circumstances of each particular case. In *Goldstein* v *Salvation Army Assurance Society* [1917] 2 KB 291, where it was held that a tombstone *could* be a reasonable funeral expense, McCardie J stated (at p. 297) that a judge 'must remember the station in life, the occupation, and the creed of the dead person, and the general circumstances of the case, and he ought not to allow as a funeral expense anything beyond these reasonable and proper limits'. In *Stanton* v *Youlden* [1960] 1 All ER 429, it was held that payment for a minister (religious rather than political) to attend a funeral was a reasonable funeral expense, but not payment for his attendance during the seven says of mourning (the deceased was of the Jewish faith). Moreover, the erection of a marble memorial stone was held not to be a reasonable funeral expense on the facts, but a simple gravestone was considered reasonable. The wishes of the deceased as to his burial are clearly relevant although not decisive — they must be reasonable in the circumstances.

The sufficiency of the assets is a crucial factor in determining what are reasonable expenses. If the estate is insolvent — or should be anticipated as such — it seems that only necessary expenses are likely to be considered reasonable: 'At law where a person dies insolvent, the rule is, that no more shall be allowed for a funeral than is necessary' (*per* Hardwicke LC in *Stag* v *Punter* (1744) 3 Atk 119; 26 ER 872). However, the court will not adhere to this rule strictly if the executor had good grounds to believe that the deceased died solvent. In determining what are necessary expenses, 'regard must undoubtedly be had to the degree and condition in life of the party': *Hancock* v *Podmore* (1830) 1 B & Ad 260; 109 ER 783, at 785.

It seems that 'testamentary and administration expenses' comprise all the expenses that can be properly incurred in the administration of the deceased's estate. That would include the costs of seeking legal advice and employing an agent (such as a solicitor) to carry out the administration. Also included are the costs of legal proceedings properly undertaken for the benefit of the estate. If the assets are insufficient to pay all the funeral, testamentary and administration expenses, the funeral expenses have priority: *Sharp* v *Lush* (1879) 10 Ch D 468.

The relative positioning of funeral, testamentary and administration expenses within the current insolvency order of priority is not altogether clear. Such expenses have traditionally been regarded as having priority over all other debts, even where the estate was administered in bankruptcy: *Re Walter* [1929] 1 Ch 647 (applying the then current legislation, the Bankruptcy Act 1914). Nevertheless, it would be difficult to maintain that the traditional position still obtains when the current statutory regime indicates otherwise (see Williams, Mortimer and Sunnucks, *Executors, Administrators and Probate,* 1993, pp. 623–40).

(e) *Preferential debts.* These are debts which have priority over ordinary debts by virtue of sch. 6 (as amended) of the Insolvency Act 1986: for example, money owed to the Inland Revenue by way of income tax which the deceased was liable to deduct from remuneration paid to employees and building sub-contractors; money owed to Customs and Excise, e.g., VAT and car tax; social security contributions owed by the deceased; money owed to employees. All preferential debts rank equally between themselves and thus abate proportionately if the assets are insufficient.

(f) *Ordinary debts.* This class of debts consists of all debts which are not in any of the other categories. All ordinary debts rank equally and abate proportionately.

(g) *Interest on preferential and ordinary debts.* Such interest is payable for the period during which the debts were outstanding since the deceased's death. For this purpose preferential and ordinary debts rank equally.

(h) *Deferred debts.* This class includes certain loans made to partnerships and debts owed by the deceased in respect of credit provided by his or her spouse.

10.2.3.5 Solvent estates

In a solvent estate all the creditors will be paid, but rules are required to determine the order in which the assets are to be used to pay the debts. The order is specified by s. 34(3) of the Administration of Estates Act 1925. But if a debt is secured, a special rule may apply by virtue of s. 35. It is convenient to deal with the special rule first and s. 34(3) in a separate section.

According to s. 35(1), if a testator by his will disposes of an interest in property, which at the time of his death is charged with the payment of money, that interest shall be primarily liable for the payment of the charge. The most common scenario is where the deceased's estate includes a mortgaged house: the effect of s. 35(1) is that the devisee of the house will be liable for the repayment of the mortgage. Where the outstanding mortgage exceeds the value of the house — 'negative equity' — the devisee stands to lose the house, and the creditor may prove for the balance of the mortgage (as an ordinary debt). For s. 35(1) to apply the property must be charged with the debt at the deceased's death. In *Re Birmingham* [1959] Ch 523, the deceased's solicitors completed the purchase of property in Brighton which she had agreed to buy before her death. Their costs were held to be an ordinary, unsecured debt and not a charge on the property conveyed (since their entitlement to costs arose after her death).

Section 35(1) applies subject to a contrary or other intention signified by will, deed or other document. Such an intention is not signified by a general direction to pay debts out of the testator's estate unless 'such intention is further signified by words expressly or by necessary implication referring to all or some part of the charge': s. 35(2). In *Re Valpy* [1906] 1 Ch 531, the testator directed that his residuary estate should bear all his debts, except 'mortgage debts' on Blackacre. The issue was whether a mortgage on Whiteacre should be borne by the residuary fund or by Whiteacre itself. The court held that the clear implication of the testator's direction was that all mortgage debts other than those of Blackacre were to be paid by the residue: thus a contrary intention was established. Compare, however, *Re Wakefield* [1943] 2 All ER 29, CA, where the testator devised his realty to his nephew, William Wavell Wakefield (the outstanding England rugby captain of the 1920s), and later contracted to buy a farm but died before completion. Prior to his death he had sent a cheque to his solicitors with a letter stating that the cheque was for the balance of the purchase money. The letter showed that the testator intended the balance to be paid by the cheque, but it was held that the intention disclosed by the letter could not affect events occurring after the testator's death: the letter did not refer to such events, and was simply a mandate to solicitors which necessarily ended on his death. Consequently s. 35 applied to the payment for the farm.

What if the testator does show an intention that a debt should be paid by some fund other than the property charged, but the fund is insufficient? The rule is that the property charged is exonerated only to the extent that the specified fund is sufficient. In *Re Fegan* [1928] Ch 45, the testator mortgaged certain life insurance policies, the proceeds of which he had partly bequeathed to his daughters. He directed that all his debts should be paid from a particular fund, thereby showing a contrary intention. But, as the fund was unable to bear all the debts, it was held that the insurance policies had to meet the mortgage debts to the extent that the latter had not been satisfied by the specified fund.

10.2.3.6   Section 34(3) of the Administration of Estates Act 1925

(a)   The statutory order   Apart from the possible application of s. 35, the payment of the funeral, testamentary and administration expenses, debts and liabilities of the deceased in a solvent estate is governed by s. 34(3), which directs that, subject to the provisions of the will, the deceased's assets are to be applied in the order specified in Part II of the First Schedule of the Act:

1.   Property of the deceased undisposed of by will, subject to the retention thereout of a fund sufficient to meet any pecuniary legacies.
2.   Property of the deceased not specifically devised or bequeathed but included (either by a specific or general description) in a residuary gift, subject to the retention out of such property of a fund sufficient to meet any pecuniary legacies, so far as not provided for as aforesaid.
3.   Property of the deceased specifically appropriated or devised or bequeathed (either by a specific or general description) for the payment of debts.
4.   Property of the deceased charged with, or devised or bequeathed (either by a specific or general description) subject to a charge for the payment of debts.
5.   The fund, if any, retained to meet pecuniary legacies.
6.   Property specifically devised or bequeathed, rateably according to value.
7.   Property appointed by will under a general power, including the statutory power to dispose of entailed interests, rateably according to value.
8.   The following provisions shall also apply —
   (a)   The order of application may be varied by the will of the deceased....

It is possible for certain property to fall within more than one paragraph in the order, in which case it will be treated as belonging to the earlier mentioned paragraph (unless the will shows a contrary intention). Property 'undisposed of by will' (para. 1) includes property which the deceased tried, but failed, to dispose of — for example, a lapsed share of residue: *Re Lamb* [1929] 1 Ch 722, where the testator left his residuary estate to four persons, one of whom predeceased him. It was held that the lapsed share was 'undisposed of' for the purposes of the statutory order. The order specifies that a fund has to be retained from the property undisposed of to meet any pecuniary legacies; similarly as regards residue (para. 2), if the property undisposed of is insufficient for the purpose. Thus it is possible for all the property in paras 1 and 2 to be set aside for the payment of pecuniary legacies; but such a fund then ranks fifth in the order for paying debts. The statutory order is not exhaustive in its description of the assets available for paying debts. It appears that property appointed by deed under a general power may be used as a last resort; so may the subject-matter of a *donatio mortis causa* (see 10.2.3.3). Moreover, in *Re Eve* [1956] 2 All ER 321, it was held that property subject to an option to purchase could be used for paying debts — as a last resort — even though such property is not specifically mentioned in the order. It is not clear what is the order of priority between these various candidates for use in the 'last resort'.

(b) Variation Paragraph 8(a) above emphasises that the order may be varied by the deceased, thus reiterating the general direction in s. 34(3) that the order applies subject to the provisions of the will. But the difficulty lies in the fact that property which the testator specifically devises, bequeaths or charges for the payment of debts falls into paras 3 and 4, whereas one might have expected it to be used first if the testator's wishes were being followed. This paradox has caused the courts some problems.

The central issue is — what is required to vary the order? Clearly a mere appropriation or charging of the debts onto particular property is insufficient (since such property will rank only third or fourth). The cases indicate that there must appear in the will an intention, express or implied, to exonerate some other category of property disposed of by the testator. In *Re James* [1947] Ch 256, the testator gave his house in Monmouth and some other assets on trust for sale, and 'after payment of my just debts funeral and testamentary expenses' to invest the proceeds on certain trusts. He left the residue to his wife (there were no other gifts in the will). The issue was whether the residue (para. 2) was the primary fund for paying the debts, as *per* the statutory order. It was held that by directing debts to be paid out of the specific gift the testator had shown an intention to exonerate the residue, the only other gift. *Re Meldrum* [1952] Ch 208 was similar: the testator bequeathed his deposit account in a Dartmouth bank 'after all legacies debts funeral and other expenses have been liquidated' to his daughter, and by a later clause gave the residue to her and to his son. It was held that the deposit account was primarily liable since the testator had intended to exonerate the residue. Both these cases were consistent with *Re Littlewood* [1931] 1 Ch 443, where there was a charge of debts on specific bequests followed by an absolute gift of residue (which was held to be exonerated). Maugham J stated (at p. 445):

> ... if a testator chooses to charge debts by his will on certain specific items of personal estate, and then gives his residue to some person other than the legatee of the specific property, there can be no doubt, on the construction of the will, that he intends the specific property to be primarily applied in payment of the debts, to the exoneration of the person to whom the residue is given.

Consider, on the other hand, *Re Gordon* [1940] Ch 769: the testatrix bequeathed a necklace to a friend, and the balance of a pecuniary legacy to the Rationalist Press after the payment of her debts. There was no other disposition, hence she died largely intestate. Should the debts have been paid out of the undisposed-of property (para. 1) or the pecuniary legacy (para. 4)? It was held that the statutory order had not been varied since there was no possible intention to exonerate any other gift. Bennett J stated (at pp. 775–6):

> Where a solvent testator has made by his will a disposition of property which falls either within para. 3 of the Schedule or within para. 4, and has made no other disposition of his property and has not otherwise indicated his intentions, there seem to me to be no grounds for a conclusion that such a testator has intended to vary or interfere with or alter the order in which the statute has said that assets are to be applied for the payment of debts and funeral and testamentary expenses.

What if the testator directs payment of debts to be made out of residue but a gift of a share of the residue lapses? Should the lapsed share (undisposed-of property) be used first to pay the debts? According to the statutory order the lapsed share should be used first unless the will directs otherwise. The cases suggest that the order is varied if the residuary gift is so worded that shares in the residue are not ascertainable until the debts are paid. In *Re Kempthorne* [1930] 1 Ch 268, the testator bequeathed his residuary personalty 'subject to and after payment of my funeral and testamentary expenses and debts' in shares to his siblings, two of whom predeceased him. At first instance it was held that the lapsed shares should be the first to be used to pay debts. But the Court of Appeal held that by directing that the debts should be paid out of residue before its division into shares amongst the residuary beneficiaries, the testator had shown an intention to vary the order inasmuch as the net residue available for distribution could not be ascertained until the debts had been paid. Lawrence LJ stated (at p. 300):

> In the present case we find that the testator expressly makes the whole of his personal property, which he bequeaths in the form of a residuary gift, subject to the payment of his funeral and testamentary expenses, debts and legacies; and only directs a division of his residuary personalty into shares after those expenses, debts and legacies have been paid. Consequently, the only bequest

to each residuary legatee is a bequest of a share in the net residuary personalty remaining after the payment thereout of the funeral and testamentary expenses and debts and legacies.

This decision was followed in *Re Harland-Peck* [1941] Ch 182, CA, where the testatrix left her residuary estate, 'subject to the payment of' her funeral and testamentary expenses and debts, to two beneficiaries, one of whom predeceased her. It was held that the statutory order had been varied by the testator's wording ('subject to'), which was similar to that in *Re Kempthorne* ('subject to and after'); the difference in the wording was described as 'insignificant'. Hence the debts were payable out of the whole residuary estate and not out of the lapsed share first. But the statutory order prevails where the will simply directs debts to be paid without charging them on the residue as a whole. In *Re Lamb*, (above), the testator directed that his debts should be paid 'as soon as possible' after his death, made some specific gifts and left the residue between four relations, one of whom predeceased him. It was held that the lapsed share should be primarily liable for the debts: there was no variation since the testator had not indicated which property was to bear the debts. This decision was followed in *Re Sanger* [1939] 1 Ch 238, where a testatrix bequeathed pecuniary legacies, gave the residue to five beneficiaries (two of whom predeceased her), and then directed that all the duties payable on her death should be discharged out of her estate. The court held that her debts were to be paid primarily out of the lapsed shares of residue. Simonds J stated (at pp. 248–9) that he found it difficult to distinguish between a gift of property subject to and after payment of debts and, on the other hand, a direction to pay debts followed by a gift of residue. In *Re Harland-Peck*, (above), the court acknowledged the difficulty, but attempted the following distinction:

It seems to us, however, that the two classes of cases may properly be distinguished on the ground that in the first class of case there is an express charge of the specified items upon the subject-matter of the gift, while in the other class there is merely a direction to pay the specified items unsupported by any charge express or to be implied. (*per* Luxmoore LJ, at p. 190)

(c) Marshalling The statutory order specified by s. 34(3) regulates the incidence of debts between beneficiaries, but does not bind creditors: they are entitled to payment out of any of the deceased's assets, as a general rule. So what is the position where assets are used *out of order* to pay debts? The personal representatives must then make adjustments between the beneficiaries so as to ensure that the proper order prevails as between them. This process is known as 'marshalling the assets'. It normally involves compensating a beneficiary out of the property which should have been used before his to pay debts. In *Re Broadwood* [1911] 1 Ch 277, the testator bequeathed a specific gift of shares to his son on attaining the age of 21. The executors used some of the shares (para. 6) instead of the residue (para. 2) to pay the debts. It was held that the son was entitled to compensation from the residue for the extent of his loss, namely, the value of the shares when he became entitled to them (on attaining 21).

10.2.4 Distributing the assets

The distribution of the remaining assets (after the payment of debts) to the beneficiaries entitled under a will or on intestacy will often be the last major task of the personal representatives. Although they are not bound to distribute the estate *before* the expiration of one year from the deceased's death, they will normally do so if the administration of the estate is straightforward.

10.2.4.1 Ascertaining the beneficiaries
In order to distribute the assets the personal representatives must ascertain who are the beneficiaries entitled to take. This will normally be clear from a will, but on an intestacy inquiries will be necessary to establish who are the next-of-kin. In either case, various problems may arise. For example, a beneficiary may have disappeared, or a will may require interpretation by the court as to who were the intended beneficiaries.

What should personal representatives do in such circumstances? They will usually advertise their intention to distribute, and thus will secure the protection of s. 27 of the Trustee Act 1925 (see 10.2.3.2). In cases of doubt it is appropriate to seek the help of the court, which might, for example, conduct an inquiry to ascertain the beneficiaries, or give directions as to how the personal representatives are to proceed. In *Re Benjamin* [1902] 1 Ch 723, the testator divided his residuary estate equally between his 13 children. The executors were unable to trace one of his sons, who had apparently disappeared whilst returning from a holiday abroad. Following the executors' application to the court, an order was made directing them to divide the son's share 'upon the footing that' the son had not survived the testator. Such an order — where the court gives directions 'on the footing that' — is commonly called a '*Benjamin*' order. It is a highly useful order in practice since it allows the distribution of the estate (or part of it) to proceed: personal representatives are protected if they distribute in accordance with the order. In *Re Gess* the principle of *Re Benjamin* was extended to the ascertainment of debts (see 10.2.3.2). But what if the assumption on which the order was made is later shown to be false? Suppose that Arthur was a recluse whose estate was distributed under a *Benjamin* order on the footing that he died childless, but it later transpires that he was survived by several children. Have they a claim? The position is that the claimants may be able to trace the distributed property since a *Benjamin* order does not destroy entitlement, as emphasised in *Re Green's WT* [1985] 3 All ER 455. The testatrix's son went missing while on a bombing raid over Berlin in 1943. Neither his plane nor any of the crew were ever seen again. The Air Ministry certified that he must be presumed to have died in the raid. The testatrix, never accepting that her son was dead, made a will in 1972 in which he was made a major beneficiary. Following her death, the court granted a *Benjamin* order enabling the executors to deal with the estate on the footing that the son had predeceased the testatrix. Nourse J stated (at p. 462):

The true view is that a *Re Benjamin* order does not vary or destroy beneficial interests. It merely enables trust property to be distributed in accordance with the practical probabilities, and it must be open to the court to take a view of those probabilities entirely different from that entertained by the testator.

10.2.4.2 Appropriation

Section 41 of the Administration of Estates Act 1925 gives personal representatives the power to appropriate any part of the estate in or towards satisfaction of any legacy bequeathed by the deceased, or of any interest or share in his property, as may seem just and reasonable to them, according to the respective rights of the persons interested in the property of the deceased. Although the power to appropriate is widely stated in s. 41, applying to both wills and intestacy, there are some restrictions on its exercise. For example, if an appropriation is made in respect of any settled legacy, share or interest, consent is required from either the trustee or the person entitled for the time being to the income: s. 41(1)(ii). Consequently, professionally drawn wills often contain provisions conferring a wider power of appropriation than that allowed by s. 41.

A duly effected appropriation has several consequences. For example, the other assets of the estate are cleared for distribution, which may ease administration. An appropriation binds all persons interested in the property of the deceased whose consent is not required: s. 41(4). And the beneficiary's interest lies henceforth in the appropriated assets — the value of the interest may therefore fluctuate with the assets: *Ballard* v *Marsden* (1880) 14 Ch D 374 (East Indian Railway stock appropriated to pay for a pecuniary legacy).

10.2.4.3 Assents

An assent is the instrument or act whereby a personal representative effectuates a testamentary disposition by transferring the subject-matter of the disposition to the person entitled to it (*per* Pennycuick J in *Re King's WT* [1964] Ch 542, at 547).

It will be recalled that the deceased's estate devolves on his personal representatives prior to its distribution (see 10.2.1.1). The assent is the method whereby the deceased's property is vested in the beneficiaries under the will or intestacy — until then they do not have a beneficial interest in the property. The position regarding assents differs according to whether the property in question is pure personalty (when common law rules apply) or land, in which case s. 36 of the Administration of Estates Act 1925 applies.

In order to make an assent as regards pure personalty, the personal representatives must indicate, expressly or impliedly, that the property is not required for administering the estate and that it may pass under the will. The indication may be in writing or expressed orally, or by implication through conduct. In *Barnard* v *Pumfrett* (1841) 5 My & Cr 63; 41 ER 295, the executor wrote a letter to a legatee (Philip) in which he recited that a number of legacies had been bequeathed to several legatees, including Philip. The letter continued: 'The above legacies I assure you, my dear Philip, shall be most cheerfully paid to you all, in just compliance with your late dear uncle's bequests.... I shall, as soon as the legal time arrives for payment, give you a line, so that you may please yourself in what way you would like best to receive it.' It was held that the content of the letter amounted to an assent since the executor had implied that there were sufficient assets to pay the legacies.

On the other hand, an assent in respect of land must be in writing (signed by the personal representative) and must name the person in whose favour it is given: s. 36(4) of the Administration of Estates Act 1925. Where a personal representative is also entitled in some other capacity — such as devisee or trustee — he may not hold the interest in that other capacity unless he makes a written assent to himself: *Re King's WT* (above). Moreover, such vesting 'necessarily implies that he is divesting himself of the estate in his original capacity' (*per* Pennycuick J, at p. 548). The decision provoked some criticism since it appeared to be complicating the process of administration. The impact of the case was somewhat reduced, however, by *Re Edward's WT* [1982] Ch 30, CA. The testator succeeded to his wife's property when she died intestate. Her estate included a house which the testator occupied for the 20 years between her death and his. He had obtained letters of administration, but had never executed any assent in writing in his own favour in respect of the realty that he inherited. Buckley LJ stated: 'An assent to the vesting of an equitable interest need not be in writing. It may be inferred from conduct' (p. 40). The husband's long occupation of the house constituted such conduct.

Section 36 helps purchasers of a legal estate in land from a personal representative. A statement in writing by the latter that he has not made an assent or conveyance in respect of a legal estate shall be 'sufficient evidence' of that fact in favour of the purchaser; hence a conveyance on that basis operates to transfer the legal estate as if no previous assent or conveyance had been made by the personal representative: s. 36(6). Clearly it is vital for purchasers to satisfy themselves that a personal representative has not assented previously since, if he has, he will have divested himself of title to sell in that capacity. Moreover, s. 36(7) provides that an assent or conveyance by a personal representative in respect of a legal estate is 'sufficient evidence' that the person in whose favour the assent or conveyance is made is the person entitled to have the legal estate conveyed to him. But a purchaser is not protected by either s. 36(6) or (7) if notice of a previous assent or conveyance affecting the legal estate had been placed on or annexed to the probate or administration. Moreover, the facts related in both subsections are deemed to be only 'sufficient evidence' in favour of the purchaser. In *Re Duce and Boots Cash Chemists (Southern) Ltd's Contract* [1937] Ch 642, it was held that 'sufficient' does not mean 'conclusive', so that a vesting assent should not be regarded as sufficient evidence of something which the purchaser has reason to believe is contrary to the fact.

10.2.4.4 Position of the beneficiaries during administration

It is well established that the estate being administered by a personal representative is the personal representative's property ... no legatee, devisee or next-of-kin has any beneficial interests in the assets being administered. (*per* Ungoed-Thomas J in *Re Hayes's WT* [1971] 2 All ER 341, at 347)

Beneficiaries have no legal or equitable title to the deceased's property until the personal representatives have made the required assents. Until then the legal and equitable title is vested in the personal representatives. In *Commissioner of Stamp Duties (Queensland)* v *Livingston* [1965] AC 694, PC, a wife was left a share in her husband's residuary estate but died while the estate was being administered (and before the residue was even ascertained). It was held that she had no beneficial interest in the property, prior to her death, for succession duty purposes since the entire ownership of the unadministered assets was in the hands of the executors. In *Eastbourne Mutual Building Society* v *Hastings Corporation* [1965] 1 All ER 779, a widower inherited his wife's home on her intestacy but never obtained letters of administration. A compulsory purchase order was eventually made with a view to clearing the site where the house was situated. The issue was whether the widower was 'entitled to an interest in the house' for the purposes of assessing the compensation payable under the Housing Act 1957. It was held that he did not have an interest in the house as it formed part of the wife's unadministered estate.

So what interest, if any, does a beneficiary have prior to the vesting of the property in him? He has the right only to bring an action to compel the due administration of the estate. It appears that what constitutes due administration may depend on the wishes of the beneficiaries. In *Crowden* v *Aldridge* [1993] 3 All ER 603, all the residuary beneficiaries signed memoranda agreeing to vary the testator's will so as to increase the totally inadequate gift to his housekeeper. Each signatory stated that he was 'prepared to enter into a deed to formalise this gift', but several later changed their minds. It was held that a unanimous direction by residuary legatees to an executor was effective to vary his obligations to administer the estate, and that the memoranda were binding on all concerned for this purpose (see 7.2.3.4).

10.2.4.5 Minors

The general rule is that personal representatives cannot obtain a valid receipt from a minor for payments to which he is entitled from the deceased's estate; nor can the adult spouse, parents or guardian give a binding receipt on the minor's behalf. Moreover, personal representatives remain generally liable for assets in their hands to which a minor is absolutely entitled until they obtain a proper discharge (see below) or account for and pay them over to the beneficiary on his attaining his majority: *Harvell* v *Foster* [1954] 2 All ER 736, CA.

The general rule is subject to exceptions. For example, the will may authorise payments to be made directly to the minor, or to his parents or guardian. A married minor can give a valid receipt for any entitlement to *income*: s. 21 of the Law of Property Act 1925. And if the property has not been given to trustees for the minor, the personal representatives can appoint between two and four trustees or a trust corporation to hold the property for him: s. 42(1) of the Administration of Estates Act 1925. On such appointment the personal representatives are discharged from any further liability in respect of such property (unless they have appointed themselves as trustees, as they may). But s. 42(1) applies only if the minor is entitled to an absolute interest under the deceased's will or intestacy.

10.2.4.6 Income, apportionment and interest

(a) Income The general rule is that specific gifts carry with them all the income, profits and accretions arising from the date of the testator's death. The rule applies not only to immediate specific gifts, but also to contingent or future specific gifts (in which case they carry the *intermediate* income: s. 175 of the Law of Property Act 1925). All residuary gifts, apart from future residuary bequests, likewise carry all the income, profits and accretions from the testator's death. These rules are subject to any contrary direction or disposition in the testator's will. Any income, profits or accretions to which the above rules do not apply pass to the residuary legatees as a general rule.

(b) Apportionment The rules of apportionment — a mix of equitable principles and statute — have the laudable aim of attempting to ensure, subject to the provisions of the will, fair and equal treatment of all beneficiaries. But the complexity of the rules, and their occasional failure to achieve their aim, have resulted in their frequent exclusion from professionally drawn wills. Accordingly, the rules will be considered in the briefest outline. The equitable rules of apportionment apply to certain beneficiaries who are entitled *in succession* to the same property. The rule in *Howe* v *Earl of Dartmouth* (1802) 7 Ves 137; 32 ER 56 applies where residuary personalty is settled by will for persons in succession: the rule imposes a duty on trustees to convert wasting, hazardous or unauthorised investments, and reversionary interests, into authorised income-bearing investments (thus protecting both the life tenant and the remainderman). The rule in *Re Earl of Chesterfield's Trusts* (1883) 24 Ch D 643 is concerned with how to apportion the proceeds, between the life tenant and the remainderman, when a reversionary interest is sold. A calculation is made to determine what sum, invested at 4 per cent compound interest at the date of the testator's death, would produce the amount actually received on the sale of the reversion. The calculated sum is treated as capital, whereas the difference between it and the sum actually received is treated as income. The life tenant takes the sum treated as income; the remainderman takes the rest. The rule in *Allhusen* v *Whittell* (1867) LR 4 Eq 295 is that a life tenant is not entitled to income from the parts of the estate required for payment of debts and legacies.

Section 2 of the Apportionment Act 1870 provides that income is treated as accruing from day to day 'and shall be apportionable in respect of time accordingly'. Thus an apportionment is necessary whenever entitlement to income changes, an inconvenient consequence. It appears that the statutory rule too is commonly excluded from professionally drawn wills. The Law Reform Committee recommended that s. 2 should not apply unless expressly included in the will (LRC Report No. 23, 1982, para. 3.40).

(c) Interest At common law, general and demonstrative legacies carry interest at 6 per cent per annum from the time when they become payable, subject to the contrary intention of the testator. A legacy normally is payable at the end of the executor's year in the case of an immediate legacy, but on the date when the contingency is satisfied if the legacy is contingent or future. In some exceptional cases, however, legacies carry interest as from the date of the testator's death — for example, where a testator gives a legacy to a minor who is his child (or to whom he is *in loco parentis*), or where a legacy is given to a creditor in satisfaction of a debt. As regards annuities, the basic position is that, unless the testator directs otherwise, an annuity is treated as commencing on the testator's death, the first payment becoming due a year later. Interest is not payable on the arrears of an annuity, but such interest has exceptionally been allowed where, for example, the arrears have accumulated through the misconduct of the party charged with the duty to pay the annuity.

10.2.4.7 Payment of pecuniary legacies
This is a controversial topic. The relevant statutory provisions lack precision and appear to conflict. The case law is partly irreconcilable and notable for the absence of binding decisive authority. One would have expected that the payment of legacies would have been squarely addressed by the sweeping 1925 property legislation, but it is arguable that the pre-1926 rules still largely apply. Because of these uncertainties, it is advisable that the will should contain provisions expressly dealing with the incidence of pecuniary legacies (the testator's intention prevails over the statutory and pre-1926 rules).

(a) The pre-1926 rules Before 1926 the rules as to which assets could be used for the payment of pecuniary legacies — and in which order — were relatively clear. The general rule was that pecuniary legacies were payable only out of general personalty unless the will indicated a contrary intention. If this fund was insufficient, the legacies abated proportionately: *Robertson* v *Broadbent* (1883) 8 App Cas 812. The general rule was subject to two exceptions. First, if the residue of the realty and personalty was given in one mass, the testator was taken to have intended that the realty could be used if the personalty proved insufficient: *Greville* v *Browne* (1859) 7 HLC 689; 11 ER 275. Secondly, if the testator created a mixed fund of realty and personalty out of which he directed the legacies to be paid, the realty and personalty were proportionately liable for paying the pecuniary legatees: *Roberts* v *Walker* (1830) 1 Russ & My 752; 39 ER 288. The basic question is whether these rules have been altered by the Administration of Estates Act 1925. There are two relevant provisions: s. 33(2) and s. 34(3).

(b) Section 33(2) It will be recalled that when a person dies intestate, his estate is held in trust by his personal representatives with the power to sell it: s. 33(1). Section 33(2) provides that they shall pay — out of the ready money of the deceased (so far as not disposed of by his will, if any) and any net money arising from disposing of any other part of his estate (after payment of costs) — 'all such funeral, testamentary and administration expenses, debts and other

liabilities as are properly payable'. And 'out of the residue of the said money' they 'shall set aside a fund sufficient to provide for any pecuniary legacies bequeathed by the will (if any) of the deceased'. The clear direction in s. 33(2) that a fund be set aside to pay for pecuniary legacies appears to alter the pre-1926 rules where there is a *partial* intestacy: the pecuniary legacies must be paid 'out of the residue of the said money', which may include the proceeds of sale of realty. In *Re Worthington* [1933] Ch 771, the testatrix bequeathed pecuniary legacies and left her residuary estate, both real and personal, to two beneficiaries equally, one of whom predeceased her. That share lapsed and went on intestacy. At first instance it was held that the pecuniary legacies should be paid in accordance with the rule in *Greville* v *Brown* (above), but the Court of Appeal held that the legacies were payable primarily out of the lapsed share, applying s. 33(2). *Re Worthington* was followed on this point in *Re Berrey's WT* [1959] 1 All ER 15.

Unfortunately it is not clear what happens where s. 33(2) is applied but the undisposed-of property is insufficient to meet the pecuniary legacies. Moreover, what if in a partial intestacy there is an operative *express* trust for sale created by the testator? For example, the testatrix in *Re Worthington* might have left her residuary estate to trustees on trust for sale to hold the proceeds for the two beneficiaries equally. The existence of the express trust in a partial intestacy excludes the statutory trust since the latter can only have effect subject to the provisions of the will: s. 33(7). Thus s. 33(2) would appear to have no application to any proceeds arising under the express trust.

(c)   Section 34(3)   We have met s. 34(3) before: it regulates the use of assets to pay debts by applying the order in Part II of the First Schedule of the Administration of Estates Act 1925 (see 10.2.3.6). The crucial issue is whether s. 34(3) applies to the payment of pecuniary legacies as well. If it does not, then it would seem that the pre-1926 rules apply in all situations to which s. 33(2) does not apply; namely, where the testator dies fully testate, or where he dies partially intestate and either there is an express trust or the undisposed-of property is insufficient to meet the legacies. Remarkably — and regrettably — it is not clear from s. 34(3) whether it applies to legacies. The section provides that the deceased's real and personal estate is applicable towards the discharge of his 'funeral, testamentary and administration expenses, debts and liabilities', subject to the provisions of his will. No mention of legacies there, unless it can be argued that 'liabilities' includes legacies. That would be a strained argument. It is scarcely credible that the draftsman would have omitted the simple and well-understood word 'legacies' if he had intended s. 34(3) to apply to legacies. Moreover, the interpretation of 'liabilities' as including legacies is really precluded by consideration of s. 33(2), above, which contains a direction to pay 'debts and other liabilities' *followed by* the setting aside of a fund to meet any pecuniary legacies. Clearly 'liabilities' and 'legacies' are being used in totally different senses in s. 33(2), and it is hardly arguable that the meaning has radically altered in the very next section in the Act.

On the other hand, is it credible that the 1925 legislation would have left the pre-1926 rules unaltered, apart from the application of s. 33(2) on partial intestacy? And there is express mention of legacies in the order in Part II of the First Schedule — paras 1, 2 and 5 (see 10.2.3.6). However, the fact that legacies are mentioned — as they have to be — in an order dealing with the payment of debts does not necessarily lead to the conclusion that the order applies to the payment of legacies. Nor is the language used in paras 1 and 2 — 'subject to the retention ... of a fund sufficient to meet any pecuniary legacies' — sufficiently clear and direct had the draftsman intended the order to apply to the payment of legacies as well as debts.

What do the cases say? They do not speak with one voice. First, consider the cases which support the view that s. 34(3) does not apply to the payment of pecuniary legacies. In *Re Thompson* [1936] Ch 676, the testator gave pecuniary legacies and left his residuary realty and personalty to hospitals in Buxton. For tax purposes it was necessary to decide out of which property the pecuniary legacies should be paid. It was held that they were payable primarily out of the residuary personalty in accordance with the rule in *Greville* v *Browne*. Clauson J expressly rejected the view that s. 34(3) applied to the payment of legacies:

> The provision does not say so, and the provision is not concerned with any such matter. The provision is concerned with the way in which funeral testamentary and administration expenses, debts and liabilities are to be met. There is no indication that there is any intention of altering the law in respect of the rights of the legatees as against those interested in the residuary personalty and residuary real estate, or in respect of the rights *inter se* of those interested in the residuary realty and personalty respectively, as regards bearing the charge of legacies. (p. 682)

Re Thompson was applied in *Re Anstead* [1943] Ch 161, where it was held that the first thing to be done in administering a solvent estate was to set aside a fund out of residue to meet pecuniary legacies, and that the residuary personalty was primarily liable for this purpose in accordance with the pre-1926 rules. In *Re Beaumont's WT* [1950] Ch 462, Danckwerts J stated (at p. 466) that s. 34(3) 'has in effect made no provision with regard to such things as legacies' and that the position of legacies 'depends on the old law'. He held on the facts that pecuniary legacies were not payable primarily out of a lapsed share of residue (as *per* para. 1 of the statutory order) but out of the whole of the residue before division (the pre-1926 position). A similar decision was reached in the last reported case on the issue, *Re Taylor's Estate* [1969] 2 Ch 245, where the interpretation of s. 34(3) was fully considered and the conflicting authorities reviewed in a judgment expressing indebtedness to Professor Ryder's article, *The Incidence of General Pecuniary Legacies* [1956] CLJ 80, in which he concludes that s. 34(3) does not apply to the payment of legacies. The practical consequence of this view is that a fund to meet pecuniary legacies should be retained under paras 1 and 2 only to the extent that it would have been liable to apply to legacies under the pre-1926 rules.

What of the contrary authorities? In *Re Worthington*, above, there appears to have been unanimity that s. 34(3) does govern the payment of legacies as well as debts. For example, Hanworth MR stated (at p. 775) that the provisions of the statute (s. 33(2) and s. 34(3)) 'indicate that unless there is some provision in the will which negatives the prescribed order of administration, that order of administration must apply both to legacies and debts'. But the facts of *Re Worthington*, were concerned with a partial intestacy to which s. 33(2) clearly applied and was sufficient to dispose of the case. It was thus unnecessary for the court to comment on s. 34(3) — such remarks must be considered as *obiter*. *Re Gillett's WT* [1950] Ch 102 purported to follow *Re Worthington*, but is an unsatisfactory authority to the extent that it was conceded by counsel and *assumed* by the court that the statutory order applied to legacies. In *Re Midgley* [1955] Ch 576, the testatrix gave pecuniary legacies and left her residuary estate on an express trust for sale in favour of six beneficiaries. She later revoked the residuary gift to one of them but made no substitutional provision. Thus a share of the residue was undisposed of. It was held that the statutory order applied with the result that the pecuniary legacies were payable primarily out of the undisposed-of share. Harman J based his decision on the apparently mandatory direction in para. 1 that a fund was to be retained for the payment of pecuniary legacies. The same approach was adopted in *Re Martin* [1955] Ch 698, where there was a partial intestacy as to an undisposed-of share, but no express trust for sale. Section 33(2) thus clearly applied, and the case could have been decided accordingly. But the decision was based largely on s. 34(3), the judge holding that it was clear from para. 1 that it applied to legacies — there would be no point in setting aside a fund from undisposed-of property unless it was to be used to meet legacies. *Re Martin* would have been a stronger authority if the judge — Danckwerts J — had not already reached the opposite conclusion in *Re Beaumont's WT*!

On balance the authorities supporting the view that s. 34(3) does *not* apply to legacies are stronger: it is hard to escape from the conclusion that had s. 34(3) been intended to apply to legacies, the word 'legacies' would have been clearly stated in the subsection rather than being mentioned obliquely in Part II of the First Schedule.

10.2.5 The position of personal representatives

10.2.5.1 Remuneration and expenses
It is clear from the foregoing pages that personal representatives have several major and potentially onerous duties to perform in the administration of an estate. But is it necessarily all work and no reward? The general rule is that personal representatives are not entitled to remuneration for executing their duties: 'It is trite law that an executor or trustee is in general entitled to no allowance for his care and trouble' (*per* Vinelott J in *Re Orwell's WT* [1982] 3 All ER 177, at 179). There are several exceptions to the general rule. The most important in practice is where the testator authorises executors to charge for their services under a 'charging clause' in the will. Such clauses commonly appear in wills which appoint professional executors. Since charging clauses are regarded as conditional legacies, executors who wish to benefit should not witness the will: s. 15 of the Wills Act 1837. Charging clauses are construed strictly, as a general rule: *Re Orwell's WT* (concerning the entitlement of the

literary executor of George Orwell's widow). Further, personal representatives may claim remuneration if authorised to do so by a contract with the beneficiaries. And the court may authorise remuneration in special circumstances — for example, where there are assets abroad — or under a number of statutes (such as the Trustee Act 1925 when the court appoints a corporation to act as personal representative). In any case, testators frequently give executors legacies (sometimes conditional on the acceptance of the office).

Personal representatives are entitled to be reimbursed for all expenses properly incurred in the administration of the estate. The expenses are borne by the estate as 'administration expenses'; but expenses incurred in the upkeep of a specific gift are the responsibility of the beneficiary: *Re Pearce* [1909] 1 Ch 819 (see 7.1.2.4).

10.2.5.2 Acting alone?

As a general rule personal representatives may act severally. This means that where there are two or more personal representatives, each may act independently in the proper course of administration, such acts binding the estate and the other representatives. However, a conveyance of land requires an order of the court or the concurrence of all the personal representatives to whom a grant was made in respect of that land: s. 2(2) of the Administration of Estates Act 1925. The same rule applies to contracts to convey land if made after 30 June 1995: s. 16(1) of the Law of Property (Miscellaneous Provisions) Act 1994. Contracts made before that date do not need concurrence to be binding. If persons are appointed to act as executors *and* trustees, they must act jointly when disposing of property as trustees.

Need personal representatives perform their duties *personally*? Although the general principle is that they cannot delegate, there are important statutory exceptions. The most important is s. 23(1) of the Trustee Act 1925, which provides:

> Trustees or personal representatives may, instead of acting personally, employ and pay an agent, whether a solicitor, banker, stockbroker, or other person, to transact any business or do any act required to be transacted or done in the execution of the trust, or the administration of the testator's or intestate's estate, including the receipt and payment of money, and shall be entitled to be allowed and paid all charges and expenses so incurred, and shall not be responsible for the default of any such agent if employed in good faith.

The practical significance of s. 23(1) is enormous. Few lay representatives will be confident enough to administer an estate personally without resort to the services of a solicitor or bank. Section 23(1) enables such resort to be made, the cost chargeable to the estate as administration expenses. It appears from s. 23(1) that personal representatives are protected in delegating provided that they act 'in good faith'. Under s. 23(2), personal representatives may appoint agents to act in respect of assets held outside the United Kingdom. Unlike the case with s. 23(1), they may delegate to the agent the execution of 'any discretion or trust or power' vested in them. Section 25 enables personal representatives to delegate temporarily, by power of attorney, the exercise for a period not exceeding 12 months of any duty, power or discretion vested in them. And s. 9 of the Trusts of Land and Appointment of Trustees Act 1996 enables personal representatives to delegate certain functions to beneficiaries (see 10.2.2.3).

10.2.5.3 Accounting
It will be recalled that personal representatives must exhibit an inventory and render an account of their administration whenever required to do so by the court (see 10.2.2.2). Consequently, they must keep accurate accounts of receipts and payments. Persons interested are entitled to inspect the accounts. The accounting which the court may order can take various forms. For example, it may relate to the whole of the administration, or to a particular period, type of transaction or specified assets. Or it may be ordered on the footing of wilful default — accounting for assets which would have been received but for the personal representative's breach of duty. Although the last major task of personal representatives is to distibute the assets, administration is normally completed by submission of the final estate accounts.

10.2.5.4 Administration proceedings
Administration proceedings may be commenced by anyone interested in the estate — beneficiaries, creditors and personal representatives. The proceedings are not necessarily contentious; for example, personal representatives may seek guidance from the court on the performance of their duties. There are two main types of administration proceedings. The applicant may seek to determine a particular administration issue, or, less commonly, an action may be brought for the administration of the estate by the court under a general administration order. Applications are normally made to the Chancery Division, but the county court (estates not exceeding £30,000) and the bankruptcy court (insolvent estates) also have jurisdiction. Once a general administration order has been made, the court supervises the personal representatives: they cannot exercise their powers without the court's permission. The costs of administration proceedings are borne, as a general rule, by the estate. Because of the cost involved in supervision by the court, a general administration order is likely to be made only if there is no reasonable alternative. Instead of bringing administration proceedings, creditors and beneficiaries may be able to sue personal representatives directly where appropriate (below).

10.2.5.5 Liability of personal representatives
The liability of personal representatives may arise in various ways, as already seen. It will be recalled that all causes of action subsisting against the deceased survive against the estate and become the responsibility of the personal representative (see 10.2.3.2); but they are liable only to the extent of the deceased's assets. Moreover, personal representatives may be liable in some circumstances for a breach of trust — for example, by making an unauthorised profit from their office. But the most likely cause of liability is a breach of duty resulting in a loss of assets, termed *devastavit* ('he wasted'), for which personal

representatives are personally liable to the creditors and beneficiaries of the estate. *Devastavit* may take many forms; for example, failure to collect and preserve the deceased's estate, to pay debts with due diligence (and in the prescribed order if the estate is insolvent), or to distribute the assets to the rightful beneficiaries. Spending an excessive amount on the deceased's funeral is a *devastavit*; so is improper conversion or investment of the assets. *Marsden* v *Regan* [1954] 1 All ER 475 was one of the clearest examples — wrongfully giving away the deceased's furniture and bedding. In *Re Kay* [1897] 2 Ch 518, payment of a small legacy (out of a large estate) before advertising for creditors was held to be a *devastavit*. The test is not whether the personal representative is culpable, but whether there has been a loss of assets caused by a breach of duty.

What if a creditor or beneficiary acquiesced in the *devastavit* (or breach of trust)? The general rule is that acquiescence is a defence: the personal representative is not liable to anyone who acquiesced in his acts with full knowledge of the facts. Under s. 62 of the Trustee Act 1925, the court has power to impound the interest of a beneficiary who instigated a breach of trust or consented to it in writing.

10.2.5.6 Defences and relief

It will be recalled that personal representatives are protected from liability in the execution of their office in various circumstances — for example, where they advertise in accordance with s. 27 of the Trustee Act 1925 before paying debts and distributing assets, or where they act under a *Benjamin* order. There are also a number of potential defences, some of which have already been considered (such as acquiescence in a *devastavit*). Personal representatives may plead limitation as a defence under the Limitation Act 1980, the relevant periods being the same as those generally applicable in litigation — for example, six years for actions founded on contract or tort (but three years for personal injuries) and 12 years for actions for recovery of legal or equitable interests in land. *Devastavit* is regarded as a tort for these purposes. Limitation cannot be pleaded as a defence against a beneficiary if the personal representative has committed fraud or holds assets claimed by the beneficiary.

The defence of *plene administravit* ('he fully administered') is important in practice as a means of limiting the liability of personal representatives when sued for a debt by creditors. It is an assertion that all the assets have been distributed, which has the effect (unless disproved) of limiting the personal representative's liability to assets coming into his possession after the date of the judgment in the action. Or a plea of *plene administravit praeter* ('he fully administered except') may be entered, asserting that all the assets have been distributed except assets admitted to be in the personal representative's hands. That plea, if not disproved, limits liability to the admitted and the future assets. Failure to plead these defences is regarded as an admission that the personal representative had sufficient assets to satisfy the claim: *Midland Bank Trust Co. Ltd* v *Green (No. 2)* [1979] 1 All ER 726. Thus, if those assets are not forthcoming, a *devastavit* will be presumed to have occurred.

Relief from liability for breach of trust may be granted by the court under s. 61 of the Trustee Act 1925 if it appears that a personal representative 'has acted honestly and reasonably, and ought fairly to be excused for the breach of trust and for omitting to obtain the directions of the court in the matter in which he committed such breach'. The onus is on him to show that he has satisfied the statutory requirements. Whether relief is granted depends on the particular facts of each case. In *Re Gale* [1941] Ch 209, the testator left property to trustees for DL 'during her widowhood'. The trustees carried out his wishes, but it later transpired that DL was a spinster and had never married. She had however called herself 'Mrs' and had deliberately fostered the belief that she was married. In the circumstances relief was granted under s. 61.

10.2.5.7 Following the assets

If a personal representative wrongfully distributes assets, the deprived beneficiary (or creditor) may be able to follow the assets into the hands of their holder. There are two potential remedies (the details of which are outside the scope of this book). First, the beneficiary may trace and recover the assets — if identifiable — from the holder, even if the latter was not the recipient from the personal representative. But it is not possible to trace against a *bona fide* purchaser of the assets for value without notice. The beneficiary may well have remedies against the personal representatives, but need not have exhausted them in order to trace. However, whatever has been recovered from them must be set off in the tracing action: *Re Diplock* [1948] Ch 465, CA. Secondly, the beneficiary can claim a refund from the *recipient* of assets wrongfully paid by personal representatives provided that all remedies against them have been exhausted. In *Ministry of Health* v *Simpson* [1951] AC 251, the testator left residuary estate to such 'charitable or benevolent' objects as executors might select. The executors, believing the gift to be valid (it was later held to be void for uncertainty), distributed over £200,000 among 139 charities. The testator's next-of-kin recovered £15,000 from the personal representatives (thereby exhausting their remedies against them) and sought the balance from the charities, claiming the right to trace and to a refund. Both remedies were held in *Re Diplock* to be applicable, but the Ministry of Health appealed on behalf of one of the charities, a hospital. The House of Lords held that tracing was not possible in that particular case since the hospital had spent its gift on new buildings; but the claim for a refund succeeded, the claimants having exhausted their remedies against the personal representatives.

10.2.5.8 Personal representative and trustee

If property has to be held on behalf of beneficiaries until a certain time, trustees will normally be necessary — for example, where there is a life or minority interest. There are some similarities between personal representatives and trustees stemming from the fact that both are in a fiduciary position, their powers and duties partly governed by similar or identical statutory provisions and case law principles. It is common — where trusts arise under a will — for testators to appoint the same persons to act in both capacities. However, a person generally cannot hold and deal with assets in both capacities simultaneously. It is thus important to draw a distinction between the position of personal representatives and trustees and to be able to determine in which capacity a person (appointed to both offices) is acting at any particular time.

The function of a trustee is to hold the property of beneficiaries under a trust until the trust ends; that of a personal representative is to administer the estate as a whole. The latter retains the function for life — he must deal with any relevant matters arising after the apparent completion of the administration. Trustees may retire from office, but personal representatives have no general right to do so. Trustees have extensive powers to appoint new trustees, but personal representatives have not. Trustees must always act jointly (except for a trust corporation), whereas personal representatives may generally act severally. And different limitation periods apply: an action against a trustee must normally be brought within six years of the cause of action accruing, whereas the usual period in the case of personal representatives is 12 years.

It is important in practice — where a person is appointed in both capacities — to determine when the transition occurs from personal representative to trustee. It is clear that an assent by a personal representative to himself as a trustee brings about the transition. In *Attenborough* v *Solomon* [1913] AC 76, the testator (died 1878) appointed his two sons, A and B, to be his executors and trustees. He gave some pecuniary legacies and then left his residuary estate to his sons on certain trusts. They paid all the debts and legacies, and prepared the estate accounts within a year. In 1892, A pawned some silverplate (part of the residuary estate held on trust) without B's knowledge and misappropriated the proceeds. Following A's death B discovered what had happened and claimed the return of the plate. The case turned on whether A held the plate as an executor when he pawned it or as a trustee. In the former case he could have validly acted alone and thus passed good title to the pawnbroker; in the latter case he could not have passed title since trustees can only act jointly. The House of Lords held that A and B held the residuary property as trustees once they had assented (which can be done informally or impliedly through conduct in the case of personalty). That had occurred when they prepared the residuary estate accounts since they thereby showed that they were assenting to the dispositions of the will taking effect. Hence B's claim was upheld.

There is some authority for the view that the transition from personal representative to trustee occurs *automatically* — without the need for any assents — once the debts have been paid and the assets distributed. For example, in *Re Cockburn* [1957] 2 All ER 522, it was held that once executors or administrators have completed administration, they become trustees holding for the beneficiaries under a will or intestacy. They can then exercise the power to appoint new trustees. The same view was taken in *Re Ponder* [1921] 2 Ch 59: the deceased died intestate survived by his widow and two infant sons. As administratrix she paid the debts and divided the residue in accordance with the pre-1926 intestacy provisions. It was held that she thereby ceased to hold the assets as administratrix but held them as trustee (thus allowing another trustee to be appointed). However, *Re Ponder* was doubted in *Harvell* v *Foster* [1954] 2 QB 367, where the Court of Appeal emphasised that the transition to trustee does not terminate the personal representative's office (it lasts for life) and that retaining property in trust for a minor is part of the duty of the representative.

10.2.6 Taxation

The concept of taxing inherited wealth goes back to the ancient world. The Emperor Augustus, for example, made himself decidedly less popular with his fellow Romans on introducing estate duty. In current English law the deceased's estate may be involved in the payment of three taxes in the course of administration: income tax, capital gains tax, and inheritance tax. These taxes will be considered in outline only (the details are outside the scope of this book).

10.2.6.1 Income tax

Any income tax owed by the deceased prior to his death is a debt of the estate. Personal representatives thus have a duty to pay the amount owing, and will need to submit accounts to the Inland Revenue for the relevant assessment to be made. Income from the estate arising after the deceased's death but prior to the completion of administration is also taxable, but only at the basic rate.

10.2.6.2 Capital gains tax

This tax is now charged under the Taxation of Chargeable Gains Act 1992 on profits arising from certain transactions which are not subject to income tax, such as sales of land and shares. The tax is not charged on income profits made in the course of business — they are covered by income tax or corporation tax — but is charged on profits made from the sale of a business. There are a number of exemptions and reliefs, most notably those affecting the disposition of owner-occupied housing. And the tax is applicable only when a taxpayer's gains exceed a certain annual level (£6,300 in the 1996–7 tax year). On death the deceased is treated as having disposed of all of his assets at their market value at the date of his death. However, tax is not charged as a result of that disposal.

The property of the deceased devolves on personal representatives at its market value at the date of death. They will have no liability at that stage for capital gains tax. However, if they sell assets for administration purposes for a sum exceeding the market value, tax is payable on the profits (subject to an annual exemption below £6,300 for each of the three tax years commencing with the year of the deceased's death). The personal representatives may set off the expenses incurred in selling against the gains made. If assets are transferred to the beneficiaries entitled under the will or on intestacy, the latter are treated for capital gains tax purposes as having acquired them at their market value at death.

10.2.6.3 Inheritance tax

Inheritance tax is the main form of taxation occasioned by death. Its principles are derived from two earlier taxes, estate duty and capital transfer tax. The former, introduced by the Liberal Government in 1894, was a graduated tax on the value of the deceased's estate. It could be avoided by the deceased disposing of his property *inter vivos* provided that he survived for seven years thereafter. Capital transfer tax — which replaced estate duty in 1975 — was intended to reduce tax avoidance. The idea was to tax 'transfers of value', which included not only succession on death but also lifetime transfers. Inheritance tax replaced capital transfer tax and is now governed by the Inheritance Tax Act 1984. It is a hybrid tax, retaining some of the characteristics of both the previous taxes. Much of the form and terminology of inheritance tax is derived from capital transfer tax, but in substance it more closely resembles estate duty, because of the broad exemption of lifetime transfers.

The basic concept is that inheritance tax is charged on the value transferred by transfers of value made by an individual. A transfer of value is any disposition — lifetime or on death — which reduces the value of the transferor's estate. Death is treated as a transfer of value — the deceased is regarded as having made a transfer of value 'equal to the value of his estate immediately before his death': s. 4(1) of the Inheritance Act 1984. Transfers of value are progressively aggregated. Once the cumulative figure exceeds £215,000 (the threshold as from 6 April 1997) tax is charged at 40 per cent. No tax is charged on aggregate amounts below the threshold (the 'nil-rate tax band'). Because transfers are cumulated progressively, earlier transfers may be within the nil-rate tax band. In practice tax is payable only in the minority of cases: the value of most deceased estates is insufficient — even when added to lifetime transfers — to attract inheritance tax (in 1995–6, the number of estates subject to the tax was only about 18,000).

It is a fundamental rule in the operation of inheritance tax that it is not charged on *potentially exempt transfers*. These are *inter vivos* gifts made by individuals to other individuals or certain trusts after 18 March 1986 (when the introduction of the tax was announced). No tax is payable provided that the transferor dies more than seven years after the transfer. However, such transfers are chargeable if the transferor made a gift subject to reservation of benefit. These are gifts where the transferor parts with legal title to property but continues to derive some benefit from it. The benefit must have been obtained in the period of seven years prior to the transferor's death in order for the gift to become chargeable as a gift subject to reservation. If the transferor was enjoying the benefit when he died, he will in effect be treated as having owned the asset for tax purposes.

There are a number of exemptions and reliefs by which liability for inheritance tax is avoided or reduced. By far the most important exemption concerns spouses — all transfers between them are exempt (with minor exceptions) whether made *inter vivos* or on death. Also exempt are gifts to charities, gifts for national purposes or for the public benefit, and gifts to political parties (defined as parties which had at least two MPs elected at the general election preceding the gift, or one MP and a minimum of 150,000 votes for members of that party). These exemptions apply, as in the case of spouses, to gifts made *inter vivos* or on death. In addition there are some exemptions confined to lifetime transfers. For example, individual taxpayers are entitled to an annual exemption (comparable to an income tax personal allowance); small gifts are exempted; also certain gifts made in consideration of marriage.

Reliefs generally operate by *reducing* the amount of tax payable on transfers of certain types of property (but where a 100 per cent relief applies, the effect is similar to an exemption). The most important reliefs relate to agricultural and business property. Agricultural relief applies if the transferor occupied the property for agricultural purposes during the two years preceding the transfer, or owned it for seven years preceding transfer provided that it was occupied by himself or another throughout that time for agricultural purposes. The relief reduces the tax payable on the agricultural value of the property by 50 or 100 per cent depending on the nature of the transferor's holding. Business relief applies where there is a transfer of business property by a person who has owned the business for the two years preceding the transfer. The relief reduces the value of the business for tax purposes by 50 or 100 per cent depending on the extent of the transferor's holding.

Where inheritance tax is payable on death it should be paid promptly, especially as a grant of representation cannot be obtained until payment is made (see 10.2.1.2). It is the personal representatives who are usually accountable for its payment. The tax will rank as an administration expense and will normally be paid from the residuary estate. But the testator can provide otherwise and direct, for example, that certain gifts should bear their own tax. If a potentially exempt transfer becomes liable for tax because the transferor dies within seven years, the transferee bears the tax payable and is accountable for it (not the personal representatives).

10.2.6.4 Tax planning

It is obviously sensible for testators to consider arranging their affairs so as to minimise the amount of tax payable after death. And certainly their legal advisers have a duty to point out the tax implications of the provisions of a will, or at least to refer clients to financial consultants. Finch *et al.*, *Wills, Inheritance and Families* (1996) found that the latter option is very popular (surprisingly few solicitors seem to profess expertise in tax matters). Of course, not every testator whose estate might be subject to tax liability will regard tax avoidance or mitigation as of great concern. Some might even take the view that since tax revenue is supposedly used for the public good — the funding of the welfare state, for example — its zealous avoidance is hardly the mark of the public-spirited citizen.

The intricacies of tax planning lie well outside the scope of this book, but some basic observations can be made. It is important to keep in mind the total potential tax liability rather than focusing simply on the effect of one tax. Thus the interaction between inheritance tax and capital gains tax may be crucial. For example, the acquirer of property will need to consider whether he should avoid selling it prior to death, thus avoiding capital gains tax but increasing possible inheritance tax liability. As regards inheritance tax, effective tax planning will encompass the maximum utilisation of exemptions and reliefs, consistent with the manner in which the testator wishes to distribute his estate. The wealthiest testator may avoid inheritance tax liability altogether if he leaves all his property outside the nil-rate tax band to charity; but if he has a spouse and children, they may not be amused, so such an option is usually unrealistic. It is obviously important to ensure that the nil-rate tax band is used effectively in conjunction with the exemptions and reliefs. Hence property attracting the nil-rate band or qualifying for relief should not be given (for tax purposes) to exempt transferees since this duplicates the exemptions or reliefs. Consider, for example, the basic scenario where a testator is survived by a spouse and two children. Suppose that he leaves his estate (value £415,000) to his wife, and that there are no chargeable lifetime transfers. No inheritance tax is payable on his death because transfers between spouses are exempt. But if the widow later leaves the property to the children, £80,000 will be payable in tax (i.e. 40 per cent of £200,000, the rest falling within the nil-rate band). However, suppose that instead the testator left £200,000 to his children and £215,000 to his wife, who later leaves that sum to the children. No tax is payable on the testator's death since the gift to the children falls within the nil-rate band and the gift to the widow is exempt. Nor is tax payable on her death because her gift will be in the nil-rate band. Thus a considerable saving will be made simply through the way in which the assets are distributed (the saving achieved in our example by greater utilisation of the nil-rate band in respect of the children).

Tax planning is also possible after the deceased's death. Provided that beneficiaries under a will or on intestacy are *sui iuris* and that they agree, the distribution of the estate can be varied, and tax savings made thereby. A variation or disclaimer must be made in writing within two years of the deceased's death to be effective for tax purposes: s. 142 of the Inheritance Act 1984. Provided that the Inland Revenue is informed within six months, the variation is regarded as having been effected by the deceased. Similar provisions operate with regard to capital gains tax under the Taxation of Chargeable Gains Act 1992.

Index